The Age of Eclecticism

The Age of Eclecticism
Literature and Culture in Britain, 1815–1885

Christine Bolus-Reichert

The Ohio State University Press
Columbus

Copyright © 2009 by The Ohio State University.
All rights reserved.

Library of Congress Cataloging-in-Publication Data
Bolus-Reichert, Christine, 1969–
The age of eclecticism : literature and culture in Britain, 1815–1885 / Christine Bolus-Reichert.
p. cm.
Includes bibliographical references and index.
ISBN 978-0-8142-1103-8 (cloth : alk. paper)—ISBN 978-0-8142-9201-3 (cd-rom) 1. English literature—19th century—History and criticism. 2. Eclecticism in literature. 3. Tennyson, Alfred Tennyson, Baron, 1809–1892—Criticism and interpretation. 4. Kingsley, Charles, 1819–1875—Criticism and interpretation. 5. Arnold, Matthew, 1822–1888—Criticism and interpretation. 6. Pater, Walter, 1839–1894—Criticism and interpretation. 7. Hardy, Thomas, 1840–1928—Criticism and interpretation. I. Title.
PR451.B64 2009
820.9'008—dc22
2009015109

This book is available in the following editions:
Cloth (ISBN 978-0-8142-1103-8)
CD-ROM (ISBN 978-0-8142-9201-3)

Cover design by Janna Thompson-Chordas
Text design by Juliet Williams
Type set in Adobe Granjon

CONTENTS

Acknowledgments		vii
Introduction		1
PART I	TOWARD AN AGE OF ECLECTICISM	
Chapter 1	History's Diverse Beauties	19
Chapter 2	The Philosophy of the Nineteenth Century	65
Chapter 3	Eclecticism and Literary Modernity	102
PART II	ECLECTIC VICTORIANS	
Chapter 4	Alfred Tennyson: The Originality of Medley	139
Chapter 5	Charles Kingsley: The Alexandrian Age	169
Chapter 6	Matthew Arnold: The Second Best Life	190
Chapter 7	Walter Pater and Thomas Hardy: "Triumph in Mutability"	223
Afterword		248
Notes		257
Works Cited		278
Index		289

ACKNOWLEDGMENTS

Many thanks to those who were present as teachers, readers, and friends in the early stages of this project—to James Eli Adams, Patrick Brantlinger, Matei Calinescu, Kathleen Foster, Oscar Kenshur, and Andrew H. Miller; to my reading group partners David J. Carlson and Martin Harris; and to Katherine Gehr, who heard all about the Victorian eclectics on long walks around Bloomington, Indiana. I'm especially grateful to Andrew Miller who wrote me a very encouraging letter just before I moved to Toronto: I was to take the time to make the book what I wanted it to be. It's not exactly that, and it never could be, but it's closer to what it ought to be, thanks to everyone who was there at the beginning and to colleagues at the University of Toronto who gave me the time and the space I needed to bring *The Age of Eclecticism* to a fit ending—to Russell Brown who saw that I wanted a leave, and to Elizabeth Cowper who gave it to me. I dedicate this book, with intense gratitude, to my parents, Michael and Kathleen Bolus, and to my husband, Aaron Reichert.

INTRODUCTION

The return of "eclectic" to the critical vocabulary of art history and aesthetics in the eighteenth century signaled both a new way of understanding creativity in relation to history and an implicitly negative judgment on any work of art deserving the label. "Eclectic" and "eclecticism" were concepts that provoked anxiety about the possibility for progress in the arts, the consequences of historical belatedness, and the use of historical styles in the absence of an appropriately modern style. In nineteenth-century Britain, the connotations of eclectic were largely negative: to be eclectic was to be mediocre, undiscriminating, middle-class, confused, decadent, liberal, mixed, and unoriginal. Works of genius were not eclectic. The art of the nineteenth century, if eclectic, would not adequately represent the age to itself or to future generations. In once again reviving the language of eclecticism, this study aims to restore a way of seeing and explaining nineteenth-century culture that was typically used to denigrate the period and only rarely to acclaim its contributions to the arts. To denominate Victorian literature eclectic might seem, therefore, to risk its canonical status; but to ignore the role of eclecticism in shaping the canon of Victorian literature we have today is to overlook those qualities that make it continually fresh and accessible, that seemingly collapse all the intervening time and distance between our historical moment and that of the Victorians.

While it is never possible to select a single cause to explain a complex series of effects, in following a dominant thread, the problem of authority, one can detect a regular pattern in Victorian culture—a pattern that will help to explain the pervasiveness of eclecticism. In every aspect of life, certainty had seemingly been replaced by anxiety; reliable guides to belief and action no longer waited at the door to experience. The image of being pushed into a vast expanse of uncharted territory or onto the trackless sea recurs again and again in the literature of the nineteenth century, figuring the modern sense of historical ruin and isolation. The Established Church, the intellectual elite, the aristocracy, communal traditions—none could withstand the onslaught of competing opinions or the deepening sense of the individual's prerogative in shaping his destiny; but looking one's liberated self in the mirror raised an uncomfortable and persistent question: who would validate all the choices one now had to make? If religious dissenters had the same rights as those who cleaved to the Church of England, then faith was a matter of conscience, the choice of the individual rather than an Establishment. If it was no longer the case that a small number of educated persons controlled the press or the publication of books, then authors would compete in an open marketplace for the attention of readers. If one no longer believed in the absolute right of the aristocracy to direct the economic and political forces of the nation, then new persons fit to rule would have to be chosen. If the mass migrations from country to city and from homeland to colony separated individuals from traditional communities, then a new communal fabric would have to be woven from the remnants of the old. The sense of authority lost must have been profound. The resulting eclecticism often looked like an admission of defeat or surpassing arrogance. What was the principle of selection to be?

This question was not an idle one, either for the Victorians or for those historians determined to give some account of what we now recognize to have been the first information age. In his brief preface to *Eminent Victorians*, Lytton Strachey offers some prescient advice to present and future historians of the period: "It is not by the direct method of scrupulous narration that the explorer of the past can hope to depict that singular epoch. If he is wise, he will adopt a subtler strategy. He will attack the subject in unexpected places; he will fall upon the flank, or the rear; he will shoot a sudden revealing light into obscure recesses, hitherto undivined. He will row out over that great ocean of material, and lower down into it, here and there, a little bucket, which will bring up to the light of day some characteristic specimen, from those far depths, to be examined with a careful curiosity" (9). Strachey's methodological metaphor addresses the difficulty of attaining a position of authority over so extensive a field of inquiry as the sixty-four years of Victoria's reign. In its framing it manages to align future historians with the objects of their study; for surely, the Victorians, too, must have been overwhelmed, even "submerged," by the sheer range and quantity of writing, past and present, through which they might attempt to telescope their times. In characterizing his efforts as "haphazard," made up of "fragments of truth," and motivated by "convenience and art" (9), Strachey brings into view one aspect of the eclecticism that beset the Victorian Age and his own: it was fraught with a sense of randomness and indiscriminate picking and choosing, "here and there"; in emphasizing his "careful curiosity," the necessity "of selection, of detachment, of design," and his goal of writing with "becoming brevity" (9–10), Strachey points to another understanding of eclecticism that emerged during the nineteenth century: it could also be a self-conscious process of selecting from past and present, which might lead to creative synthesis.

Strachey's analysis of the situation of the critic and historian speaks to the central issues of this study, both how I plan to articulate the problem of eclecticism in the Victorian period, and why I think it necessary to erect an imposing new conceptual framework in a field of scholarship notable for its rigorous historicism. "The burden of the past" invoked by any discussion of eclecticism is a familiar aspect of modernity, particularly in the history of literature. This study aims to reframe that dynamic, and to place it in a much broader context, by examining the rise in the nineteenth century of a manifold eclecticism. A potentially protean category, eclecticism may be a symptom of decay or renewal—or both. In this study I am especially concerned with two broad understandings of eclecticism in the period— one understood as an unreflective embrace of either conflicting beliefs or divergent historical styles, the other a mode of critical engagement that ultimately could lead to a rethinking of the contrast between creation and criticism, and of the very idea of the original. Eclecticism then and now was process *and* product, accident *and* necessity. It has never been a singular term—an idea with only one meaning consistently applied; it is decidedly multifarious, even as it takes in a set of related phenomena. Eclecticism and eclectic will not replace the more familiar terms that encompass and describe literary history (romanticism, realism, aestheticism, decadence, modernism, or postmodernism) or literature in general (hybridity, intertextuality, anxiety of influence); eclecticism is valuable as a critical and aesthetic category because it helps us to see the problems of literary creation more in line with how Victorian writers saw themselves and the dilemmas they felt were peculiar to the age in which they lived.

The secondary aim of this work is to contribute to the emerging field of transnational Victorian studies, and, in doing so, to find a way to talk about a broader, post-Romantic nineteenth-century culture. In 2003 the editors of *Victorian Studies* asked Sharon Marcus and Irene Tucker to comment on the potential of "transnational" conceptions of Victorian studies. Both writers deplore the tendency of Victorianists to be both provincial and untheoretical in their conception of the larger field. Compared with other period concepts, such as Romantic, the moniker "Victorian" provides no theory of what constitutes a Victorian work of art; something is Victorian simply by virtue of its chronological placement between two dates. In her essay "International Whiggery," Tucker points out the tendency of scholars interested in Romanticism to look abroad for an understanding of the theory underlying the field; by its very nature, Victorian studies seems to be utterly provincial. My work contributes to this long overdue comparative study of Victorian literature and culture. On the one hand, I examine the prevalence of an eclectic philosophy in France and the British responses to it. On the other hand, I argue that Victorian eclecticism is itself a comparative approach to the study of culture. Eclecticism becomes valuable as a critical paradigm because it offers a built-in theory of the literary and historical period, much in the way Romanticism does. It is particularly vital now, because so much of our language for describing the conditions of postmodernity also describes what the Victorians understood as eclecticism. In short, by reviving eclecticism as a critical term, I am trying to historicize the theoretical language available to us for describing how Victorian culture functioned, to make the terrain of Victorian scholarship international and comparative, and to create a place for the Victorians in the genealogy of postmodernism. All languages give us access to a particular way of seeing the world. I am trying to give Victorianists—and other students of nineteenth-century literature and culture—a new perspective on familiar debates that intersect in crucial ways with issues still relevant to literature in an age of multiculturalism and postmodernism, where we too seem to be sailing over a vast ocean of writing, pulling up, here and there, our little buckets.

The journey toward the acceptance and tentative celebration of eclecticism was not an easy one. For most of the nineteenth century, British writers shied away from using the words eclectic or eclecticism, and when they did use them, it was rarely in a positive sense. These words carried strongly negative connotations, which would not easily be shed, even in a time and place as manifestly eclectic as Victorian Britain. It would be difficult to claim that this sense of revulsion for eclecticism was traceable to Victor

Cousin, its first modern proponent, or to the *juste milieu* French culture his philosophy had helped to bring about. It is somewhat easier to follow the fortunes of eclecticism in the debate on architectural style, and in the broader concern of Victorians for the imprint their culture would leave on history. But eclecticism was both an intellectual and an aesthetic dilemma, arising from a growing awareness of the claims of the past in the present and resolvable only through historical synthesis or, as some few imagined, a virtually impossible break with history.

In giving order to the vagaries of history, Victorian writers tended to impose models of progress or circularity. Not surprisingly, eclectic thinkers wanted to have it both ways. History would alternate between periods of contraction and expansion, or periods of analysis and creativity; progress would go on apace for a time, before running out of ideas. At the low ebb of original ideas, we have eclecticism, the culture of analysis and excessive introspection. For the eclectic this situation was always temporary and to be regarded as an opportunity for gathering up the riches of the past in order to prepare for the future. Was it so simple as reversing what had often been experienced as decadence and ending, and calling it a new beginning? No. No one who lives through such an interregnum regards it as a blessing. Those writers most deeply affected by the ebb tides of eclecticism were often the most irredeemably pessimistic about the future—their own and the nation's. Eclecticism gave them a thread of hope, a reason to go on working, and a way to keep off, as Carlyle might have said, that night wherein no man may work.

Even Cousin, with his philosophical eclecticism, did not expect to prepare a summa of human knowledge, with the truth extracted and displayed, because he knew that eclecticism was never anything more than a method for dealing with the messiness of the past and its tentacle-holds on the present. Much like its late-Hellenic and Baroque precursors, nineteenth-century eclecticism sought to resolve conflicts between systems of thought, not in order to create its own system of the world, but rather to establish the conditions under which better and clearer thoughts might prevail. With such liberal aims as these, well adapted to the pragmatic spirit of the Britain of the Great Reform Bill, it is perhaps somewhat surprising that an eclectic philosophy, which based its appeal on common sense, was not embraced during Victoria's reign. While many versions of eclecticism can be traced in Victorian thought—and it is the aim of this study to bring them to light—the idea of eclecticism was met with disapproval almost everywhere, until very late in the century.

In making these related claims—Victorian culture was eclectic, eclecticism was a problem, this problem had to be resolved through a creative synthesis—I do not mean to argue that the nineteenth century was unique in its need to deal with the burden of the past, and therefore uniquely eclectic, or that eclecticism had never been perceived as a problem at any other point in history, or even that Victorian eclectics were prone to combine the materials of the past in more unlovely fashion than the eclectics who had gone before. I want instead to emphasize the degree to which the conditions producing eclecticism affected how the culture saw itself and its place in history, and became identified with the spirit of the age—indeed, with the innermost hopes and fears of its most articulate critics and apologists. These claims depend on two crucial assumptions, the first that eclecticism was pervasive in the culture of the nineteenth century, and widely discussed, and the second that literary eclecticism—the focus of this study—depended on cultural translation, both across cultures and across the arts.

Two significant inscriptions of the Victorian idea of eclecticism, separated by only a few years, show, when brought together, the two sides of this peculiarly modern disease—just as Strachey's preface would do for the next generation. George Somerset, the hero of Thomas Hardy's novel *A Laodicean* (1881), suffers from the "modern malady of unlimited appreciativeness"; he is indecisive and "lukewarm." In the essay on "Style" (1888), Walter Pater declares that "no critical process can be conducted reasonably without eclecticism" (16); and, since he says this about Tennyson's poetry, it is clear that Pater means one cannot write, create literary art, without being eclectic. The best writers select from among all the words of the language, with all their shades of meaning in view, the words most suited to the writer's purpose. For Hardy, the working out of the novel's plot involves lessening the pressures of plenitude through experiments in eclectic combination; while for Pater, the future of literature depends on the willingness of individual writers to engage eclectically (and critically) with literary history. What was it about their historical situation that made these two very different writers take what seemed on the face of it to be a lamentable fact, namely the burden of the past as it weighed on the present, and to transform it into the cornerstone of human creativity? Somerset's uncritical inclusiveness and Pater's critical exclusiveness are symptoms of the eclecticism that was already a significant force in nineteenth-century European culture. Having choices was both heavy and light; it signified not only the burden of responsibility for shaping the future, but also a future that was in some sense free-floating, uncertain, and radically contingent.

In Hardy's novel, eclecticism comes to be associated with a supple, forward-looking liberalism positioned against the backward-looking rigidity of the Gothic Revival. Eclecticism, by definition, cannot be conservative, but must remain open to change, and perpetually receptive to new influences. For the Victorians, liberalism, in both its humanistic and political senses, had already created a connotative conundrum. "Liberal" could mean free, open-minded, receptive, and generous of spirit, optimistic and unprejudiced; or it could mean licentious and indulgent, lax and lukewarm, middling and makeshift. Likewise in the choice of an architectural style, "eclectic" might equally describe undiscriminating mixture or stylistic synthesis. Here, the choice arises not only from an awareness of competing historical styles and their distinct meanings but also from the availability of these styles in an open marketplace. As capitalism intensifies, individuals have to make more choices commensurate with their financial standing. The richer and better educated a person is, the greater the number of decisions she will have to make. Since most people slide toward uncritical inclusiveness, rather than critical exclusiveness, their eclecticism is naïve, and driven by nothing more calculated than the happenstance of instantaneous preference (probably helped along by clever marketing and the desire to show up one's neighbors).

Just as the necessity of choosing underlies liberalism and capitalism, it becomes a more acute problem of identity with the advent of widespread, state-sponsored education. The liberal arts had always been defined eclectically, and the process of learning was necessarily a protracted one; but by the time a student reached maturity, he would be able to grasp the interrelations among disparate objects of study; that is, he would have a liberal viewpoint. For the growing middle classes, however, traditional academic subjects were treated (if possible) even more superficially, and the taste or sensibility that the upper classes acquired as a matter of course in their everyday lives continued to elude those who were scrambling to reach the vantage point of their former masters. When the middle class reached the summit and captured the castle, they registered their newfound authority and independence by renovating the venerable structure in their own image. Not much constrained by taste, they blithely mixed Gothic and Greek, Moorish and Byzantine, with old and new vernacular styles. They redecorated with paintings and sculptures drawn from every period, and artifacts from every place touched by Britain's empire. It was an age of bric-a-brac, supported by the naïve eclecticism of a class that had discovered the past and the world, and dominated them both.

As the plurality of artistic styles became more widely known, and the link between aesthetics and morality more insistent, stylistic preference could take on all the weight of religious affiliation. The affective force of *A Laodicean* depends on this link between the aesthetic and the moral; if one is stylistically eclectic, then one is probably shot all through with eclecticism and its moral ambiguities. In a conclusion that validates his characters' inconsistency, Hardy rejects the notion that moral principles must be fixed and unswerving, instead presenting lukewarmth as an important transitional phase in one's moral development. However, this liberal approach to morality was generally viewed with suspicion, because it seemed to make received wisdom or even revealed truths open to negotiation, allowing individuals to pick and choose the bits of doctrine with which they felt comfortable and to discard the rest as inessential or antiquated. One could argue that aesthetic standards changed with the times, evolving with the societies in which those standards developed; but to say that morality was subject to the same shifting proprieties as fashion would be to call into question the whole foundation on which Christian morality was based. Eclecticism in morality was the inescapable effect of historical accumulation, yet it was regarded as a violation of historical progress. The Reformation and the Renaissance had shown that it was possible to choose both one's religion and one's cultural heritage, that organic development, in its strictest interpretation, could be circumvented. Before the rise of historicism, such apparent divergences from development were not perceived as disruptive; but a deeper awareness of history, and a romantic preference for folkloric integrity, gave all such deviations the taint of artifice.

To claim eclecticism for the nineteenth century is thus paradoxical, as it did not express the age in any strictly representational sense and did constitute a break with historical development. To claim for eclecticism the exalted status of "high" art would be equally misleading. What, then, does eclecticism do for the critic and historian? Eclecticism describes a way of thinking about the historical inheritance. It gives us a glimpse of the aspirations of the middle classes during the period. And it underscores a crucial dilemma of the age: the problem of producing an original style that would represent the age to itself and to posterity. In the nineteenth century, historicism had led to the imitation of historical styles, while ever-deepening knowledge of these styles contributed to a sense that modern art was inauthentic, because inorganic and derivative. Conceptions of the artist had changed, too, which placed a new premium on originality—genius became the only acknowledged path to artistic greatness. These romantic-historicist notions put intense pressure on artists not only to produce works of individual genius but also to create a national style that was both organically coherent and culturally distinctive. But eclecticism was rooted in the artistic culture of the nineteenth century, and the only way to get beyond a damaging, naïve eclecticism—the only way to develop an individual or a national style—was to pursue a more rigorous eclecticism.

Introduction

The literary historian Walter Pater articulated the critical exclusiveness of nineteenth-century eclecticism, and overcame the intellectual and aesthetic crisis provoked by eclectic historicism, when he redefined style as "a peculiar sense of fact," rather than the exclusive property of genius. In his essay on "Style," the peculiarity of the artist bears only a superficial resemblance to the prevailing notion of the genius as a creature born not made. While "true art" does express a specific personality—"fact as connected with soul," the literary artist must be a scholar, whose sense of fact depends on selecting from a multitude of facts. Within the critical exclusiveness of eclecticism, originality becomes possible only through the extreme refinement of the writer's medium. Under the regime of choice, the writer must be both critical and self-critical. The writer finds organic completeness by submitting all words, phrases, and sentences to the unity of the internal vision, the literary architecture, which is "a single, almost visual image, vigorously informing an entire, perhaps very intricate, composition, which shall be austere, ornate, argumentative, fanciful, yet true from first to last to that vision within" (23). For Pater this submission of expression to idea is a truly "eclectic principle" (34), because it borrows from all the forms of beauty that have existed throughout time and allows for the contemporaneous existence of infinitely varied styles.

Could this rigorous eclecticism, practiced by a select few, overcome the prejudice most felt against the naïve eclecticism that continually told against progress, as it pilfered history and jumbled together its ill-gotten gain in cities and houses whose lineaments were equally confounded? In Pater's account of the sources of style, literary eclecticism coincides with a perception of historical belatedness, but does not forestall the emergence of fresh and distinctive styles; on the contrary, it is the vital requirement of all artistic creation whatever under the conditions of modernity. In this way Pater largely put to rest the doubts of his contemporaries who worried that the arts could only decline as surely as the sciences progressed. He made what looked like ending into a new beginning. The eclectic interregnum would be, for Pater, not a time for waiting, but a time for making, because analysis was only another aspect of invention.

It is possible to equate the uncritical inclusiveness of naïve eclecticism with bourgeois modernity and the critical exclusiveness of Paterian eclecticism with avant-garde modernity, with the former impelled by a liberal faith in "doing as one likes" (as Arnold puts it in *Culture and Anarchy*) and the latter driven by its "high" aestheticist opposition to that "low" form.[1] We can make several further distinctions between the two eclecticisms. All eclectics must be open to variety, but not all eclectics discriminate. One does not choose to be naïvely eclectic, although one might be content to be uncritical with respect to the historical inheritance, and happy to absorb culture from any source. Paterian eclecticism permits no such passivity, but demands painstaking scholarship, whether one is the author or reader, artist or spectator. This will limit significantly the number of persons producing works of eclectic synthesis as well as those who can appreciate them. All eclectics believe in progress, but some eclectics believe that progress happens only fitfully, or cyclically. Naïve eclectics do not recognize the burden of the past, or if they do perceive it, they tend to regard it as so much flotsam to navigate, but never as a serious threat to progress. By contrast, volitional eclectics move forward only by mapping the historical terrain, aware of every turning and branching in the road. They believe in progress *and* decadence, in the intricate patterns of *corsi* and *recorsi*. Volitional eclectics favor synthesis over development, and seek to live in synchronic, rather than diachronic, time. This does not mean they will exist always in an ahistorical present, but rather that they will exist with the synchronous consciousness of past, present, and future. Such volitional eclecticism might liberate the artist from the bourgeois "march of progress" *and* from Hegelian universal history—we do not have to develop in a particular way. All eclectics translate cultural material, but not all eclectics respect the distinctiveness of their sources. Naïve eclectics tend to appropriate the artifacts of disparate cultures, but in a manner that makes what is taken resemble the taker. Imperial plunder tells the tale of the victor not the maker; the collection of old masters displays more wealth than taste; the neo-Gothic castle or neo-Classical villa inclines to fashion rather than to history. In his translations of culture, the naïve eclectic tends to level off differences; in his art, he reaches for the readymade, mimicking the official culture and flattering national biases. At its worst, this bourgeois eclecticism, so dependent on capitalism for its circulation, produces art that is mechanical, pretentious, and thoughtless, the pap of an immature society motivated by vanity and greed. At its best, naïve eclecticism might promote cross-cultural understanding, greater self-consciousness, and an aptitude for social transformation. Creating the potential for change is the continual labor of the volitional eclectic. What Wolfgang Iser calls "the translatability of cultures" makes true eclecticism possible. If one were limited to a single language or perspective on the world, then the territory from which one selected "the best that has been thought and known"—to borrow another apt expression from Arnold—would be too narrow to yield any crop of ideas that could be so denominated. It would be as though one tried to draw conclusions about Earth's terrain without ever leaving the mountain valley or sandy isle. Thus the volitional eclectic must also be conscientiously cosmopolitan, eschewing the temptations of nationalism and organic historicism in favor of the wider view offered by comparison. This might look like a gesture of mastery that depends on an impossible erudition. Eclectic synthesis might yield what looks like a synthetic culture—derivative and artificial. But for the volitional eclectic, it is no longer a matter of choosing eclecticism, but only of choosing how to be eclectic.

The hard-won insights of Hardy and Pater did have their day; the literary and artistic culture of late-nineteenth- and early-twentieth-century Britain was unabashedly eclectic—an eclecticism that bears a complicated relationship to avant-garde modernism, in its "high" form, and to postmodernism, in its "low" form. In telling the story of getting there, the seven chapters of this study are balanced between a general account of the aesthetic and intellectual crises of eclecticism, and a more focused account of the practices of volitional eclecticism in literature.

Chapter 1 commences where this introduction began, with the reentry of "eclectic" into the critical vocabulary of art history in the second half of the eighteenth century. The purpose of this chapter is to examine the conditions giving rise to eclectic art and architecture in the nineteenth century and the extent to which these conditions might bear on the production of literary texts as well. Eclecticism became a useful concept during the nineteenth century, both as an explanation for decline in literature and the other arts and as the means for resolving their crisis. This is not to say, however, that the effects of eclecticism in literary texts were identical to those in the other arts. After all, eclecticism in language, ideas, and literary style is not as easy to *see* as an eclectic building or even an eclectic painting; nor is an eclectic literature as easy to anatomize as an art museum or international exhibition. In order to make literary eclecticism *visible,* I must borrow some of the language, images, and theories of the other arts, of architecture, in particular; in chapter 1, then, I aim to create eclectic homologies that will carry over into the chapters that follow. By way of defining the significance (and slipperiness) of the concept of eclecticism, I take up the famous controversy over the eclecticism of the Carracci, a family of late-sixteenth-century Italian painters who founded an academy at Bologna. The academic art they represent, in its theories and educational programs, and in its claim to originality as a style, provides an important starting point for an examination of the fortunes of eclecticism in the nineteenth century. The dangers of adopting eclecticism as a critical term are perhaps best illustrated by the emotional debate carried on by Denis Mahon in the 1950s, as he struggled to recover the Carracci reputation by dispensing with the idea of eclecticism. With the advent of postmodernism, however, the term is no longer shameful, and the time seems ripe for allowing the eclecticism of the Carracci to be acknowledged and appreciated once more.

In the second part of chapter 1, I bring the debate on the eclecticism of the Carracci into the British context, considering Sir Joshua Reynolds's methods of instruction at the Royal Academy, which essentially follow those established by the Carracci at Bologna. In the *Discourses,* Reynolds sets out his eclectic principles and tests their value in relation to emerging genres such as landscape. Reynolds provides an interesting case study, poised as he is on the brink of the Romantic revolution that would reject his core notion that the training of the artist depends on assimilation of the great masters for the idea that the training of the artist depends on immersion in nature. I close the section by considering Ruskin's complicated rejection of Reynolds in *Modern Painters,* as part of his defense of the Romantic painter Turner.

Keeping in mind Iser's rule that cultural translation was unnecessary as long as the historical inheritance was taken for granted, eclecticism in the modern sense could not be said to have a history before this period. Around the end of the eighteenth century, one's culture could no longer be taken for granted; the cultural inheritance was in the process of being romanticized and historicized, which accounts for the anxiety that eclecticism produced in all the arts. It is not surprising, then, that "eclectic" was the epithet most commonly applied to Victorian architecture, and, because architecture was the dominant art of the period conceptually, it became a locus of anxious projections about the future. To survey the architecture of the Victorian period is to confront the material results of eclecticism: the stylistic eclecticism adopted by (and endured by) the middle classes; the historical revivals in domestic architecture and decoration; anxiety over the status inconsistency represented by copies or imitations; the loss of distinctness of place; the ever-narrowing range of authenticity and the corresponding search for aesthetic novelty and artistic originality. The third part of chapter 1 deals with a neglected episode in Ruskin's career and in the history of Victorian medievalism. Ruskin visited Sir Walter Scott's mansion at Abbotsford in 1838 with the intention of describing it in a series of essays on "The Homes of the Mighty," but he was so dismayed by what he found there that he determined never to write about it for the public. Unlike most visitors to Abbotsford, he could not reconcile the character of the building with what he thought he knew of the author's mind. For Ruskin, Scott's mind was manifested in the novels; in the novels only, Ruskin seemed willing to suspend his preference for organic coherence and authenticity. His imagination when reading established the connections among the fragments of Scott's genius, but his imagination when seeing refused to accept the conflict among the different styles that made up Scott's mansion. Ruskin's response to Scott's house is thus characterized by desire and constraint: a desire to see the world of Scott's romances, tempered by the knowledge that one cannot recreate the past—except in books.

By the middle of the nineteenth century, medievalists had become more idealistic—more concerned with ideas than things—but dissatisfaction remained the keynote. Victorian architects and designers went on trying to imitate the medieval cultures they admired, but critics became more exacting; the freedom of the eighteenth- and early-nineteenth-century revivalists was lost in the effort to rebuild the Middle Ages according to the rules discovered by scholars and archaeologists. John Ruskin was naturally a leader of the movement to discover an authentic middle ages, but he was intensely pessimistic about the possibility of reclaiming its forms for the present age. Ruskin's position would be widely disseminated later in his career through the famous "Nature of Gothic" chapter of *The Stones of Venice:* the nineteenth century can never reproduce the architecture of the middle ages, because the culture is too different. It was a statement against imitation—against reenactment. Throughout his career, then, Ruskin found himself in the peculiar position of advocating the superiority of medieval architecture while condemning nearly every effort that was made to build it. He established a rule that still constrains neomedievalists: it is appropriate to write fictions about the past, but inappropriate to try to make them come to life. In spite of Ruskin's powerful influence, there were architects who embraced eclecticism, and it is with a brief consideration of these, and what Sir John Summerson called "the problem of failure" in Victorian architecture, that I conclude my discussion of eclecticism in the arts.

Chapter 2 explores a particularly influential framing of eclecticism as a philosophical system in the work of Victor Cousin. Largely forgotten today, Cousin in the first half of the nineteenth century was the focal point of intense debate in both France and Britain. A philosophical method that seemed by turns willful and passive, powerfully synthetic and hopelessly derivative, eclecticism complemented the historicism of the age and strengthened the Romantic movement in France (inspiring Stendhal to name eclecticism "the philosophy of the nineteenth century"), but did little to repair the crisis of faith that would define nineteenth-century culture. On the contrary, eclecticism seemed to promote skepticism and moral confusion, and critics such as Sainte-Beuve and Hippolyte Taine in France and William Hamilton and George Henry Lewes in Britain attacked its founder, Cousin, as both an intellectual dilettante and a political charlatan.

Chapter 3 takes up some of the broad understandings of eclecticism that arose in the debate over Cousin's eclectic philosophy, in particular the notion that eclecticism was inherently literary or metaphorical rather than philosophical. Turning this notion back on the conditions affecting literary creation in the early nineteenth century, I consider several aspects of literary modernity as problems of eclecticism. First, Samuel Taylor Coleridge's description of the eclectic mind in *Biographia Literaria* gives us a template for interpreting the forms of naïve eclecticism that were infecting literary culture. Second, writers of the period were becoming increasingly concerned with the multitude of voices trying to be heard in the literary marketplace. Southey, Mill, and De Quincey worried that there was no reliable method for ordering the vast quantities of printed material available and that too often, readers would turn to digested versions of text—eclectic magazines and the like—rather than encountering a work firsthand. The third significant problem of literary modernity, the burden of the past, resonates strongly with the dilemma of style typical of naïve eclecticism. William Hazlitt and Thomas Love Peacock questioned whether poetry (or any of the arts) could progress and whether any further development, apart from eclectic imitation, were possible. T. B. Macaulay also doubted the possibility for progress in literature, and warned against the danger that eclecticism posed for poetry in particular. In his essays on Milton and Dryden, Macaulay addressed a fourth aspect of eclectic literary modernity when he argued that the nineteenth century must be an age of criticism. Some of his contemporaries disagreed. In the fourth section I consider Thomas Carlyle's account of the disease of self-consciousness in literature, which he recognizes as an outgrowth of historical awareness and eclectic machinery for promoting the arts, such as academies and journals, together with Charles Kingsley's analysis of the negative consequences of widespread, naïve eclecticism in poetry that was largely driven by the poet's diseased self-awareness.

Collectively, these writers create a picture of the operations of eclecticism in literature and indicate possible solutions for overcoming it, some of which are taken up by the writers who are the focus of this study: Tennyson, Kingsley, Arnold, Pater, and Hardy. In chapter 4 we see that Tennyson offers a model of eclectic poetics that challenges the presumption that literary eclecticism heralds inevitable decline. In *The Princess* Tennyson proves that the medley form might be original. However, the poem's reception was sharply divided among those critics who believed that the formal experiment was a success and those who did not. I take up the debate between two critics in particular, Aubrey De Vere and C. P. Chrétien, who view the success or failure of Tennyson's poem as a judgment not only on the poet's reputation but also on the eclectic orientation of the nineteenth century. Kingsley's ambivalence about eclecticism (seen in his praise of *The Princess* and his condemnation of eclecticism elsewhere) makes the interpretation of his novel *Hypatia* especially difficult. Set in fifth-century Alexandria, the novel dramatizes the conflict among the diverse peoples of the city at the moment when Christianity is ascendant. Kingsley's plot works steadily toward a compromise among contending forces and frames Christianity as a religion of the *via media*. Alexandria became a watchword in the Victorian period for eclectic decadence and moral confusion, and Kingsley is at least partly responsible for disseminating the idea, which I briefly explore in writings about Britain's imperialist encounters.

The end of chapter 5 marks a turning point in the study from a focus on the problem of eclecticism in Victorian culture toward a focus on the role of volitional eclecticism in securing the future of literature. In chapter 6, I uncover the early influence of Cousin on Matthew Arnold, examine the self-conscious eclecticism of Arnold's poetry and criticism, and conclude by considering Arnold's later writings on literature and culture, which examine both the negative force of uncritical eclecticism, "doing as one likes," and the positive force of eclectic criticism, "finding the best that has been thought and known in the world." Like its ancient counterpart, modern eclecticism would consistently attempt to reconcile the divergent tendencies of Western culture: idealism and materialism, classic and romantic, beautiful and sublime, Greek and Gothic, Hellene and Hebrew. Perhaps more disturbing to nineteenth-century sensibilities, eclecticism proposed a historical model of synthesis in opposition to the preferred and virtually unquestioned model of development; and, confirming its secondary, derivative status, eclecticism seemed to be a critical endeavor preparing the way for the future, rather than a productive, creative process in its own right. A sense of literature's decline did not, however, preclude a search for solutions, and in spite of widespread opposition to eclecticism, Arnold advocated an implicitly eclectic program of literary history and criticism, a project that would finally be made explicit in the work of Walter Pater.

If the "Age of Eclecticism" can be said to begin in 1815 with Victor Cousin's first lectures at the Sorbonne in Paris, then it might be said to conclude with the publication of *Marius the Epicurean* in 1885. The novel was a watershed in Pater's career, a treatise in the form of a romance, an answer to the critics who had driven him to suppress, for many years, the "Conclusion" to *Studies in the History of the Renaissance* (1873). In his early reviews of Pre-Raphaelite poetry, Pater had discovered the aesthetic of the "mixed situation," which led him to a broad understanding of Renaissance as eclectic process. It also brought him to accept, even to prefer, the relative and the tentative to the absolute. For Pater, transitional ages were best, and he devoted much of his writing to exploring the peculiar beauties of liminally positioned writers and artists, and since life was always in flux, one could find such beauty in every time and place. In chapter 7, I also consider Pater alongside the other writer who haunts this introduction—and, in a real sense, the entire book—Thomas Hardy. *A Laodicean* and *Marius the Epicurean* have both been described as intellectual novels; they are better termed philosophical romances, for both thematically and structurally they make the formation of the self into a heroic quest. For both writers, that self can be triumphant only in his or her mutability—I'm adapting Ruskin's description of modern literature here—and the fulfillment of the quest is achieved only through volitional eclecticism, so that eclecticism as a philosophy, as a way of living, is actually figured as heroic, the best hope for survival under the corrosive conditions of modernity. But after 1885, after *Marius,* the problem of how to live is not so often represented as a problem of how to choose, or rather, it is taken for granted that the modern self is a medley.

In the concluding afterword, I bring the discussion back to the present, paraphrasing Arnold once more, to the function of eclecticism at the present time. The historical dilemma embodied by eclecticism has not dissipated; if anything, it has grown more acute with the passage of time, as the burden of the past must always do. The urge to encompass vaster reaches of geographical space compounds the difficulty of taking in perpetually receding historical time. The problem of eclecticism for literary critics and historians has often been reframed as its solution, just as it was for many Victorians. Only by becoming volitional eclectics do we avoid a worse fate—being always naïvely eclectic.

PART I

Toward an Age of Eclecticism

CHAPTER 1

History's Diverse Beauties

In his brilliant and polemical *Studies in Seicento Art and Theory* (1947), Denis Mahon identified Johann Joachim Winckelmann, one of the founders of modern art history, as the propagator of the catchword "eclectic"—"that veritable masterpiece of concise meaninglessness"—in a small work published in 1763, *Abhandlung von der Fähigkeit der Empfindung des Schönen in der Kunst, und dem Unterrichte in Derselben*. Winckelmann employed the term to denote the imitators of classical art; like the late Hellenic eclectic philosophers, these classical artist-imitators (*der Nachahmer*) caught reflections of the original masters in the inevitable cyclical movement of styles and forms through the centuries. Drawing an explicit parallel between *der Nachahmer* of late antiquity and the Baroque artists of recent history, Winckelmann initiated what in Mahon's view would become a central misunderstanding in the history of art: the Carracci would play the part of the modern Nachahmer. In other words, according to Mahon, the dominant figures of Baroque art would carry the stigma of eclectic impurity and decadence. Their supposed theory of "selection" combined with an "erudite-sounding watchword" doomed the Carracci to the category of reactionaries out of touch with their times in the modern, individualist romance of the history of art.

As Mahon saw it, the "legend" of an Eclectic School in the seventeenth century arose from a misapplication of classical art theory (on the part of

Winckelmann) to actual works of art. Classical theory "should be looked upon in light of a propagandist polemic on behalf of a minority preserving a legitimist descent: an interpretation of art [. . .] rather than an active principle animating it" (Mahon 197). Reduced to the confusing, imprecise, and negative term "eclectic," the complicated style of the Carracci, developed from a myriad of influences, was lost, Mahon believed, in a theoretical fog. He conceded that the confusion over the Carracci's use of theory began almost immediately, with their first biographers, Giovanni Battista Agucchi and Giovanni Pietro Bellori. While Mahon attempted to raise the reputation of the Carracci family by distancing them from theories imposed on their artistic productions after the fact (as he thought), earlier critics found reason to praise the Bolognese painters' profound learning and its deployment in their art.

Mahon's attitude toward eclecticism, and "classic theory," was typically post-Romantic and widespread by the middle of the twentieth century. In 1960, in terms similar to those employed by Mahon in his defense of Baroque painting, the art historian Lincoln Rothschild attempted to find an interpretation of style that would "establish direct connections between the forms of artistic expression and the patterns of human life" (6). In trying to account for those periods in which the arts did *not* seem to reflect the prevailing spirit of the age, Rothschild enumerated four conditions under which the link between art and society might be weakened or even severed: first, during "transitions of growth" in which extremes of style passed through a middle ground; second, "transitions of change, in which vestiges of previous sophistication are inevitably involved in the formulation of new expression"; third, provincialism, in which artists tried "to reproduce a style away from the metropolitan center"; and fourth, eclecticism (112). While artistic products of the first three categories still fit neatly into Rothschild's evolutionary model, clearly, the offspring of eclecticism did not. Rothschild's vehement rejection of eclecticism establishes an important link between eclecticism and varieties of conservatism on the one hand, and between eclecticism and capitalism on the other:

> A considerable variety of social maladjustments will support eclectic cultural expression as a mask or shell that may be donned complete, with little reference to the inhabitant shape. A ready-made culture suits people of immature responsibility, who can enjoy effortless leisure, freedom from necessary activity or obligation. Eclectic pretensions also frequently cast art in the role of shield or apologist for leadership entrenched beyond the limits of its social usefulness, or actively predatory and antisocial, like the personal elegance notoriously affected by racketeering gangsters; or the

palaces, and collections of old masters owned by the so-called "robber barons" of the late nineteenth century. Academic dependence on classical models also provides a convenient mode of official generalization, a dignified way of taking a stand against sin and for everything noble without committing the management or the regime to any too precise or practical program. (114)

Rothschild aimed his righteous indignation at two groups in particular: the newly rich, whose adoption of a "ready-made culture" or mimicry of an official or, worse, authentic culture proved that they "regard[ed] art as a pretentious assertion"; and the aristocracy, whose capacity to produce an authentic art had long since evaporated along with its "social usefulness." After ridiculing consumers of culture for preferring eclectic art, Rothschild turned his attention back to the producers of culture. Artists who adhered to classical models were by definition eclectic and, ultimately, irrelevant. Eclecticism was generalizing, uncommitted, and vague; it was hypocritical, conforming, and weak.

While critics such as Rothschild and Mahon made "eclectic" and "eclecticism," for a time, practically unusable terms in the history of art, the postmodern sensibility has again made it possible to examine critically the significance of eclectic periods in the history of art, architecture, and philosophy. The neglect of the term is not particularly surprising, in light of the critical and historical controversy I have just been recounting. What is surprising is that no other term has been advanced to replace it that would also describe the peculiar conditions surrounding the invention, production, and propagation of nineteenth-century art and literature. Rothschild wanted to disallow any link between eclecticism and cultural evolution; and yet the historical pattern emerging from an examination of eclecticism across cultures and across the arts suggests that it arises consistently in those times and places where there is a sense of cultural loss or stagnation and that it becomes the method by which artists and thinkers grope their way back to confidence and even, finally, to originality.

What Is Eclecticism?
Reconsidering Winckelmann's Interpretation of the Carracci

The salient facts of the Carracci history tend to support the traditional eclectic-theoretical interpretation. Most critics writing before Mahon agree that the Carracci rejected the antinaturalistic, or Mannerist, style that was popular in the second half of the sixteenth century. They advocated a return to the style and the principles of the High Renaissance and the painters they admired: Titian, Correggio, Raphael, and Michelangelo. To promote these principles among the young artists of Bologna, Ludovico Carracci founded the Accademia degli Incaminati (Enggass xi).[1] According to Frank Mather in his 1923 *History of Italian Painting,* the Carracci Academy was influenced and anticipated by the Belgian Denis Calvert's academy founded at Bologna on the same principles and with the same fund of "nostalgia for Renaissance grandeur" (458–59). These schools used then-progressive methods of comparative study, such as casts and engravings, in attempting to identify and assimilate the perfections of past masters.

Annibale Carracci, considered by most contemporaries to be the greatest painter of the family, carefully studied the methods of Raphael, Tintoretto, and Correggio, and was "launched on the impossible quest of combining with the austere grandeur of the Roman School, the charm of Venetian coloring and the emotional instability of Correggio. [. . .] [I]t was an attempt dictated by the times, and the inevitable choice of any superior spirit who wished to reknit the Renaissance tradition" (Mather 459). Lending support to the Carracci method, Agucchi, a contemporary of the Carracci, observed the successful operation of this principle in Renaissance art. *Idea* was the path to perfection for modern artists. As Rensselaer Lee explains, "Idea for Agucchi is an image of embellished nature which the painter forms in his mind by the empirical process of selecting the best from many objects" (206). In Agucchi's view, the Mannerists precipitated a decline in taste because they relied on their own imagination, on *fantasia;* the Carracci restored painting, through *idea,* by following the antique and assimilating its perfections. Bellori closely followed Agucchi's line on the Carracci, fifty years later.[2] An intellectual and antiquarian, Bellori was profoundly interested in artistic theory and praised the Carracci for achieving an idealized form of beauty, "nature perfected." The imitation of the ancients, who had "most fully grasped" "eclectical empiricism," would lead modern painters to "the perfect combination of nature and art." According to Bellori and others, Annibale had solved one of the stylistic dilemmas of the seicento by uniting *disegno* and *colore,* by combining technical perfection with fresh painterly colors (Enggass xvi). Carlo Cesare Malvasia praised the Eclectics in 1678 for taking the best from all the best artists, "form[ing] from them a brief compendium, rather a precious extract, outside of and beyond which little remained for the studious to desire," and forming from all these styles one of their own which had nothing to envy in all the others (qtd. in Mather 471). Unlike Mahon, who wants to validate the unique style of Annibale by resisting the eclectic interpretation, earlier historians of art approved it and could still allow for the development of a new style within the Carracci's critical endeavor: Baroque Classicism—the perfect unity of line and color, painting informed by knowledge.

As Rensselaer Lee points out in his review of Mahon, neither Winckelmann nor the Carracci's earlier critics would have considered their eclecticism a bad thing. The role of the Nachahmer was, in their view, admirably fulfilled: "When all reservations are made, the Eclectics had fairly done their work of correcting the disorder of the late Renaissance and of restoring something of the old decorum. They made possible the revival of the grand style at Rome, in the eighteenth century. [. . .] The Eclectics were the bridge by which the classical manner passed over into Western Europe, an indispensable link in the chain of the great Hellenistic tradition" (Mather 469). When Winckelmann explained more fully the use of "Eclectici" to describe the Carracci in his *Geschichte der Kunst des Alterthums* (1764), he noted their resemblance to the philosophers of late antiquity "who [. . .] tried to combine the ideas of previous schools, owing to their lack of vitality" (qtd. in Wittkower 152). Far from denouncing the art of the Carracci, Winckelmann rather offered up "eclectic" as an interpretation of their particular historical situation: they collected and summarized the systems of their more talented predecessors.

For centuries the concept of genius was compatible with the practice of imitation. This relationship survived as long as imitation remained free of the taint of eclecticism. Though Winckelmann may indeed have been the first to perceive Carracesque imitation as eclectic, he yet believed that imitation (and, by extension, eclecticism) was the proper course to the revival of art. His famous pronouncement—"The only way for us to become great or, if this be possible, inimitable, is to imitate the ancients" (*Reflections* 5)—bears all the contradictions of his age. As Walter Pater would later recognize, Winckelmann's classicism constituted a form of rebellion against the prevailing artistic culture of his day. To return to the source of culture (Greece, of course, for Winckelmann) and to partake of its vitality even in reflection might suffice to bring beauty back to art. In basic agreement with the theories of selection current for two centuries, Winckelmann believed "that the imitation of the Greeks [could] teach us to become knowledgeable more quickly, for it shows us on the one hand the essence of what is otherwise dispersed through all of nature, and, on the other, the extent to which the most perfect nature can boldly, yet wisely, rise above itself" (21). The greatest artists of the Renaissance had "to first feel and to discover in modern times the true character of the ancients" (39), and this recovery of an outlook no longer inevitable in modern times enabled them to produce an art both of their age and superior to it. Commentators who wished to denigrate the productions of post-Renaissance artists would say that they were mere copyists, never getting at the ideal that the Greeks captured and that Michelangelo recaptured. "Imitation" in Winckelmann has frequently been understood as the "ancient Greek method by which general ideas of beauty led ultimately to the realization of the ideal" (Fried 90), while "copying" was thought to mean the realistic portrayal of a particular object. More recently, however, the art historian Michael Fried has brought to light an often-overlooked passage from the *Reflections* that should reverse our traditional prioritizing of imitation and copying. In the section Henry Fuseli titled (in his translation) "Workmanship in Sculpture," Winckelmann tries to imagine how the Greeks managed to transfer their models from wax to marble, exactly reproducing the form of the wax model. The Greeks' elusive perfection, Winckelmann seems to say, resides in a moment of copying, not of imitating, the ideal. Without the ability to make the perfect copy, the entire enterprise would have been a failure. Fried argues that Winckelmann does not therefore denigrate the "workmanship" of sculpture, as Fuseli seems to do, but values it as an absolutely integral part of the process of creating "inimitable" art—art that is deserving of imitation (94).

The theoretical interpretation of the Carracci that has now become so disreputable originated with the understanding that in order to accomplish the restoration of painting, the Carracci must have followed two important precepts: they had to study, copy, and accept as guides the models of the past, and they had to draw upon the traditional subject matter supplied by poets and historians, whether past or present (Lee 207). The only alternatives seemed to be the direct imitation of nature (practiced by Caravaggio) or the direct transmission of the image in the mind (practiced by the Mannerists). Was painting then only the "poor relation" of literature, destined to remain forever a subordinate art? Mahon affirms that "Whether or not [painting] made its mark was to a certain degree contingent on the amount of learning and erudition displayed; hence tradition and precedent played a considerable part" (159). The "academic" view of painting identified here was, according to Lee, "an accepted and even prevailing point of view among critics and amateurs of art at the beginning of the century just as it was Bellori's at the middle and end" (207). When "academic" is equated with "eclectic" and "eclectic" with Annibale, however, Mahon and Lee part company: Mahon concludes that the classic-idealist theory was retrospective in character, that it could not "have been the driving force behind any artistic movement" (196), and that the Carracci were not especially eclectic compared with Raphael or with Poussin (painters who are never saddled with the derogatory term). By contrast, Lee contends that the Carracci were familiar with artistic theory that "counseled the method of eclecticism as part of a program for the improvement of the art of painting in what they considered its present state of decline" and that "Winckelmann, who followed Seicento opinion in this matter, was essentially right when he first named them eclectics and [. . .] there is still justification for so regarding them today" (211). Thus, Lee considers eclecticism as a way of operating (at a particular moment in history) and the Carracci method of painting as eclectic; while for Mahon, the issue turns on whether eclecticism can have any descriptive utility.[3]

Conveying little more than a general censure of seicento art, especially of the Carracci, the term "eclectic" has for a good many years dropped out of use in academic art history. Despite strong evidence pointing to the widespread use of eclecticism as a way of operating in sixteenth- and seventeenth-century art, Mahon's impassioned refusal of "eclectic" as a critical term influenced most writers on the Carracci either to remain silent on the issue or to repeat his reasons for not employing it.[4] But Mahon had inadvertently drawn attention to a thorny problem for art historians: when is "selective borrowing" eclecticism, and when is it a means for the display of genius? For Rudolph Wittkower, who is best known for his work on the genius and character of artists, *Born Under Saturn,* the issue hinges on whether the artist in question borrows silently or makes his borrowing part of a theoretical program: "the most common empirical procedure of art historians is concerned with the tracing of influences and borrowings, [. . .]. But when confronted with this very issue as an explicit theory, the same art historians paradoxically retract and stigmatize it as eclectic" ("Imitation" 154). But as one defender of the apparently discredited idea of "eclecticism" put it, we should recognize the courage of the Carracci in facing the crisis of late-sixteenth-century art head on. Instead of imitating the masters, the Carracci imitated nature with their guidance; they had to thoroughly understand the masters and understand nature as well.[5]

Defining eclecticism is notoriously difficult since there is no particular visual or literary style associated with it. Embracing eclecticism as a theory could destroy a reputation, since romantic art history turned the classical theory of selective imitation upside down. But practicing eclecticism has been unavoidable for writers, philosophers, and artists alike at least since the end of the eighteenth century. Derived from the Greek verb *eklegein* (to select) (Dillon and Long 4), "eclectic" names a *process,* that of selecting the best from among a collection of things. "Eclectic" as a negative aesthetic judgment can be traced to the particular outlook of Romantic art history in the first half of the nineteenth century. In fact, Mahon blames nineteenth-century art historians such as Henry Fuseli, Franz Kugler, and Charles

Blanc for the dissemination of the Carracci "legend" (and for the family's subsequent relegation to secondary status in the story of the progress of painting). The Carracci may have served their purpose in the revival of taste, conventional wisdom would utter, but they produced nothing really original. But the Carracci reputation was still vital in this period, and no one writing the history of Italian painting, or tracing the development of revived classicism, could afford to ignore them.

The fragile literary foundation on which the Carracci theory of eclecticism was first erected was little more than an affectionate sonnet presented at the funeral of a fellow painter, Niccolò dell'Abate. It is variously attributed to Annibale, Agostino, or an anonymous friend:

> Whoever a goodly painter seeks to be
> Should take the Romans' drawing to his aid,
> Movement from the Venetians, and their shade,
> And worthy coloring from Lombardy,
> The awesome Michelangelo must see,
> The truth to nature Titian has displayed,
> The pure and sovereign style Correggio had,
> And of a Raphael just symmetry,
> Tibaldi's basis, and his decoration,
> Invention of learned Primaticcio's own,
> And just a little grace from Parmigianino.
> But leaving so much study and vexation,
> Set him to imitate those works alone
> Which here were left us by our Niccolino. (Holt 73–74)[6]

Whether a form of conventional praise for an artist (e.g., he combines the best qualities of all the best painters) or a glimpse into the "ideas [and] critical terms" of the Carracci school, the sonnet is certainly the most damning evidence of Carracci eclecticism as mere cookery. It has nonetheless, and in spite of several incorrect attributions, profoundly influenced the historical judgment of the school at Bologna.[7] Winckelmann, when he reintroduced the term "eclectic" to describe the Carracci method of painting, picked up the ingredients of the famous sonnet from Malvasia: "They were eclectics and sought to combine the purity of the ancients and of Raphael, the knowledge of Michelangelo, the richness and exuberance of the Venetian school, especially of Paolo Veronese, and the gaiety of the Lombard brush in Correggio" ("Essay on the Beautiful in Art" 99). Having remarked on the decline that preceded the Carracci, Winckelmann contends that although they "must be regarded as imitators," they did "achieve [. . .] the fame of their masters" (99). Henry Fuseli, whose translation of Winckelmann in 1764 introduced the term "eclectic" into English, took a more severe view of the eclectic recipe for success in his lectures to the Royal Academy: "Of such advice, balanced between the tone of regular breeding and the cant of an empiric, what could be the result? excellence or mediocrity? who ever imagined that a multitude of dissimilar threads could compose an uniform texture, that dissemination of spots would make masses, or a little of many things produce a legitimate whole? indiscriminate imitation must end in the extinction of character, and that in mediocrity,—the cipher of art" (II:108–9). Disgusted by what he judged the mechanization of art and the eclipse of originality, Fuseli tried to resist, in his reform of the Royal Academy, the "compendiary method [. . .] which [. . .] has ruined the Arts of every country, by reducing execution to a recipè, substituting manner for style, ornament for substance, and giving admission to mediocrity" (II:388–89). Eclecticism, the "compendiary method" praised by classic-idealist theorists of the previous three centuries, could have played no part in the "real progress of Art" (III:4). For Fuseli, only Genius could advance the cause of Art by the direct perception of Nature and its *imperfect* transmission (III:7–8).[8] Mere craftsmen should, in his view, be asked to leave the Academy (II:388–91). But by making Art the exclusive domain of Genius, Fuseli calls into question the very existence of the academy that supports him (he'd been made professor in 1799). Founded during the waning years of the Renaissance, the academy of art served no purpose but the promotion of another rebirth through its criticism, something Fuseli reluctantly admitted: "All, whether public or private, supported by patronage or individual contribution, were and are symptoms of Art in distress, monuments of public dereliction and decay of Taste. But they are at the same time the asylum of the student, the theatre of his exercises, the repositories of the materials, the archives of the documents of our art, whose principles their officers are bound now to maintain, and for the preservation of which they are responsible to posterity, undebauched by flattery, heedless of sneers, undismayed by the frown of their own time" (III:58). That the Eclectic schools had likewise been involved in the maintenance and preservation of the "materials" and "documents" of art apparently escapes Fuseli, who reserves his admiration for productive geniuses whose places in the history of art are secure. That Fuseli recognized in Annibale Carracci the standard for academic art (III:119) and despised him for it speaks volumes about the Royal Academician's troubled relationship to the art of his own time. He wishes to take up at once the role of the critic and the role of the artist, a dual posturing that would become typical of the eclectic during the nineteenth century. In the productive slippage between Fuseli's criticism and his art production emerges a self-conscious, critical art. For the Academy to play any role in the future of art, it would have to maintain this difficult balance between promotion and invention.

Like Henry Fuseli, Franz Kugler believed that his art criticism would further the recovery of art in his own age. In his preface to the second edition of his *Handbuch der Geschichte der Malerei seit Constantin dem Grossen* (completed by Jacob Burckhardt in 1847), Kugler credits a period of "wide-spread dilettantism" early in the century with the rediscovery of the art of the Middle Ages and with the subsequent researches into all periods of the history of art (iv). Nourished by the "romantic" art thus brought to light, modern "romantics" yielded to an aesthetic position as extreme as the classical that had preceded it. If he had needed a reminder that style was a choice, this was it. Kugler felt that a revised edition of the *Handbuch* was necessary to qualify his early intolerant opinions: "The more the sources of knowledge and judgment enlarged, the more it became apparent that the modes of conception peculiar to the romantic period had confined our views within too limited a space, and that even so late as ten years previously such views had partaken too much of that contracting influence" (iv). First published in 1837, his *Handbook of Painting* was enormously influential in categorizing the different regions and periods of Italian art. His aesthetic judgments followed from this taxonomy and were thus immediately available to amateurs and professionals alike. Though he was not the first to observe the divergent tendencies in the art of the seicento, he established definitively the existence of two schools: the Eclectics and the Naturalists. Just as he was trying to mediate the extremes of the classical and the romantic, he tried to lead his readers into a position between eclecticism, which he regarded as an intense form of idealism, and naturalism: "Each class exercised in its development a reciprocal influence on the other, particularly the *Naturalisti* on the Eclectics; and it is frequently impossible to distinguish, with perfect precision, the artists of one class from those of the other" (II:481).

But distinguish them he would. Kugler's definition of eclecticism and his classification of the Carracci as Eclectics, derived from Bellori, Malvasia, and even Winckelmann, remained unquestioned for over a century. "The greater number of artists of this time (that is the end of the sixteenth and first half of the seventeenth century) are known by the name of Eclectics, from their having endeavoured to select and unite the best qualities of each of the great masters, without however excluding the study of nature. This eclectic aim, when carried to an extreme, necessarily involves a great misapprehension with regard to the conception and practice of art, for the greatness of the earlier masters consisted precisely in their individual and peculiar qualities; and to endeavour to unite characteristics essentially different at once implies a contradiction" (II:481). Not nearly as negative in his judgment as Mahon contends he was (219), Kugler actually seems sympathetic to the goals of the Eclectic school. What he describes is a scholarly practice that both takes account of the best art of the past and returns for inspiration to the original—to Nature. Though the "eclectic aim" might be carried too far, Kugler has generally good things to say about all the Carracci, even turning them into romantic heroes who "opposed fresh ideas to the exaggerated mannerisms then existing" (II:484). Of Ludovico Carracci, Kugler writes: "He passed his youth in constant and close attention to studies which had become a dead letter among the artists of the time, and which thus exposed him to much ridicule and contempt; but this only made it the more evident to him that reform was desirable, and that it had become necessary to introduce rules and well-understood principles into art, to counteract the lawless caprice of the mannerists" (II:482). Kugler had reproduced the rise-and-fall pattern of Italian painting established by Bellori in his *Lives* by denoting the fifty years prior to the Carracci as a period of decline. In his story of the progress of painting, the three Carracci were trailblazers. In youth they might have tried to realize their "patchwork ideal," but their extraordinary talent helped them to surpass "mere plagiarism" of the great masters and achieve a "thoroughly-understood and artistic appropriation of their highest qualities, bearing the character rather of rivalry than of imitation" (II:484). Like Winckelmann, Kugler saw the Carracci-as-Nachahmer as supplying an urgent need for order and as marking a high point in the history of painting. They might never be considered artists of the first rank, but they had prepared the way, both through their scholarship and through their painting, for another Renaissance, the one through which Kugler imagined he was living.

The popularizing French art historian Charles Blanc, in his *Histoire des peintres de toutes les écoles* (1865–77), also acknowledges the Carracci's role in preparing for the future of painting, but at the same time seems to denigrate them as "coldly calculating artists who had simply imitated the more truly inspired artists who had preceded them" (Goldstein, *Visual Fact* 1). Nonetheless, Blanc, like Winckelmann and Kugler before him, believes that what the Carracci produced from their eclectic style was vastly superior to anything else being done in Italy at the beginning of the seventeenth century. They put forth, in systematic fashion, an "eclecticism" that would

> [...] choisir dans chacun des maîtres de premier ordre ce qu'il a eu de mieux, étudier le dessin des grands dessinateurs, la couleur des grands coloristes, les ordonnances de celui-ci, les effets de celui-là, et se composer, de

ces qualités diverses, en les combinant, de plus, avec l'étude de la nature, un style mixte, qui serait excellent puisqu'il n'y manquerait rien et que toutes les parties en auraient été puisées aux meilleurs sources. (xiii–xiv)

[[. . .] choose in each of the masters of the first order that which he has done best, to study the drawing of the great drawers, the color of the great colorists, the rules of these ones, the effects of those ones, and to comprise, from these diverse qualities,—combining them, furthermore, with the study of nature—a mixed style, which would be excellent seeing that it would want for nothing and that all the parts had been drawn from the best sources.] (my translation)[9]

Blanc's attitude is typical of French thought in the nineteenth century; eclecticism as a method always serves a particular historical purpose. Not all periods in history are equally creative, and there are some artists whose role it is to give birth to genius and to the new age. But he cannot wholeheartedly endorse the method, any more than Fuseli and Kugler do. The romantic ideal of originality was by now firmly entrenched, so even the Carracci's volitional eclecticism seemed to violate the principles of art and it could not to be promoted or preferred as an artistic method. By the time Blanc was writing his history of painting, many artists were in revolt against academic, that is, eclectic, methods of instruction.

Given this antieclectic tradition, Denis Mahon naturally was at pains to recover the reputation of the Carracci (particularly in relation to their now more popular contemporary, Caravaggio) via their interaction with the art of their own time, in the union of naturalism and imagination that he identifies as the essence of the Baroque. By contrast, nineteenth-century historians of art constructed a retrospective theory of eclecticism to explain a way of operating shared by the Bolognese painters, while still acknowledging the pivotal role of the Carracci and their Academy in the advancement of art during the seventeenth century. They may not have been the recipe eclectics ridiculed by Fuseli, but they did self-consciously and deliberately reinterpret the elemental forms of classicism into a living language. Undaunted by the inferiority their eclecticism implies, Rensselaer Lee recognizes that "Annibale was a scholarly painter who succeeded in his eclectic aim" (212). Occupying a central position between the two poles of the classical and the Baroque (Mahon 204), the Carracci output reveals eclecticism at work, trying to reconcile contradictions and longing to hold on to the past even as the present encroaches.

This dilemma is readily apparent in Annibale's contribution to the then-lowly genre of landscape painting. That Annibale painted landscapes at all might have troubled his classicist admirers, but it no doubt delighted those twentieth-century critics who wanted to claim him for the romantic-naturalist genealogy. The companion pictures *Hunting* and *Fishing* (ca. 1585, both now in the Louvre) represent some of Annibale's most groundbreaking work, despite his clear indebtedness to the tradition of Venetian landscape, especially to Titian. At first glance these paintings would seem to belong to the genre of mythological landscape that Titian made famous (Robert Cafritz sees a close resemblance in Annibale's work to Titian's *Pardo Venus,* painted around 1560, certain works of Domenico Campagnola, and decorative paintings by, among others, Niccolo dell'Abate [85–86]). Notably absent from Annibale's work, however, is a single mythological figure. While the landscapes of both *Hunting* and *Fishing* are ideal, in the sense that they are "calculated to enhance nature aesthetically and morally," they do not allude to "classical gods and heroes to transmute physical reality into poetic invention" (Lagerlöf 7). Instead, Annibale imbues ordinary activities with transcendent significance. Collecting food becomes the window through which we catch a glimpse of the divine idea underlying nature, stretching back to the beginning of time. The men and women represent various occupations and classes; dogs and horses are as numerous as people. The recessionary planes within both pictures provide glimpses of a general prosperity. Even those who are working hardest are fully integrated into the scene; in *Hunting,* the men in charge of refreshment and a poor hunter defending his catch from a dog frame the action of the noble riders and beasts, while in *Fishing,* a woman mending nets, two men dragging a net until their muscles bulge, a boatsman, and a fisherman occupy the center of the scene, which is framed this time by better-dressed merchants and leisurely fishermen. Both scenes manage to convey a classical sensibility (Annibale's later landscapes would take up biblical and mythological themes), but within a naturalistic framework. They also share strong horizontal movement as the actions of hunters and fishermen carry them to the left or right of center. Annibale has thus taken from Titian his coloring, his composition, and his view of nature as benevolent and innocent, and he has given us a composite view, achingly nostalgic and Arcadian, and confidently modern.

In my view, Mahon's assertion that the principles of selection allegedly employed by the Carracci were commonly known and used by other painters does not bolster his subsequent claim that the charge of eclecticism is misplaced. Eclectic methods of instruction were indeed prevalent in the academies, and eclectic theories of painting were widely circulated[10]; to disavow the Carracci's knowledge of theory in order to recover their original reputation (based, as we have seen, on the very eclectic method now considered so discreditable) seems profoundly misleading. In the debate on the eclecticism of seicento painting, we witness the emergence of a discourse simultaneously critical and innovative, retrospective and speculative. Nineteenth-century critics of the Carracci tend to repeat, while denigrating, their eclectic-critical methods. Those who saw in the artistic efforts of the Carracci a phenomenon more distinctive than mere imitation or simple influence may have been thus predisposed by a series of formulations for coping with the disintegrative forces of coexistent romanticism (generally understood) and classicism; in other words, the eclecticism of seicento art represented an acceptable compromise between competing artistic ideologies.

Sir Joshua Reynolds and Eclectic Education

The history of the idea of eclecticism did not perish with the Carracci, nor did the eclectic instruction of young artists remain confined to their academy in Bologna. The man who would become the greatest promoter of eclectic education in Britain, Sir Joshua Reynolds, stood poised at the brink of a transformation in the arts that would overturn the centuries-old theory of imitation through selection on which his teaching was based.[11] Though his *Discourses* delivered before the Royal Academy from 1769 to 1790 were, in John Ruskin's words, "not well arranged, and not very *recherché* or original" (I:491), they constitute the major body of art theory in Britain with which nineteenth-century critics, including Ruskin, had to contend, and contain early arguments against nascent romanticism. Reynolds aimed the *Discourses* first of all at the students of the newly formed Academy. In fulfilling this directive, the first president of the institution solidified the course of instruction set out by the prestigious Italian academies of art. The educational (and status-raising) function of the Academy having been firmly established by the Carracci and others, Reynolds had primarily to justify adherence to a well-worn path, to argue for the value of an eclectic system of education that was already being challenged in the eighteenth century by great artists who had broken the rules.[12]

To convince students—and the public—that only an Academy could secure the progress of the arts, Reynolds promoted a theory of invention based on the careful and prolonged study of collected artistic achievement. A centralized institution, organized under royal patronage, offered the surest means for bringing together the greatest painters of the age as teachers and contributors of artworks, "to create a repository for the great examples of Art" (81): "These are the materials on which Genius is to work, and without which the strongest intellect may be fruitlessly or deviously employed. By studying these authentic models, that idea of excellence which is the result of accumulated experience of past ages, may be at once acquired; and the tardy and obstructed progress of our predecessors may teach us a shorter and easier way. The Student receives, at one glance, the principles which many Artists have spent their whole lives in ascertaining; and, satisfied with their effect, is spared the painful investigation by which they came to be known and fixed" (II:81). In founding the Academy upon these eclectic principles, Reynolds seeks to engage the "accumulated experience of past ages" in the service of the future; indeed, as Quentin Bell points out, Reynolds's primary innovation in the *Discourses* consists in his assertion that great painters, building upon "authentic models," discover their *own* styles. Thus, we might view Reynolds's academic project as a form of "creative eclecticism," an enabling process of selection and imitation, rather than the limiting of artistic freedom in the service of absolutism as later critics, such as William Blake, would have it.[13]

In Discourse II, Reynolds clearly outlines the process whereby the artist, submitting himself to years of study, at last achieves creative independence. In the first appearance of what will become one of his main tropes, Reynolds compares the acquisition of the mechanical skills of painting to that of the grammar of language. Beginning with the most basic skills, students would first learn to draw from the flat, then from the round. The human body was the subject of almost every study, and students had to copy noses, eyes, ears, and mouths, and then separate limbs and entire figures, from an accepted master such as Raphael. They would memorize proportions, the catalogue of human expressions, eventually learning light and shade and color, all from antique models. Lectures on anatomy and perspective, and the life class, would complete training in the *grammar* of the art, and "when the student's mind had been so perfectly attuned to the beauties of antiquity that the imperfections of Nature would be automatically corrected" (Bell 14), he would graduate to the second degree of proficiency.

The academies of art did not consider their educational mission concluded until the student had mastered the historical canons of painting, sculpture, and architecture—"to learn all that has been known and done before his own time" (II:89). The middle period of an artist's development requires, for Reynolds, a sort of full-blown eclecticism. The student seeks out the best art works ever produced and discovers their outstanding qualities; before he is a master, he must become a critic and a scholar. The eclectic synthesis of all that is excellent in each of his models enables the student to produce, according to his talent, a superior work of art: "Those perfections which lie scattered among various masters, are now united in one general idea, which is henceforth to regulate his taste, and enlarge his imagination. With a variety of models thus before him, he will avoid that narrowness and poverty of conception which attends a bigoted admiration of a single master, and will cease to follow any favourite where he ceases to excel" (II:89). In the discourses that follow, Reynolds continually emphasizes the need for comparison and selection as the only sure means of avoiding deformity and exaggeration: "A man is as little likely to form a true idea of the perfection of the art, by studying a single artist, as he would be to produce a perfectly beautiful figure, by an exact imitation of any individual living model" (VI:163). This raises, of course, one of the problems attendant on an eclectic method—the tendency to deviate from nature in the pursuit of excellence; so it was not only the loss of originality that troubled critics such as Fuseli but also the loss of truth—a sacrifice that would be too great for one of Reynolds's sharpest critics, John Ruskin.

The third and final stage of the artist's training requires still more discipline: moving beyond the combination of various excellences to the discrimination of incompatible styles. Reynolds in effect answers the critics of Carraccesque eclecticism who claimed that the Bolognese painters' combination of elements of different styles created monstrous deformities, Frankenstein's monster *avant la lettre*. Students of the RA would be trained in the art of "know[ing] how or what to choose, and how to attain and secure the object of [their] choice" (VI:160). Far from seeing the Carracci as servile imitators (their reputation had not yet suffered Romantic attack), Reynolds saw in their "liberal style of imitation" evidence of "men who extended their views beyond the model that lay before them, and have shown that they had opinions of their own, and thought for themselves, after they had made themselves masters of the general principles of their schools" (VI:165). In fact, Reynolds invokes the Carracci, especially Ludovico, as "model[s] for style in Painting" (II:96), praising his ability to take "only as much from each [school] as would embellish, but not overpower, that manly strength and energy of style, which is his peculiar character" (V:139); more importantly, Reynolds credits the Carracci with laying the foundation of the Grand Style at their Accademia when they revived the example of Michelangelo (XV:326–27). As later critics have suggested, Reynolds might have been mounting a defense of his own methods and demonstrably imitative, eclectic portraits.

The success of academic eclecticism depended, of course, on Reynolds's belief that all truly great artists learn from the art of the past, that geniuses are not born, but made. Central to his refutation of Edward Young's influential "Conjectures on Original Composition" (1759) was the notion that

"Invention, strictly speaking, is little more than a new combination of those images which have been previously gathered and deposited in memory: nothing can come of nothing: he who has laid up no materials, can produce no combinations" (II:91). Rather than relying on ineffable inspiration, the artistic genius sustains himself on "The daily food and nourishment [. . .] found in the great works of his predecessors" because "There is no other way for him to become great himself" (XII:273). Reynolds harshly refutes Young's fashionable assertion that "genius is from heaven, learning from man" with practical knowledge: "It is very natural for those who are unacquainted with the *cause* of any thing extraordinary, to be astonished at the *effect,* and to consider it as a kind of magick" (VI:152). Only the "ignorant," "from their entire inability to do the same at once," could believe that great art is produced without effort (VI:152). While Reynolds acknowledges the power of imagination at work in his heroes, Raphael and Michelangelo, he continually emphasizes their diligent labor, the years of practice their work must have cost them. Convinced that "by imitation only, variety, and even originality of invention, is produced" (VI:154), Reynolds recommends that students follow Raphael's example. Raphael's first works reveal his devotion to his master, Pietro Perugino, but, says Reynolds, he soon formed "higher and more extensive views" and "imitated the grand outline of Michael Angelo; he learned the manner of using colours from the works of Leonardo da Vinci, and Fratre Bartolomeo: to all this he added the contemplation of all the remains of antiquity that were within his reach; and employed others to draw for him what was in Greece and distant places. And it is from his having taken so many models, that he became himself a model for all succeeding painters; always imitating, and always original" (VI:164). Reynolds's reading of Raphael echoes and explains Winckelmann's assertion in *Reflections:* one becomes great—inimitable—only by imitating the ancients. These critical contemporaries would agree: it was Raphael's eclecticism that made him great, and only a falling off from the study of the art of the past could have brought the Renaissance to a close and ushered in the degeneracy of art that we call Mannerism.

Eighteenth-century critics such as Reynolds and Winckelmann would have seen in those deformed and exaggerated figures the operation of pure fantasy, of uncontrolled imagination. The opposite tendency, Reynolds felt, also had to be resisted: the Dutch painters produced exact copies of whatever appeared before their eyes, but in their servility to reality they made no appeal to the mind. And only by appealing to the intellect could painting achieve the status of a liberal art. The ascendancy of poetry over painting in the hierarchy of the arts had everything to do with the eclectic nature of literature compared with the mechanical nature of painting, and with the fact that the production of great literature resulted from prolonged study of ancient models and the assimilation of an historical canon, while great painting (that is, works appealing to the eyes alone) could be produced by skilled copyists. In the academic view, painting could be neither a divine gift nor a mechanical trade. If painting were to become the equal of poetry, then its practitioners had to emulate the poets: Reynolds flatly declares, "He can never be a great artist, who is grossly illiterate" (VII:175). The store of humanistic learning had to be shared with artists who, in addition to mastering the mechanical part of the art and its supporting sciences, would be conversant in poetry, philosophy, history, and religion; they must be admitted into learned society, where their recreational reading would be supplemented with brilliant conversation (VII:175); and they must travel in order to obtain the storehouse of images and ideas necessary for the creation of great art.

One can easily imagine Reynolds's paternal tone in Discourse XII when he addresses youthful art students about to embark on their first trip to Italy. Indeed, the Grand Tour was arguably a larger part of the humanistic training than it was of the artistic. Polonius-like, he enumerates the careless habits to be corrected, the forms of inattention to be avoided, the dangers of seeing too much, and the necessity of nourishing the mind upon variety. At last he arrives at the central issue: "young Students should not presume to think themselves qualified to invent, till they [are] acquainted with those stores of invention the world already possesses" (XII:277). To this iteration of a familiar point Reynolds adds a warning against emulating the *Pittori improvvisatori* whose spontaneous productions dazzle the eye and instead suggests beginning with an exercise called the *Pasticcio*. The student's pastiche would "encompass the different excellencies which are dispersed in all other works of the same kind" (XII:278); not stopping there, the student would learn the art of selecting what is excellent in art and in nature (XII:279). The *Pasticcio,* while consistent with Reynolds's eclectic program of education, raises the problem of the element of chance in shaping a synthesis of sources. In the introductory paragraphs of the twelfth discourse, Reynolds alludes briefly to a general condition of travel: "we must take what we can get, and when we can get it" (263). But how much more is this true of the process of canonization? How susceptible to chance is the selection of the models employed at the Academy itself? Though Reynolds never questions the classical norm on which he bases his teaching, the eclectic methods outlined in the preceding pages certainly could have led students to artworks and styles other than those selected by the Academy. Expansively, he admits that the artist must find the beauty in all ages and in all schools, in what is great and in what is little, in East and in West (VI:170). Given these conditions, academic eclecticism would undermine, eventually, its own standards of imitation and invention, of what is perfect in art. Conceding that what is recognized as genius varies over time, Reynolds must have entertained some doubt that genius would always manifest itself as neoclassical.

It is likely that Reynolds was aware of the dangers posed by an increasing knowledge of the history of art, and must have guessed that the problem of creating (or rather choosing) a style to express the age could only be compounded by eclecticism. In order to stave off the threat of competing aesthetic systems, the academies established standards of taste by promoting an internally coherent style. At first this had meant purging the excesses of the Baroque in an attempt to create a purer classical model. Selecting the most suitable models for imitation, the academies were able to produce a "grand style" or *beau ideal* that passed as universal. For Reynolds in Discourse III, intellectual dignity and ideal beauty superior to what is found in nature define the Grand Style. With a gesture that sweeps away Dutch and Flemish and any merely imitative art, Reynolds avers that "a mere copier can never produce anything great" and that the "genuine painter [. . .] must endeavour to improve [mankind] by the grandeur of his ideas" (III:103). He proceeds to lay out the path to the Grand Style, a road, one might say, cleared of all its random growth and exhibiting only enormous landmarks in the form of past masters. As Reynolds repeatedly contends throughout the *Discourses,* the student must engage in a "laborious comparison" of these works so that he "acquires a just idea of beautiful forms; he corrects nature by herself, her imperfect state by her more perfect" (III:106). He learns to see nature through the eyes of the ancients and so arrive at a "central form [. . .] from which every deviation is deformity" (III:107). Though he admits that a variety of figures may be beautiful, none of them exhibits the highest perfection. In *The Schools of Design,* Bell agrees that the creation of a composite perfection was central to academic training. He recounts the oft-told story of Zeuxis, the Greek painter commissioned by the people of Crotona to paint Helen. In order to create an image of the legendary beauty, Zeuxis chooses the twelve most beautiful girls in town, makes nude studies of each, and eventually picks the five most beautiful models of the group. At last he combines their separate features to make one figure more beautiful than any individual could be (Bell 3–4). Bell, who is favorably disposed to eclecticism, connects such a synthetic process with the cosmetic industry: "it is possible to imagine the beautification of a form through the readjustment of individual members" (4). While most Romantic and post-Romantic critics would reject the destruction of organic unity in the individual human body, academicians such as Reynolds regarded the elimination of accidents and deformities (in nature as well as in fashion) as the mission of an art addressed to the mind.

In an essay on the *Discourses* typical of Romantic criticism, William Hazlitt exposes inconsistencies in Reynolds's advocacy of the Grand Style and his belief in the power of diligent labor to produce great art. Hazlitt's arguments in favor of the power of genius will be familiar: "all the great works of art have been the offspring of individual genius, either projecting itself before the general advances of society or striking out a separate path for itself; all the rest is but labour in vain" (127). The proof is in Reynolds's pudding, Hazlitt claims, somewhat erroneously: does *he* not return continually to those originators who "unfold [. . .] new and exquisite powers of their own, of which the moving principle lay in the individual mind" (128)? So Hazlitt points to all those statements in which the academician notices the special genius of one artist or another, and argues that Reynolds is just leading his students on when he tells them that hard work will supply any deficiency in their natural talent. Much more complicated and important for the development of art criticism in the nineteenth century is Hazlitt's contention that Reynolds's precepts regarding the Grand Style are plainly flawed and illogical. Taking issue with the key passage in Discourse III, where Reynolds claims that "a mere copier of nature can never produce anything great," Hazlitt poses an argument that Ruskin will expand in *Modern Painters:* Reynolds seems to discount the greatness of effect possible in nature herself, implying that she "is a heap of disjointed, disconnected particulars, a chaos of points and atoms" (Hazlitt 134–35). One of Reynolds's own contemporaries, Edmund Burke, had suggested the extent to which a lack of clarity in atmospheric effects gives birth to the sublimest views in nature; but Reynolds was not very interested in landscape or nature generally because it seemed to him unintellectual, less likely to achieve the grandeur of *Istoria*—or to raise the status of his profession. As a recent editor of the *Discourses,* Pat Rogers, notes, Reynolds seems not to have been influenced by Burke's aesthetic treatise and does not really attempt to integrate his famous distinction between the sublime and the beautiful into his theory of the Grand Style—a serious omission, and one that undoubtedly diminished Reynolds's influence in the nineteenth century.

In this respect, landscape again makes for an interesting test of eclectic principles, as it did in the case of Annibale Carracci. In his 1993 essay "The Public Prospect and the Private View," John Barrell attempts to reconnect assumptions about genre to their original context by considering the rise of landscape painting in terms of its ability to express public virtues. Taking

Reynolds's comments on landscape as his starting point, where the academician asks whether landscape has the right to aspire so far as to reject depicting what painters call the "accidents of nature," Barrell points out that landscape as a genre had usually been associated with private virtues. He summarizes two types of landscape representation that became dominant in the eighteenth century. First, there was the panoramic landscape, which was the analogue of the social and the universal, and which is surveyed, organized, and understood by disinterested public men who regard objects in the landscape in terms of their relations, and who are enabled to do this by their ability to classify and generalize. Second, there was its opposite, the occluded (or confined) landscape, belonging to the private man, whose experience is too narrow to permit him to abstract from it. The occluded view conceals the general view by concealing the distance; a characteristic image of this category would be a cottage within a stand of trees, whose larger setting appears only in spots through the foliage. For Barrell then, landscapes during this period are generally constructed as either private or public, and were understood to appeal to private or public interests respectively, or to two spheres in the life of a citizen.

Landscape would first gain in authority as it catered to public interests. Like history painting, landscape now aimed to appeal to the broad and comprehensive vision, and the ability to abstract representative from actual nature that would become the chief qualification for citizenship (rather than a disposition to perform acts of public virtue). Reynolds was profoundly interested in how changing generic distinctions within painting would affect the status of artists. In his Fourth Discourse, Reynolds compares the trends in landscape painting on the Continent. The Dutch School, he argues, though adept at producing faithful portraits of particular places, should not be imitated by students who wish to achieve greatness in painting. By contrast, Claude Lorrain had achieved in his landscapes something akin to history painting by representing *general* nature and avoiding local detail: his truth is founded on the same principles as those by which the history painter achieves perfect form. Reynolds's advocacy of ideal landscape makes sense in terms of Barrell's argument outlined above. Even though Reynolds would admit to liking the more particularized views of his contemporary Gainsborough, as the first president of the Royal Academy, Reynolds worked hard to raise the professional status of artists in general, and saw that the best way to achieve his goals for art would be to ally painting with literature and philosophy. In other words, the ideal landscape, informed as it was by literary precedents, provided a more certain route to professional acceptance. If a painter was obviously a scholar, then he was no longer a craftsman.

Throughout his discourses Reynolds acknowledges the tardiness of painting compared with its sister art, poetry. Painting must learn to appeal to the mind, rather than to the eye; that is why nature must be considered in the abstract, for particulars would only distract the eye. The painter, by studying the literature of all nations and periods, must divest himself of prejudices in favor of his age or country, which could lead him to depict the local and the temporary rather than the universal and timeless qualities of his subject.[14] For a literary model of this process, Reynolds could look close to home. In *Windsor-Forest* (1713), Alexander Pope had described a particular place in language that elevated it to a representative type. Seeing "order in variety," Pope unified all the parts of the landscape by the principle of *concordia discors*. Undaunted by nature's incredible variety and changeability, the poet made the particular details of the place allude to a larger narrative of progress from waste to plenty, and the expansion of a nation from the old world to the new.

In spite of the persuasiveness of Reynolds's arguments in the *Discourses,* the seeds of doubt that would make artists permanently anxious about eclecticism had already taken root. Depending on the elimination of particularities and the "accidental" deformities of nature, the Grand Style's separateness from nature would form the basis of Ruskin's critique of academic authority in *Modern Painters*. Though Ruskin would eventually return in his *Lectures on Art* to something like Reynolds's eclectic outlook, he begins his career by tearing down the central theory of the *Discourses,* that in striving after perfection, the Grand Style reaches an intellectual dignity equal to the art of poetry, and in its appeal to the mind, raises humankind from a lowly condition. By contrast, Ruskin would argue that the Grand Style, which is eclectically constructed from nature and from the masters of the past, cannot mean anything in the present age: "if we are to produce anything great, good, awful, religious, it must be got out of our own little island, and out of these very times, railroads and all" (*Works* III:231). In the preface to the second edition, Ruskin attacks even more directly the idealizing ambition of academic painting. Painting something as it ought to be, rather than as it appears, is morally wrong, and he mounts his defense of modern landscape painting on the basis of its truthfulness; before Turner, the landscape painter attempted "to modify God's works at his pleasure, casting the shadow of himself on all he sees, constituting himself arbiter where it is honour to be a disciple, and exhibiting his ingenuity by the attainment of combinations whose highest praise is that they are impossible" (III:25). The Grand Style displayed "clumsiness of combination," and ultimately became a "monstrous creature," opposed to nature. In attempting to perfect the forms of nature,

Ruskin complains, the painter has forgotten nature altogether—has left it out of the picture.

Ruskin would overturn Reynolds's understanding of perfection by referring it back to nature: "Now there is but one grand style, in the treatment of all subjects whatsoever, and that style is based on the *perfect* knowledge, and consists in the simple unencumbered rendering, of the specific characters of the given object, be it man, beast, or flower. Every change, caricature, or abandonment of such specific character is as destructive of grandeur as it is of truth, of beauty as of propriety" (III:25). Even while Ruskin rejects any effort to combine separate beauties, he does not altogether abandon the Platonic ideal of archetypal forms. The deep study of nature will bring the painter "perfect knowledge" of the specific character of every living thing, a character reaching perfection if not subject to accident or disease. Again demonstrating his debt to Reynolds, even as he breaks with his core values, Ruskin does not advocate the servile imitation of nature, such as he perceives in the Dutch School. He calls them "professional landscapists" and "dextrous imitators of certain kinds of nature, remarkable usually for [their] perservering rejection of whatever is great, valuable, or affecting in the object studied" (III:188). He reacts to one of his contemporaries, Constable, much as Reynolds might have done, abhorring his "morbid preference" for low subjects, but respects his works for their honesty and originality, their manliness of manner. Ruskin cares nothing for a descriptive record of a place or a moment, but expects the landscape painting to provide him with a glimpse of God. Only by the incorporation of mystery, that obscurity he so loves in Turner, can a painter raise a "holy thought" in him. Ruskin thus agrees with Reynolds as to art's mission—the improvement of the spectator—but eclecticism in its crass assemblage of parts fails to capture the essential perfection of a unified creation.[15] This tendency to infuse style with moral meaning would be Ruskin's most enduring contribution to the history of art, and certainly the feature of his writing that helped to make architectural eclecticism a cultural problem.

For the early critics of the Carracci, and for academic artists across three centuries, eclecticism was not an accident but a necessity, not failure but success. Post-Romantic critics uncomfortable with the designation, and all that it implied of derivation and recipe mixtures, gradually made the term unusable in the history of art, at least through the middle decades of the twentieth century. The situation in architecture shared many of the same features, but with these significant differences. The awareness of eclecticism in architecture came later than it did in painting, around the turn of the nineteenth century, arising with the Battle of the Styles, which brought with it the consciousness of stylistic choice. There was no sustained period of acceptance—within a half-century the playfulness of "Gothick" had been supplanted by the serious search for a purer, unmixed Gothic. The professionalization of the architect naturally played its part in the quest for authenticity, bound as it was to expand knowledge of historical forms and styles and to create a demand for demonstrable expertise. Debates about architecture were inevitably more public than debates about painting, and tended to make the issue of style a moral one, an index of national character. Twentieth-century critics of Victorian architecture did not need to overturn the judgments of their predecessors in order to claim their aesthetic independence; indeed, when they wished to denigrate the built environment of the previous century, they had only to invoke the angry critics who had been first on the scene. This is not to say that Victorian architecture was derided solely for its eclecticism, but that eclecticism—especially naïve eclecticism—was symptomatic of a lack of progress in the arts, the dominance of capitalist values, and the loss of a faith that, in earlier ages, had underwritten great architecture.

As J. Mordaunt Crook argues in *The Dilemma of Style,* choice has been at the root of architectural style, at least since the Renaissance, when it was first understood as "a conscious system of design, a visual code, a postvernacular language of forms" (13). This transformation offered both freedom and the burden of choice—a burden that became heavier as the Victorians' "acute awareness of history clashed with the results of evolutionary thinking" (131). For some architects this meant trying to recover the line of development that had been severed with the rise of classicism by adapting Gothic to present uses, but even those architects who embraced a broader, synthetic eclecticism had to decide "what to 'eclect'" (126). Eclecticism as idea and practice is often used to explain what John Summerson in 1968 called "the problem of failure" in Victorian architecture. In accepting that it was "horribly unsuccessful" ("The Evaluation of Victorian Architecture" 2), he is relying on "the documented self-criticism of the age itself"; to find a point of view from which it all makes sense (and succeeds) would be, he argues, a "fraud" (18). Anyone who looks at Victorian architecture, therefore, has to confront "the problem of failure," which is directly traceable to the pervasive "doubt" of practitioners and critics in the period, to the ambiguities in their conception of architecture, especially the question of style: "Every Victorian building of any consequence is a statement of stylistic belief—either a belief in one style, or in the peaceful coexistence of styles (eclecticism), or in the efficacy of a mixed style" (6). Sir Joshua

Reynolds would have recognized in these latter-day, latitudinarian architects a little of his own prescription with respect to history: "To find excellencies, however dispersed, to discover beauties, however concealed . . . can be the work only of him . . . who has extended his views to all ages and all schools" (VI:170). But Ruskin's revulsion for the "monstrous creatures" of the Grand Style extended to the "accursed Frankenstein monster of, indirectly, [his] own making" (*Works* X:lvi). Of course, he was referring to the usually vulgar imitations of Gothic that had sprung up across England after the success of *The Stones of Venice* (1851–53). As Summerson reminds his readers, Ruskin never called for the revival of Gothic, but rather for something much harder to define—a new style that would mean the same as Gothic, would have the same integrity, both moral and aesthetic. In *Stones of Venice,* his plates were "illustrations of principle, not . . . things to copy" (9). Summerson says that Ruskin was looking for modernism, but that he did not know what it was. Out of this freedom grew a "latitudinarianism" that was neither Gothic nor eclectic; I would rather describe the latitudinarians who looked to Ruskin as volitional eclectics who were self-consciously mining what Reynolds might have termed "history's diverse beauties" in order put together a new style; and while at first it might have looked like "Frankenstein's monster," by the end of the century Victorian architecture revealed a kind of hybrid beauty entirely its own.

A Thing to Dream of, Not to Build
Ruskin at Abbotsford

For most architectural historians the genealogy of the Gothic Revival in Great Britain is interwoven with Romantic literary culture, and popular literature is often blamed for the misdirection of national architecture during the nineteenth century. Charles Eastlake, one of the movement's early historians, wrote in 1872 that there had been three major influences on the Gothic Revival—literary, religious, and antiquarian—and that Walter Scott had been responsible for "awaken[ing] popular interest in a style which had hitherto been associated with ascetic gloom and vulgar superstition" (113). Drawing attention to the "romantic side of archaeology," Scott, according to Eastlake, kept alive architecture's "one solitary and flickering flame, [. . .] the Lamp of Memory" (115). In 1928 Kenneth Clark's history of the Gothic Revival sought to correct and restrain Eastlake's original assessment of Scott's importance.[16] While giving a central place in his account to literary medievalism, Clark emphasizes that the Gothic Revival was well under way before Scott arrived on the scene, and grew out of the whole Romantic Movement. But it was indeed the revival of interest in national, medieval literature that gave rise to the architectural revival: "Literary men with no particular architectural bent had started a demand for Gothic which was largely satisfied by amateurs" (80). As Megan Aldrich points out in *Gothic Revival,* Scott's Gothic pushed the Revival in a more realistic direction (140). His medievalism was to Walpole's what Pugin's Gothic was to Strawberry Hill. The eighteenth-century revival had been, as Clark admits, a hybrid, bred from classical tastes and "Gothick" fantasy. As Eastlake emphasized, Scott's literary architecture formed part of the rich texture of his novels (113). His realistic depiction of character and setting gave his readers a more substantial impression of medieval life, and made it, on some level, habitable. (Aldrich believes that the Eglinton Tournament would never have occurred without the example of *Ivanhoe.*)

In *A Writer's Britain,* Margaret Drabble credits Scott with doing for Scotland what Wordsworth had done for the Lakes: "he praised her beauties, created a new vision, and encouraged the tourist trade. He also restored the country's history and dignity" (171). With the publication of *The Lady of the Lake* in 1810, the enthusiasm for Scottish travel reached epidemic proportions. As Drabble relates, "On all the roads leading to the Trossachs was suddenly heard the rushing of many chariots and horsemen. Inns were crowded to suffocation. Post-hire permanently rose. Every corner of that fine gorge was explored, and every foot of that beautiful loch was traversed by travellers carrying copies of the book in their hands, [. . .] repeating passages from it with unfeigned rapture" (172). In his novels Scott "covered the country from coast to coast," and the tourists followed him everywhere he went. Even Queen Victoria pursued the pleasure of Scott and Scotland by touring the scenes of the poems and novels, and finally purchasing Balmoral as her country retreat. As Ian Ousby points out in *Literary Britain and Ireland,* Scott "wrote at a time when the taste for wild landscape and for picturesque evidence of the medieval past was in the ascendant, and he gave this taste a local form and shape" (346). Above all, Scott made Scottish history fashionable, and set his seal most firmly upon its medieval phase when he purchased Abbotsford (a farmhouse with classical portico) in 1812 and began to refashion it according to his vision of the Gothic, demolishing the original house by 1822.

Located near ancient Melrose Abbey, Abbotsford "satisfied Scott's ambition of becoming a laird, the founder of a dynasty, and the life he led there smacked more of the country gentleman than the relentlessly busy novelist" (Ousby 348). Over the years Scott transformed the house into a Scottish baronial mansion and filled it with arms, armor, heraldic devices, and a diverse collection of mementos of the famous. In 1824 Scott wrote to a friend, "You should come and see Abbotsford which as Augustus said of Rome (I love magnificent comparisons) I found of Brick and have left of marble. It is really a very handsome old manorial looking place both without and within, with a fine library, a Gothick hall of entrance and what not. But in truth it does not brook description any more than it is amenable to the ordinary rules of architecture—it is as Coleridge says 'A thing to dream of not to tell'" (qtd. in Daiches 92). Scott's entire career seems to underscore the intimacy between historical romance and the archaeological pursuit of history, to make history a "thing to dream of." In his seminal essay "Three Kinds of Historicism," Alan Colquhoun clarifies the "confusion" surrounding the term "historicism" in this period. It is "a theory that all sociocultural phenomena are historically determined and that all truths are relative"; it is "a concern for the institutions and traditions of the past"; it is "the use of historical forms" (3). As a theory of history, an attitude, and an artistic practice, the Gothic Revival embodies all three kinds of historicism. The Revival could not exist without the new theory of history that saw all time periods as distinct and the artifacts they left behind as belonging to them in an organic sense; it could not prosper without an attitude of reverence and humility toward the past, and a desire to preserve its remains; finally, it could not become a movement if artists did not try to make the past live again in the present.

Ruskin and his contemporaries quickly realized that gathering up the fragments of the past with an eye toward rebuilding led inevitably to eclecticism, both in the coexistence of different styles and in the mixing of styles from different periods and countries. The growth of these hybrid, eclectic "monsters" was, to paraphrase Bruno Latour, a consequence of the modern effort of classification (to which Ruskin himself contributed); in this case, the antiquarianism of the Gothic Revival and its popularization in literature, painting, and architecture were necessarily at odds, but they inevitably co-evolved. As Colquhoun puts it, "historical thought [. . .] clearly revert[s] to eclectic practice" (12) when it sets up one period as a paradigm, as nineteenth-century historicism did with Gothic. An indelible feature of modernity, historicism exists at war with itself, longing to bring the past to life, and then despising its own creations.

Yet reproduction or imitation of the desired object had been a salient feature of medievalism since the eighteenth century. The antiquarian Horace Walpole had his Gothic Revival house, Strawberry Hill, and his Gothic romance, *The Castle of Otranto;* his contemporary William Beckford built his Gothic dream house, Fonthill Abbey, and wrote his neomedieval-orientalist fantasy, *Vathek;* and Walter Scott began his career by collecting traditional ballads (and writing some better-than-fair imitations), carried on by writing a slew of historical novels including *Ivanhoe;* and, when he had amassed (almost) enough funds, began transforming Abbotsford into a medieval castle.

Most visitors to Walter Scott's mansion at Abbotsford considered it the perfect outward expression of the famous author's mind. John Ruskin's 1838 letter to John Claudius Loudon records a very different experience. At this time, Ruskin was writing a series of articles for Loudon's *Architectural Magazine* on "The Poetry of Architecture." This early work already hinted at Ruskin's later preoccupations with nature and authenticity, and art as the expression of Zeitgeist. But this first project was also explicitly touristic in nature, composed of leisurely pieces meant to delight and inform armchair travelers. The ambitious young man—he was only 19 at this time—had plans for a further series on "The Homes of the Mighty," in which Scott's mansion would appear as the first number. Traveling to Abbotsford with this project in mind, Ruskin found that Scott's dream house would not make a suitable subject for one of his essays; he was therefore not an uncritical tourist but a desiring subject possessed with a longing that Abbotsford could not satisfy. He might have assumed, too, that his visit to the author's house would give him access to the space of the Waverley novels consumed in his youth. In his search for this authentic experience he was disappointed; but, as Michael Brooks has written, this was the first important step for Ruskin in recognizing that his beloved Gothic architecture would never be successfully translated into a modern setting (13). Instead of finding the embodiment of the literary past, Ruskin found a modern, eclectic monument. His bitterness is audible in the letter to Loudon: "Had Abbotsford *one* point about it deserving of praise, or even admitting of toleration—or had it shown the slightest evidence of the superintendence of that mind whose plaything, whose sucking coral, it had been—the case would have been different; but it does not—and what purpose could it possibly serve to endeavour or pretend to cast a stain upon a part of Scott's reputation, insignificant enough, it is true, but which might perhaps give pain to some of those whose affections are gathered in his memory, and which, while it would have been daring to have hurled it at the light of his *living* name, it would be only base to cast upon the marble of his sepulchre?" (*Works* I:16). In this letter Ruskin both denies the connection between the house and the man (he does not see the "slightest evidence of that mind whose plaything it had been") and affirms it when he concludes that attacking Abbotsford would be like "pointing out the deformity of his limb or triumphing over the one weakness which was the cause of his ruin and his death" (I:16). Blaming Abbotsford for bringing Scott to the point of bankruptcy in 1826 and for hastening his death, Ruskin regards the house as he would any destructive vice. An air of compulsiveness hangs about the place where no sign of discrimination, of "superintendence," is visible. The garden is classical, an Italian fountain attaches to a baronial gateway, the house commences with "a horrible-looking dungeon keep"; worst of all, the grand front "is a splendid combination of the English baronial, the old Elizabethan, and the Melrose Gothic—a jumble of jagged and flanky towers, ending in chimneys, and full of black slits with plaster mouldings, copied from Melrose, stuck all over it" (I:17). This place of defense, as Ruskin calls it, indicating his displeasure at seeing both military and ecclesiastical architecture appropriated for a dwelling place, is "fitted up as if it were as large as the Louvre" (I:17). Ruskin is struck by the copy of an arch from the cloisters at Melrose: "This arch, designed for raising the mind to the highest degree of religious emotion, charged with the loveliest carving you can imagine, and in its natural position combining most exquisitely with the heavenward proportions of surrounding curves, has been copied by Scott in plaster, and made a *fireplace*" (I:17). For Ruskin this misuse of the sacred arch of the Gothic cathedral in the domestic hearth proves "that Scott, notwithstanding all his nonsense about moonlight at Melrose, had *not* the slightest feeling of the real beauty and application of Gothic architecture" (I:17).

By the time he is writing of Scott as "the great representative of the mind of the age in literature" in *Modern Painters III* (1856), Ruskin clearly has had time to ponder the relationship between Scott's literary genius and his genius for living in the nineteenth century. In his chapter "Of Modern Landscape," Ruskin works hard to justify his elevation of Scott to the pantheon of Homer, Dante, and Shakespeare. His argument depends on establishing Scott's modernity, which he does by delineating the characteristics of modern landscape painting, and then tracking them in Scott's work. His comparative study of Greek, medieval, and modern landscape art leads Ruskin to conclude that the moderns are expected to take pleasure in "things which momentarily change or fade; and to expect utmost satisfaction and instruction from what it is impossible to arrest, and difficult to comprehend" (V:317). Ruskin finds evidence of this "triumph in mutability" in the modern obsession with clouds, a preoccupation that suggests, metaphorically, the loss of belief in God. He writes, "[M]uch of the instinct, which, partially developed in painting, may be now seen throughout every mode of exertion of mind,—the easily encouraged doubt, easily excited curiosity, habitual agitation, and delight in the changing and the marvellous, as opposed to the old quiet serenity of social custom and religious faith,—is again deeply defined in those few words, the 'dethroning of Jupiter,' the 'coronation of the whirlwind'" (V:318). The worship of wind and clouds—of chance—betrays ignorance, perhaps willful, perhaps endemic, of stable facts. As he does throughout his entire corpus, Ruskin draws upon the explanatory power of Greek mythology and culture. Referring to the *Clouds* of Aristophanes as the only serious study of the subject in the ancient world, Ruskin borrows the poet's conclusions: "[clouds] are 'great goddesses to idle men'"; "whoso believes in their divinity must first disbelieve in Jupiter, and place supreme power in the hands of an unknown god 'Whirlwind'"; this god makes his disciples "'to speak ingeniously concerning smoke'" (V:318). The modern age is marked, as no other has ever been, by the pervasiveness of unbelief. The love of fog, clouds, smoke, and somber colors in modern landscape painting suggests to Ruskin a darkness of heart caused by the loss of faith. On the whole Ruskin believes that the modern age is properly called the Dark Age, compared to the bright Middle Ages, because "On the whole, these are much *sadder* ages than the early ones; not sadder in a noble and deep way, but in a dim wearied way—the way of ennui and jaded intellect, and uncomfortableness of soul and body" (V:321). The positive valence of modern uncertainty is the love of liberty and wildness; it is levity, even profanity, before nature; it is the romantic love of beauty, which the moderns find in history or nature, but never in themselves.

For Ruskin, Scott exhibits, more than any other modern writer, this strange mixture of the "elements of progress and decline" (V:327). There are other poets greater than he, whose genius belongs more to the next age, but Scott's genius is peculiarly of the moment. First, Ruskin claims, "Nothing is more notable or sorrowful in Scott's mind than its incapacity of steady belief in anything" (V:336). For proof Ruskin takes Scott's ambivalence toward the supernatural and toward Catholicism (an attitude typical of Gothic novelists such as Ann Radcliffe). He is Presbyterian, Ruskin says, because that is the most sensible thing to be when one wishes to live in Edinburgh, even though he finds Roman Catholicism "more picturesque."[17] Second, Scott has the weakness of "looking back, in a romantic and passionate idleness, to the past ages, not understanding them all the while, nor really desiring to understand them" (V:336). This is the most serious charge Ruskin levels against his childhood hero. For many Victorians Scott was the first poet whose use of history had been in the service of realism, and not merely as a colorful backdrop. He had also been the first in literature (as Georg Lukács has argued in *The Historical Novel*) to link social customs to historical development. Ruskin, however, does not see Scott's treatment of historical material as anything but interested. His best characters and scenes are "sketched from nature," but, Ruskin contends, "his romance and antiquarianism, his knighthood and monkery, are all false, and he knows them to be false; does not care to make them earnest; enjoys them for their strangeness, but laughs at his own antiquarianism, all through his third novel,—with exquisite modesty indeed, but with total misunderstanding of the function of an Antiquary. He does not see how anything is to be got out of the past but confusion [. . .]" (V:337). Ruskin is obviously bothered by what he considers Scott's carelessness toward his historical material (specifically his lack of understanding of architecture), and he goes on to reiterate his experience of Abbotsford, to make the point that Scott is representative of his age in his ignorance about art. Having only a "confused love of Gothic architecture," Scott cannot "tell the worst from the best, and built for himself perhaps the most incongruous and ugly pile that gentlemanly modernism ever designed" (V:338). For Ruskin, Abbotsford embodies Scott's modernity in its "mingling of reverence with irreverence" (V:338). By misusing the arch from Melrose Abbey, Scott shows an attitude to history that Ruskin has begun to reject: that we can own history, consume it indiscriminately. Scott the "pure modern" (as Ruskin calls him) "admires, in an equally ignorant way, totally opposite styles" (V:338). Scott is eclectic, in the common usage, irreverent even as he is sorrowful, desiring intimacy with a more colorful past that is gone forever. Ruskin instinctively felt, and tried hard to justify his opinion, that Scott's novels—and even his home at Abbotsford—were "adequate" expressions of the age in which they were produced, largely because of their eclectic historicism.[18]

The fact that Scott's eclecticism made him essentially, supremely modern did not, however, lead Ruskin to accept eclectic historicism as the way forward in architecture. It was inorganic, and often ignorant; it falsified the architectural record; it threatened to extinguish the lamp of memory. But it was only many years after his visit to Abbotsford that Ruskin became truly convinced that Gothic architecture was a thing to dream of, and not to build—when he decided that his writing on architecture, in assisting the revival of Gothic, had done more to degrade, than to exalt, the original. He had made people of varying abilities and insight long for what he described, to long, as he and Scott had done, for the chance to inhabit a medieval world. Eclecticism was essentially romantic, yes; but it was also always acting—playing a part rather than being in time. This made Scott's choice of Gothic an ethical one. It also exposed a tension in the period about the proper uses of the past that would not be resolved until the end of the century.

It is significant that another of Ruskin's idols, Turner, for whom he wrote *Modern Painters,* became the most famous illustrator of Scott. In 1838, the year of Ruskin's visit, Turner produced a watercolor of Abbotsford. The Gothic Revival mansion is hazily, though distinctly, drawn against a hill in the right of the picture, its towers mimicking the forms of trees and rocks. The scene is one of integration, even reconciliation: humans in harmony with animals in the foreground, architecture in harmony with external nature. Turner's aesthetic modernity is proven by his sympathy with Scott, in a way that might have pleased even that finicky tourist, Ruskin.

The "Problem of Failure"
Eclectic Revivals in Architecture

At the same time that John Ruskin was expressing, privately, his dismay at Scott's eclecticism, A. W. N. Pugin, perhaps the most notorious propagandist of the Gothic Revival, who had already converted to Roman Catholicism in order to align his religious and aesthetic values, was making the choice of style, very publicly, a moral issue. In *Contrasts* (1836) he took on the entire classical inheritance and the Protestant Reformation that, in his view, came along with it. What neoclassicists deemed the elevation of taste should have been condemned for what it was, the expression of modern unbelief: "Almost all the researches of modern antiquaries, schools of painting, national museums and collections, have only tended to corrupt taste and poison the intellect, by setting forth classic art as the summit of excellence, and substituting mere natural and sensual productions in place of the mystical and divine" (16). As Pugin recognized, moreover, the mere collecting of things did not confer understanding or belief. A society seeking to recover its faith in God by building Gothic churches was doomed to fail, because only faith could create such enduring monuments. Religious ideas and ceremonies had always had the profoundest influence on the development of style, because style was the outward expression of inner faith. Therefore, Christianity had found its perfect expression in pointed architecture. If "the architecture of the nineteenth century [was] that extraordinary conglomeration of classic and modern styles peculiar to the day" (v), then it could not express a belief in anything higher than having the liberty or the means to choose. Patrons request what they like or what they believe will convey their status to others, and that is what architects build.

Pugin strikes against this laissez-faire tendency of modern architecture in his "Illustration of the Practise of Architecture in the 19th Century on New Improved and Cheap Principles." Arranged as a collection of advertisements, it satirizes various aspects of the profession, including the spread of amateurism that allowed patrons to dictate to designers: "Shortly will be published Architecture Made Easy, or Every Man His Own Architect by which Gentlemen Amateurs May Easily Acquire Every Information Respecting Design and Practice." He ridicules public lectures on architecture that promote outlandish styles such as "Mechanicks Institute, A Lecture on Antideluvian, Babylonian, Greek, Roman and Gothic Architecture by Mr. Wash Plasterer" or that gloat over the mechanization of design as in "Mechanicks Institute, A Lecture on a New Designing Machine Capable of Making 1000 Changes with the Same Set of Ornaments by A Composition Maker." These mock-lectures highlight for Pugin what had become a central problem in the profession: since neither the architects nor their patrons had any allegiance to a particular style—proof that they did not possess the religious faith Pugin believed ought to underwrite any national style of architecture—British architecture could never be more than a mishmash of borrowed styles bearing the imprints of vanished believers. Architects bragged that they could design "Buildings of Every Description [. . .] Gothic or Grecian on Moderate Terms" and such architectural freaks as

> A Moorish Fish Market with a Literary Room Over an Egyptian Marine Villa
> A Castelated Turnpike Gate
> A Gin Temple in the Baronial Style
> A Dissenting Chapel in the Plain Style to Serve Occasionally for a Lecture or Reading Room
> A Monument to Be Placed in Westminster Abbey—a Colossal Figure in the Hindoo Style Would Be Preferred and No Regard Need be Paid to Locality
> A Saxon Cigar Divan. (*Contrasts*)

The principal targets of *Contrasts* are well known—the Renaissance and the Reformation—but Pugin's diagnosis of what was ailing modern architecture extends to the democratization of taste. While most of his work attacks the decadent, sensual, and classical taste of the upper classes, he recognizes another threat from below—the indiscriminate mixing of styles by the newly wealthy and partially educated. The architectural freaks in Pugin's list were meant to outrage and even disgust his readers, but the attack on eclecticism was less likely to persuade than were his illustrations of medieval and modern cities and institutions (the "contrasts"). By exposing the weakness of a nation in which belief no longer dictates the choice of style, he also forged a connection between style and belief that would trump for many the pleasure of having a choice.

While Pugin's *Contrasts* is properly a work of the Battle of the Styles (Greek versus Gothic), to which the satirical attack on professional eclecticism is secondary, his most important successor, Ruskin, eventually moved beyond the morality of the styles to an examination of what it means to have a choice—the only article of faith that Pugin could discover in nineteenth-century architecture. Asked by the citizens of the northern industrial city of Bradford to assist them in choosing a style for their new Exchange, Ruskin begins his 1864 lecture "Traffic" by informing his audience that he cannot speak about their new Exchange because he does not care about it. Worse yet, he cannot care about it because they do not. They may be about to spend £30,000 for an imposing new building, but they mean nothing at all by it: "[You] think you may as well have the right thing for your money. You know there are a great many odd styles of architecture about; you don't want to do anything ridiculous; you hear of me, among others, as a respectable man-milliner; and you send for me, that I may tell you the leading fashion; and what is, in our shops, for the moment, the newest and sweetest thing in pinnacles" (*Works* XVIII:434). Like the eclectic patrons scorned by Pugin, these industrialists can afford to purchase whatever style they choose, and they are acutely aware that they do, in fact, have a choice. Ruskin's savage tone and outright dismissal of any good intention behind inviting him to speak proceed from his unshakeable Romantic conviction that "architecture is the expression of national life and character" (XVIII:434). Merely asking the question "which style?" betrays the disease in a nation in which already several styles vie for ascendance. "I notice that among all the new buildings which cover your once wild hills, churches and schools are mixed in due, that is to say, in large proportion, with your mills and mansions; and I notice also that the churches and schools are almost always Gothic, and the mansions and mills are never Gothic. May I ask the meaning of this? for, remember, it is peculiarly a modern phenomenon. When Gothic was invented, houses were Gothic as well as churches; and when the Italian style superseded the Gothic, churches were Italian as well as houses. [...] But now you live under one school of architecture, and worship under another" (XVIII:440). For Ruskin this association of style and function, far from indicating a reverence for the space of worship, rather indicates that they "have separated [their] religion from [their] life" (XVIII:440). By making Gothic the exclusive style of churches, but rarely choosing to employ it in other contexts, the citizens of Bradford appear to make religion a surface matter only, not something shot all through the fabric of life. The separation further implies that the Sunday Gothic-church-goers do not believe that their houses, factories, and hills are sacred, too: "in calling your churches only 'holy,' you call your hearths and homes 'profane'" (XVIII:442). Underlying this typology of style, Ruskin recognized a convenient compartmentalization of values; on Sundays, we believe and act according to these Christian values, and during the week, we believe and act according to these economic values.

Unfortunately for Ruskin, those who heard his lecture thought he meant they ought to choose Gothic, in order to affirm their faith, missing the vitally important distinction "do you mean to build as honest Christians or as honest infidels?" (XVIII:443). The eclectic architecture of the nineteenth century by its very nature could never proclaim a "common purpose"; having a choice only institutionalized doubt. To demonstrate effectively the universality of his claim that all great architecture results from great religion, Ruskin identifies the three great religions that have underwritten the three great European styles: the Greek worship of the God of wisdom and power, the medieval worship of the God of judgment and consolation, and the Renaissance worship of the God of pride and beauty (XVIII:445). All of these having passed, he argues, the English have now supplied a fourth deity of their own: the "Goddess of Getting-on" or "Britannia of the Market" (XVIII:448). They have a nominal religion, Christianity, and an actual religion, capitalism, with its goddess of the marketplace, to whom all "great architectural works are, of course, built" (XVIII:448): "It is long since you built a great cathedral; and how you would laugh at me if I proposed building a cathedral on the top of these hills of yours, to make it an Acropolis! But your railroad mounds, vaster than the walls of Babylon; your railroad stations, vaster than the temple of Ephesus, and innumerable; your chimneys, how much more mighty and costly than cathedral spires! your harbour-piers; your warehouses; your exchanges!—all these were built to your great Goddess of 'Getting-on'; and she has formed, and will continue to form, your architecture, as long as you worship her; and it is quite vain to ask me how to tell you how to build to *her;* you know far better than I" (XVIII:448). Apart from the revival styles with their confused attempts to declare allegiance to the values of the past, Victorian architecture expressed for the most part its faith in profit and progress, and the practical values of getting ahead in life by any means necessary. The revived styles of the Greek, medieval, and Renaissance gods could be subsumed, as Pugin recognized, under the values of commercial culture and would indeed be employed as the signs and tokens of success, piety, fidelity, patriotism, liberty, democracy; but for Pugin and Ruskin, the very coexistence of these competing deities meant that none of the revived styles could truly express the age, because the values each expressed would always be in conflict—and no clever representation of belief could supply its lack. Eclecticism was thus entirely at odds with the values of the Gothic Revival, as represented by its moralists, because it sought to resolve conflict and to preserve the best parts of the past for the future, rather than acknowledging that they constituted contradictory views of life.

In their effort to reestablish a single style for the national expression that was architecture, aesthetic purists such as Pugin failed to understand that the majority of people would always remake any historical style in their own image, as Sir Walter Scott did, never allowing it to express one idea only. Like Pugin, the Gothic Revivalist George Gilbert Scott blamed the Civil War for breaking up national traditions and hastening the uniform adoption of classical styles; but his recommendation that Gothic—as "the style whose traditions have the strongest possible claims upon our affections"—replace classicism ignored the fact that architects would be replacing one imported style with another (6–7). Choosing Gothic over Greek was still choosing. And by the end of the century, everyone agreed that Gothic was a dead style, which survived only in eclecticism: Gothic had become "one ingredient in an ever-evolving eclecticism" (Crook 160). Disillusioned Goth J. P. Seddon complained, "Eclecticism! Eclecticism! What horrors have been perpetrated in thy euphonious name" (qtd. in Crook 179). J. D. Sedding's diagnosis was more precise: "What we call Victorian architecture is nothing in fact but a retrospective art, an art of plagiarism and odds and ends... historic art made histrionic" (qtd. in Crook 180). It was the same charge of inauthenticity that Ruskin had leveled at Walter Scott, which pointed to a lingering crisis of identity. The organic relationship between style and nation once taken for granted had been lost, and that was what rankled most. As Sedding put it, Victorian architecture was "composed of what naturalists call 'illegitimate crosses'" (qtd. in Crook 180). Even when it was intentionally designed, eclectic architecture continued to be regarded as monstrous and unnatural, or as histrionic and frivolous.

Balancing the unease about eclecticism, naïve or volitional, was the emergence of a new (debased) "native" architecture sprouting like mushrooms out of every speculator's suburb. It was ugly, practical, and cheap: the architecture of commercial competition. The only real architecture we have, William Morris acknowledged in "The Revival of Architecture" (1888), is laboriously eclectic. Thoughtful architects realized that an exotic Gothic style would not thrive in the nineteenth century: the economic system was incompatible, and would not allow workers to express their individuality; and most builders would opt for cheaper, mass-produced materials. So the revivalists would try a Gothic of slightly later date, always thinking to get closer to the "spirit of the age" the later they chose to dig for style. It was not a crazy idea, but it should have pointed out the essential problem with Revival styles: they did indeed belong to their ages, and the saddest thing about the nineteenth century—but also its compensatory gift, Morris thought—was its awareness of history. Like Hardy's Laodiceans, they all knew too much; they could not invent, but could only adapt—the debate on architectural style had made this clear. Ruskin's essay on "The Nature of Gothic" marked the beginning of the end of the Revival for Morris, by making the contrast between the nineteenth century and the fourteenth century so great that it was obviously impossible to bridge the gap. In sharp contrast to eclectics such as Morris, James Fergusson, in the *History of the Modern Styles of Architecture* (1891), despaired of their ever matching the forms and tendencies of their art to the greatness of their engineering. Whether in the revivalist or the modernist camp, most critics shared the conviction that nineteenth-century architecture went horribly wrong when it revived historical styles; this revulsion only deepened as ever-cheaper and less-authentic imitations spread across the landscape.

The aesthetic revisionism that had commenced with the Gothic Revival of the eighteenth century was brought to fruition in 1834 when the British government called for a competition to rebuild the destroyed Houses of Parliament and asked only for Gothic or Elizabethan designs. Their reasons were compelling: the new buildings would be on the site of the ancient Palace of Westminster, and could incorporate what remained of it; they would also be close to Westminster Abbey, one of the great medieval monuments; and, finally, Gothic was thought to be a truly English style and thus would best represent the nation to the world (Clark 108–21). With this grand gesture, the competition signaled the end of the dominance of varieties of classicism across the spectrum of English culture. Though the disciples of Gothic would attempt a takeover of style as complete as Neoclassicism had once enjoyed, never again would any style of architecture, painting, or the decorative arts achieve such ubiquity.

Several factors contributed to the end of the tyranny of a single style. While the confrontation of Gothic and Greek styles had energized supporters on both sides, moderates found a productive, if controversial, middle road. By selecting elements from various historical styles, from the beautiful and the sublime, the ideal and the natural, architects satisfied an apparently contradictory desire for individual freedom within the social order. "Picturesque," the peculiar growth of the Revolutionary period, exemplifies this eclectic aim to reconcile cultural extremes. In its most popular forms the picturesque aesthetic exhibited the best qualities of the new moderate liberal outlook, what was termed in French politics the *juste milieu* or middle course. For many intellectuals of the day, the eclectic *juste milieu* was less a philosophical system than a sensibility and an aesthetic. In his study of the French painter Thomas Couture, Albert Boime emphasizes that the artist under the influence of eclecticism wished not to overthrow classicism but to infuse it with passion and imagination by looking everywhere for inspiration and meaning (16): "Nothing is given but everything is assembled (and open potentially to reassembly). The eclectic borrows variously and pieces together representative elements in another place. All ideas in this system have value not by virtue of any single writer or thinker, but by virtue of their ready-made distinctiveness and capacity to be reconciled as an ensemble" (22). In this view the styles of the past and of other countries were equally available for incorporation into living works of art, an art that would express a new relationship to history, to country, to colony—an art tolerant, open, and already meaningful.

Coming only two years after the Great Reform Bill, the rebuilding of Westminster in accordance with popular taste marked the opening up of the rarefied realms of personal style and the fine arts to the middle classes. As the knowledge of historical and foreign styles increased through public museums, exhibitions, pamphlets, and periodicals, the newly empowered classes gained access to the intricacies of the languages of style—to a vocabulary that could be deployed in self-representation. The picturesque developed into a complicated, eclectic, aesthetic mode whose elements were easily adapted to differing economic conditions.

No architect was more successful than John Claudius Loudon in disseminating the picturesque at all levels of British society. Throughout his life, Loudon was preoccupied by the two fundamental questions of his profession: use and beauty. Initially a disciple of Uvedale Price (author of *Essay on the Picturesque*, one of the most important treatises on the subject), he adapted the principles of landscape painting as guides for designing and laying out real landscape. But he had also "imbibed the principles of utility" from Bentham, and he liberalized Price's teachings by taking into account the needs of those cottagers whose dwellings had been appropriated (and neglected) as elements of picturesque scenery (Simo 6). According to his biographer, Melanie Louise Simo, Loudon believed that true taste in the British rural style should be founded on the best of indigenous cottages, castles, and villas; but his *Encyclopedia of Cottage, Farm, and Villa Architecture,* which went through numerous editions during the century after its initial publication in 1833, presented designs that showed him to be impartial on the question of style. The fitness of the style—its characteristic elements designed for particular uses—was more important than its being Gothic or Greek.

The first section of the *Encyclopedia* offers designs of "Cottage Dwellings in Various Styles." Alongside the numerous Gothic and Italianate or classical designs, Loudon gives space to German Swiss, Elizabethan or Old English, Indian Gothic, and Chinese. Many of the designs are hybrid creations, but Loudon accepts even these awkward contributions into the *Encyclopedia,* as long as the architect has made the house fit for living in. For example, in his Remarks to Design XIX Loudon wonders, "What then, is the style attempted? Those who have viewed the buildings of all the countries of Europe with an architectural eye, or those who have studied the cottage buildings in the pictures of the Italian landscape painters, will best be able to determine this question" (82). Allowing for the understanding of picturesque principles that some readers will bring to the design, Loudon concedes that "no characteristic of any style or manner ought to be servilely imitated, when that imitation would prove inconsistent with utility," but the spirit of the original ought to be retained even as the architect adapts the structure to its new location (82–83). Loudon seems unable to explain how the strange, domed cottage might be deemed a legitimate occupant of English soil, but it is his particular genius to allow any style at all that is beautiful and functional into his pantheon of models without trying to rationalize its inclusion on moral grounds, as the acolytes of Gothic or Greek were wont to do. Loudon's eclecticism encourages liberal practice in a profession just emerging from its long dependency on aristocratic patronage. He sums up this way one of the most important factors in his own approach to design: "The time has gone by for one class of society to endeavour to mark another with any badge whatever; and therefore we could wish all architects, when designing cottages, to abandon their received ideas" (1183). In 1805, he goes on, a prominent architect wrote that the moldings and ornaments of the "regular" styles of architecture should never be applied to cottages, but now, in 1840, we see progress in the moldings and ornaments carefully placed in the smaller dwellings. Thinking and reading beings, clearly, all have the right to style.

Unlike Loudon, who saw eclecticism as the by-product of a rational architecture, George Wightwick built an altogether different foundation for his eclecticism—it would be "Beautiful," "Poetical," and "Romantic." In this endeavor he tried to emulate Walter Scott: his "romance"—which he named *The Palace of Architecture* (1840)—would be to architecture what Scott's novels were to history (vii). As Wightwick recognized, much of the pleasure of reading Scott was attributable to his powerful evocation of the architecture and landscapes of the past. Scott's readers could occupy the historical spaces opened up by his novels, both imaginatively through reading and physically by traveling to the famous places he described. By making the most scientific and mathematical of the arts into a romance and bringing to life the entire history of architecture as a single eclectic palace, Wightwick encouraged his readers to inhabit imaginatively whatever pavilion or room they fancied after being guided through by the "Prince Architect." Just as the Great Exhibition of 1851 would collect the decorative arts of the world under a single roof, so Wightwick collected the world's architecture into a single book, having faith that such a "congress" would conspire to create a brighter future for the art: "You will see, within this domain, an epitome of the Architectural world. Mine is, as it were, a palace of congress, wherein you will be successively addressed by humble (but, it is hoped, characteristic) representatives of the great families of Design in ancient and Mahomedan India, China, Egypt, Greece, ancient and modern Italy, Turkey, Moorish Spain, and Christian Europe" (3). On their journey, Wightwick's readers would learn to recognize the importance of architecture as a vehicle of association—its pictorial romance and material poetry (4). As a precursor to his ambitious program, the Prince Architect claims Hadrian's villa at Tivoli, where the emperor, after traveling for six years around his empire, "resolved on imitating all the monuments, the magnificence or splendour of which had excited his imagination" (5). Preoccupied with architecture as testimony to the character of nations, as (to paraphrase Pugin) the history of the world, Wightwick bravely acknowledges, "The numerous architectural abortions to be found in many a modern city, however detestable in themselves, are, nevertheless, testimonies to the existence of that *spirit,* and of those *means,* which, under the guidance of knowledge, would produce monuments worthy of pretension, instead of gew-gaws, manifesting pretension only" (10). Part of Wightwick's eclectic purpose is to learn from this sometimes bewildering accumulation of styles the true path for the future of architecture: "in every new work, we seek to express, not only the limited excellence of what now *is,* but the anticipated virtue of a day not yet arrived" (11). By selecting and comparing what he imagines to be the most characteristic structures of various nations, Wightwick hopes to uncover what links spirit, means, and beauty; and ultimately, in the testing of new combinations, perspectives, and groupings, to find at last a suitable dwelling place for his country and his age.

Like Wightwick, A. J. Beresford Hope, who would eventually become president of the Royal Institute of British Architects (RIBA), as well as a leader in the revival of the Church of England, based his aspirations for the future of architecture as a fine art on the adoption of an eclectic program. In his 1858 lecture "The Common Sense of Art," Beresford Hope makes the essential unity of all architecture—all the styles of different lands—his first principle, but he also recognizes local significance and development and so chooses the Gothic as the pattern of future architecture. This choosing of a particular style, he knows, makes him eclectic: "the only style of common sense architecture for the future of England, must be Gothic architecture, cultivated in the spirit of progression founded upon eclecticism" (10). The progressive architect must search everywhere for material and for inspiration; all of England's Gothic, all the Gothic in Europe will not be sufficient for the task: "To be truly eclectic, we must be universally eclectic—we must eclect from everything that has been collected; and we must assimilate and fuse everything that we eclect, for without such fusion the process remains after all only one of distributive collection" (13). Like the eclectic philosophers in France, Beresford Hope had faith in the common sense that would guide his choices. Common sense would tell him to stop "eclecting" when he could no longer assimilate the style. If the architecture of the past—mixed and hybrid as it was—was the natural and spontaneous response of human beings to their environment, then the architecture of the future would be responding to an environment that included the architecture of other ages and other nations, as well as new materials and new technologies for building. Believing that only primitive societies developed "total styles," he embraced a theory of evolution for the arts that incorporated the vital feelings of association on which successful architecture depended. The Crystal Palace was a great building because its ornamentation was continuous with English "Perpendicular" Gothic; it inspired patriotic feelings because it embodied English history and carried it forward in time. The rational latitudinarianism that informed Beresford Hope's judgment made "Progressive Eclecticism" a mid-Victorian catchphrase (Crook 161).

Proceeding on assumptions similar to those adopted by Sir Joshua Reynolds in the training of young artists, the eclectic revivalists adopted an "art for art's sake" position, against Pugin and Ruskin, who insistently linked eclecticism with degraded morality. In France the theorist, restorer, and Gothic revivalist Eugène Viollet-le-Duc reached a similar conclusion that the architect's education must proceed from the careful analysis of the masterpieces of the past to an original synthesis of those achievements, allowing for the conditions of, and using the materials dictated by, his own age (Summerson, "Viollet-le-Duc" 141). This analytical process often began with the simplest structures and progressed to the most ornamentally complex. The primitive hut had been a favorite instructive image since the eighteenth century in which architects had hoped to discover absolute structural necessity, a pure and unadorned response to the laws of nature (Viollet-le-Duc 23). Viollet-le-Duc imagines that the first shelter was a tree, and that when storms became strong enough to disturb its protective canopy, people heaped more material over the spreading branches. For Ruskin, as for Viollet-le-Duc, this spontaneous, rational development of the primitive dwelling underscores the connection between national landscape and architectural forms, and, as Ruskin would have it, "the prevailing turn of mind by which the nation who first employed it is distinguished" (*Works* I:5). Such a conclusion ordinarily leads to the rejection of eclecticism. For example, in *The Poetry of Architecture* Ruskin argues for the specificity of architectural language; it cannot be translated across cultures or exported indiscriminately without a calamitous loss of meaning. Indeed, his desire to prohibit the exportation or mechanical revival of any style would make the primitive hut or the picturesque cottage impossible for all nonpeasants. Writing of the search for a style of the nineteenth century, Viollet-le-Duc also tries to link style to language; just as language is something all human beings possess, we all have style, or inspiration (215); but Viollet-le-Duc acknowledges the loss in translation even while imagining the recovery of meaning. Though we have progressed far beyond the rudiments of language, "those simple and true ideas that lead artists to invest their conceptions with style," we need only recall the want our art was created to satisfy in order to have true style again. Pushed to their extremes, both Ruskin and Viollet-le-Duc signal the coming end of historical (eclectic) styles; but Ruskin and Viollet-le-Duc reach, via similar theoretical and historical models, the same conclusion: the new style will be the child of eclectic historicism.

Ruskin devotes half of *The Poetry of Architecture* series, which he wrote, significantly, after his visit to Abbotsford, to the study of the cottages of various nations, but not in order to recommend them as homes for the middle classes. Like most of Ruskin's output, *Poetry* is meant to be instructive, not prescriptive. And as is usually the case, his intention is enthusiastically misunderstood. Ruskin acknowledges only three cases in which a cottage might be designed by an architect: when a nobleman or man of fortune erects dwellings for his domestics on his own property, when a landlord exercises influence over the houses of tenants for the sake of improvement, and finally "when ornamental summer-houses, or mimicries of wigwams, are to be erected as ornamental adjuncts to a prospect which the owner has done all he can to spoil, that it may be worthy of the honour of having him to look at it" (*Works* I:66–67). While he is willing to advise interested parties in the first two cases, he considers the third circumstance to be barbarous and not worthy of his consideration. This prohibition against a *cottage ornée* as a kind of substitute for the primitive hut ("wigwam") is particularly severe, since Ruskin's ideal cottage closely resembles the *designed* version, and completely disregards the reality of most laborers' cottages: "A few square feet of garden and a latched wicket, persuading the weary and dusty pedestrian, with excessive eloquence, to lean upon it for an instant and request a drink of water or milk, complete a picture, which, if it be far enough from London to be unspoiled by town sophistications, is a very perfect thing in its way. The ideas it awakens are agreeable, and the architecture is all that we want in such a situation. It is pretty and appropriate; and if it boasted of any other perfection, it would be at the expense of its propriety" (I:12). The "proper" features of English picturesque cottages were thought to be smallness, rusticity, and simplicity; the shape and color of the dwelling had to be harmonious with the landscape from which the materials for building were extracted; and the internal necessities were to determine its irregular, external boundaries. Ruskin calls forth a host of images associated with rural pleasures, and betrays a continued infatuation with "the presumed innocence and simplicity of a 'primitive' life, passed in harmony with nature" (Archer 68).

Why then does Ruskin disallow this more perfect form of dwelling for members of his own class? Because the *cottage ornée* has been torn from its social fabric. Ruskin recognizes that the period of the primitive hut has passed him by, and although he purchases a whitewashed cottage on the shores of a beautiful English lake, he improves and enlarges the original structure until it is an appropriate and typical dwelling for a member of his own class. It seems that Ruskin found his way to authentic dwelling by incorporating—eclecting—past forms into the contemporary. The ambivalent transition between the cottage and villa sections of his first book is revealing:

> And now, farewell to the cottage, and with it, to the humility of natural scenery. We are sorry to leave it; not that we have any idea of living in a cottage, as a comfortable thing; not that we prefer mud to marble, or deal to mahogany; but that, with it, we leave much of what is most beautiful of earth, the low and bee-inhabited scenery, which is full of quiet and prideless emotion, of such calmness as we can imagine prevailing over our earth when it was new in heaven. We are going into higher walks of architecture, where we shall find a less close connexion established between the building and the soil on which it stands, or the air with which it is surrounded, but a closer connexion with the character of its inhabitant. We shall have less to do with natural feeling, and more with human passion; we are coming out of stillness into turbulence, out of seclusion into the multitude, out of the wilderness into the world. (I:73)

The peculiar relation of the cottage to the primitive hut, enshrined by architects as the first dwelling, is strongly evident in Ruskin's delineation of the territory of the two houses. The evocation of a building that no architect has ever seen, and which the peasants themselves do not use for their own cottages, locates the artificial cottage not in the wilderness but in the suburbs. Built into the form of the cottage is a longing for the (small) space of childhood, what architects regarded as the childhood of the whole race. In the small dwelling one is more vulnerable and, at the same time, more aware of one's security. Taking pleasure in the experience of vulnerability, the inhabitants of the *cottage ornée* shed their heavy clothes, their formal speech, and renew physical contact. Gaston Bachelard recognizes the original house as an unchanging space that is always familiar; the ornamented cottage, although inauthentic, can be understood as an attempt to rebuild the primitive hut. Situated on the boundary between the primitive hut and familiar domestic space, the *cottage ornée* opens onto memory, onto memories of houses. The villa opens onto other memories—of travel, literature, and painting. The villa not only contains collections of experiences and artifacts, like those Ruskin saw in Abbotsford, but is also itself an eclectic form, the imitation of the memory of a house built somewhere else. Evaluated against the characterization of the primitive hut as a pure, unadorned response to nature, the copy cottage can only fail. But the villa is always already dissociated from its national origin. The key difference for Ruskin is in the inhabitant of each:

> Man, the peasant, is a being of more marked national character than man, educated and refined. For nationality is founded, in a great degree, on prejudices and feelings inculcated and aroused in youth, which grow inveterate in the mind as long as its views are confined to the place of its birth; its ideas moulded by the customs of its country, and its conversation limited to a circle composed of individuals of habits and feelings like its own; but which are gradually softened down, and eradicated when the mind is led into general views of things, when it is guided by reflection instead of habit, and has begun to lay aside opinions contracted under the influence of association and prepossession, substituting in their room philosophical deductions from the calm contemplation of the various tempers, and thoughts, and customs, of mankind. (I:74–75)

For Ruskin this displacement of national feelings in favor of general ideas opens the way to eclecticism in art: "the more polished the mind of its designer, the less national will be the building" and the less unified will be the building and its scenery (I:75). The implications of Ruskin's analysis are significant for the larger questions raised in this chapter: the growth of the middle classes came about as a result of massive displacement from the land. Living in cities where no native style prevailed, and confronted with unfamiliar aesthetic systems, ordinary citizens created a profoundly ordinary, symbolic-ornamental, and eclectic architecture.[19] These newly available languages of art encouraged novel expressions, what Eagleton might call aesthetic bonding, an imaginative exchange of identities (24).

While the seemingly ideal synthesis of styles represented by the picturesque did not satisfy the guardians of high culture, it has been consistently employed in domestic architecture for two centuries. For commentators such as Ruskin, the picturesque could never create a true *juste milieu* because it corrupted the essential character of each style from which it borrowed. The liberalization of style would lead to the bastardization—the mongrelization—of artistic style generally; the lack of any one style to represent the character of the age was proof of its corruption, its surrender to the pressures of supply and demand in the market of culture. Rather than adhering to a single style (as one might to a single religion), architects would design buildings in any style their patrons demanded, however inappropriate or ridiculous.

It is tempting to conclude by saying that the common-sense eclecticism envisioned by Loudon and Beresford Hope won the day—that architects such as Norman Shaw, C. F. A. Voysey, and Edwin Lutyens represented the future. But the eclectic synthesis they achieved proved temporary with the advent of modernism, when the stars of purity and authenticity were again in ascendance. It may be, however, that modernism itself was the interregnum—an anomalous moment in which we pretended not to have a choice.

As proof, it is worth pointing out that two of the most influential architectural writers of the early twentieth century were apostates when it came to the Victorians. Both Kenneth Clark and John Betjeman began their careers by despising Victorian architecture, and ended by respecting—if not loving—it. Clark wrote his "classic" (Crook's word in the 1995 preface) *The Gothic Revival* just after his graduation from Oxford. When his publisher suggested reprinting the 1928 edition, Clark responded nervously: "I expected to find the history inaccurate, the entertainment out of date, the criticism relatively sound. But it is the criticism which has worn least well" (1). In the letter, reprinted in later editions, Clark explains how he had set out to validate the architectural doctrines that were current in the 1920s but had ended up being "persuaded by what [he] set out to deride" (2). He worried that later generations could not possibly understand the hatred of Victorian architecture that had once existed—it was universally ridiculed. Even in the 1920s Clark knew that he was doing something radical in mounting even a half-hearted defense—it was "interesting" though never "agreeable"—of the aesthetic and moral positions of the Victorian built environment. The best to be hoped from a reprinting, he concluded in 1949, would be to show the "very great change which my attitude towards all the arts has undergone in the last twenty years, and which began with my reading of Ruskin's *The Nature of Gothic*" (4). Though Ruskin had been a devastating critic of his own age, Clark recognized that Ruskin had guided the best architects toward a reconsideration of the moral meaning of architecture, and to the production of a few works of enduring genius. Even Summerson would ask in 1968 whether "failure" was a fair label when the Victorians had labored so hard, and with such seriousness, to improve the art of architecture.

For steering the larger populace toward an appreciation of Victorian architecture, Clark assigns the most credit to John Betjeman. In his 1970 introduction to *Ghastly Good Taste* (originally published in 1933), "An Aesthete's Apologia," Betjeman tells of the incipient fascination with Victorian art and literature that blossomed in his youth but was restricted in one important sense: "Their architecture I thought then was not to be taken seriously, as it was purely imitative and rather vulgar" (xxi). Indeed, the book concludes (in both editions) with this death knell: "Except for the fine streak in domestic architecture [. . .] building ceased to be of anything but commercial importance in England after 1860" (105). Betjeman had blamed the lamentable fall of a great art on "self-conscious stylism"—in other words, architecture declined because it lost its organic connection to the society that produced it. It fell because it was eclectic. And yet, in the revised edition, in a footnote, the apostate Betjeman acknowledges that Norman Shaw, whose work he had once derided as "sham classicalism," "was our greatest architect since Wren, if not greater" (104). The only other part of *Ghastly Good Taste* to be altered for 1970 was the huge foldout "Street of Taste," which was originally dominated by the nineteenth century, stretched between two principal modes, "Educated Class State-Conscious" and "Middle-Class Self-Conscious." The architectural mode of the twentieth century up to 1933 was still worse—"Big Business and Chaos." Modernism, for Betjeman, had been "A misinterpretation of simplicity" and not the salvation of the art. Things became bleaker still in 1961 (in the extended version of the "Street"), when one of the icons of Victorian self-consciousness, Euston Station, was demolished. This section Betjeman titled "In Memoriam." The Victorian Society that Betjeman helped to found in 1958 lost the battle for Euston, but it went on to win public opinion and countless other battles, notably for the eclectic, aesthetic suburb of Bedford Park.[20] After Euston, the "problem of failure" would be no longer in the Victorians, but in ourselves.

CHAPTER 2

The Philosophy of the Nineteenth Century

If Victor Cousin had looked to his legacy, he might have been wiser not to connect his name with an idea that was in the air, everywhere in Europe, by 1816. Though both the man and the word were largely forgotten by the end of the nineteenth century, Cousin would forever be linked with the idea of eclecticism. It is unlikely that an eclectic philosophy would have attracted any followers or exerted any influence were it not for Cousin's extraordinary gift for propaganda and for the predisposition of his contemporaries toward a nondogmatic philosophy. Hippolyte Taine, who was no admirer either of Cousin or of eclecticism, wrote, "Ce n'est point faire injure à un siècle ni à une race que d'expliquer ses croyances par ses inclinations primitives et par ses habitudes générales; ce n'est point faire injure à l'éclectisme que d'expliquer sa réussite par le génie et par les inclinations de son pays et de son temps" (290). ["It insults neither a century nor a race to explain its beliefs by its primitive inclinations and its general habits; neither does it insult eclecticism to explain its success by the genius and by the inclinations of its country and its time"] (my translation). Most accounts of the period, including Cousin's own reflections on his early career, invoke the spirit of the age to explain the brief but sweeping popularity of eclecticism.

Cousin would often tell the story of his life as an exemplary tale of the revolutionary generation; in many points, it also exemplifies the eclectic mentality of the age. As his first biographer and sometime student Jules Simon explains, Cousin always believed he had a great destiny to fulfill. He was born in 1792 in comparative poverty but was elevated to the middle class and won a chance at an education when he saved a richer boy from bullies. He must have felt like a necessary man, plucked as he was from the very cradle of his studies and transformed almost overnight into a professor of philosophy. After the revolutionary wars, the dearth of capable scholars meant that anyone with potential was drafted into immediate service. France and French culture had to be reconstructed. This would become the keynote of Cousin's philosophy; if the previous age had brought about this necessary and destructive revolution, then the mission of his generation would be rebuilding. The spirit of the age also led him to question the primacy of French philosophy—of all philosophical traditions—and to leave his country in search of new resources. By the time he went to Germany in 1820, exiled by the restored monarchy for being rather too popular a teacher, Cousin had already formulated his eclecticism. He had to make eclecticism seem to be destiny, to be natural, because he saw the justification for any system in its existence. For Cousin success was the proof of greatness, and when his eclecticism was threatened, or even challenged, by an articulate opponent, he readily adapted to the new conditions, ensuring its survival. In philosophy and in life, he chose what was true for his own use, much as one highlighting or annotating a text might note only those points memorable or important to oneself, rather than trying to discover the purpose or overall argument of the author. In spite of his limitations as a thinker or a cultural hero, Cousin is important because his eclectic philosophy forced his generation to confront the problems of originality, progress, and history.

Wherever it appears, eclecticism has always been associated with picking and choosing from seemingly opposed systems of thought; in Cousin it was also a search for lost treasures and a political faith in compromise. Eclecticism became, by 1830, the undeclared official national philosophy, because it offered the powerful and growing middle class a practical compromise between republicanism and ideology on the one hand, and Catholicism and the monarchy on the other.[1] For his opponents within and beyond the borders of France, Cousin seemed to compromise his philosophy by his involvement with politics. Blithely opportunistic, the eclectic Cousin mined the works of his immediate predecessors in France, his contemporaries in Germany, and the common-sense philosophy of Scotland. He managed to please the middle-class intellectuals, while provoking the ire of the chief philosophical schools, even as he became a government official in charge of education and a published apologist for the "bourgeois monarchy." In his pamphlet "Justice et charité" Cousin argued that justice consisted in preserving natural rights, but he did not believe in equality and taught that the state had but limited obligations to its citizens (Boas 223). In attempting to cope with the realities of post-Revolutionary and, in fact, post-Restoration French society, Cousin offered his people an eclectic solution, a way of looking at their religious and philosophical history that would heal the deep wounds opened by the intense ideological conflicts of the time. For this he was denounced as anti-Catholic by the Abbé Bautain, who said, "The mixed position, which the philosophy of today is trying to assume, is not tenable. There is no golden mean for eternal truths" (qtd. in Boas 215). From the point of view of the traditionalists, eclecticism was vague and incoherent, unable to distinguish between true and false, good and evil. Cousin fared no better with the radical, anticlerical left. Flaubert's Sénécal thought Cousin was worse than the Jesuits, for "eclecticism taught one to draw certitude from reason, developed egoism, and destroyed solidarity" (qtd. in Boas 220). In 1852 George Henry Lewes advised a friend to read Cousin, but not to trust him, "to take no single fact on his authority," to get his book but to "read it with the utmost caution" (Letter 139:203–4). Back in France, Lerminier claimed that Cousin was not a philosopher at all, but merely an "erudito"; the positivist Auguste Comte called him a "fameux sophiste"; and Sainte-Beuve at last "could scarcely mention him without a shudder" (qtd. in Boas 220). The twentieth-century historian George Boas merely charges Cousin with "buil[ding] his philosophy on motives of utility and convenience" (251), an enterprise Norman Klein credits as being the first "that attempted to cope with the implications of modern society" (ii). For all the opposition to his eclecticism—and it was considerable—Cousin struck a resounding chord with his "philosophy of the nineteenth century."

Against System
Cousin and the Spirit of the Age

In a striking passage from his early lectures on the history of modern philosophy, delivered in 1816 and 1817, Victor Cousin imagines himself a laborer in the ruins of history: "I come to bring my stone; I come to do my work; I come to extract from the midst of the ruins what has not perished, what cannot perish" (*Lectures* 32).[2] This is the essential image of what Cousin took to be the process of eclecticism. All that was true in the history of philosophy retained its solidity, even with the destruction of the system of which it had been part, and could be recovered for the foundation of a new philosophy. This new philosophy would have neither a beginning, because its component parts predated the new structure, nor an end, because the work of building eclectically was not utopian, but recursive. If the eighteenth century had been the age of destruction, he believed "the nineteenth century should be that of intelligent rehabilitations" (31). The "spirit of party" would be succeeded by the "spirit of conciliation"—as it had so many times before; but the historical recursiveness of eclecticism troubles Cousin, even as he faithfully carries the stones that will build a new century. A similar "state of disorder" had been seen "at the decline of the ancient beliefs, and before the triumphs of Christianity, when men wandered through all contraries without power to rest anywhere [. . .]" (31). Centered in Alexandria, but affecting the entire Roman world, the first wave of eclecticism failed to produce a synthesis.[3] If an eclectic method was to gain any credence among his contemporaries, Cousin had to distinguish his "enlightened" eclecticism from "that blind syncretism which destroyed the school of Alexandria, which attempted to bring contrary systems together by force" (33). What would make Cousin's eclecticism "enlightened" and "intelligent" rather than "blind," volitional and critical rather than naïve and accidental? He would have to make an antisystematic system the core of his new philosophy—to inhabit a structure whose dissolution was part of its design.

The few published accounts of eclecticism left by Cousin alternate between confidence in a better future shaped by his method and the cosmic pessimism that demands it—he has to believe that no further progress in philosophy is possible without eclecticism. All three major systems of thought arising in the eighteenth century—the materialist, idealist, and common-sense schools—had reached their pinnacles of insight and success, and were in unmistakable decline, with disciples producing only mannered versions of the masters. Unwilling to calculate the probability of an entirely new system of thought appearing on the scene, Cousin posits that progress will occur only through combining elements of the old. To choose any other course of action would deprive philosophy of both its autonomy and its future: submitting to the "ancient authority" (i.e., the Church) would mean a return to the Middle Ages; pursuing the conflict between schools would result in their mutual destruction. To get at the raw material worth saving, he would have to "disengage what [was] true in each of these systems" ("Destiny" 45), and get on with the hard work of rebuilding. Eclecticism therefore looked like "somewhat of a desperate resource" (50)—a salvage operation—but Cousin offered it up as the common-sense solution to a philosophical stalemate. His ambition, however, surely exceeded his common sense as he aimed to "construct a philosophy superior to all systems" (45) from the ruins of exploded doctrines. Like many of his generation, Cousin feared dogmatism more than inconsistency and believed there was more danger in loving the theory than in loving the truth—however multifarious its forms.

Looking to his own development as to a golden mean, Cousin discovered that it was easier to swallow a piece of every school than to take any of them whole. If his favorite teachers disagreed, then like a good son Cousin would find a way to reconcile them, rather than having to bid either farewell; when they objected to sharing the same room, Cousin would beg them "to lay aside their tyrannical pretensions" (50). It was tyrannical to advocate for any exclusive system since, as Cousin believed, every system that had ever achieved any currency in human thought must be able to lay claim to some portion of truth. (The naïve corollary to this proposition was that systems of thought were true on the points where they agreed and false where they disagreed.) Eclecticism would first have to deconstruct "all systems by the fire and steel of criticism" in order to reconstruct "a new system which [was] the complete representation of consciousness in history" ("Exposition of Eclecticism" 101–2). Cousin's claim for the superiority of eclecticism rested mainly on its being creative—even redemptive—where "sensualism" had been only destructive; but significantly, his starting point—psychology—was the same, and his analytical method—observation—was originated by the same materialist philosophers whom he professed to supersede.

The true beginning of all knowledge had to be the perceiving self, but Cousin assumed that this imperfect instrument could be turned from self-reflection to take in a larger panorama: "I am now on the summit of the mountain, from which a vast horizon is displayed before my eyes, but I come from the depth of an obscure valley, and can still perceive and point out to others the way which has led me to the point on which I stand, so as to aid and encourage them to rise to the same eminence with myself, instead of letting them believe and of persuading myself that I have fallen upon it from the clouds" (61). Ambitious in its scope, but humble in its conception, eclecticism, more than most philosophies, internalized the contradiction between seeing the whole and being part of the whole. Even as the perceiving subject tries to step outside of history in order to survey the panorama of human experience and thought through time, he has to remember that he also stands within it. The two views—given by the eye and the mind's eye—coalesce so that Cousin can claim impartiality in the eclectic process of picking and choosing from history's ruins. Unlike the partial views afforded by other systems, eclecticism succeeds "by a patient and profound observation, and an induction at once comprehensive and scrupulous [. . .] in embracing all the elements of consciousness and reality" (100). Eclecticism builds itself up from details, or partial views, to general ideas and the mastering vision. This principle of induction informs all of Cousin's subsequent efforts in philosophy: translations, scholarly editions, and teaching the history of philosophy—all have value insofar as they "terminate in a new recomposition [. . .] and sooner or later engender a new universal history of philosophy" (*Introduction* 410). History taught Cousin that all systems had arisen in response to "certain problems" within "the spirit of man," and he believed that an eclectic history of philosophy would "account for all the requisites of thought" (421). The search for a unified solution was a common-sense proposition: the age demanded it and the human mind required it. Unlike the tyrannical systems that it sought to replace, eclecticism offered not the unity of a theory, but rather "the harmony of all contrarieties" (416); it derived its power not from exclusion, but rather from extension.

Cousin wanted to bypass periods of ideological conflict altogether, by being mindful of the truth on all sides of any question. Mistrusted by all factions for what seemed like extreme moral relativism, he was forced to expend considerable effort defining and limiting the role of eclecticism *in* philosophy and eclecticism *as* philosophy. Throughout his fragmentary writings on the subject, Cousin variously names it a principle, a method, a system, a philosophy, and an application of philosophy. In 1817 Cousin, assigned to present a course of lectures on the history of philosophy, commences by declaring that the "criticism of systems almost demands a system, so that the history of philosophy is constrained to first borrow from philosophy the light which it must one day return to it with usury" (*Lectures* 36). Philosophy will teach him to recognize what is true and what is false in each of the systems that he surveys: whence comes this light? If eclecticism is the light that Cousin borrows from philosophy, then he conceives of it as a system worthy of criticizing other systems of thought—it is to be his "guide." His love of philosophy compels him to study its history, so that he might bring back more light from the past. Eclecticism will help Cousin "to deduce from the study of systems, their strifes, and even their ruins, a system which may be proof against criticism" (37). Not yet the end of philosophy, eclecticism promises to discover its new beginning. It is "the true historical method" (35), but not the object of study. Eclecticism is thus already a problem for Cousin: he wants to make it into a system that can bring order to the chaotic past. It is more than method and less than philosophy. It borrows from philosophy so that it might enrich philosophy.

After his triumphant return to teaching in 1828, he expresses his hope, in "Destiny of Modern Philosophy" (1829), that "Eclecticism may serve as a guide to the French philosophy of the nineteenth century," which will be an "Eclectic philosophy" (53). Not surprisingly, eclecticism will lead to an eclectic philosophy, appropriate to the spirit of the age, that he does not yet name.[4] In its best sense eclecticism represents "philosophical toleration," which "after the long reign of fanaticism, . . . calls forth the desire and the taste for a profound study of every system" (53, 54). Bringing every system under the probing gaze of the scholar, eclecticism recovers the lost treasures of human thought, which, like herbs concealed in a rain forest, will meliorate future ills. In the "Exposition of Eclecticism" (1833), it is again named a system, but Cousin at last gives a fuller account of its powers: "It is not compelled to proscribe all systems, in order to justify itself; it is satisfied with disengaging the inevitable portion of error that is mixed with the portion of truth, which forms the life and strength of each of them; and by pursuing the same course with them all, enemies as they were by their contrary errors, it makes them friends and brothers, by the truths which they contain, and thus purified and reconciled, it composes with them a vast whole, adequate to the expression of complete and universal truth. Not this method, at once philosophical and historical, which, in possession of truth, is able to find it scattered here and there in all systems, is Eclecticism" (101). As Cousin imagines it, eclecticism is a method that begins and ends in breadth. From the start, it takes in all other systems, sifting them for the valuable nuggets of truth, which it recognizes by their solidity and endurance—these are the stones that remain when the supporting framework of an old system fails. Instead of casting out any philosophy, which once influenced human action, it makes room for all that was beautiful, good, and true in each. The system underlying eclecticism, "which serves it as a point of departure and a principle in the labyrinth of history" (101), depends on observation and induction; it wields "a rigid criticism" as the instrument by which it decomposes all other systems and reconstructs the fragments "in a new system which is the complete representation of consciousness in history" (102)—the "complete and universal truth." Despite the bombast of "complete" in both phrases, Cousin qualifies the outcome of eclecticism with words such as "expression" and "representation"; eclecticism cannot be allowed to become the dogmatic replacement for exclusive doctrines. By nature it is the enemy of all systems and schools; if it becomes a system or a school, it goes against its nature. Eclecticism can only "express" and "represent," because it is an ever-changing picture of accumulated human experience.

Even with such natural restraints on the power of eclecticism, Cousin's critics saw only the provocative arrogance of a young philosopher who claimed to have penetrated the open secret of the universe that everyone else had somehow overlooked. Protesting that he was receiving calumnies in exchange for a gift freely given, Cousin yet understood well the vulnerable points of a system of thought that claimed to be independent of system and, systematically, to unite all contraries. In the "Exposition" he takes time to defend his "principle" and "instrument" from attack, asking whether it was "the dream of a deceived mind, which unable to produce a system for itself demands one of history?" (102). With the intention of persuading his critics of eclecticism's spontaneous ascendancy, Cousin rather airily responds to each of the most serious criticisms of his method: "All these objections will vanish of themselves before the slightest examination" (102). Eclecticism is *not* a syncretism that mingles together all systems; rather it is choice and discrimination, not mixture and confusion, because it leaves no system intact. Eclecticism does *not* approve everything, confounding true and false, good and evil; rather it distinguishes true and false and makes use of only the truth in each system. Eclecticism is *not* fatalism; to say that man with his "noble but limited intelligence" grasps but a portion of the truth is not fatal. Eclecticism is *not* the absence of all system; rather it is the application of a system from which it stands apart. In eclecticism, Cousin concludes, "the spirit of the nineteenth century has recognised itself" (105). Even Cousin's most severe critics might have concurred with this final claim. The malady of the nineteenth century could be traced to its inability to represent itself consistently, to its incapacity to decide on one mode of governance or a single faith. For Cousin, however, the true Eclectic in no way resembled the naïve, accidentally eclectic person. In fact, eclecticism was to be his cure for this common ailment, the means of coping with the sum of history.

Historian of Philosophy and Philosopher of History

When Victor Cousin laid claim to eclecticism, it was not virgin territory, but, much like the Western Hemisphere, it had always been there, affecting the weather, shaping the ocean currents, even when it was unknown by the Europeans who felt its presence. Eclecticism was a kind of standing offer in the history of ideas, an approach that could be taken with more or less intention behind it. Two periods that modern historians have often designated "eclectic" probably influenced Cousin's adoption of the term: the late- or post-Hellenistic and the early modern. However, Cousin was uneasy about the "blind syncretism" of ancient eclecticism, and he was silent on the eclecticism of Enlightenment authors such as Jakob Brucker and Denis Diderot, preferring to see all philosophy after Descartes and

Locke (and before Kant) as having an empiricist orientation. In spite of these doubts, Cousin proudly acknowledges, "Eclecticism is not of yesterday" ("Exposition" 104). It had been practiced, whether openly or not, by philosophers from Plato to Leibniz, and it was present in the new historicism of German philosophy. Distrustful of novelty and deeply pragmatic, Cousin gives his eclecticism an entirely commonplace origin: "It was born the moment that a sound head and a feeling heart undertook to reconcile two passionate adversaries, by showing them that the opinions for which they combated were not irreconcilable in themselves, and that, with a few mutual sacrifices, they might be brought together" (104). Being eclectic for Cousin was like breaking up a fight between friends—you want your friends to get along so you don't have to choose between them. As a historian of philosophy, Cousin looked for new friends and for ways to keep his old friends happy. As a philosopher of history, Cousin believed in alternating periods of conflict and compromise, high and low creativity, and, optimistically, that differences could always be sorted out in the end.

Characterized by its supposed loss of vigor and creativity, the period between the reigning Hellenistic philosophies of Stoicism, Epicureanism, and Skepticism and the emergence of Neoplatonism (50 B.C.–A.D. 200) has long borne the negative label "eclectic," at least since Eduard Zeller's authoritative 1883 study *A History of Eclecticism in Greek Philosophy*.[5] While recent efforts to expose the limitations of Zeller's analysis have contributed to a better understanding of ancient philosophy, his work still gives us the clearest picture of nineteenth-century attitudes to what was then understood as philosophical eclecticism.[6] In Zeller's reckoning, eclecticism arose as a means to reunite the Hellenistic philosophies that had their common origin in Aristotelian thought. Largely in agreement with Cousin's explanation of the emergence of modern eclecticism, Zeller offered a psychological explanation for the eclectic impulse. The first founders of separate schools, and their immediate followers, cling more tenaciously to points of doctrine, seeing every variation, every point of disagreement, as grounds for further dispute. Schools in their first and second generations tend to be exclusive, but this state of perpetual conflict inevitably declines, leading to a reassessment of points held in common and finally an attempt at fusion. Zeller repeatedly characterizes eclecticism as natural and universal—a permanent feature of the human mind, and a recurrent historical process. While Zeller's initial characterization differed little from Cousin's, his subsequent analysis of eclecticism (and all those thinkers caught up in its processes) was, for the period, typically ambivalent. Natural though it might be, eclecticism could produce two vastly different outcomes, leading to revolution and progress or to exhausted thought and irreversible decay.

In another significant parallel to his own century, Zeller saw that philosophy was transformed by cultural exchange. Romans generally assessed the value of philosophy in terms of its practical utility. They asked what philosophy could contribute to moral education and selected from the various systems what they deemed serviceable, "careless of the deeper interconnections of particular definitions" (16). Every individual would choose out of the various systems "that which [was] true for his own use[, which] presupposes that each man carries in himself the standard for decision between true and false" (18). For Zeller this appeal to the immediately certain made eclectic philosophy distinctive and important; but it was also a symptom of "scientific decay" and "the exhaustion of thought" (19). To ignore the intermediate stages by which we come to know a thing is unphilosophical, because it causes us to regard as innate that which is actually learned. The combination of systems based on the individual's selection would not provide a long-term solution or obviate the need for a new system: positive conviction would again be necessary. Understood as a stage in a recurrent historical process, eclecticism would either revive the philosophy of direct revelation from God (such as did occur with the rise of Neoplatonism) or lead to skepticism—the utter loss of faith in what is given.

Though he is frequently unsympathetic to the aspirations of eclectic philosophy and positively contemptuous of its professed methods, Zeller does concede the value of eclecticism in education. Most learning requires, to some degree, the application of eclectic principles, whereby the student learns first to imitate, then to combine, and finally to synthesize, the raw material of any subject. For three centuries teaching in academies of art had adhered to such eclectic principles. Far from being seen as a trammel on creativity, eclecticism in its conceptual openness freed the student to canvass all of history; to avoid being overwhelmed by it, he would have to approach the past critically. In the definition of eclecticism most likely to have influenced Cousin, Diderot eulogizes the eclectic philosopher as one who has embraced the utmost freedom of thought:

> The eclectic is a philosopher who, trampling underfoot prejudice, tradition, antiquity, general agreement, authority—in a word, everything that controls the minds of the common herd—dares to think for himself, returns to the clearest general principles, examines them, discusses them, admits nothing that is not based on the testimony of his experience and his reason; and from all the philosophies he has analyzed without respect and bias he makes for himself a particular and domestic one which belongs to him.... There is no leader of a sect who has not been more or less eclectic..... The Eclectics are among the philosophers who are the

> kings on the face of the earth, the only ones who have remained in the state of nature, where everything belonged to everyone. (*Encyclopédie,* art. "Éclectisme," vol. 5; trans. A. A. Long; qtd. in Donini 19)⁷

Paolo Casini has argued that in this article we find a self-portrait of Diderot at a crucial turning point in his career (35–36). Though he borrows the substance of the article from other writers, Casini points out that Diderot effaces the nuanced accounts of earlier eclectics in order to make the general type of the eclectic philosopher into a freethinker (38). Against those who would oppose the project of the *Encyclopédie,* and its mapping of human knowledge, Diderot argues not only for the necessity of being skeptical with respect to authority, but also for a constructive eclecticism.⁸ He will not only doubt and tear down, but he will also respect truth when he finds it and build up something new—"a particular and domestic [philosophy] which belongs to him." Diderot elevates experience to equality with reason, just as Cousin would do, and thereby avoids the emptiness of abstract ideas that too often lacked any meaningful connection to lived experience. When he claims that the leaders of every school must have been eclectic, he is valorizing the essential creativity of the eclectic process. The homely image of the philosopher as king in a world "where everything belonged to everyone" would have appealed to the post-Revolutionary generation, trying to salvage something from the general wreckage. The emphasis in the *Encyclopédie* was on the history of ideas, on accumulated knowledge and its practical uses, which linked it with at least one aspect of Enlightenment thought. As Wilhelm Schmidt-Biggemann has argued, "The plane of experience for practical reason is the area of history. In the historical concept, which is essential for eclecticism, facts and topoi of history could be selected and applied to practice" (548). Although Cousin fails to acknowledge the example of the Encyclopedists, the idea of the utility of history underlies his eclecticism.

Despite its close connection with the practical uses of history, if eclecticism had any right to be called a philosophy in the early nineteenth century, it was still best understood as a philosophy of history. As a theory of history, Cousin's eclecticism borrowed the model of alternating periods of high and low creativity from Enlightenment philosophers such as Voltaire, and infused his belief in progress. Periodically, the eclectic philosopher would have to step into a historical impasse, and discover the foundation of a compromise that would generate historical change. In the hands of Cousin, therefore, eclecticism was a tool for both interpreting and transforming human development through time. Though the influence of Hegel was indisputably strong with Cousin, his eclectic philosophy of history was formulated before he knew Hegel and was probably more directly influenced, as I have argued, by Diderot's conception of the philosopher as independent thinker. This is not to say that Cousin did not adapt his eclectic philosophy of history to later developments. His eclecticism demanded perpetual rethinking and accommodation. For example, it is likely that Michelet's 1827 translation of Vico's *Scienza nuova* (1744) had a profound influence on the 1828–29 lectures on the history of philosophy.[9] Although Vico's theory of history is usually described as cyclical, he did not imagine that every return caused an identical series of effects. This model of "the course nations run," built on the succession of ideas informing social practices, would have justified the study of history that was so central in Cousin's work. Even as the appearance of eclecticism signaled the exhaustion of ideas or weariness with conflict, a volitional eclecticism was the best method for choosing how the next cycle of history would develop. To see Cousin's eclectic philosophy of history only in terms of German historicism, which was clearly to become the most powerful influence in shaping nineteenth-century historiography, is to overlook the lesser stream of eclecticism that continues to shape ideas about the historical inheritance throughout the century. Organic historicism made eclecticism a problem, not a solution.

Regarding Cousin as a philosopher of history in the tradition of Vico and as a historian of philosophy in the tradition of Diderot helps to account for his shifting notion of progress. While he clearly saw the nineteenth century as having a unique role to play in history, such as might shape future progress in all fields of knowledge, later in his career he turned to writing the stories of the great women of the seventeenth century, France's Golden Age. It was an age of organic completeness, in which all the elements of science, politics, philosophy, and the arts cooperated to make France the greatest nation in the world. What made Cousin imagine that a society reconstructed eclectically from the ruins of history could approximate the achievements of the seventeenth century? How could eclecticism produce anything other than monsters? Cousin wanted progress in philosophy to match that of the sciences, but it would have to get beyond the cycle of destruction and reconstruction. Eclecticism, pushed to its logical extreme, made progress into an illusion. In some ways this accorded well with the critical spirit of the age; but if naïve eclecticism was a problem of history, then deeper investigations into history and the bringing forth of more material might exacerbate the problem. To overcome the practical limitations of his program, Cousin appealed to the sensibilities of the age.

In his lectures before the "noble youth of the nineteenth century," Cousin promised he would deliver to them a system that would be accepted by their hearts, as well as by their reason (*Lectures* 37). If Proclus was the work of Cousin's heart, as his biographer Jules Simon claimed, then it was because he imagined himself a modern-day Proclus, making the stand for a rational idealism in opposition to the forces of skepticism and empiricism. Being open, as Proclus had been, to new kinds of historical understanding, Cousin believed that he could contrive a philosophy that would better represent the age than any that had come before. As a "necessary man," Cousin imagined that he was fulfilling his destiny when he found that which had been lost—eclecticism. In spite of opposition from all exclusive doctrines, his singular efforts would allow the nineteenth century to realize its true character and take its rightful place in history: "This word, long since fallen into deep oblivion, scarcely uttered by a single voice, has echoed from one end of Europe to the other, and the spirit of the nineteenth century has recognised itself in Eclecticism" ("Exposition" 105). The word would echo across Europe and Europe would have to answer back, uniting in the common purpose of building the age to come. Every nation would answer by carrying its stones—to return to Cousin's metaphor of rebuilding—bringing forward its best, most enduring ideas. Sounding a call for European unity in an age of nationalism, Cousin's eclecticism was self-consciously cosmopolitan. Taking his cue from Madame de Staël's *De l'Allemagne* (1813), Cousin traveled to Germany to meet the great idealist philosophers, whose work he was instrumental in disseminating in France. He dismissed the idea that to be true to itself, the French spirit must remain ignorant of "the philosophical schools which flourish in other parts of the great European family" (80). He believed that traditional rivals France and Germany would find common ground "in this still feeble mingling of idealism and realism" and that "a true eclecticism [was] silently forming in European philosophy" (*Introduction* 428). After the fashion of his friend Hegel, he read intellectual developments as signs of national development: "the state of speculative philosophy in an epoch is equally relative to the general state of society in that epoch" (429). The proper historical role for eighteenth-century French philosophy had been as inspirer of revolutions—revolutions that had to be suffered and won for the good of all humanity. Cousin believed that eclecticism promised its own epoch-making combination of imagination and action, which would lead to a still more perfect mode of government, capable of inspiring cultural rebirth.

What Cousin might rightly have deemed the institutions of eclecticism—schools and universities; societies for the promotion of art, literature, and science; museums, encyclopedias, exhibitions, and anthologies—were thriving in nearly every part of Europe and were on their way to promoting a general form of culture such as the Western world had never seen. Having a habit of speaking of "the nineteenth century and its mission," Cousin would often be overcome with enthusiasm for a future that held out the promise of kaleidoscopic unity, such as that contained in the French constitution: "the throne and the country, monarchy and democracy, order and liberty, aristocracy and equality, all the elements of history, of thought, and of things" (439). Situated between the old and the new worlds, Europe's governments would inevitably reflect a mixture of old and new institutions. Literature, too, reflected the age's propensity to mix and mingle, bringing together "classic legitimacy and romantic innovation" (440). In short, it was impossible for philosophy to "avoid being eclectic when all that [was] around it [was] so" (440). The institutions and ideas of the nineteenth century would mutually reinforce and reflect each other. As a philosophy of moderation, eclecticism could come to fruition only when the moment of crisis (the revolution) was past; spontaneity *and* reflection were then possible, and together would usher in an age of progress. To be eclectic—to swim with the current of the times—not only would fulfill philosophy's historical role but would make all Cousin's work ramifying and productive. He could not choose his place in history, but by choosing eclecticism Cousin thought to make time pay. It was a typically eclectic compromise between liberty and necessity.

Thus Cousin sounded the reveille for a new century. His generation would have a vital part to play in history—"that of being just toward all systems and the dupe of none of them" ("Exposition" 50)—which required a distinctive style of thought. In coping with the burden of the past, Cousin sought to exercise "reflective choice" in order to reshape and improve on the century's intellectual inheritance. Without any pretension to originality, he selected from the history of philosophy what was most congenial to the spirit of the age, what seemed "true and productive," rather than "sterile and false" (*Lectures* 25). Eclecticism was to be the "breath of life" making the "sterile results of erudition . . . prolific, and thus productive of an universal history" (*Introduction* 410). Eclecticism was to be the handmaiden of genius, standing at its side and gathering up the "prophetic chants that ring from age to age" ("Exposition" 151). The eclectic philosopher was to play the role not of a mere critic, but of an intimate friend or lover; philosophy was "not to separate itself from the people, but to sympathize and identify itself with them, to labor for them, while it place[d] its foundation in their hearts" (151). At the most fundamental level eclecticism was for Cousin the process of binding together both individuals and ideas: when we see too many differences "between one individual and another, one country and another, one epoch of humanity and another, we feel a profound melancholy" (150). Eclecticism makes us feel better about history, Cousin argued, because we see that it is not waste, solitude, and longing, but rather abundance, unity, and fulfillment. His frequent recourse to the sexualized imagery of reproduction was in keeping with his view that eclecticism, though not a primary creation, was the secondary level of creation that generated historical change. In this way, Cousin roused the passions of his generation for compromise and gradual reform, not revolution, for the *juste milieu,* not utopia.

Literary Assessments in France

In his 1853 preface to *Lectures on the True, the Beautiful, and the Good,* Cousin seems to revise the nature of his contribution to philosophy. While admitting that eclecticism is the "doctrine" most often linked with his name, he professes that his "true doctrine" and "true flag" is spiritualism, a philosophy whose genealogy he traces from Socrates and Plato through the Gospels, Descartes, and Madame de Staël. Practical man that he was, he no doubt saw that enthusiasm for eclecticism was waning and that he needed to strengthen his position with posterity. Spiritualism, by the early 1850s, seemed to have had more influence in shaping the literature and art of the Romantic generation, but in reality they were first entranced by the promise of eclecticism, from which Cousin's vague spiritualism had evolved. In seeking a foundation for eclectic judgment, Cousin had most often resorted to common sense, sensibility, and emotion—to the heart. He concluded nearly every lecture with an inspiring evocation of divine power not only as an effort toward theodicy but also as an indication of his "acceptance of a preeminence of the divine as the source and foundation of human excellence" (Bénichou 153). As Paul Bénichou has written, Romantic spiritualism optimistically "combin[ed] faith in God and faith in man" and looked to the aesthetic as the primary means of communication with the divine (153). While spiritualism seems to arise naturally from Romantic preoccupations, Romantic eclecticism would seem to be almost a contradiction in terms, given the Romantics' exaltation of originality; but Cousin gave Romantic writers license to broaden their subject matter, to place new emphasis on psychology, to import foreign ideas, and to experiment with a variety of genres. Moreover, it was particularly characteristic of French Romanticism to embrace novel expressions of genius while preserving a proud and comforting past.

In an incisive 1827 review of Cousin's *Oeuvres de Platon* that appeared in *Le Constitutionnel,* the novelist and critic Stendhal wondered what made the nineteenth century so receptive to the works of Plato and why after many years of neglect Plato's message had taken hold. He expresses the surprise Cousin must have felt when this age "réputé si frivole" and "plein de lui-même et aussi affairé" received the philosopher's gift with enthusiasm, and when he saw his work crossing the boundary between the intellectual elite and the ordinary bourgeois—"Un livre qui [. . .] a charmé jusqu'aux femmes" ("Sur Victor Cousin" 205). A partial answer, Stendhal believes, is in the century's curiosity and love of the exotic, but the complete explanation is far more complex; Plato's own philosophy was ahead of its time and found its spiritual match in the nineteenth century, with its "double character." Far from regarding the century's mixture of beliefs as symptomatic of decline, Stendhal perceives it as a cause for celebration:

> Oserons-nous rendre un si bel hommage à notre siècle, et sa modestie voudra-t-elle l'accepter? Lui, qui croit ne pas avoir de philosophie, en a une; et entre la philosophie de Platon et la sienne, il y a une analogie intime et une sympathie profonde. (206)
>
> [Do we dare to offer such a beautiful homage to our century, and will its modesty want to accept it? It believes that it does not have a philosophy, but it has one; and between the philosophy of Plato and that of this century, there is an intimate analogy and a deep sympathy.] (my translation)

The close analogy between the philosophy of Plato and that of the nineteenth century originates in their mutual effort to reconcile materialist and spiritualist philosophies, a project Stendhal interprets as an attempt to get beyond the historical cycle of alternating ascendancy:

> La destinée de ces deux factions a été de lutter toujours, de se détrôner chacune à leur tour, et de dominer alternativement sur les esprits; et la raison en est simple: le monde et toute chose en lui ayant réellement deux principes, l'un matériel et visible, l'autre invisible et immatériel, la philosophie qui nie ou méprise l'un de ces éléments ne peut longtemps satisfaire la conscience du genre humain; son insuffisance se fait sentir le jour même où elle est adoptée, et le lendemain commence une réaction au profit de la doctrine opposée. [. . .] L'histoire des opinions humaines n'est qu'une série de réactions semblables, qu'ont exercées alternativement l'une contre l'autre quelques grandes idées exclusives. (206)
>
> [The destiny of these two factions was always to fight, to dethrone each other by turns, and to dominate alternately the spirit of the age; and the reason for it is simple: the world and all things in it have really two prin-

ciples, one material and visible, the other invisible and immaterial, the philosophy which denies or mistakes one of these elements cannot long satisfy the conscience of humanity; its insufficiency is felt the very same day that it is adopted, and the following day begins a reaction that profits the opposite doctrine. [. . .] The history of human opinions is only a series of similar reactions, where exclusive ideas are exerted alternately one against the other.] (my translation)

Like Cousin, who believed both in historical cycles and in progress, Stendhal believed that the nineteenth century would be unique in its ability to overcome the reactionary impulse that sets in following the dominance of one ideological phase or another. He admits that the post-Revolutionary reaction against the materialism of the eighteenth century was indeed spiritualist in nature, and that Romantic spiritualism simply marked another swing of the pendulum of ideas; but with the advent of Cousin and his introduction of foreign thinkers (Greek, German, and Scottish) into French, Stendhal imagines that a new epoch of human thought is commencing, where the old distinctions—classical and romantic, materialist and spiritualist, conservative and republican—will fall away, and that his age will not be "une triviale répétition de tous les siècles" (207). The "lumières" of the new mixed philosophy will teach that "il y a du vrai et du faux dans toute les opinions" (208) and that one must neither scorn any system nor adhere fanatically to any other.

Accepting this truth makes progress possible: "[. . .] l'enfance de l'espèce humaine a été la proie des doctrines exclusives, et que si l'âge d'or est devant nous, et non point derrière, c'est que l'éclectisme est réservé à sa maturité" ["the childhood of humanity was prey to exclusive doctrines, and if the golden age is before us, and not behind us, it is because eclecticism is reserved for its maturity"] (my translation) (208). Stendhal believed that humanity progresses only by escaping the current of reaction, something that had happened only rarely throughout history under the guidance of eclectic visionaries; the cultural situation of the nineteenth century was analogous to that of earlier transitional periods, where eclecticism had overcome ideological warfare. Those eras saw progress because they were eclectic, but like Cousin, Stendhal is uncertain about the degree to which the age can choose to be eclectic. He fancies a "génie de la conciliation" soaring over Europe, a spirit that "est celui de l'éclectisme, et il est l'enfant légitime des lumières" (209). As the philosophy of the nineteenth century, eclecticism would complete the work of the Revolution that had freed citizens from tyranny over their bodies, at last liberating the mind from the tyranny of exclusive ideas. The age required a philosophy whose doctrines would complement the new institutions. A government that would take eclecticism for its guiding spirit and have "le bon sens d'obéir à ses inspirations" would win over the intellectual elite of Europe and become the benefactor of all humanity (209). Whether Stendhal delighted, as Cousin would do, in the mixed government of Louis Philippe, or still anticipated political institutions that would genuinely reflect the diversity of the French people of the nineteenth century, he had articulated the desirable link between eclecticism and the national character or Zeitgeist, and in so doing made clear the powerful appeal that Cousin had for intellectuals of his generation.

In reflecting on the achievements of the first half of the nineteenth century, and the Romantic movement in particular, the literary critic Sainte-Beuve singled out Victor Cousin as one of the three academicians who had "la plus grande influence sur la direction des esprits des études en France," calling him one of "les régents de cet âge" ("Villemain" 161). Sainte-Beuve's admiration was tempered, however, by shrewd realism, and an awareness of the shortcomings of nineteenth-century culture when measured against past achievements.[10] Cousin, he contends, is not a true philosopher, and when we remove the varnish (*le vernis*) of the prestige conferred upon modern genius, Cousin appears in his real form—"le plus éloquent des *sophistes* dans le sens antique et favorable du mot"—but still a sophist (162). Contemporary praise distorts the worth of men such as Cousin, just as it overlooks their flaws. By restoring their true character and contribution, we see that "Ce sont là du reste les plus belles gloires réservées encore aux époques dites de décadence" (162). In those years marked for decline, critics must still judge their contemporaries as posterity will judge them: as inferior though influential men, forgettable in spite of the seeded ground they leave behind them.

While the melancholy mood of second thoughts intrudes upon many assessments of Cousin's legacy in later-nineteenth-century French criticism, nowhere is this tone more pronounced than in Sainte-Beuve's 1847 review of a collection of Cousin's lectures dating from 1815 to 1820. In these early lectures Cousin promises to dethrone the reigning materialist and sensualist philosophy almost with the force of his personality alone, an energy that yet permeates even the written expression of his early romanticism and that provokes in Sainte-Beuve a struggle between his heart, once captured by Cousin, and his head, long free of the great orator's spell. Perhaps as much as the loss of his own youthful naïveté, Sainte-Beuve regrets Cousin's naming of the new philosophy *l'éclectisme,* a designation that instantly complicated its reception and damaged Cousin's credibility, if not within his packed lecture halls, then certainly outside them, and most unfortunately beyond the borders of France. Reflecting on what eclecticism meant to Cousin's enthusiastic auditors, he recalls its enduring association with the long ago and far away, and with an intellectual curiosity that would take its practitioners outside the narrow confines of their native milieu:

> Qui dit éclectisme suppose la curiosité des opinions du dehors et le goût des voyages intellectuels. 1816 se trouvait un moment bien choisi pour inoculer ce goût à l'élite de la jeunesse. C'était l'heure où l'on allait commencer à sortir de chez soi, non plus pour se combattre, mais pour se connaître. ("Victor Cousin" 1023)
>
> [Whoever says eclecticism assumes curiosity about the opinions of the outside world and a taste for intellectual voyages. 1816 was a moment well chosen to inculcate this taste in the elite youth. It was at the moment when they were going to leave home, no longer to fight, but to know themselves.] (my translation)

Sainte-Beuve rightly links the success of eclecticism among the youth of France to Cousin's post-Revolutionary moment. Cousin gave students a model for self-cultivation and an example of intellectual curiosity that they could take beyond the borders of France. Indeed, Cousin's role in bringing the works of foreign thinkers into French changed irreversibly the course of nineteenth-century culture, first with the German and Scottish influence on Romanticism (an effort begun, of course, by Madame de Staël, whose work Cousin acknowledges) and then with his Greek translations, which helped to promote a second revival of Classicism in philosophy and the arts. This effort to recover the most important philosophical matter from history was entirely consistent with Cousin's eclectic principles. Sainte-Beuve criticized the historical approach for its limited productivity, but recognized its labor as central in the eclectic philosophy:

> Comme toute étude d'ailleurs qui porte sur l'histoire, l'éclectisme a sa réalité, indépendante même de la philosophie particulière à laquelle il s'appuie. Quand on ne le considérait, après tout, que comme une méthode historique pour aborder l'examen des systèmes de philosophie dans le passé, il faudrait reconnaître qu'il a produit de positifs et féconds résultats. L'Antiquité dans ses grandes écoles, le Moyen Âge et la scolastique, la Renaissance et les hardis rénovateurs italiens, ont été successivement mis en lumière, interprétés selon leur véritable esprit; et dans ces voies diverses où s'avance chaque jour une studieuse élite, on retrouve partout à l'origine le passage lumineux, le signal et l'impulsion du maître. (1023)

[As with any study that is supported by history, eclecticism has its reality, independent even of the particular philosophy on which it rests. When one only considers that, after all, as a historical method used to take up the examination of past systems of philosophy, it must be acknowledged that it produced some positive and fertile results. Antiquity in its great schools, the Middle Ages and the scholastics, the Renaissance and its bold Italian renovators, were successively brought to light and interpreted according to their true spirit; and by these diverse routes where each day a studious elite advances, one finds everywhere in the beginning the luminous passage, the signal and the impulse of the Master.] (my translation)

The "positive and fruitful results" of eclectic historical study were everywhere apparent in the schools, where the "studious elite" benefited from the example of Professor Cousin, but the dilemma posed by mere eclecticism remained. Everyone could agree that in philosophy, as in most other fields, the relatively new attentiveness to and practice of history were leading to great discoveries, but of a dry and archival sort; in France, where people expected philosophy to offer more than a catalogue of past achievements, a collection of biographies of great men, or an anthology of the wisdom of the ages, Sainte-Beuve thought that the eclectic's progress was an illusion, a synthetic "doctrine" for an artificial age.

All too conscious of the tendencies of the national character, he worried that prejudice against the idea of eclecticism would drive underground all Cousin's achievements, and the better portion (in Sainte-Beuve's reckoning) of his philosophy, *le spiritualisme:*

> Pour les esprits superficiels et qui jugent sur l'étiquette, l'éclectisme n'a souvent paru désigner qu'un procédé extérieur qui va par le monde, quetant et glanant les vérités à droite et à gauche, sans les avoir avant tout approfondies en soi. (1023)

[For the superficial spirits and those who judge by the political label, eclecticism often appeared to indicate only an external process which passes through the world, collecting and gleaning the truths on the right and on the left, without first having really understood them oneself.] (my translation)

The "thoughtless bias" against the Eclectic method, which seemed but "questing and gleaning" after bits of truth, ignored the depth of Cousin's commitment to the study of psychology (then a science of low reputation) and the requirements of the human spirit.[11] In addressing these early lectures to the youth of France, "[. . .] à vous qui formerez la génération qui s'avance; à vous l'unique soutien, la dernière espérance de notre cher et malhereux pays" (qtd. 1021), Cousin links moral liberty to political liberty and makes both contingent on their openness to the doctrine of eclecticism. Philosophers could no longer require ideological "servitude" from their followers or preach a materialism that made slaves of everyone. Cousin recommended eclecticism to those who could deliver France from the stern conflicts of the Revolutionary generation, even as they brought about a conceptual revolution of their own. Sainte-Beuve clearly regretted the lost opportunity that Cousin's original conception of eclecticism represented for his generation.

The literary historian Hippolyte Taine, writing in 1857 after the total victory of eclecticism and the *juste milieu,* and perhaps with a more realistic view of its capacities and shortcomings, explains not only the success of "la philosophie régnante" with intellectuals and its particular charm for members of the French middle class, but also its failure to live up to France's own philosophical tradition. Whereas Stendhal had welcomed eclecticism as the principle that would restore balance to history and end the cycle of revolutions in philosophy, Taine rejected it as a mechanical principle, a seductive machine that swallowed up some of the best minds of his generation. In his study of eclecticism's rise to power, Taine emphasizes the significance of the post-Revolutionary mood in bringing down the philosophy of the eighteenth century, and goes even further than Stendhal in citing those writers who were most responsible for the mind-altering declarations that produced the conditions necessary for eclecticism and an eclectic philosophy: Rousseau, who authorized sentiment, consecrated the ideal, and proclaimed the invisible; Madame de Staël, who preached exaltation and enthusiasm; Chateaubriand, who recovered the beauty of Christianity, changed God into a decorative artist, and overcame science with sympathy (296–97). These revolutionaries differed from those of previous generations in that they retained certain proclivities of their grandparents:

> S'ils avaient perdu les habitudes d'analyse, ils avaient gardé la passion de la métaphysique; ils étaient à la fois sentimentaux et systématiques, et demandaient des théories à leur coeur. Cela produisit un style singulier, inconnu jusqu'alors en France, le style abstrait. Composé d'expressions vagues, il convient au "besoin d'idéal" et au rêve. Composé d'expressions élevées et grandioses, il contente le besoin d'élévation et de grandeur. Composé d'expressions philosophiques, il semble introduire partout la philosophie. On l'employa, parce qu'on était rêveur, sublime et philosophe. (297–98)

[If they had lost the habit of analysis, they retained the passion for metaphysics; they were at the same time sentimental and systematic, and demanded theories for the heart. That produced a singular style, unknown hitherto in France, the abstract style. Composed of vague expressions, it suits the "need for the ideal" and for the dream. Composed of elevated and grandiose expressions, it contents the need for elevation and grandeur. Composed of philosophical expressions, it seems to introduce philosophy everywhere. It was employed, because one was a dreamer, sublime and philosophical.] (my translation)

Already joined within them were these opposing tendencies, and the desire to make a science of the knowledge of the heart, to produce a philosophy of sentiment, and to build future liberty upon the foundation of diversity; but their science was unscientific, their philosophy unphilosophical, and their future a fantastic utopia. In Taine's prose, we can sense his disgust with the dreams that carried away the previous generation—dreams that, after all, only resembled the reality they sought to embody—grandiose language instead of grand ideas, philosophical expressions instead of philosophy. The "abstract style" created by combining the desire for system with rampant sentimentalism allowed its practitioners to imagine that they inhabited an ideal compromise, which, in fact, had eluded them.

The two passions of their "renaissance" were dream and abstraction, which imposed on all their theories the necessity of being consoling and poetic, and on the dreamers the obligation of believing in theories without having any proof (298). The romantics were at once "sceptique, idéaliste, mystique, indien, païen, chrétien, humanitaire, manichéen, en stances, en versets, en alexandrins, en petits vers, en couplets croisés, en rimes continues" (299). This mixture of creeds infused a variety of literary genres and, indeed, entirely mixed works. Taine laments the popularity of plays and novels that make claims appropriate only in scientific treatises, and the representation of characters within them as instances of universal humanity and historical epochs, or of the need for social and political reform: "Nul poëte ne daigna être simplement poëte" (299). Taine argues that the dilemma of style in French culture before Cousin prepared the nation for his consoling philosophy, which allowed it to continue in its chosen track; in the "style abstrait et sublime," Taine recognizes the roots of eclecticism and of its success:

Les motifs qui persuadaient les maîtres persuadaient les disciples; le même besoin régnait dans la chaire et dans l'assemblée; l'auditoire était converti d'avance; on lui prouvait ce qu'il avait envie de croire; dans les sentiments du professeur, il applaudissait ses propres sentiments. (300–301)

[The reasons which persuaded the masters persuaded the disciples; the same need reigned in the pulpit and the assembly; the audience was converted in advance; one proved to it what it wanted to believe; in the sentiments of the professor, it applauded its own sentiments.] (my translation).

France was ready for Cousin, and his primary genius lay in his ability to satisfy the wants of a population yearning to believe in something. Throughout his essay "Pourquoi l'éclectisme a-t-il réussi?," Taine resorts to the language of seduction to explain the force of Cousin's eclecticism as it swept over France and "subjugated" its people. Nascent romanticism, and especially the German influence,[12] combined with Cousin's "sonorous" monologues to transform the public into an empty vessel to be filled with the "mists" and dreams of the Eclectic philosophy: "[. . .] et le public, emporté sur un nuage, était ravi de planer avec lui au dessus de l'univers" (301). Cousin's appeal was particularly seductive because, Taine concedes, he possessed real genius.

As we have already seen, Cousin's endeavors received their impetus from the historicism that became the dominant mode of viewing the past and coping with its legacy. In looking at the profit Cousin made from the "nouvel esprit" that transformed the study of history, Taine at once admires the way Cousin "réunit à sa philosophie l'histoire de la philosophie" and regrets that "le philosophe usurpa l'estime que méritait l'historien" (304). In describing the way this man born of working-class parents during the Revolution climbed into the ranks of the powerful, Taine sees Cousin "availing" himself of "la faveur et [. . .] les services de l'histoire et du libéralisme" and at the same time "maneuvering" into the good graces of the public with "la variation perpétuelle de sa doctrine et l'allure ondoyante de son esprit" (304). When eclecticism was thus "défendu par des hommes de talent, [. . .] il devait tout abattre et tout subjuguer" (301), and this was even more the case after 1830, when Cousin was engaged in continually modifying his philosophy to suit the various interests of the mixed government he underwrote with his own work. He excised all of those elements of his philosophy that seemed too foreign or anti-Christian or republican in order to conciliate the offended parties of the nationalists, the Church, and the aristocracy. At this point Cousin begins to merit the accusations once hurled only at his eclecticism; such modifications and emendations were certainly opportunistic, and we can measure the disappointment some of his adherents must have felt when we compare the power of Cousin's early

1815 address (keep in mind Cousin was no more than 23 years old at the time) to his later sophistic capitulations. Taine wrote of the same early lecture that had provoked Sainte-Beuve's nostalgic recollections:

> Son succès fut d'autant plus grand qu'à ses forces naturelles il ajouta des forces artificielles; il profita des circonstances accidentelles commes des circonstances permanentes; avec ses armes propres il eut des armes étrangères, et, en premier lieu, l'amour de la patrie et de la liberté. Écoutez ce passage, sentez ce style, et dites si un Français de 1815 pouvait y résister. (301)

> [Its success was all the greater since to its natural forces it added artificial forces; it benefited from accidental circumstances as if they were permanent circumstances; to its own weapons it added foreign weapons, and, initially, the love of the fatherland and freedom. Listen to this passage, feel this style, and tell me whether a Frenchman of 1815 could resist it.] (my translation)

The address in which Cousin exhorts the youth of France to save their country by embracing his "beautiful doctrines"—his philosophy of the nineteenth century—struck both Sainte-Beuve and Taine with its power of enthusiasm. Philosophy and history joined together would enter the sphere of action, and be no more separated from the people who needed them; but Taine is deeply critical of what seem to him to be conflicting aims: the study of philosophy and the improvement of society, *or* the writing of literature and the reform of politics. For Taine, the proof of the failure of Cousin's project to save France with philosophy came in the modification of those doctrines in the face of intense criticism (what happened to the Cousin who went into exile during the 1820s to avoid persecution by the Restoration monarchy?). By surrendering certain of his beliefs in the 1830s, Cousin irreparably damaged his philosophy (such as it was), even as he managed to seduce more followers into his camp:

> Il eût été bien difficile de ne pas réussir avec tant d'adresse, avec tant de soin pour séduire, amuser, entraîner et ménager les esprits, avec tant de précautions pour suivre ou devancer leur marche. (308)

> [It would have been quite difficult not to succeed with such an address, with so much calculated to seduce, amuse, involve and handle the spirit, with so many precautions to follow or precede their functioning.] (my translation)

With these "variations utiles," Cousin had the power of a political party behind him, the credit of his historical researches, the silence of his foes, the sympathy of the spirit of the age, and his own great talent. How could he fail to please?

The problem with eclecticism was apparent, then, even at its height. In 1857 Taine could see that the reigning philosophy tottered on its last legs. The public approval had turned cold, and if the public attended to the Eclectics at all, they did so to revel in "son beau style" (311). Was the doctrine ineffectual because of Cousin's compromises of 1830? Was it stagnant because it failed to engage with any opposition? Eclecticism always backed away from conflict, preferring to see in everyone's ideas something of the truth, something it could use. Had this openness to diversity finally destroyed eclecticism? Cousin had warned against eclecticism ever becoming a school, because it could exist only as a method or principle of inquiry, but when it became at least the quasi-official philosophy of the ruling party, it abandoned its prime directive. Of course, Cousin would have disagreed with this interpretation, seeing its adoption by the July Monarchy as a sign of the new regime's openness to competing or foreign ideas; but its welcoming attitude did not foreshadow a renaissance in French philosophy. Early in his essay on the success of eclecticism, Taine blames the philosophy of Cousin for knocking down "la philosophie philosophique" and for reducing "la science à une machine oratoire d'éducation et de gouvernement" (291). Unlike the Positive philosophy that would follow eclecticism, it proved nothing and knew nothing except at a distance or within the trammels of the heart. Most critics of eclecticism would not admit it was any kind of philosophy worth the name; further, they worried that it resembled, and acted as, a machine for processing ideas. What emerges from the machine of eclecticism—or factory with all its laborer-historians—is necessarily a synthetic product, a secondary creation. The question, then, of why eclecticism found favor among artists and writers remains to be answered.[13]

With its dual emphases on history and universality, eclecticism freed artists and intellectuals from the dominance of a single, classical tradition. It demonstrated the relativity of rules and styles over time, even as it professed to retain access to those universal qualities that would make a work of art eternally appealing. Stendhal, whose infatuation with Cousin comes through very strongly in *Racine et Shakespeare,* argued that all great artists had been romantic in their time (a notion that would be taken up by the openly eclectic Walter Pater), and so the "genius of conciliation" that eclecticism brought to Europe freed artists to be what they had always been, the cultural innovators, those important persons who were able to see through to new combinations.[14] This hope of seeing things as they were derived from Cousin as well, from his importation of Platonic philosophy into French culture and his emphasis on the powers of the imagination: "The Platonic ideal could be attained by an imaginative leap beyond the concrete object, and Cousin claimed that the intuitive faculty underlay all knowledge of the world" (Boime 16). Cousin offered the Romantics a way to be philosophical that was compatible with being artistic. The Romantics were disposed to be impressed by the talent of eclecticism for combination, by its willingness to recognize and unite opposing styles. In 1828 Cousin thrilled the Romantics in the audience by legitimizing their project: "the eclectic spirit in literature is shown in the accord of 'classical legitimacy with romantic innovation'" (Boime 16). Echoing Cousin, Lamartine wrote that "one must be classical in expression and romantic in thought" (qtd. in Boime 16). In his famous account of the novel, Balzac places himself within the "school, which must be named that of *literary eclecticism*" and keeps company there with Walter Scott, Madame de Staël, James Fenimore Cooper, and George Sand. According to his definition, the literary eclectic "demands a representation of the world as it is," thus combining the leading features of the literature of imagery and the literature of ideas (Balzac 127, 130). In his "painting" of modern society, Balzac cannot limit himself to the rigid prescriptions of the seventeenth century, because life has become so much more complex: "The introduction of the dramatic element, imagery, picturesqueness, description, dialogue, seems to me indispensable in modern literature" (131). Balzac summed up the affinity that the modern writer had for eclecticism: "perfection requires a total view of things."

Cousin in Britain

The Scottish philosopher Sir William Hamilton perhaps felt obliged to contradict Cousin's work after hearing of the French philosopher's astonishing popularity following his lectures of 1828–29, and though Hamilton's chief purpose was not to undermine eclecticism, those portions of Cousin's philosophical teachings that he chooses to challenge are contiguous to those his contemporary S. T. Coleridge objected to as characteristic of eclectics.[15] Hamilton's 1829 review of *Cours de philosophie: Introduction à l'Histoire de la Philosophie* (1828) commences with expressions of admiration for Cousin's success in "awakening" in his hearers "interest unexampled since the days of Abelard" in the "exposition of doctrines unintelligible to the many" (194). Slyly, Hamilton indicates that the pretensions of his doctrine are proportionate to the attention it has received (but what kind of attention?—that of the crowd unaccustomed to the language of philosophy): "It professes to offer nothing less than to be the complement and conciliation of all philosophical opinion" (194). The popularity of Cousin's doctrine betrays to Hamilton its weaknesses; he wins approval not from those colleagues capable of disputing the foundation on which he constructs his philosophy, but from receptive students on whom the effect of his bombastic language is greater than the meaning behind it. However, Hamilton ventures to meet Cousin on terms of equality, as one philosopher to another. Rather than cast aspersions on his character, Hamilton examines the philosophical tradition in which Cousin establishes himself and whether its underlying doctrines are at all sound.[16]

In common with Cousin's French critics, Hamilton recognizes that Cousin belongs to the phase of reaction against eighteenth-century sensualism, a reaction that is dominated by German "Rationalism." Cousin believes, with the rationalists Fichte and Schelling, that human reason is the source of truth and reality, and that "Experience affords only the occasions on which intelligence reveals to us the necessary and universal notions of which it is the complement; and these notions afford us at once the foundation of all reasoning, and the guarantee of our knowledge of existence" (196). Like Kant, Hamilton rejects the idea that human beings can have any knowledge of the Absolute; but men such as Cousin refused to be circumscribed by the narrow limits of "a philosophy of observation" and, according to Hamilton, revived "a bolder and more uncompromising Rationalism" than any that had come before. These new rationalists reject a philosophy of experience as "unworthy of the name of science"; since experience is transitory and contingent, it cannot be relied upon as "a proper basis of certainty": "Philosophy must, therefore, either be abandoned, or we must be able to seize the one, the absolute, the unconditioned, immediately and in itself; and this [the rationalists] profess to do by a kind of intellectual vision. In this act, reason, soaring not only above the world of sense, but beyond the sphere of personal consciousness, boldly places itself at the very centre of absolute being, with which it is, in fact, identified; and thence surveying existence in itself, and in its relations, unveils to us the nature of the Deity, and explains, from first to last, the derivation of all created things" (197). Hamilton concedes that Cousin is not devoted exclusively to "Rationalism," but in fact attempts to "combine the philosophy of experience, and the philosophy of pure reason, into one" (198). Hamilton does not explicitly link the privileged position offered by "Rationalism" with the eclectic's need to occupy the "very centre of absolute being," but it is clear that Cousin's philosophy cannot exist without such egocentrism. The ideal perspective of the eclectic exists outside of the transitory viewpoints of other systems, because it must be the judge of them all. If the eclectic cannot reproduce the transcendent vision of the Absolute, then he or she will not be able to escape the confines of the Zeitgeist; however, it is the paradox of eclecticism as Cousin formulates it not only to be the philosophy, even the spirit, of the nineteenth century but also to overcome the specific conditions of the age in order to find truth wherever it existed throughout time. Hamilton, of course, denies that any person can achieve a perspective outside of time, such as must belong to the Deity alone.

While the target of Hamilton's attack is not eclecticism, he attempts to destroy the foundation on which Cousin has erected his philosophy: the sovereignty of human reason. Cousin teaches that reason has three integrated elements: 1) unity, absolute cause, the infinite (what Hamilton calls the unconditioned); 2) plurality, relative cause, difference (the conditioned); and 3) intelligence, which is composed of unity and plurality as cause and effect, the realization of the one through the other (198). The logical outcome of this doctrine is to recognize "Man [as] the microcosm of existence" and reason as divine, since it is "a revelation of God in man" (199). When we create, we mimic the divine nature, and activate the "free causality" that exists within each human mind; the principles that created the universe are still at work within us, the "law of expansion" that moves unity toward variety, and the "law of attraction" that returns variety to unity (199). Hamilton cannot accept the premise that human reason can have any grasp of the Absolute or the Infinite, in other words, of God, and at best, human reason comprehends only the "conditionally limited" (203). Such a proscription makes philosophical inquiry impotent and irrelevant, at least according to those Rationalists who believe that philosophy can exist only as the study of the unconditioned.[17] By contrast, Cousin seeks to enlist psychology in the service of philosophy, in order to prove that the Absolute is indeed knowable and conceivable by the human mind through reflection, "under relation, difference, and plurality" (202). It is this manner of knowing the one unity, the Absolute, or God, that gives Hamilton the ammunition for his attack: "it is asserted to be known as absolute unity, i.e.[,] as the negation of all plurality, while the very manner by which it is known, affirms plurality as the condition of knowledge itself" (217). On this basis Hamilton announces that eclecticism is a "signal failure" because Cousin's "reliance on the powers of man" can "end only in disappointment" (220). Human beings can indeed reflect upon the nature of existence, thus separating and distinguishing its elements, but they cannot put it back together again—they cannot create unity from variety. Hamilton perceives the sin of the eclectic to be one of overreaching, of believing that what we labor to attain, we have in fact accomplished.

The specific features of Hamilton's objections are significant considering the shape eclecticism would take in Britain. As Hamilton builds his case against the conceivability of the Absolute, he lights on Cousin's equation of human reason with the divine, specifically the way Cousin uses this premise to construct the ideal perspective of the eclectic. Cousin's eclecticism depends on difference, relation, and plurality, on being able to reproduce the action of the reflective mind, which separates and distinguishes; and, more substantially, it must mimic the activity of the creative mind, which joins together what has been torn asunder. Hamilton perceives the relation in Cousin's philosophy between reflection in the individual, and the practice of history, and the necessity of a history of philosophy "with all its elements, with all their relations, and with all their laws, represented in striking characters by the hands of time and of history, in the visible progress of the human mind" (201). This endeavor provides Cousin with the lofty vantage point he needs to discern the relations among previous systems, to overcome the partiality of reflection, and of history, and to reunite the dispersed products of human intelligence. The arrogance of the eclectic in his appropriation of God's singular view looked very much like atheism or, worse, a boundless confidence in humanity that would render "God as a necessary postulate for proper moral action"[18] completely irrelevant.

Sir William Hamilton suffered, after his death, the same ignoble fate as Cousin, which was to be thoroughly refuted and utterly forgotten, but he did make an early and significant contribution to the debate on eclecticism in Britain. By far the most important opposition, however, came from the pen of philosopher and critic George Henry Lewes, who wanted to expose eclecticism as a mirage and its founder as a dangerous charlatan. In his 1844 review "The Modern Metaphysics and Moral Philosophy of France," he endeavors to explain the current state of philosophy in a country known only for its "sensualism and atheism" and to guide readers through the errors of various systems to the truth of positivism. The occasion of the review allows Lewes to launch the positive philosophy of his hero Auguste Comte in Great Britain, but this goal necessitates the defeat of positivism's chief rival to the title "philosophy of the nineteenth century." Whereas Hamilton focused on the tendency of eclecticism to promote unbelief through its arrogant assumption of a god's-eye view, Lewes exposes its tendency to be unscientific when it advances metaphorical explanations of phenomenological problems. Lewes commences his critical survey of French philosophy with a brief analysis of what all nineteenth-century philosophical systems do share, namely that they are "dogmatical and constructive" where the philosophy of the eighteenth century had been "sceptical and destructive," spiritual rather than material, religious rather than opposed to religion. The method of nineteenth-century philosophy is historical, where that of the last century "invert[ed] the results of historical experience, and boldly asserted that civilization was the gradual process of degeneration [. . .] placing the golden age in the past, instead of the future; and calling on mankind to return to that primitive state" (355). Emancipated from this "misconception of the nature of social organisation," the philosophy of the nineteenth century proceeds on the assumption that society is "inseparable from man" and that "in its perfection we must seek the perfection of mankind" (355). For Lewes this healthy historicism is as characteristic of the eclectics as it is of Auguste Comte (and all the other new schools). Since all hold these values in common, Lewes builds the case for positivism by destroying eclecticism's right to call itself a science—and without the prestige of the "positive" sciences attached to it, eclecticism and all other philosophies would disappear, no longer having any "practical bearing" on the development of society.

Like Hamilton, whose essay on Cousin he cites here, Lewes identifies the first error of the eclectics as their presumption that human beings can have knowledge of anything but phenomenological laws. Seeking knowledge of essences, the eclectics are led into the familiar trap of believing that their naming of a thing has made it comprehensible. Cousin and his chief follower Théodore Jouffroy claimed that the mind could be "an object to itself" that would be observed by the mind's eye, the "oeil interne." Lewes declares this notion "too palpably absurd" (366), and ridicules Cousin and Jouffroy as "caricatures of men" (364) who bring the doctrines of legitimate philosophers (such as Thomas Reid and Dugald Stewart) into contempt. How can the internal eye observe what is passing in the mind, when the instant it does so, the mind can contemplate only the effort at observation taking place? Lewes compares such an effort to the eye trying to see itself seeing. (Would it matter to Lewes that we can observe ourselves seeing simply by looking in the mirror? This could be a metaphor for the reflexiveness of the mind's eye.) He seems to quibble over the basis of psychology when he accepts that the mind can be known to itself in recollection, when the facts of consciousness are repeated often enough that we become aware of the pattern, but not so long as we are trying to catch ourselves in the act of thought (365). As will often be the case in Lewes's critique of eclecticism, he objects to Cousin's use of metaphors where only facts ought to be relevant or admissible; but Lewes's approach overlooks the extent to which human beings still depend on metaphorical explanations of things beyond the reach of ordinary understanding. In fact, Lewes's support of Comte depends in large part on his acceptance of Comte's evolutionary scheme of the mind, which posits that understanding is first supernatural and fictitious, then metaphysical and abstract, and, finally, positive and scientific. Cousin's abstractions do not belong to a scientific age—they might even be a form of primitive knowledge—and seem to limp far behind the verifiable matter of those sciences that do claim to have a practical bearing on society.[19]

Using metaphors to fill the void of absent facts is one of the aspects of Cousin's style to which Lewes most objects, but this continual recourse to literary tropes points to a problem in Cousin of much greater proportions, his showmanship. Lewes names Cousin "the most showy [of living metaphysicians]," in whose writing one finds "splendour of diction; a richness, variety, and purity of exposition; an enthusiasm in manner, and an erudition extensive though inaccurate"—"The style of Cousin is very near perfection" (367–68). What worries Lewes is the way Cousin takes in his audience with what amounts to a brilliant performance in the *role* of philosopher, a profession for which Cousin claims few qualifications and little training, having taken over the Chair of Royer-Collard at the age of twenty-three. Lewes challenges Cousin's seemingly unassailable claim to fame, those well-known products of his erudition: the editions and translations of the great works of philosophy. Even Hamilton was taken in, Lewes says, by Cousin's reputation "as the translator of Plato and the editor of Proclus and Des Cartes; as the expositor of Kant and Hegel" (368), and so long as one looked only at his reputation, admiration was still possible; but as soon as one inspected the basis of this reputation, Lewes warns, one would discover that his reputation was as much a tissue of lies as his philosophy: "When we look into [his reputation] and see how it was obtained, a feeling of something very like contempt can hardly be restrained; for it then turns out that Cousin did *not* translate Plato; did *not* write the 'Leçons sur Kant;' [sic] and that his doctrines are the unacknowledged pillage of Hegel and his friends, joined to a caricature of the method of Stewart" (368). Lewes relates how he discovered, during a visit to Paris, the actual translators of Plato, capable but poor young men, "glad of employment, and glad of [Cousin's] patronage" (369), who were enlisted to do the hard work of rendering Plato's ideas intelligible (370), while Cousin merely went over the completed translation, "correcting and polishing the style (as he alone can polish), and wrote the argumentary prefaces" (369). Anxious to remove even the smallest credit from Cousin, Lewes adds that "these prefaces often display a curious misunderstanding of the nature of the dialogues they precede!"—that is to say, Cousin did not bother to read the work carefully before adding his fictions to it. The work on Kant evolved in a similar fashion, Lewes claims, with a young man laboring at the exposition of Kant's ideas and Cousin polishing the style, contributing "two chapters of perfectly written gossip, named criticism," and placing his name on the title page (369). At this point Lewes can barely contain his rage against the man whose outward brilliance cast a man of Comte's talents into the shadows: "It is difficult to preserve the respect due to a man of M. Cousin's unquestionable ability and attainments, when we see them coupled to such acts of *charlatanerie;* and we are the more anxious to call attention to these facts, because they enable us to understand the contradictions of his philosophy, and to trace in that a kindred mode of operation" (369).[20] In Lewes's opinion, Cousin has contributed nothing to philosophy, stealing all of his ideas from original thinkers, and varnishing them with his exquisite style. "Faithful" to no master, Cousin's enthusiasm for each of his successive subjects carries his students along; but his exposition "has always more or less misrepresented, sometimes caricatured, the doctrines he professed to expound" (370). Perhaps intending to deliver the final blow of the wrecking ball, Lewes declares that the "striking predilection for literature" Cousin manifested when a student at the École Normale should have carried him into an altogether different career, where this talent would "have procured him a brilliant and more honourable success" (370). As Lewes argues, Cousin's flaws as a philosopher—his plagiarism, literary and showy style, and unscientific approach—all feed into and upon his eclectic principle. In particular, the charge of being overly literary will become important as we contend with the problem of verifiability that Lewes perceives in eclecticism.

Following his destruction of Cousin's reputation, Lewes embarks on the demolition of Cousin's only substantial contribution to philosophy and the mental development of the species, his eclecticism. In his *Biographical History of Philosophy,* Lewes wants to dismiss eclecticism as "nothing but a misconception of Hegel's 'History of Philosophy'" (773), but grudgingly proceeds, as he does in his 1844 review, to analyze its usefulness in writing the history of philosophy and in philosophical inquiry more generally. Lewes readily concedes that Cousin does not profess to be original but "rests his claim as a thinker on the development of a method which is to reconcile all thinkers and which is to resume in one body of doctrine all the truths that lie scattered through the incomplete systems of others" ("The Modern Metaphysics" 374). By way of clarifying his master's dictates, Jouffroy explains that this method would operate by juxtaposition: with all the great monuments of philosophy arrayed alongside one another, made known by the labors of the historians and translators, it would be the task of the eclectic to organize them properly, with "the questions [. . .] arranged in their legitimate order, with the truths discovered concerning each by the different philosophers, so that the whole should form a methodical science, in which we could perceive at a glance both what we know and what remains to be discovered" (qtd. 374). With the troops thus assembled, the eclectic would have merely to point out the weaknesses in each individual system, and set them aside, leaving the strengths to grow together. Lewes seems to shake his head in wonder at the naïveté Jouffroy exhibits here, an ingenuousness that seems genuinely unaware of the need for a "criterion of truth." The first problem with the eclectic operation Jouffroy describes stems from the definition of error, which Lewes calls "fallacious": "Error is *often* an incomplete view of the truth, but not *always*" (375). By way of example, Lewes reminds his readers that Newton did indeed burden his laws of attraction with the medium of ether (an error), but he'd got the laws right; on the other hand, Descartes developed a theory of vortices that was altogether wrong, and contained no salvageable truth. Since only some systems contain portions of truth, while others have none at all, how will the eclectic "select those systems which do contain them" (376) and not preserve error from those which do not into the bargain? What if the farmer does not know the wheat from the chaff? "He can only separate it by virtue of his previous knowledge," Lewes argues, and therefore, the eclectic must know the truth already, at least by its relation to those truths that he has already ascertained, "and then he is in possession of a philosophy in which he includes the discoveries of others, as the chemist includes any discovery made in any other quarter of the globe" (376). According to Lewes, the eclectic is in a vicious circle, seeking a system of philosophy by arranging the truths of other systems, but to do this he must already know these truths and thus be already in possession of a system; and, further, as in all the sciences, the discoveries of others will help him on his way. No one has ever been completely original, Lewes acknowledges, so what makes eclecticism special? It makes others do all the work! Lewes jokes at Cousin's expense. Actually, eclecticism is nothing more than "a *subsidiary* process" in any field of inquiry, and is essential to the student's success. The idea that eclecticism could become primary, let alone the philosophy of the century, strikes Lewes as ridiculous.

Lewes destroys any pretension eclecticism could have to be a system, but he is unable to arrest its force as a tendency of the age, a way of operating in response to a potentially overwhelming historical inheritance. He does not attempt to explain *why* Cousin, despite his unscientific assertions and careless plagiarisms, exerted such a powerful attraction over his audience, or *why* eclecticism, with its ethereality and outrageous hubris, nonetheless satisfied the need for both psychological explanation and practical application. Whether Lewes means to denigrate the literary when it is found in association with the eclectic is unclear; more likely, he wishes to establish philosophy on scientific grounds by wresting it out of the hands of the idealists and humanists. When Lewes equates being literary with being eclectic, as in the case of Cousin, he implies that the opposition between the culture of science, represented in philosophical terms by positivism, and the culture of arts and letters, or the humanities, represented in philosophical terms by eclecticism, runs deeper than mere methodological disagreements. W. M. Simon, writing on the "two cultures" in nineteenth-century France, sees Comte's attack on the psychological foundation of Cousin's eclecticism, specifically its use of "introspection"—or *l'oeil interne*—as exemplifying their differences. For Comte introspection was unscientific (48), and he denied that it could have any value for the study of mental phenomena. Lewes believed that unscientific philosophical inquiry had no value for a society that had passed into the third stage of mental development, the positivist. Positivism would also be instrumental in overcoming the "intellectual anarchy of Europe" (396), the condition of being uncritically or naïvely eclectic. The metaphorical abstractions of Cousin seemed to linger behind in the transitional age; indeed, most eclectics understood their activity as transitive, getting society, or a particular art form, from one stage of development to the next, but they are much less specific than Lewes was about what the new society ought to look like, though he did not doubt that positivism would supply all the religion and art that a *scientific* culture might require.

Not all Britons responded negatively to the eclectic philosophy imported from France. A decade after Cousin's death, William Angus Knight, a professor of moral philosophy at the University of St. Andrews, Scotland, addressed his students on the reviled system of philosophy known as eclecticism, and the need to recover its spirit in modern practice. How far Cousin had fallen in the fifty years since delivering his sensational 1828–29 lectures to some two thousand auditors at the Sorbonne is betrayed by Knight's avoidance of Cousin's name in an exposition that probably owed a great deal to his eminent precursor. Knight follows Cousin in recognizing eclecticism to be more than a philosophical system. Where Cousin had defined eclecticism as both "a principle in the labyrinth of history" and "an instrument [of] rigid criticism sustained on a solid and extensive erudition," Knight taught that "It is both a system and a tendency; a formal philosophical doctrine, and a spirit of philosophizing" (44). In the 1878 lecture "On Eclecticism," he clarifies its essential nature as a constant mode of thought, rather than focusing on its historical outlines: "What I wish to put before you is its general speculative drift, its leading features, and permanent tendency. These may be seen, not only from the phases it has assumed as a coherently developed doctrine, but even more characteristically from its unconscious presence, within the lines and under the limits of the systems which have ignored it. Wherever the effort to reconcile the claims of rival doctrines has taken the place of a one-sided advocacy of special views, the result, to the extent of the reconciliation, has been eclectic" (44). Knight directly echoes Cousin here, who had earlier claimed that eclecticism was not new, but has been around forever, as compromise and reconciliation. Conceding that the propositions of eclecticism seem "self-evident," and that there is always truth on both sides of every great controversy, Knight imagines eclecticism as scales keeping the sects in balance. Periods of compromise inevitably follow from periods of controversy. The chasm between opposing views widens until each forgets the truth to which the other lays claim. While Knight's conception of the historical rhythm of ideas is not uncommon in the nineteenth century, he firmly positions eclecticism as an essential element within this pattern: "A state of perpetual controversy amongst the sects [. . .] would do no particular good, if it did not lead to a better appreciation of their respective merits; and we find that an eclectic or reconciling movement generally follows, and is produced by, the controversies of the schools" (47–48). Positing that eclecticism always follows periods of conflict, Knight echoes the prediction and hope of many of his contemporaries that criticism would lead ultimately to new sources of inspiration: Macaulay perceived that Dryden's eclecticism allowed him to develop new talents as a critic that led to the founding of a critical school of poetry, while architectural historian Robert Kerr observed that eclecticism had at last produced a synthesis of styles, giving birth to the style of the nineteenth century.

In answer to the charge of dilettantism leveled at eclectics, Knight emphasized, as Cousin had done, the rigorous critical process and vast erudition that underlay his philosophical method. Knight has to make his stand for eclecticism by taking on its dilettante reputation. People have misunderstood eclecticism, Knight proposes, because the term seems "to indicate the really elementary process of gathering together bits of systems, and arranging them in what must be at the best an artificial patchwork. No wonder that the result of a mere collection of *memorabilia*, however carefully made, should be a product without unity, coherence, or vitality. A system that resolved itself into a 'golden treasury' of elegant extracts would deserve the neglect of all competent logicians, and of every serious thinker" (45). The dangers of this low form of eclecticism—this mere anthologizing of choice tidbits of wisdom—were apparent in the arts as well as in politics and philosophy, during the nineteenth century. Cheap imitations and popular collections threatened the "unity, coherence, [and] vitality" of the arts, by compromising artists' original creations, tearing apart coherent styles, and vitiating the power of complete poems, novels, and essays. How was an eclectic to prove he or she was not being, according to common usage, eclectic?

Eclecticism could never be content with "mild and hazy commonplaces" but would conserve "every intellectual difference that is the outcome of distinctive thought, and of a true interpretation of the universe; only, it makes room, alongside of each interpretation, for others that have usually been held to be inconsistent and incompatible with it" (50). The eclectic does not mix up systems, or create a "golden treasury" of the best bits of others' ideas, but preserves the integrity of each idea on the road to finding the greatest sum of truth. Since history had shown "uniformity of belief" to be impossible, and that disagreement would persist as long as humanity did, the eclectic would be there to push the adversaries through the stalemate. "With every cycle will come a new phase of insight, a new attitude of feeling towards the universe," and the absence of controversy "would imply the decadence of the intellect, the withering of the imagination, and the stoppage of the pulse of the human heart" (51). Eclecticism would have to be an ongoing process that would never cease while controversy remained or ideas flourished; eclecticism and controversy would always be with us because of human diversity and because of the unity of human nature. Unity within diversity "constitute[s] the root or ground of eclecticism" (53). If eclecticism could not rest upon any Utopian plateau of human knowledge and achievement, then it could never become a "school" in its own right. Knight warns that in "laying the foundation of a school, the eclectic becomes sectarian, and thus commits an act of intellectual suicide" (59). More a "regulative principle in all systems, and the outcome of all" than the "distinctive badge" of any one, eclecticism must reach its perfection in its utility, impartiality, and variety. Knight believed that far from leading to "inaction" or "supineness" as critics feared, eclectics would be ever alert to changes in society, restless in the quest for truth, and exacting in the study of history.

Eclecticism seemed "literary" to Lewes because it operated metaphorically and comparatively, secured its followers on the basis of its beautiful style, and had impetus from what he and other critics such as Taine and Stendhal considered a "literary reaction" against the materialist culture of the eighteenth century. As part of his effort to tear down the lofty claims of eclecticism, Lewes had compared Jouffroy's eclectic maneuver to that of the chemist, who of necessity consulted all those works that had bearing on his own experiments; but for the scientist this was not a matter of juxtaposing treatises and waiting to be inspired by their truth. Although Lewes intended to demonstrate that eclecticism was in no way an original idea or anything more than the common-sense procedure followed by any sensible scientist, was it just possible that eclecticism could offer a model whereby the humanities could mimic the progress of the sciences? In his famous essay on Milton, T. B. Macaulay argues that scientists progress by building on the discoveries of their predecessors, while artists generally experience a diminution of energy and creativity in response to the marvelous works of their precursors. What if Cousin and Jouffroy did indeed offer an alternative model of creativity, in which the historical inheritance itself would become the source of inspiration? As Taine suggests, eclecticism simply developed from impulses already present in the culture of the nineteenth century, so its imitation of scientific culture is not surprising; however, it is not a philosophy intended for the use of scientists but an idea meant to help those engaged in the humanistic disciplines to organize knowledge and those practicing art to deal with the anxiety of influence.

CHAPTER 3

Eclecticism and Literary Modernity

As the eclectic idea crossed the Channel to grapple with manifest eclecticism, resistance to the philosophy grew in direct proportion to the rapidity with which British culture was becoming fundamentally eclectic. Not crippled by polarized ideologies as France had been, British philosophers and critics did not feel the powerful attraction to Cousin's teachings that had once moved Stendhal to name Cousin the greatest philosopher of the age for his ability to overcome the destructive cycle of reaction and revolution. The culture of nineteenth-century Britain seemed to be under assault from the very forces of diversity and difference that Cousin harnessed to his catholic theory of eclecticism. The Victorians would become eclectic as the study of history promoted relativism and stimulated the adoption of multiple historical styles. They would become eclectic as a capitalist economy made the products of past and present, colonial and Continental cultures available to the middle classes through cheap reproduction. They would become eclectic as modern latitudinarianism overcame religious intolerance and encouraged acceptance of competing systems of belief. And they would become eclectic as widespread education propagated superficial knowledge and spread the veneer of civilization and taste over classes once distinguished by unequal access to culture. Self-conscious eclecticism was certainly at work in the organization of such characteristically Victorian institutions as the museum of art and natural history, the public lecture series, the collection of biographies, the literary anthology, the keepsake and treasury, and the international exhibition. Advancing with the tide of changes that were decentering and diffusing national identity, eclecticism, aimed as it was at the educated classes, looked as though it would overflow the last remaining stronghold of British culture—its press. If the literati succumbed to the sweet nothings of Cousin, then nothing remained but to give over responsibility for culture to the masses and to submit to the dictates of popular opinion.

Although Cousin's writings were translated into English and widely reviewed in Britain, few philosophers would have been willing to avow publicly any allegiance to the French thinker, or to consider themselves part of an Eclectic school. This reluctance to embrace Cousin's eclecticism cannot be explained only by its weaknesses (which were discussed on both sides of the Channel); indeed, Cousin offered both a cogent analysis of and a solution for handling the new cultural situation common to both countries. Yet eclecticism was not embraced in England, as it was in France, and Cousin was despised even though he was proposing and advocating the same kind of "glorious revolution" that had already been successful in Britain. His *juste milieu* was automatically mistrusted at least partly because he was French—because it seemed to represent all those tendencies of French thought against which the English defined their own national identity. As late as 1840 John Stuart Mill, in a review of Tocqueville, feels compelled to address the general unwillingness of British readers to engage with French philosophy (to which Tocqueville makes "a brilliant exception"): "At a time when the prevailing tone of French speculation is one of exaggerated reaction against the doctrines of the eighteenth century, French philosophy, with us, is still synonymous with Encyclopedism. The Englishmen may almost be numbered who are aware that France has produced any great names in prose literature since Voltaire and Rousseau" (214). Mill, who was early influenced by Cousin, laments the "insular" tendencies of British thought, which, in spite of French being "almost universally cultivated on this side of the Channel," prevent his countrymen from being drawn into "The general movement of the European mind" (214). At the time of Mill's review, the "prevailing tone" of French thought and the "general movement of the European mind" had been established by Cousin, who was also firmly in control of higher education in France, and Mill's unwillingness to speak his name is indicative of the uneasiness about Cousin in Britain. Mill's reference to Voltaire is significant, in light of his place in the negative Gallic stereotype that was still in force well into the

Victorian period. As historian Gerald Newman has written, "The chief intellectual components of the Gallic stereotype, Britain's distorted image of revolutionary France, were evidently the ideas of destruction, license, abstract political thought, atheism, and impious mockery" (389). In the nineteenth century the Gallic stereotype was applied to "*analogous* tendencies of unbelief, moral laxity, ridicule, generalizing philosophy, and cosmopolitanism" (397; author's italics)—all of which might have been associated with Cousin and eclecticism. Developed during the revolutionary period, the Gallic stereotype was used from the start to "uproot international ideas," and eclecticism embodied an ideal of internationalism that Britain could not easily accept. That British writers could not acknowledge the French contribution to understanding the cultural situation, however, does not mean they did not take up the same ideas or face the same problems. The Gallic stereotype was linked to elitist decadence *and* mass culture, a dualism that parallels Victorian responses to eclecticism, particularly in the emerging discourse about literary modernity.

The Eclectic Mind

The history of the idea of eclecticism has been repeatedly punctuated by the same accusation: in seeking to find the best in everything and everyone, the eclectic bankrupts meaning. In an early critique of modern eclecticism, Samuel Taylor Coleridge challenges the foundation of the "philosophy of the nineteenth century." Writing his *Biographia Literaria* between 1815 and 1817, Coleridge might have got wind of Victor Cousin's lectures of the same period in which the Frenchman first advanced the modern theory of eclecticism.[1] In the biographical miscellany, Coleridge is concerned to construct and justify his conservative opinions in the wake of an attack by Hazlitt on the poet's early support of the French Revolution; thus he is careful to distance himself from any hazy or confused doctrines, of which eclecticism could easily become an example. Coleridge borrowed the essential material of his statement against eclecticism from Schelling:

> But the worst and widest impediment [to metaphysics] still remains. It is the predominance of a popular philosophy, at once the counterfeit and the mortal enemy of all true and manly metaphysical research. It is that corruption, introduced by certain immethodical aphorising Eclectics, who, dismissing not only all system, but all logical connection, pick and choose whatever is most plausible and showy; who select, whatever words can have some semblance of sense attached to them without the least expen-

diture of thought, in short whatever may enable men to talk of what they do not understand, with a careful avoidance of every thing that might awaken them to a moment's suspicion of their ignorance. This alas! is an irremediable disease, for it brings with it, not so much an indisposition to any particular system, but an utter loss of taste and faculty for all system and all philosophy. (167)

Like Schelling, Coleridge wants to explain why his contemporaries had lost their taste for philosophy. Eclecticism was partly to blame, because it substituted an "impotent sham philosophy" for analytical study and "aphoristic" wisdom for patient philosophical inquiry (*Works* 7.1:292). Coleridge adds depth to Schelling's briefer description with terms that would become essential in later critiques of eclecticism. First, he indicates that eclecticism is "popular"; even if he was unaware of Cousin as a rising star in philosophy, he could have predicted the wide appeal that the eclectic principle would have, how it would soothe minds tortured by the difficult choices offered by ideologies. As Scottish philosopher William Angus Knight would later concede, eclecticism's chief proposition is an obvious one: there is generally truth on both sides of any question. Coleridge must have seen how the ordinary mind reaches for the indisputable truth, the easy resolution, and then shows it triumphantly before the bickering ideologues and academics, asking, "what are you fools arguing about? Your battles are pointless, your foes imaginary. Join us here in the practical world!"

Coleridge next identifies eclecticism as the "counterfeit" and "enemy of all true and manly metaphysical research" (167). All of Cousin's major critics in Britain—Sir William Hamilton and George Henry Lewes in particular—would expose what they believed to be his false assumptions and exhortatory style that served to mask the emptiness of his propositions. They would complain, in much the same terms used by French critic Hippolyte Taine, that he convinces his auditors with grand schemes and epic generalizations that but mimic, or counterfeit, genuine philosophical inquiry. For Coleridge, the eclectic method is "unmanly" because it bypasses rigorous analysis in favor of historical presentations and uses the work done by others in a haphazard manner to forward its own agenda. "Manly" research involves, it seems, stern self-discipline, perhaps even the sacrifice of one's health and happiness, to discover a fragmentary truth—a truth that will have been earned, not stolen. The ambivalence in some criticism toward Cousin and his eclectic principle would stem from the recognition that he labored over his history of philosophy, over all those editions and translations, but that he expended little thought (to paraphrase Coleridge) in putting his system together. In fact, the eclectic seems to justify his historical study by claiming for it a power to change lives that history as such does not normally possess. Hamilton would go so far as to say that Cousin did not understand what he was talking about. Coleridge believes that this was true of all Eclectics, but that their system allows them to proceed without "awaken[ing] them to a moment's suspicion of their ignorance" (167). This "irremediable disease," as Coleridge describes it, of a mistaken belief in one's own powers of discernment encourages a person to rely on himself alone for judging true and false, good and evil, moral and immoral.

Third, Coleridge introduces the theme of "corruption," which for him signifies the destruction of system and "all logical connection." Corruption would also come to be synonymous with decadence, one of the chief complaints against eclecticism in the arts, and with a presentiment of cultural decline. Critics of eclecticism do not always distinguish whether this fall would be the result of a venal or a cardinal sin—another valence of corruption for Coleridge—whether from pollution of the old systems by foreign influences, such as those from the rising classes of the anarchistic Continent, or from open rebellion and blasphemy. Certainly, eclecticism was intended to be a conciliatory philosophy, but once people began to "pick and choose," and to decide for themselves which portions of a doctrine they found agreeable enough to retain, then the integrity of any particular system would be destroyed. Of course, this picking and choosing would be most problematic when it came to one's religion. For example, could one still be a faithful member of the Church of England if he or she decided that the style of medieval Catholicism better expressed the essence of Christianity? Were all those Gothic stone churches expressive of a resurgent core belief, or did they simply reflect the trend toward superficiality in worship? More specifically, if one rejected, say, the doctrine of transubstantiation but believed all the rest of the teachings of the Church of Rome, could one still be Catholic? If people began to ignore the organic development and coherence of a system, and to select only "whatever is most plausible [or] showy," or proper to the spirit of the age, then what is to prevent them from inventing their versions of each doctrine and each system, just as it suits them? (One could argue that this is ultimately what has happened with religion in the twenty-first century, where we see the endless splintering of religious sects, the mixing of pop culture with religion, or selective obedience on the part of members of mainstream religions.) For conservatives, eclecticism signifies a catastrophic disregard of traditional authorities. For liberals, eclecticism represents emancipation of the individual mind. For radicals, eclecticism portends the reign of mediocrity.

Coleridge's encapsulation of the opposition to eclecticism draws upon both conservative and radical opinions. Seeing that such a principle tends toward disintegration, rather than the ideal unity in diversity imagined by Cousin, toward the appearance of truth rather than the true, and toward indecision rather than decisive action, a philosopher-artist such as Coleridge would necessarily place his trust in traditional authority for holding negative social impulses in check and in the individual imagination for generating creative ideas. However, it would be misleading to overlook the eclectic qualities of Coleridge's own work. In an amusing echo of his denunciation of "immethodical" Eclectics, he refers to his own *Biographia* as "an immethodical miscellany" (qtd. in Leask xxviii)—part biography, part literary criticism, part metaphysics, part literary theory, part history of philosophy, part philology, part exhortation, and part apology. The multiplicity of purpose matches the diversity of method and style employed in discovering and communicating his opinions. In the chapter on metaphysics, he exhibits great admiration for certain of the doctrines of Leibniz, the very same upon which Cousin constructed his idea of eclecticism. Leibniz taught that true philosophy would consist in "explain[ing] and collect[ing] the fragments of truth scattered through systems apparently the most incongruous" and that the "deeper [. . .] we penetrat[ed] into the ground of things, the more truth we discover in the doctrines of the greater number of the philosophical sects" (*Biographia* 148).[2] Since truth is often "masked" and "mutilated," the task of the philosopher must be to seek it everywhere, without regard to the strange places in which he might find it. In an eclectic tour de force that would have delighted Cousin, Coleridge (following Leibniz) catalogues the truths to be found in opposing sects:

> The want of *substantial* reality in the object of the senses, according to the sceptics; the harmonies or numbers, the prototypes and ideas, to which the Pythagoreans and Platonists reduced all things; the ONE and ALL of Parmenides and Plotinus, without Spinozism; the necessary connection of things according to the Stoics, reconcileable with the spontaneity of the other schools; the vital-philosophy of the Cabalists and Hermetists, who assumed the universality of sensation; the substantial forms and entelechies of Aristotle and the schoolmen, together with the mechanical solution of all particular phenomena according to Democritus and the recent philosophers—all these we shall find united in one perspective central point, which shows regularity and a coincidence of all the parts in the very object, which from every other point of view must appear confused and distorted. (148–49)

Cousin had, of course, followed Leibniz closely in his original formulation of eclecticism, even borrowing this aphorism (which Coleridge quotes in the original French): "J'ai trouvé que le plupart des sectes ont raison dans une bonne partie de ce quelles avancent, mais non pas tant en ce quelles nient" (149).[3] The really attractive part of eclecticism is its promise to be the key to all mythologies; nothing has to be excluded when one's philosophy exemplifies the principles of inclusion and tolerance. Eclecticism assumes, as Coleridge does here, that it is possible to achieve "one perspective central point" from which all systems might be viewed as they really are. But how that ideal viewpoint is to be found is not clearly explained either by Leibniz or by Cousin. The dilemma of the individual's self-reliance remains, which may explain why, only a few pages further on, Coleridge comes out against eclecticism.

The Multitude of Voices

Despite eclecticism's obvious attractions, uneasiness about it persisted. Apparently fueled by two of the most dangerous tendencies of the age—superficial learning and latitudinarian attitudes—eclecticism wore by turns the aspect of the philistine bourgeois, the pantheistic bohemian, and the cosmopolitan dilettante. Eclecticism focused attention on the problem of judgment, specifically how people who were only partially educated, by chance or by inclination, would determine which of the "prophets" of the age spoke the truth, or at least parlayed a recognizable version of the contemporary situation.

In an 1829 essay for the *Quarterly Review* on the "State and Prospects of the Country," Robert Southey worries about the "progress" in the literary marketplace that every year makes more books available for sale. The increase is an obstacle to literature and education because no individual could possibly read and judge them all. The first of the two factors making the age an unpropitious one for concentrated study can be characterized as historical; living at a late period in history, a scholar is naturally more burdened by the sheer number of texts demanding his or her attention in any field of study—not to mention the "new" knowledge of those disciplines invented in modern times, which are jostling for prominence with traditional studies:

> The Greeks had no other literature than their own, enriched with what little they had gleaned from Egypt; the Romans had no other than that of Greece; and, till within the last fifty years, the learning of a well-read per-

son was confined to that of Greece and Rome, a few of the most celebrated Italian, French, and Spanish writers, and a limited selection from the works published in our own language. To these languages, German must now be added; and in each of them, a list of authors of celebrity might be drawn up, whose works it would require the lifetime of a laborious student to digest. In addition to this, the sciences of agriculture, natural history in all its branches, mechanics, chemistry, mineralogy, and geology, have either been created or exceedingly extended. To master all this is impossible. No perseverance can toil through such a mass, nor memory retain it. (118–19)

Sounding almost panicked at the prospect of being overwhelmed with the "mass" of knowledge, Southey has captured one of the characteristic ideas of his century, namely that human learning had reached such dimensions in modern times that new institutions and organizations will be needed to cope with it all, to order it, to reduce it to more human dimensions. Yet the impulse toward reductive models gives rise to the second great difficulty facing scholars, and all reasonably educated people, in the nineteenth century: can the "new systems, manuals, and abridgements [. . .] conveying knowledge more easily, simply, or compendiously than before" (119) be relied upon to transmit the same ideas and information as the original authors would have done? The encyclopedias, dictionaries, anthologies, digests, periodical reviews, eclectic journals—in short, all those publications that promised to purvey the important knowledge of the day in swift and painless fashion—bypassed the labor and sacrifice once thought to compose the essential quality of the scholarly life.[4] Even if digested knowledge sufficed for the merely educated person, how could these shortcuts ever satisfy the genuine seeker after truth? But without some guide through the vast tracts of human knowledge, how could any one person hope to cover any portion of it in his or her lifetime? Southey worries that the average reader will "give up profound and systematic application in despair, and betake [himself] to works of a subordinate character" until that person "becomes a mere living dictionary." The tendency of the age is to substitute "mere knowledge, for the power of saying and doing that which is fit, which, more than anything besides, contributes to stamp this the age of moderate men, and to render the existing state of society so unfavourable to every sort of extraordinary excellence" (119). In Southey's view the power to say and do "that which is fit" seems to derive from encounters with ideas at first hand, since the already digested knowledge emerges with the strong coloring of an interpreter's opinions, making it difficult, if not impossible, for the twice-removed reader to capture the original spirit of the text. In the *Biographia Literaria,* Coleridge is even more severe in his judgment on the worth of periodicals and digested knowledge. Satirically thanking the "anonymous critics" who had made his name famous, he jokes that readers will not "distinctly remember[ ] whether [his name] was introduced for an eulogy or for censure": "And this becomes more likely, if (as I believe) the habit of perusing periodical works may be properly added to Averrhoes's catalogue of ANTI-MNEMONICS, or weakeners of the memory" (32–33). Far from improving the understanding of the average reader, the "habit of perusing periodical works" leads to a kind of degeneration of knowledge, where all the conflicting opinions offered in various journals lead one further into confusion.

John Stuart Mill did not share their Conservative politics, but he agreed with some of the poets' diagnoses of the leading characteristics of the age. One of the great dangers of what Mill called the "age of transition" was the advent of false prophets who would try to supplant the ancient institutions and fill the void of absent authority. In an inventory of its shortcomings, a transitional age must record its lack of consensus; the old authorities are divided among themselves or against each other, resulting in a "mixed state without received doctrine" ("Spirit of the Age" 28). While the "diffusion of superficial knowledge" is the "grand achievement" of the age, it is not the cause of transition; it is the tendency of people to discuss and question ideas, rather than embrace them, that gives the age its transitional character (6–8). In his essay on "Civilization," Mill specifies how the increase of reading and the growth of commercial publishing exacerbate this "intellectual anarchy." Demonstrating that the individual has less influence in a civilized society in which more decisions are made by "the movements of masses" (90), Mill argues that all classes ought to be prepared for the responsibilities of rule. Following Southey, Mill observes that civilization promotes a "relaxation of individual energy," with wealth as the sole inducement to concentrated activity (97–98), and a reliance on opinion, without any reliable guide to judge what is true and what is quackery or puffing (100–101). The fate of literature in a civilized society, then, is not surprising:

> It is not solely on the private virtues, that this growing insignificance of the individual in the mass, is productive of mischief. It corrupts the very fountain of the improvement of public opinion itself; it corrupts public teaching; it weakens the influence of the more cultivated few over the many. Literature has suffered more than any other human production by the common disease. When there were few books, and when few read at all save those who had been accustomed to read the best authors, books were written with the well-grounded expectation that they would be read carefully, and

if they deserved it, would be read often. A book of sterling merit, when it came out, was sure to be heard of, and might hope to be read, by the whole reading class; it might succeed by its real excellencies, although not got up to strike at once; and even if so got up, unless it had the support of genuine merit, it fell into oblivion. The rewards were then for him who wrote *well*, not *much;* for the laborious and learned, not the crude and ill-informed writer. But now the case is reversed. (102)

Driving the destruction of literary values is the desperation of an author to succeed, to be noticed at all among the million competitors willing to do anything to capture, ever so briefly, the public's attention. With the sheer mass of publications stacked up against any writer, he can no longer rely even on history to rescue him from oblivion. Advertising now trumps merit, and the press of opinion tramples genuine ideas. Both Southey and Mill recognize that time is working against even the most diligent readers, and without a track through the wilderness of opinions no one can hope to collect, even in the most ample of "golden treasuries," the best works of the age. Mill's scheme for overcoming the "system of individual competition" (105) in literature depends on exploiting the tendency of the age toward combination. In order to arrest the decay of literature and the reign of ignorant opinion, Mill proposes "organized co-operation among the leading intellects of the age, whereby works of first-rate merit, of whatever class, and of whatever tendency in point of opinion, might come forth with the stamp on them, from the first, of the approval of those whose name would carry authority" (106).[5] This patently eclectic project would depend first of all on the "regeneration of individual character among our lettered and opulent classes," a cultural sea change requiring the complete reformation of the university system—a notion Mill might have derived from Cousin, with whom he corresponded and who was a noted author on educational reform. Since "great minds" were never formed by institutions whose purpose was the reproduction of their own narrow values, the universities would have to become nonsectarian, both in admission policies and in teaching: "all thinkers, much above the common order, who have grown up in the Church of England, or in any other Church, have been produced in latitudinarian epochs, or while the impulse of intellectual emancipation which gave existence to the Church had not quite spent itself" (108). With the rooting out of the "principle [. . .] of dogmatic religion, dogmatic morality, dogmatic philosophy" (109), it might at last be possible to produce graduates "qualified to seek truth ardently, vigorously, and disinterestedly" (107)—those individuals who would eventually be capable of judging ideas on their merits. Teachers, Mill writes, would not be expected to conceal their opinions for the sake of becoming eclectic or undogmatic, but would hold those opinions more firmly for "know[ing] all creeds, and, in enforcing [their] own, stat[ing] the arguments for all conflicting opinions fairly" (110). He concludes: "In this spirit it is that all the great subjects are taught from the chairs of the German and French universities" (110). In this reference to Cousin's eclecticism, Mill acknowledges his debt to the eclectic paradigm and advocates an educational program founded on eclectic principles. Seeing in eclecticism a principle of democracy—a democracy that was anyway advancing relentlessly over the nineteenth century—Mill recognizes that the only cure for the "common disease" of the age, its intellectual confusion or eclectic *tendency,* is in the application of a rigorous principle of eclecticism. The pretension to knowledge would be supplanted by authentic knowledge, and the pretension of hack writing to literary values would be replaced by literature's hard-won truths.[6]

Of all the statements on the intellectual anarchy of the nineteenth century, and its need for eclecticism, Thomas De Quincey offers perhaps the most prescient analysis of the future of human learning. In a brief 1824 essay, De Quincey concedes that "this is the age of superficial knowledge" of which the greatest proof is the encyclopedia—but "prodigious *extension* implies a due proportion of weak *intension;* a sealike expansion of knowledge will cover large shallows as well as large depths" ("Superficial Knowledge" 449). Unlike Mill, however, De Quincey does not imagine a vanguard of intellectuals emerging to guide confused youth through the literary wilderness; instead, he perceives that the proliferation of knowledge in all fields is leading to the division of intellectual labor. He even recommends that this specialization continue, as profundity is to be preferred over comprehensiveness (for the sake of knowledge itself); but as is typical of his writing, De Quincey severely qualifies this recommendation by offering an extremely appealing model of individual development as its opposite: "Let all the objects of the understanding in civil life or in science be represented by the letters of the alphabet: in Grecian life each man would separately go through all the letters in a tolerable way; whereas at present each letter is served by a distinct body of men. Consequently, the Grecian individual is superior to the modern; but the Grecian whole is inferior: for the whole is made up of the individuals; and the Grecian individual repeats himself. Whereas in modern life the whole derives its superiority from the very circumstances which constitute the inferiority of the parts [. . .]" (452). The question, then, for the history of the idea of eclecticism is whether, as a principle and a tendency, it will operate more like the modern machine, where each person contributes his bit of skill to the overall operation, or whether, as a principle and a tendency, it will operate more like an educated Greek, who considers all the issues raised by all fields of knowledge, and determines for himself the truth in each. Clearly, *time* has become a factor in a way that it never could have been for that ancient Greek, whose whole world revolved around Greece and who saw only a noontime shadow of history beneath his feet. The multiplicity of modern life—and the fantastically long expanse of history trailing behind us—has catastrophically limited our ability to comprehend any subject at all. Now scholars are taught to be specialists, as De Quincey predicted we would be, and the impulse toward comprehensiveness is wisely laid aside. The eclectic, even in the nineteenth century, risks the integrity of his or her knowledge for the sake of that expansive vision.

The Burden of the Past

In his 1836 sketch of the architectural profession, A. W. N. Pugin satirized the tendency of his colleagues to sell their skills to whoever could afford them, and at whatever cost to their own aesthetic and moral principles. Architecture suffered from the influx of capital and from the spread of superficial knowledge about styles that gave the average man or woman license to demand a building or renovation in whatever style he or she fancied. The writer suffered similar indignities, resulting from the boom in reading and publishing, so that De Quincey's vision of the fate of the scholar in the nineteenth century might also have predicted the fate of the artist. With the disappearance of traditional authorities, public opinion, transmitted through the organ of the press, became increasingly important, and literature was absorbed into this new function. Because writers who wanted readers had, on some level, to satisfy the demands of their public, they would often produce great quantities of historical poems, fictions, and biographies, or sensational novels and tales; though, of course, one of the extraordinary aspects of Victorian culture was the willingness of people to listen to men such as Mill, Carlyle, Ruskin, and Arnold berate them for their mistaken attitudes and careless actions. Certainly, the intellectual anarchy and pervasive unbelief these men found so troubling were manifested in the literature of the day, and nowhere was the situation more dire than in poetry. Everyone agreed that poetry had evolved at the beginning of civilization; the humanist philosopher Giambattista Vico even proposed that poetry made civilization possible by naming the phenomena of nature and transforming them into law-giving deities.[7] Poetry seemed to spring from the human impulse toward belief in a transcendent reality, and when that belief was lost, so too was the poetic faculty. The proliferation of competing belief systems and the geometrical increase in reading materials tended to erode the faith on which traditional institutions depended for their continued dominance; the crowd overwhelmed individual voices and limited the influence they might have; and so the poem and the poet faded into inconsequence.

For at least a century preceding William Hazlitt's trenchant explanation of why poetry can only decline, poets and critics had offered various explanations for its demise.[8] In fact, Walter Jackson Bate sees the growth of criticism in the mid-eighteenth century as an attempt "to reground the entire thinking about poetry in the light of one overwhelming fact: the obviously superior originality, and the at least apparently greater immediacy and universality of subject and appeal, of the poetry of earlier periods" (48). Eighteenth-century critics were the first to explain the superiority of ancient poetry historically; that is, they saw that the ethos of the ancients, with its passionate directness, was more conducive to the growth of poetry than were the affectations of civilized societies. At the head of the Romantic movement, Wordsworth believed that poetry might be renewed by returning to its sources: nature, simplicity, and common life. As Bate points out, however, the Romantic poets were in the minority. Most critics "assume[ed] that the door [was] closed" (49). Belief in the marvelous and the heroic had vanished with Christianity, science, and the "well-ordered State"; language had become specialized, and less metaphorical, with the growth of analytical writing; the arts in general had become detached from ordinary life; and the subdivision of genres had contributed to the narrowness of the artist's practice (49–52). As the reading audience grew larger, so did its "mediocrity of taste" (53). Finally, eighteenth-century critics blamed their own stock-in-trade, criticism, for intensifying self-consciousness and timidity in poets; but the growth of criticism was "considered inevitable as a culture grows older, and part of the price paid for the spread of literacy" (54).

A new emphasis in discussions of poetry's decline appeared in the nineteenth century, with the comparison of progress in the sciences to progress in the arts. Hazlitt, in his brief essay for the *Round Table* (1817), "Why the Arts Are Not Progressive," rejects the analogy between science and art as altogether false and dismisses the remedies for art's tardiness—namely "study of the antique, the formation of academies, and the distribution of prizes"—as likely to do more harm than good: "When that original impulse no longer exists, when the inspiration of genius is fled, all the attempts to recal it are no better than the tricks of galvanism to restore the dead to life" (158). The galvanic solutions that Hazlitt mentions were precisely

Chapter 3: Eclecticism and Literary Modernity

those being employed in painting and architecture, and were actually creating (some thought) a great deal more confusion than had existed before. Now instead of a single model worthy of imitation—the classical—artists of the nineteenth century confronted at least two—the classical and the medieval. The institutionalization of the fine arts (painting and poetry for Hazlitt) and the professionalization of artists generally produce rules and criticism, but not, he believes, great art. According to Hazlitt, only that which is "mechanical, reducible to rule, or capable of demonstration, is progressive, and admits of gradual improvement: what is not mechanical or definite, but depends on genius, taste, and feeling, very soon becomes stationary, or retrograde, and loses more than it gains by transfusion" (158). Like many of the writers of the Romantic period, Hazlitt aligns poetry with nature, and thus excludes the possibility of progress except by drawing upon that source. Science advances by building on previous discoveries, while the arts, depending on individual genius, "leaped at once from infancy to manhood" and "have in general declined ever after" (159). The great artists were not only in direct communication with nature; they also were unhampered by criticism from any but those who genuinely inclined toward art. Only those with "natural genius" attempted either poetry or criticism, while other great minds were employed with wars, religion, and politics—there were none of those connoisseurs and "pretenders to taste" whom the modern artist confronts as a rule, as soon as his work reaches the world. Hazlitt reminds the cheerleaders of progress that "The diffusion of taste is not the same thing as the improvement of taste" (161), and while institutions certainly promote the former, there is little evidence that they can affect the latter: "The number of candidates for fame, and of pretenders to criticism, is thus increased beyond all proportion, while the quantity of genius and feeling remains the same; with this difference, that the man of genius is lost in the crowd of competitors, who would never have become such but from encouragement and example; and that the opinion of those few persons whom nature intended for judges, is drowned with the noisy suffrages of shallow smatterers in taste. The principle of universal suffrage, however applicable to matters of government, which concern the common feelings and common interests of society, is by no means applicable to matters of taste, which can only be decided upon by the most refined understandings" (161). Hazlitt assumes that only persons born with an understanding susceptible of "refinement" can develop as critics and artists, which seems to make art forever undemocratic in a society that will eventually become democratic in its government. Denying that the "public taste is capable of gradual improvement," Hazlitt apparently denies the efficacy of democratic education, a surprising assertion from one whose own writing aimed to improve his readers with straightforward discourse on the chief topics of the day. Unlike the Romantics in France, who believed that anyone could be educated into understanding, though not into genius, Hazlitt wants to erect a barrier against incursions into fine art by the insensible and uncultivated, whose opinions on works of genius ought to be deflected, leaving them intact for the judgment of those whom nature has qualified for the task. If the proper judges are left to their work, then those works worthy of attention will reach public notice, while those with merely flashy presentation and little substance or art will end up in the dustbin of history.

Thomas Love Peacock's wicked little treatise on *The Four Ages of Poetry* (1820) proposes a historical trajectory similar to the one offered by Hazlitt—poetry peaks in the second period of civilization, the Golden Age, soon after the mechanical aspects of the art have caught up with the brilliant expressions and vivid ideas of the Iron Age—but is much less forgiving of those latest entrants into the annals of literary history, the Lake Poets. Contemporary poets are living in what Peacock considers the second Brass Age, the modern period having four ages of its own, all dimmer reflections of the ancient ages of poetry. Blaming the obsession with picturesque beauty for driving budding poets back into nature, Peacock argues that these modern poets "convert[ed] the land they lived in into a sort of fairy-land, which they peopled with mysticisms and chimaeras" and inspired with their nonsense a whole host of "desperate imitators, who have brought the age of brass prematurely to its dotage" (15). Peacock views the embracing of history by poets with as much skepticism as their ecstatic return to nature, and contrasts their collective delusion with other fields of knowledge:

> While the historian and the philosopher are advancing in, and accelerating, the progress of knowledge, the poet is wallowing in the rubbish of departed ignorance, and raking up the ashes of dead savages to find gewgaws and rattles for grown babies of the age. Mr. Scott digs up the poachers and cattle-stealers of the ancient border. Lord Byron cruises for thieves and pirates on the shores of the Morea and among the Greek islands. Mr. Southey wades through ponderous volumes of travels and old chronicles, from which he carefully selects all that is false, useless, and absurd, as being essentially poetical; [. . .]. Mr. Wordsworth picks up village legends from old women and sextons, and Mr. Coleridge, to the valuable information acquired from similar sources, superadds the dreams of crazy theologians and the mysticisms of German metaphysics, and favours the world with visions in verse, in which the quadruple elements of sexton, old woman,

Jeremy Taylor, and Emmanuel Kant, are harmonized into a delicious poetical compound. (16)

The critique here is unmistakably aimed at the eclecticism of the Romantic poets, who, in drawing inspiration from numerous sources, fail to promote—in Peacock's opinion—any coherent ideas of their own. Far from representing progress in poetry, which would be a recovery of the originality of the ancient poets, the Romantics have proven that any return to the Golden Age of poetry is absolutely impossible. The Romantic is undiscriminatingly "eclectic" and therefore not a true eclectic at all. In effect, Peacock argues that the *poets* fail to follow the example of a *scientifically oriented* eclecticism: "The brighter the light diffused around [the modern poet] by the progress of reason, the thicker is the darkness of antiquated barbarism, in which he buries himself like a mole, to throw up the barren hillocks of his Cimmerian labours. The philosophic mental tranquillity which looks round with an equal eye on all external things, collects a store of ideas, discriminates their relative value, assigns to all their proper place, and from the materials of useful knowledge thus collected, appreciated, and arranged, forms new combinations that impress the stamp of their power and utility on the real business of life, is diametrically the reverse of that frame of mind which poetry inspires, or from which poetry can emanate" (17). Peacock makes it perfectly clear that the ill-considered, indiscriminate, and eclectic combinations of the Romantics will not "impress the stamp of their power and utility on the real business of life." Though the two processes of collection Peacock describes might at first seem to advance toward equally rewarding ends, the poet's self-burial in "the darkness of antiquated barbarism" does not have the same potential for progress that the philosophical eclectic's has—and here is the crux of the problem in interpreting Peacock's attitude toward eclecticism. He recognizes that there are two kinds of eclecticism, but cannot imagine that they would have anything in common, or would constitute similar ways of operating in response to a historical crisis of decline. For him, the mental attitude of the eclectic philosopher must be diametrically opposed to that of the frantic and mystical poet of the modern Brass Age—but not to the mental attitude that brought about the second Golden Age, around the time of the "revival of learning." At that time, the collection of the scattered materials of the medieval troubadours and rediscovered Greek and Roman literature "resulted in a heterogeneous compound of all ages and nations in one picture; an infinite licence, which gave to the poet the free range of the whole field of imagination and memory" (12). The richness of Renaissance eclecticism derived from an ability to combine diverse influences effectively and correctly; the bizarreness of Romantic eclecticism results from combinations that are jarring and offensive. Peacock's ambivalence toward eclecticism is typical of nineteenth-century literary critics, whose horror at the misbegotten monsters of their own day gives way before the intricate eclectic beauties of the past. Hazlitt had called Milton the greatest imitator and greatest borrower to have lived, and, as Peacock intimated, his perfection resulted from his ability to combine the energy and power of the Golden Age with the "studied and elaborate magnificence" (13) of the Silver.

Thomas Babington Macaulay thought to set the capstone on the tomb of poetry when he wrote in 1825 that the most wonderful proof of Milton's genius was the age in which the poet of *Paradise Lost* had lived. Like Macaulay himself, Milton lived in an age when poetry was becoming impossible—an enlightened age of scientific progress when analytical ability overtook poetic wisdom. Under these conditions, Milton's education might have crippled him, as it gave him full knowledge of ancient models whose originality "def[ied] imitation" ("Milton" 3) and made him "regret [. . .] the ruder age of simple words and vivid impressions" (4). While Macaulay is concerned to demonstrate Milton's Zeitgeist-defying genius, he also explains, without regret, the diminishing power of poetry in the nineteenth century: the steady advance of knowledge in one field—science—compensates for the loss of strength in another—poetry, or the arts in general. The key for Macaulay is in recognizing the opposing means by which art and science achieve perfection. Poetry thrives in the infancy of the race and springs from the wonder and mystery people feel when confronted with the natural world; science works to dispel mystery and thus improves gradually over the centuries: "Even when a system has been formed, there is still something to add, to alter, or to reject. Every generation enjoys the use of a vast hoard bequeathed to it by antiquity, and transmits that hoard, augmented by fresh acquisitions, to future ages" (4). In Macaulay's view, imagination and knowledge are poised on great cosmic scales, and as the weight of accumulated knowledge grows heavier with each passing year, it steadily depletes the force and sharpness of imagination.

Few artists and poets rejoice at the accumulation of a "vast hoard" of works of genius. What to the scientist represents the foundation on which he will raise a still more durable structure to the artist signifies the towering obstacle of accomplished revelation. All that remains to the poet burdened with his inheritance is the ornamentation and ceaseless refinement of the "palace of art." As Macaulay recognizes, science gains by refinement of its theories, while poetry almost always loses: "In an enlightened age there will be much intelligence, much science, much philosophy, abundance of just classification and subtle analysis, abundance of wit and eloquence, abundance of verses, and even of good ones; but little poetry. Men will judge and compare; but they will not create" (6). In negative judgments of eclecticism in painting and architecture, the accusation of excessive scholarship was always the centerpiece. To paraphrase Macaulay, artists who "judge and compare [. . .] will not create," and the tendency of civilized art to be refined, scholarly, and unoriginal would seem to support the (usually) Romantic opponents of eclecticism. The search for originality either paralyzed artists or provoked an eclectic compromise. Some artists attempted to strip away their civilized sensibilities in order to recover something of the purity of ancient expression. Straining against a treacherous language that betrays thought as it emerges, the poet has a still harder task ahead of him:

> He who, in an enlightened and literary society, aspires to be a great poet, must first become a little child. He must take to pieces the whole web of his mind. He must unlearn much of that knowledge which has perhaps constituted hitherto his chief title to superiority. His very talents will be a hindrance to him. His difficulties will be proportioned to his proficiency in the pursuits which are fashionable among his contemporaries; and that proficiency will in general be proportioned to the vigour and activity of his mind. And it is well, if, after all his sacrifices and exertions, his works do not resemble a lisping man or a modern ruin. We have seen in our own time great talents, intense labour, and long meditation, employed in this struggle against the spirit of the age, and employed, we will not say absolutely in vain, but with dubious success and feeble applause. (7)

In the image of the modern poem as "a lisping man or a modern ruin," Macaulay has captured the effect of the poet's speaking a borrowed language. In attempting to translate his modish ideas into a language of the heart, the poet's tongue grows large and clumsy in his mouth, as if to hold back insincere words. But the modern poet is also a modern ruin, a structure built to mimic natural processes and accumulated beauty. His language reflects the knowledge of his age and can be antique only by fraudulent means.

Macaulay perpetuated a legend of Milton that became a commonplace in the nineteenth century; his greatness "in an age so unfavourable to poetry" must "in some degree be attributed to his want of sight" ("Dryden" 20). Living blind and isolated from the mainstream of taste, Milton avoided its pollution. By contrast, Dryden swam in it, drank down its influences, and fed its strength with his own limited genius. Macaulay's review of Dryden's poetical works complements the essay on Milton; though these two poets were proximate in time and space, their artistic lives could not have been more different. For Macaulay, Dryden was the "greatest of [. . .] the critical poets" (21), while Milton was the last of the great imaginative poets. All of Dryden's disadvantages can be traced to the age in which he lived—"On no man did the age exercise so much influence" (21)—and all of his abilities are commensurate with an advanced stage of civilization.[9] From the earlier essay, Macaulay retains this guiding principle, "that the creative faculty, and the critical faculty, cannot exist together in their highest perfection" (3–4), and builds from this premise a case against Dryden, which is also peculiarly a defense of the best of the second-rank poets.

Making the familiar argument that "critical discernment is not sufficient to make men poets" (5), Macaulay brings forward the issue that had been nagging at the literary pessimists for more than a century: "It is by giving faith to the creations of the imagination that a man becomes a poet [and] by treating those creations as deceptions, and by resolving them, as nearly as possible, into their elements, that he becomes a critic" (5). The earliest poets are best because they were all, in Bate's term, just "postprimitive." As Peacock argues in *The Four Ages of Poetry,* it was this second, golden age of humankind that produced the greatest works of art, when the knowledge of the mechanical part of the art was mastered, when the imagination was still young, and when belief was still possible. More than a theory for Macaulay, this was the law of human nature: "Our judgment ripens, our imagination decays" (8). Such a historical pattern might imply that there was very little hope for the future of art, since art seemed to depend on a state of naïveté impossible to sustain with the advancement of knowledge. Art could thrive only in the briefest of human moments, and what came after was a kind of living fossil. The fundamental problem was unbelief, not specifically a lack of faith in religion, but an inability to suspend disbelief, to suppress the critical faculty: "We should act in the same manner [as the ancients] if the grief and horror produced in us by the works of the imagination amounted to real torture. But in us these emotions are comparatively languid. They rarely affect our appetite or our sleep. They leave us sufficiently at ease to trace them to their causes, and to estimate the powers which produce them. Our attention is speedily diverted from the images which call forth our tears to the art by which those images have been selected and combined. We applaud the genius of the writer. We applaud our own sagacity and sensibility, and we are comforted" (9). Neither modern audiences nor modern poets actually believe in the emotions—let alone the marvelous actions—represented in art. The pleasure for the spectator, Macaulay contends, now comes from his or her awareness of the machinery, technique, and composition involved in creation. Paradoxically, this improvement in technical knowledge comes at the expense of imaginative content: "The progress of language, which was at first favourable, becomes fatal to it, and, instead of compensating for the decay of the imagination, accelerates that decay, and renders it more obvious" (11). Increasingly abstract language is comparable to money, another circulating medium, a formal resemblance that might highlight the decreasing actual value of language (12); but we already know that for Macaulay, advances in science compensated for the loss of imagination and belief. Despite these apparent shortcomings, Dryden occupies an important place in literary history, and Macaulay's contempt for Dryden's lesser abilities as a poet turns into a celebration of his capacity for criticism.

Another compensation for the loss of poetry is evident in the gains of criticism, which improves as science improves; but as Macaulay tells the story, Dryden struggled to reach even this height above the decadence of mainstream taste. Dryden commenced his career at a time when English literature had just suffered the withering influence of the Protectorate, and was about to sink further under the weight of a "foreign yoke": "It was to please Charles that rhyme was first introduced into our plays. Thus, a rising blow, which would at any time have been mortal, was dealt to the English Drama, then just recovering from its languishing condition. Two detestable manners, the indigenous and the imported, were now in a state of alternate conflict and amalgamation. The bombastic meanness of the new style was blended with the ingenious absurdity of the old; and the mixture produced something which the world had never before seen, and which, we hope, it will never see again" (19). Before 1678 (the year Macaulay marks as the turning point in Dryden's long career), Dryden falls under the spell of the court and develops an eclectic style, which combines the "bombastic meanness" and "ingenious absurdity" of new and old, foreign and native. Macaulay criticizes three chief failures of Dryden's early manner: unrealistic, unbelievable characters; bombastic, ornate speeches; and excessive, undiscriminating flattery—all of which either cause or result from Dryden's eclecticism. As an example of the inferior Dryden, Macaulay chooses *Annus Mirabilis,* a work, he says, that has "no claim to be called poetry" since "It is produced, not by creation, but by construction" (22). Brandishing his Homeric standard, Macaulay speedily dispatches Dryden's poem, remarking on how his description of a sea battle with the Dutch is rendered "not by an act of the imagination, at once calling up the scene before the interior eye, but by painful meditation,—by turning the subject round and round,—by tracing out facts into remote consequences" (22). Macaulay suggests here that Dryden simply has not got the imagination to bring the sea fight to life for his readers; instead, like a critic, he turns a once-living historical fact into lifeless abstraction. By way of example, Macaulay supplies this "favourable instance":

> Amidst whole heaps of spices lights a ball;
> And now their odours armed against them fly.
> Some preciously by shattered porcelain fall,
> And some by aromatic splinters die. (qtd. 22)

Objecting to the way "preciously" and "aromatic" "divert our whole attention to themselves," Macaulay complains that the image of the battle "dissolves" before the excessive color of the words used to describe it. Compounding the fault of overly ornate language is the tendency to bombast, to violent language all out of proportion to the "abject tameness of the thought" (27). Dryden once wrote that audiences demanded these "rants," but Macaulay disallows such a defense as "unworthy of a man of genius" (27). Of course, one could please without ranting, and this further instance of disjunction between language and thought leads to the troubling question of whether audiences even perceived how inappropriate Dryden's language was. His characters, Macaulay argues, never seemed real, not because he wrote speeches for Moors and Americans, but because they, too, are abstractions, without variation and complexity: "As is the love of his heroes, such are all their other emotions. All their qualities, their courage, their generosity, their pride, are on the same colossal scale" (26). Mimicking ancient tragedy, Dryden fails to capture its emotion; he creates characters who tower over his modern audiences by their words and deeds, but who have no more apparent emotion than trees have. He admired the wildness of Shakespeare, Dante, and Homer, and thought to reach their perfection by "daring sublimity": "he attempted, by affected fits of poetical fury, to bring on a real paroxysm; and [. . .] he got nothing but his distortions for his pains" (27–28).

As Bate recounts in *The Burden of the Past,* Dryden late in life recognized how futile were these attempts to match the long strides of his ancestors:

> Strong were our Syres; and as they Fought they Writ,
> Conqu'ring with force of Arms, and dint of Wit;
> Theirs was the Gyant Race, before the Flood;
> And thus, when *Charles* Return'd, our Empire stood.

Chapter 3: Eclecticism and Literary Modernity

> ...
> Our Age was cultivated thus at length;
> But what we gain'd in skill we lost in strength.
> Our Builders were, with want of Genius, curst;
> The Second Temple was not like the First.
> ("To Mr. Congreve" 1694, qtd. in Bate 1)

Struck forcibly by the futility of trying to equal the genius of their ancestors, the best of Dryden's generation turned their powers to criticism. Macaulay attributes this shift to Dryden's superior taste, which "gradually awakened his creative faculties" (31). It was also his propensity for excessive flattery and undiscriminating admiration that propelled him toward the founding of a critical school. While Macaulay does not draw attention to the role of Dryden's catholicity in pushing him toward criticism, this trait is important in light of Dryden's early eclecticism. Macaulay looks with revulsion upon the excessive flattery that he perceives in Dryden's poetry, but is willing to overlook its presence even in the later period for the sake of his brilliant critical works. In this somewhat puzzled recognition of Dryden's particular genius, Macaulay lights, I think, on the source of his power as a critic:

> His literary creed was catholic, even to latitudinarianism; not from any want of acuteness, but from a disposition to be easily satisfied. He was quick to discern the smallest glimpse of merit; he was indulgent even to gross improprieties, when accompanied by any redeeming talent. When he said a severe thing, it was to serve a temporary purpose,—to support an argument, or to tease a rival. Never was so able a critic so free from fastidiousness. He loved the old poets, especially Shakespeare. He admired the ingenuity which Donne and Cowley had so wildly abused. He did justice, amidst the general silence, to the memory of Milton. He praised to the skies the school-boy lines of Addison. Always looking on the fair side of every object, he admired extravagance, on account of the invention which he supposed it to indicate; he excused affectation in favour of wit; he tolerated even tameness, for the sake of the correctness which was its concomitant. (32)

By Macaulay's account Dryden was willing to search high and low for the best expressions that his and previous ages had to offer. More specifically, I think it was this early practice of trying to combine "diverse beauties" that led him to found a "critical school" in the spirit of that early Carracci academy that emphasized selection and combination. Macaulay himself characterized critical poetry as the "poetry of courtesy, [. . .] to which the memory, the judgment, and the wit, contribute far more than the imagination" (12). This "different species" of poetry thrived, in eclectic fashion, on mining and combining all that was usable from earlier works; and if sometimes Dryden's compositions failed to evoke the emotion of those antecedents, then he contributed to his age a style of expression, and the consciousness of the diversity of past ages of poetry. By employing something of the old manner and something of the new, Dryden demonstrated how the literature of the past could be used eclectically in the present.[10]

Turning his attention to the literature of his own age, in 1830 Macaulay railed against the poetic stylings of Robert Montgomery, the very type of the "modern ruin." Popular in his day, and forgotten (as Macaulay predicted he would be) in ours, Montgomery's work is puffed up by "the unsupported assertions of those who assume a right to criticize" (374); the reading public fearing to look foolish buys up in large numbers the works of the latest "master-spirit of the age" (376). Seeking to enhance his reputation by stealing ideas and images from greater talents, Montgomery even failed "to turn his booty to good account" (377). Macaulay dissects Montgomery's plagiarized verses in order to expose the careless ignorance behind the praise heaped upon him. Two examples of Macaulay's catalogue will suffice to demonstrate the vulgar eclecticism at work here. Addressing the sea, Byron wrote, "Time writes no wrinkle on thine azure brow," while the thief Montgomery rendered the image ridiculously thus: "And thou, vast Ocean, on whose awful face / Time's iron feet can print no ruin-trace" (378). From Walter Scott, Montgomery lifted this lovely comparison, "The dew that on the violet lies, / Mocks the dark lustre of thine eyes," and made it his own: "And the bright dew-bead on the bramble lies, / Like liquid rapture upon beauty's eyes" (378). Montgomery's reckless thievery underscores the importance of responsible, informed criticism; one must learn how to select from the ever-increasing mass of literary production that which deserves praise and emulation. Macaulay pauses over Montgomery because "literature must be purified from this taint" (387) of plagiarism and eclecticism: "And this is fine poetry! This is what ranks its writer with the master-spirits of the age! This is what has been described, over and over again, in terms which would require some qualification if used respecting Paradise Lost! It is too much that this patchwork, made by stitching together old odds and ends [. . .] is to be picked off the dunghill on which it ought to rot, and to be held up to admiration as an inestimable specimen of art" (385). Macaulay opposes the "patchwork" brand of eclecticism that would raise a modern ruin and revel in the circulation of fraudulent treasures. But as real treasures accumulate, how is art to progress, if not by the operations of eclecticism? Macaulay the critic offers no solution for the aspiring poet—probably because he did not see any. Typical of his age, Macaulay was willing to grant science the benefit of critical selection and comparison, but poetry and the other arts would have to proceed by dint of pure invention and imagination. Montgomery was indeed a terrible poet; I believe, however, that his fault lay not in imitating Scott and Byron, but rather in doing so incompetently.

Self-Consciousness as Disease

That Thomas Carlyle worried over the passing of poetry is apparent in his 1829 essay "Signs of the Times." In it he famously diagnoses the malady of the nineteenth century as an imbalance between "dynamic" and "mechanic" forces. An overemphasis on mechanistic explanations and endeavors has precipitated the decline of religion, poetry, and morality: "There is a science which treats of, and practically addresses, the primary, unmodified forces and energies of man, the mysterious springs of Love, and Fear, and Wonder, of Enthusiasm, Poetry, Religion, all which have a truly vital and *infinite* character; as well as a science which practically addresses the finite, modified developments of these, when they take the shape of immediate 'motives,' as hope of reward, or as fear of punishment" (72). Like Macaulay, Carlyle allows for a shifting balance of these forces over time; but he is not willing to admit that gains in mechanistic knowledge compensate for the loss of other kinds of wisdom. Nor is he deceived into thinking, by the proliferation of institutions and societies supporting the arts, that the arts are in fact healthy: "In defect of Raphaels, and Angelos, and Mozarts, we have Royal Academies of Painting, Sculpture, Music; whereby the languishing spirit of Art may be strengthened, as by the more generous diet of a Public Kitchen" (66). Rather, it is increasingly clear to Carlyle and many others that the formal organization of national culture generally signals a decline in cultural production. Just as Henry Fuseli contends that the academies are symptoms of art in distress, Carlyle refuses to see the proliferation of institutions as anything more positive than the mechanization of art. After all, were science and art "indebted principally to the founders of Schools and Universities?" (73). In his view schools existed as machines for the preservation and transmission of knowledge; and no great work of art or poetry could be created by a machine: "Again, were Homer and Shakespeare members of any beneficed guild, or made Poets by means of it? Were Painting and Sculpture created by forethought, brought into the world by institutions for that end? No; Science and Art have, from first to last, been the free gift of Nature; an unsolicited, unexpected gift; often even a fatal one. These things rose up, as it were, by spontaneous growth, in the free soil and sunshine of Nature. They were not planted or grafted, nor even greatly multiplied or improved by the culture or manuring of institutions. Generally speaking, they have derived only partial help from these; often enough have suffered damage [. . .]. They originated in the Dynamical nature of man, not in his Mechanical nature" (73). Carlyle believed, with most of his thoughtful contemporaries, that works of original genius could have been produced only in a simpler age still in touch with the invisible, spiritual aspects of nature. As the histories of art and science took on more precise outlines in the early nineteenth century, it was evident that human creativity depended on the mysterious operations of unnamable forces; but Carlyle was willing to name these powers dynamical and to link them to religion, worship, morality, and wonder. Without an attitude of humility toward nature and its infinite diversity, human beings reduced themselves to digestive, reproductive machines, unable to create. Most distressing from Carlyle's point of view, religion—the proper foundation of humility—was itself taking on a mechanical character, as people began to place their faith in the machines of practical science: "Religion in most countries, more or less in every country, is no longer what it was, and should be,—a thousand-voiced psalm from the heart of Man to his invisible Father, the fountain of all Goodness, Beauty, Truth, and revealed in every revelation of these; but for the most part, a wise prudential feeling grounded on mere calculation; a matter, as all others now are, of Expediency and Utility; whereby some smaller quantum of earthly enjoyment may be exchanged for a far larger quantum of celestial enjoyment. Thus Religion too is Profit, a working for wages; not Reverence, but vulgar Hope or Fear" (79). Carlyle found the "true Church of England" in the "preaching" of the daily newspapers, which inflict "moral censure" and impart "moral encouragement, consolation, edification" (80). As religion shares with the press its aim and its audience, it takes on its nature, which is to make profit by telling people what they want to hear, or to move the populace to action in some cause, whether it be right or wrong; unity of purpose cannot endure, virtue is a matter of "Public Opinion," and the moral compass spins in its case. Being then of a "fundamental character" Unbelief spreads to the offspring of religion—literature. No longer a "thousand-voiced psalm" or "vesper hymn to the Spirit of Beauty," poetry is "a fierce clashing of cymbals, and shouting of multitudes" (80). Many of these discordant voices possess talent, but in such a noisy age who will hear them? The disturbing answer is that only the loudest—the best-advertised, so to speak—will penetrate the tumult. Under these conditions, poetry will need not inspiration, but flash and *style*—which explains why bad poets sell: they need only the demeanor of the poet to convince a gullible public of their poetic nature; they require but the *sturm und drang* of the Romantic to raise a storm cloud of approbation around their heads.

Despite having similar views on the state of contemporary poetry, Carlyle and Macaulay bring divergent perceptions of progress in art and science to bear on their explanations of poetry's decline. Macaulay judged advances in science to be the result of centuries of study, while rare artistic geniuses (most of whom lived long ago) conjured up occasional miracles. By contrast, Carlyle located the ground spring of inspiration for both art and science in the individual. His own age was sick because the arts and sciences continued to produce without any reference to a higher motive force than the "force of circumstances." The works of individual genius were reduced to little more than mechanistic theories or recipes of three parts environment stirred into one part heredity. The painter Henry Fuseli saw in eclecticism and its recipes the mechanization of art; Carlyle compared the creation of a modern poem to another mechanical process, bricklaying: "We enjoy, we see nothing by direct vision; but only by reflection, and in anatomical dismemberment. [. . .] We have our little *theory* on all human and divine things. Poetry, the working of genius itself, which in all times, with one or another meaning, has been called Inspiration, and held to be mysterious and inscrutable, is no longer without its scientific exposition. The building of the lofty rhyme is like any other masonry or bricklaying: we have theories of its rise, height, decline, and fall,—which latter, it would seem, is now near, among all people" (79). Carlyle and Fuseli observed that the collection and theorization of art in institutional settings tended to produce lackluster reflections of original works of genius—or worse, the dismembered horrors of a Robert Montgomery. And yet, toward the end of "Signs of the Times" Carlyle acknowledges that the "admiration of old nobleness, which now so often shows itself as a faint *dilettantism,* will one day become a generous emulation, and man may again be all that he has been, and more than he has been" (83–84). From the Carracci to Winckelmann, and from Dryden to Macaulay, the idea that careful study and emulation could "save" art had been a powerful one; but with the proliferation of criticism, scholarship, reviews, and, above all, poetry, reaching the attention of a partially educated public, who would judge the soundness of the "third temple"?

This ambivalence toward criticism actually forms the basis for Carlyle's next major essay on the spirit of the age, "Characteristics," in which he questions whether all of this "self-contemplation" can really be healthy.

Two major premises inform the essay, both of which have important bearing on nineteenth-century attitudes to eclecticism: "The beginning of Inquiry is Disease" (40) and "the end of Understanding is not to prove, and find reasons, but to know and believe" (43). In formulating his theory that all speculation is a kind of sickness, Carlyle assumes that "the first condition of complete health is, that each organ perform its function unconsciously, unheeded; let but any organ announce its separate existence, were it even boastfully, and for pleasure, not for pain, then already has one of those unfortunate 'false centres of sensibility' established itself, already is derangement there" (39). Since the unexamined body is the only healthy body, the only healthy society must be a precritical one. Carlyle dwells nostalgically on ancient "republics" and monarchies where every "organ"—or person—"perform[ed] its function unconsciously" and where

> Society was what we can call *whole,* in both senses of the word. The individual man was in himself a whole, or complete union; and could combine with his fellows as the living member of a greater whole. For all men, through their life, were animated by one great Idea; thus all efforts pointed one way, every where there was *wholeness.* Opinion and Action had not yet become disunited; but the former could still produce the latter, or attempt to produce it, as the stamp does its impression while the wax is not hardened. Thought, and the Voice of thought, were also a unison; thus, instead of Speculation we had Poetry; Literature, in its rude utterance, was as yet a heroic Song, perhaps, too, a devotional Anthem. Religion was everywhere; Philosophy lay hid under it, peacefully included in it. Herein, as in the life-centre of all, lay the true health and oneness. Only at a later era must Religion split itself into Philosophies; and thereby the vital union of Thought being lost, disunion and mutual collision in all provinces of Speech and Action more and more prevail. For if the Poet, or Priest, or by whatever title the inspired thinker may be named, is the sign of vigour and wellbeing; so likewise is the Logician, or uninspired thinker, the sign of disease, probably of decrepitude and decay. (50)

Like many of his contemporaries, Carlyle imagined a prelapsarian state in which men and women existed in harmony with each other and with their environment. Differences in opinion arising from speculation fractured these thoughtlessly ideal societies; people no longer shared a single idea, worked toward a common purpose, or worshipped in one church. Diverse populations lack the unity of Carlyle's "antique Republic"; antagonistic religions undermine the solidarity of the "feudal monarchy"; and museums, libraries, and universities exacerbate the mood of self-contemplation.

Philosophies divorced from religion in particular draw Carlyle's attack, because they first encourage skepticism toward traditional value systems and then give birth to the most damaging of modern ailments, unbelief. In his sketch of the precritical society, Carlyle shows religion in harmony with philosophy, not yet "split into Philosophies," and literature in service to religion, a "heroic Song" or "devotional Anthem," not yet disintegrated by speculation. The "inspired thinker" creates unconsciously, while the "uninspired thinker" *manufactures* consciously (51). Taking up once again his preferred diagnosis of modern life, Carlyle equates the "Division, Dismemberment, and partial healing of the wrong" (40) in society with mechanization, and machinery with speculation. Instead of art, we have theories of art; instead of poetry, we have reviews of poetry—these secondary creations are but the machinery of logic, "sign[s] of decrepitude and decay."

Carlyle's second major premise in the essay is, of course, almost inseparable from the first: that the goal of understanding is not to know, but to believe. Modern poets cannot match the sublimity of their ancestors, because they no longer believe in their creations. Instead of awaiting some species of divine inspiration, they collect, assemble, and imitate the "treasures" of the past; essentially they gather up old poems for raw material and manufacture new ones, no matter that they cannot feel or know what ancient poets knew and felt about the words and ideas they used so effectively. Listening hard for the sounds of genius, modern poets forget, Carlyle says, that "genius is ever a secret to itself": "The Shakespeare takes no airs for writing *Hamlet* and the *Tempest,* understands not that it is anything surprising: Milton, again, is more conscious of his faculty, which accordingly is an inferior one. On the other hand, what cackling and strutting must we not often hear and see, when, in some shape of academical proclusion, maiden speech, review article, this or the other well-fledged goose has produced its goose-egg, of quite measurable value, were it the pink of its whole kind; and wonders why all mortals do not wonder!" (42). Consciousness produces art of inferior quality—for Carlyle, no other outcome is possible. But does it follow that academics, reviewers, and second-rate poets should cease producing work? If one cannot be Shakespeare, should one give up the art? Has literature reached the end of its history? Certainly not. In many of his writings, Carlyle demonstrates his commitment to a cyclical model of history that predicts the eventual spiritual renewal of society, a rebirth that will mean the dawning of a new era of poetry, in its broadest sense. Surrendering to the irony of his position as reviewer, he acknowledges that "the diseased self-conscious state of Literature [is] disclosed in this one fact, which lies so near us here, the prevalence of

Reviewing!" (57). But he asks more pointedly whether self-consciousness is more than a symptom, whether "it is also the attempt towards cure" (54). As with his hope that the "admiration of old nobleness" might lead to "generous emulation," Carlyle here trusts that in doing this "sick thing" and "listen[ing] to itself," Literature might return to a healthier state. Despite Carlyle's opposition to eclecticism and specifically to its modern representative, Victor Cousin (66), his most optimistic pronouncement on the future of literature takes a very eclectic-historicist view of the present situation, anticipating that the best part of the past will always be with us:

> The true Past departs not, nothing that was worthy in the Past departs; no Truth or Goodness realized by man ever dies, or can die; but is all still here, and, recognised or not, lives and works through endless changes. If all things, to speak in the German dialect, are discerned by us, and exist for us, in an element of Time, and therefore of Mortality and Mutability; yet Time itself reposes on Eternity: the truly Great and Transcendental has its basis and substance in Eternity; stands revealed to us as Eternity in a vesture of Time. Thus in all Poetry, Worship, Art, Society, as one form passes into another, nothing is lost: it is but the superficial, as it were the *body* only, that grows obsolete and dies; under the mortal body lies a *soul* that is immortal; that anew incarnates itself in fairer revelation; and the Present is the living sum-total of the whole Past. (65)

For Carlyle in his role as historian, the key to revitalizing the present was *collecting* the biographies of great men whose words and actions would inspire people the way religion once did; since "the Present is the living sum-total of the whole Past," the present actually benefits from "increased resources"—from the "new wealth which the old coffers will no longer contain" (65). The forms of past art survive, even when the inspiration and belief is lost, and so the question for Carlyle becomes, as it did for most critics and historians of the arts, what will be the new foundation of our belief? Will we have an accidental, indiscriminate mixture of past forms and ideas driven by marketplace forces? Or will we achieve a considered, critical selection of past art that will assist us in developing the style by which the age will truly express itself?

With a few exceptions, most reviewers and literary critics judged the poetry of the mid-nineteenth century severely and retained the pessimistic tone of their eighteenth- and early-nineteenth-century precursors. Far from benefiting from the "increased resources" of history and world culture, Victorian poets seemed to travel in the old ruts, to be imitative in a way that was antithetical to the growth of a new style of poetry. Charles

Kingsley's 1851 article in *Fraser's,* irritably titled "The Prevailing Epidemic," is typical of the response to contemporary poetry and its incoherent eclecticism. Kingsley commences his review of "nine new books of poetry, whereof only two, if as many, are of such merit as to make it conceivable to us why they should have been published" by iterating a great Carlylean truth: "If a man has a single new fact, or thought, or metre, to add to the accumulated treasure-heaps of mankind, let him bring it, and we will welcome him as a benefactor, however small his gift [. . .] but if all he can do is to say over again things which have already been said a great deal better, let him be silent" (492). Not only does Kingsley betray concern over the enormous crowd of publications vying for his attention at *Fraser's;* he also worries over the lack of "sound and sterling critic[s]" who will stem the torrent of amateur and ill-considered literary offerings. Although he will not promise to read through all the works he will review, he yet maintains that "a book may be worth reviewing, though not worth publishing,—even as a great many actions are fit to be punished, which are by no means fit to be done" (493). Acting on this principle, he attempts "to take the most and the least faulty [works] before us, and by exposing, through them, some of the common poetic mistakes and superstitions of the day, try, if possible, to warn others from the road which leads to Limbo Patrum, the region of failures and abortions" (509). Kingsley lists as the most egregious fault of aspiring poets the total lack of art or manner in the poetry—a consequence, he feels, of the widespread belief that sincerity of feeling is sufficient to merit any assemblage of words whatever: "Now, is this a book to be read through? especially when the author informs you in the preface that it has no plot, and has actually been made as you make chairs and tables, bits at a time, jotted down in a note-book, 'altogether unpremeditated either in design or otherwise'" (494). According to Kingsley, such scribblers are not called to poetry; they do not feel any stirring joyfulness in the play of language, nor do they have any grand ideas to bequeath to humanity.

Compounding the thoughtlessness that allows amateur productions to reach the public is the noticeably sloppy language of which they are composed. In his dissection of W. R. Cassels's poem "Pygmalion," Kingsley draws attention to the particular weaknesses of the modern poet. First, Cassels errs by his imprecise word choices, which Kingsley demonstrates by citing passages that hint at a careless and wasteful mimicry of romantic images. The offending poet stumbles with the phrase "verderous pleasure" (Kingsley queries, "What sort of pleasure is that?"), with "That heaven sets lambent on its imaged self" (Kingsley begs to know, "What in heaven, or its imaged self either, does that mean?"), and "Upon each limb / Grace laid its sweet commandment lovingly" (Kingsley wonders, "Why lovingly? Did grace love the statue? If so, what is grace?") (495). Second, Cassels falls prey to a habit that Kingsley regards as the most offensive of the modern poet, namely frequent reference to the wistful longings, unique powers of observation, and all-around incomparable genius of the Poet. In "Pygmalion" he envisions streams "Calling forth flowers from the slumbering earth, / Like 'thoughts from the dream of a Poet,'" (495); in another poem Cassels tells the story of a poet disappointed in the world who comes back to his first love in the country (496). While Kingsley does not detest this latter poem as much as Cassels's others, he wishes it had any other person as its hero. The hackneyed image of the poet that the Victorians inherited from the Romantics cannot be blamed entirely on the wave of feeling that washed out traditional poetic values earlier in the century. The Romantic poets seemed to offer a kind of generalized notion of the poetic nature, whereby any reasonably thoughtful individual might lay claim to heightened perception and feelings. One of the works Kingsley reviews accordingly contains no fewer than four poems about poets—"The Poet's Bride," "Poesie," "The Poet," and "Sonnet—The Outer and Inner Life of a Poet" (498)—a density that prompts the critic to complain that poetry is suffering from an epidemic of "poets": "Why will he run into the modern cant of young authors on this point too? Instead of writing poetry now-a-days, people write spoilt prose about poets, and think that will do as well. Poetry about Poets!–a folio commentary on a bank-note! If they know so perfectly what poets ought to be, why don't they go and *be* it, and let the poor world, not over-stocked with 'world-singers' just now, see what it is like? Just as the unfortunate Germans are, or were, overrun with scribblers of 'Kunst-novellen,' who could not draw a cow if they were asked, so we are with poet-scribblers who can't write poetry" (498). In all of these examples, Kingsley sees a gap between theory and practice, saying and doing—there are novels about artists written by people who know nothing about art, poems about poets written by people who know nothing about poetry. The pervasiveness of poetry about poets (and the corresponding evacuation of genuine thought or feeling) is symptomatic of the drift in modern poetry toward a vague and eclectic spiritualism.

In the nineteenth century, Kingsley complains, it suffices to look like a thing in order to be it—modern poets substitute the re-presentation (or the theory) for the act. Since the audience for poetry no longer understands the impulse behind it or the words that compose the great poems of the past, the modern poet's superficiality might escape detection. As long as he collects enough of the catchphrases, loads his poem with the usual images, and assumes the appropriately wistful attitude, most casual observers will reckon him a poet: "It is a sad style, this, which too many young men have got into now-a-days, in prose and verse: one part Carlylese, one part Tennysonian, one part Bulwerean, one part third-hand Fichtean, and seven parts Anna-Matilda Slipslop, stolen apparently from her well-known ballad in the *Rejected Addresses;* everybody's peculiarities, and nobody's beauties; great, big, huge stock-words, every one of them a hoary sinner about town these ten years, substituted for a thought in every line, except where the young poets forget themselves a moment, and their dyed wigs get awry, and the native baldness peeps out" (497). In revealing the recipe mixture for most modern poems, Kingsley foregrounds one item in the list: pretentiousness. The use of "stock-words" in place of authentic thought can be blamed in part on the spread of superficial knowledge, which encourages individuals to lay claim to a more expansive territory of knowledge than is really wise, given their limited resources for holding onto it. Kingsley detects a misunderstanding of the most basic philosophical precepts in David Holt's *Lay of Hero-Worship* when the poet writes "Out of the Real the Ideal springeth," and he counters—no matter whether the poet meant to be cleverly paradoxical—"Nonsense! [. . .] The ideal is the real, and the only real, according to all philosophies which acknowledge an ideal, and not a mere nominal abstract" (497). Since the poet has "filched" these terms (and many others that Kingsley lists) from philosophy, "they must be used rightly, and not wrongly" (497). But Holt exhibits a far more dire brand of pretentiousness for Kingsley when he claims that he can construct a "basement upon which to build a bright / Edifice of Divine imaginings" (497). Here Kingsley recognizes the hated spiritualism of the age with its "Every-man-his-own-God-maker-cant" (498) and blasts Holt for invoking the Divine as a means to glorify the poet and *his* imaginings, "just as you would intense or gorgeous, or 'utterless,' or any other word from the stock-cant vocabulary" (497). Kingsley caps his argument against the pseudoreligious feeling of so much contemporary poetry with a diatribe against the thoughtless eclecticism of the age: "Seriously, the prevalence of this sort of—what shall we call it?—Pseudo-Spiritualistico-Eclectico-Hypoplatonico-Pantheistico-Pamborborotaractic Sentimentalism, infecting the greater part of our bad poetry, and too much of our good, is an ugly sign of the 'unreality,' as the modern phrase is—the lying, as our forefathers used to call it, in their coarse way—which is abroad in the world;—nasty foul out-croppings of Mr. Carlyle's universal 'Liars'-rock substratum,' in the very sanctuary of God, as poetry once was and will be again, but never to those who persist in this fashion of writing" (498). Kingsley asks these poets to give up writing poetry, to come into contact with one "fact," and to quit pretending to illumination that they do not possess (499). Such pretending contributes to the spread of a dangerous state of unreality, particularly in the upper classes, who seem most disposed to write nonsense, and who are most likely to be estranged from any "simple, universal word, or thought, or feeling, of human nature" (499).

The spread of superficial knowledge, false religious feeling, philosophical confusion, rampant literary borrowing, and intellectual laziness are familiar symptoms of eclecticism. Kingsley adds one more feature to the idea of eclecticism at mid-century: its effeminacy. Coleridge and Lewes might have laid the foundation for Kingsley's diagnosis, but this muscular Christian made unmanliness a central feature of the (literary) spirit of the age. In fact, Kingsley links almost all of the negative characteristics of modern poetry to its unmanliness. He first employs sexual language in his critique of Cassels's poem "Pygmalion." Glossing the final lines, in which Pygmalion finally enjoys the warm contact of his Galatea ("He clasped the maid unto his beating heart, / As father might the daughter of his love"), Kingsley complains, "Oh, most lame and impotent conclusion!" (496). While playing up the humor of a climax driven by paternal love, Kingsley also speaks to the lack of poetic consummation. Instead of feeling the fire of sexual passion, Cassels supplies only "dim wonderment," a conclusion Kingsley dismisses as "vapid, gaudy, wordy, misty bombast and slipslop, without definite images, sound manful thought, or even correct use of language" (496). Cassels is unable to satisfy the poetic promise raised by his borrowings from more "virile" sources such as Carlyle, Tennyson, and Bulwer Lytton, being, Kingsley mocks, "seven parts Anna-Matilda Slipslop" (497). Not surprisingly, Kingsley holds out the "poetess" as the ultimate failure for the young men whom he primarily addresses in this essay. The "quasi-metaphysical verbiage" of so many modern poets bypasses the "severely philosophic method" of the always masculine scholar (501). The "Autotheistic" position (the false religious feeling and poet-worship Kingsley detests) betrays a deep-seated cowardice, barely separated as it is "from sheer, blank, honest, manful Atheism—honest and manful because it wears no rouge, and has courage to look steadily at the reflection of its own skeleton face" (498). Kingsley implies throughout "The Prevailing Epidemic" that the "sanctuary of God" in which true poetry dwells can be retaken only by honest, "manful" language, which has been lost, he believes, in the imprecise, perplexed vocabulary of modern life.

Just as Macaulay reviewed the work of a bad poet in order to remind critics of their obligation to serve the public, Kingsley rehearsed the faults of modern poetry in order to arrest the decline of the art. He hoped that poetry would come to reflect the age in a significant way or even to transcend it by a mastery of traditional form—a mastery that could come only with a return to the beliefs that shaped tradition. But how were these foundational beliefs to be recovered and restored? In the second part of this book, I consider five writers (including Kingsley) who struggled to create in an age of eclecticism. Most writers discovered the necessity of compromise. The conditions of literary modernity demanded it. Just as Ruskin tried to find principles for modern architecture that would be like Gothic, but different, writers had to understand both the structure and the spirit of past literature. Old forms might be infused with new meanings, or combined to create new styles, and new modes of expression might equal the force of the antique; but this could not happen ex nihilo. In the ordinary sense, every writer born in the nineteenth century was eclectic. But if these writers wanted to use that vast inheritance, they had to learn how to be eclectic.

PART II

Eclectic Victorians

CHAPTER 4

Alfred Tennyson
The Originality of Medley

Given Charles Kingsley's dissatisfaction with the eclecticism of much post-Romantic poetry, it is remarkable that he regarded *The Princess*—a self-consciously eclectic work—as a great synthetic achievement: "[Tennyson] makes his 'Medley' a mirror of the nineteenth century, possessed of its own new art and science, its own new temptations and aspirations, and yet grounded on, and continually striving to reproduce, the forms and experiences of all past time" (250). Tennyson avoids what Kingsley identifies as the chief errors of his fellow poets—superficial knowledge, false religious feeling, philosophical confusion, rampant literary borrowing, and intellectual laziness—all familiar symptoms of a pervasive, naïve eclecticism. He works with the same materials and under similar exigencies to create unity from potentially chaotic variety, and to make a "Medley" of the discordant music of his age. Aubrey De Vere's October 1849 review of *The Princess* for the *Edinburgh Review* likewise praises Tennyson's capacity for capturing the spirit of the nineteenth century, and for doing what no one else seemed capable of doing: rendering the age a fit subject for poetry. The genius of Tennyson's synthesis, as Kingsley saw it, was in grounding the "temptations and aspirations" of the nineteenth century on "the forms and experiences of all past time." De Vere's analysis extends the idea of the age as "medley" when he credits

Tennyson with writing a poem that successfully combines widely different genres and moods. In asserting that the poem partakes of the eclectic character of the age, De Vere pays tribute to Tennyson's ability to evoke of one of the defining features of modern life:

> If a man were to scrutinise the external features of our time, for the purpose of characterising it compendiously, he would be tempted, we suspect, to give up the task before long, and to pronounce the age a Medley. It would be hard to specify the character of our Philosophy, including as it does fragments of all systems, sometimes at open war, and sometimes eclectically combined. Not less various is the texture of Society among us, in which time-honoured traditions are blended with innovations which a few months make antiquated. [. . .] As heterogeneous in its character is Art among us. Here we have an imitation of the antique, there a revival of the middle ages; [. . .]. By what term could we describe the architecture of the day? In our rising cities we find a Gothic church close to a Byzantine fane or an Italian basilica; and in their immediate neighbourhood a town hall like a Greek temple, a mansion like a Roman palace, and a clubhouse after the fashion of Louis XIV. The age in which we live may have a character of its own; but that character is not written in its face. (204)

As was so often the case during the nineteenth century, critics would invoke the heterogeneity—or outward eclecticism—of Victorian architecture in an effort to describe the inner character of the age. Here De Vere equates architectural with philosophical eclecticism, and connects them both to a more expansive "texture of Society," which readily combines the antique and the innovative. By designating his poem "A Medley," Tennyson captures the particular quality of an age that cannot be characterized easily in any other way. It is tempting to see, as De Vere does, Tennyson's classification of *The Princess* as part of an overall design—a poem that self-consciously "resembles the age," speaks the age's eclectic dialect, and performs its attendant crises. But not all readers of *The Princess* were willing to see "depths where there [were] none" (Chretien 203). C. P. Chretien's April 1849 review in the *Christian Remembrancer* raises an uncomfortable question about the poem, which has never been resolved: was the appellation of "medley" an afterthought, a kind of justification for the long poem's obvious, unresolved heterogeneity? Or is "medley" meant to draw attention to the "unity of purpose which methodises its variegated exterior" (De Vere 204)? In other words, does the poem merely reflect the eclecticism of the age, or is it coping with that eclecticism self-consciously through its eclectic form?

Two oft-quoted anecdotes from Tennyson's life reveal his ambivalent feelings about the most-revised of his long poems. In late December 1847 he wrote to his friend Edward FitzGerald, "My Book is out and I hate it and so no doubt will you" (*Letters* I:281). During the weeks leading up to the publication of *The Princess: A Medley* on Christmas day, Tennyson was visiting Carlyle, who wrote to Emerson about the poet and the poem: "a truly interesting Son of Earth, and Son of Heaven,—who has almost lost his way, among the will-o'wisps, I doubt; and may flounder ever deeper, over neck and nose at last among the quagmires that abound!" (qtd. in *Letters* I:281n). Carlyle worried, too, that "spinning rhymes" and calling them "high Art" would never furnish Tennyson with the great task he needed (281n). As Arnold would later say about writing poetry in general, the times were against him. Hallam Tennyson records in the *Memoir* that FitzGerald and Carlyle "gave up all hopes of him after 'The Princess'" (I:253). Serious poetry, it was thought, should not muddy itself too much in the present age, or it would not outlast its generation; but was the poem serious—was it original—because it arrested for a moment the fast-flowing stream of the present? His son also records a conversation Tennyson had with Frederick Locker-Lampson in 1869 in which "He talked of 'The Princess' with something of regret, of its fine blank verse, and the many good things in it: 'but,' said he, 'though truly original, it is, after all, only a medley'" (*Memoir* II:70–71). If Locker-Lampson's memory of the poet's phrasing is accurate, Tennyson, like many of his reviewers, was forced to acknowledge an irresolvable something at the heart of this strange poem. It was original—it was "only" a medley. The originality of the poem lay precisely in using the medley form to represent what was unintelligible by any other means—and by no other means could he extricate himself from the "quagmire" of the present.

Contrary to what was widely believed at the time and to what still passes as common knowledge on the subject, *The Princess* was not a critical failure.[1] Granted, Tennyson was disappointed at the poem's reception—at the consensus that *The Princess* did not live up to the expectations raised by the *Poems* of 1832 and 1842. But the majority of critics who weighed in between January 1848 and October 1849 liked the poem, even as they lamented the misapplication of Tennyson's remarkable powers to what seemed more a collection of headlines than a work of art. Even those critics who praised the beauty and sentiment of *The Princess* could find little justification for its extreme heterogeneity, both thematic and formal. Rather than debating the controversial content of the poem, many reviewers found themselves embroiled in controversy about form and style. Even his staunchest supporters conceded that they would have to wait still longer for the great moral poem they believed their hero would produce.

In its bare outline, *The Princess* looked like it would supply this lack. The main poem relates the story of a young prince who was betrothed at birth to Princess Ida, who, having reached the age suitable for marrying, is instead intent on founding a university for women over which she will preside. Despite the promise of an epic struggle between male and female that is finally resolved to everyone's satisfaction, reviewers were uneasy about the juxtaposition of comic and tragic elements, and modern and traditional values. And some critics wondered why Tennyson presented his serious message about the education and status of women in the form of a burlesque. The Prologue even in its shorter 1847 incarnation did explain the poem's formal structure, and many reviewers complained that *The Princess* lacked unity of purpose. The unusually broad range of sources informing the poem—debates on the Woman Question, discoveries in the sciences, classical mythology, the *Arabian Nights,* to name just a few—provoked attacks on the poem's anachronisms and moral confusion. But as John Killham in his study of Tennyson's sources concedes, the poet's "eclecticism in choice of materials represented the state of current taste and thinking" (276). We do indeed see a world of differences at Vivian Park (the setting of the framing story), but we see that its diverse elements do not clash. We witness the breakdown of communication between tradition and modernity and between men and women, but we see commonalty and continuity reestablished between them. Tennyson's eclecticism in this poem works on two levels: first, he canvasses "the state of current taste and thinking" (the manifest eclecticism of Victorian culture, apparent in its art, philosophy, religion, and politics) and brings that variety into the poem; and then he blends these diverse elements in order to achieve a progressive synthesis of past and present, male and female, heroic and mock-heroic. The poem thus provided critics with an occasion to rehearse the principal arguments for and against eclecticism. Two critical responses in particular, those of Chretien and De Vere, show that in the debate over the nature of Tennyson's genius, and the success or failure of this poem in particular, eclecticism was becoming as serious an issue in poetry at mid-century as it was already in architecture and philosophy.

Eclecticism at Cambridge

In the late 1820s, when Tennyson was at Cambridge, a professor at the Sorbonne, Victor Cousin, delivered a series of blockbuster lectures on the history of philosophy. Underlying Cousin's narrative was the conviction that by analyzing the history of philosophy eclectically, one could identify the truths unifying the different schools. It was simply a matter of discovering what was constant in this history, and putting aside what did not seem to fit. The philosophical battles that had, he felt, falsely opposed German idealism, Scottish common sense, and French psychology would cease; and the ideological détente that followed would provide the foundation for a political *juste milieu*—a happy medium that blended republican principles with monarchical rule. Although Cousin himself was always careful to describe eclecticism as a method rather than a school, he became identified personally with an eclectic philosophy whose fortunes were inextricably linked to the July Monarchy. As a philosophical approach, eclecticism was equated in British minds entirely with what they regarded as the instability of the French nation in the post-Revolutionary period. More seriously, the eclectic method of discovering truth struck some British philosophers, such as William Hamilton and George Henry Lewes, as an unhealthy compound of dilettantism and pedantry, without the element of genuine conviction. In Britain the rise of eclecticism signaled a loss of faith in authority, combined with a sense of the wholeness of the past seen against the fragmentariness of the present. Could an eclectic method overcome the naïve eclecticism of a society that seemed to pick and choose at random from the past, unaware of how this style clashed with that or how this idea was irreconcilable with that one? In spite of the unpopularity of French thought in Britain, eclecticism became the most congenial intellectual tool of a pragmatic age. The eclectic looked for compromises and avoided conflicts, which explained the predominance of liberalism in politics and latitudinarianism in religion, of mixed styles in architecture and painting, and of hybrid genres, such as the novel, in literature.

During his years at Cambridge, Tennyson became involved with the "Apostles," a society of gifted undergraduates who had embraced the spirit, if not the letter, of the eclectic philosophy that was thriving across the Channel.[2] The early influence of F. D. Maurice had instilled within successive generations of members a consistent set of liberal values and a "spirit of the society" that Henry Sidgwick described as the "belief that we *can* learn, and a determination that we *will* learn from people of the most opposite opinions" (qtd. in Allen 4). Maurice's own spiritual development represents an extreme version of the transformation most Apostles experienced. The son of a Unitarian clergyman whose tolerance of all beliefs worked against the effectiveness of his own teachings, and the brother of several evangelical sisters, Frederick Maurice spent his life searching for unity and avoiding controversy: "He came to think that every form of human belief might be seen to contain elements of truth that might be discovered by close analysis of the form and by an attempt to sympathize with those who held to it" (Allen 70). The process of "painfully honest self-scrutiny" (70) undertaken by all Apostles was merely the first step toward social regeneration; the Apostles' educational program, a crucial supplement to the narrow curriculum of Cambridge, included the study of modern literature, from which one would gain an understanding of the operations of the divine principle at work in the world. Like Cousin of the Sorbonne, who found his political middle way in the July Monarchy, Maurice eventually found his theological *juste milieu* in the Established Church, which was broad enough, he felt, to include all Christian believers. Cousin and Maurice taught their followers to canvass a range of opinions and finally to rest in compromise and unity, comfortably in the middle.

Peter Allen's intimate account of the Apostles' early years offers compelling portraits of the many young men who underwent such spiritual transformations as a result of their association with the "Conversazione Society." A category of experience that might rightly be described as eclectic, the dialectical self-scrutiny undertaken by the Apostles carried individuals from the point of (generally) radical beliefs to confusion and uncertainty to inclusively liberal beliefs. Jane Carlyle, one of the less charitable critics of Maurice and the "mystics," said that members such as John Sterling simply "wanted back-bone" (89). Thomas Carlyle preferred to call his friend's susceptibility to new influences and impressions a "gift for imaginative sympathy" (89). Both Sterling and Maurice wrote novels about young men whose spiritual quests led them to adopt and to reject one system of thought after another; but this was a process of spiritual awakening that would fit them for the vital project of social regeneration—they were to join Coleridge's "clerisy." The necessity of eclecticism in youth was central to educational projects from the Royal Academy of Art to Newman's *Idea of a University*. Only by canvassing a range of belief within a controlled environment could a youth emerge as an individual whose opinions might genuinely be described as his own. At the very least, then, the Apostles gave Tennyson a "loosely consistent set of values" with which his work would enter into conversation.[3] The "spirit of the society" haunted the twilight space wherein the poet described a moment of waking to consciousness again and again—a moment of waking that was essential to what I characterize as the Apostolic transformation. In *The Princess* Tennyson gave this spiritual transformation a generic form—the medley.

The Eclectic Poetics of *The Princess*

Even as Tennyson inclined toward eclecticism intellectually and temperamentally, he did not find it easy to rest in the condition of being eclectic. In

Part V of *The Princess,* it is difficult not to hear an echo of his earlier poem on the dangers of solipsism, "The Palace of Art," when Princess Ida rages, "Far off from men I built a fold for them [women]; / I stored it full of rich memorial; / I fenced it round with gallant institutes, / And biting laws to scare the beasts of prey, / And prosper'd, till a rout of saucy boys / Brake on us at our books, and marr'd our peace,..." (V:380–85). While the Princess's university is no "lordly pleasure-house" ("Palace" 1), she does create a space in which women might "reign ... apart" (14) and where the world's treasures of knowledge and art have been sifted to create a self-reflecting, self-fulfilling narrative. If Cousin's image of the eclectic philosopher was an internal eye, then in "The Palace of Art" Tennyson gives us the soul as an all-seeing, self-sustaining eclectic: "I take possession of man's mind and deed. / I care not what the sects may bawl. / I sit as God holding no form of creed, / But contemplating all" (209–12). The Princess does not pretend to be above professing a creed, but, in establishing the university, she extricates herself from the entanglements of history and family, to sit in judgment on the world. Consequently, both the Princess and the feminized soul of the earlier poem succumb to a kind of "death in life"—a stagnation or loss of consciousness worse than death—before reengaging with the world. Tennyson keeps the dangers of eclecticism firmly in mind for the reader, even as the overall movement of the poem supports the Princess's eclectic aim. Instead of an enclosed, self-devouring eclecticism, Tennyson models the dialectical eclecticism of the Cambridge Apostles; and, as a careful reading of the poem will demonstrate, the medley is anything but an indiscriminate collection of the age's tropes and artifacts.

As Tennyson sets the stage for the entertainment that is the core narrative of *The Princess,* he draws upon the collegiate model of the debate in a story passed among several narrators, each of whom might inflect the story with his own interpretation or alter its course toward a particular outcome.[4] In practice, we have in *The Princess* a single poet-narrator who has unified the seven parts of the story in a single style, leaving the characters' voices to provide the dialectics.[5] The auditors and narrators of the framing story (and inevitably the readers who are pulled into that frame) are likely to sympathize with the troubles of the characters and to identify with the various positions taken by them. Sympathy, and even susceptibility, were vital elements in the character of a Cambridge Apostle, especially in his approach to handling controversy, and Tennyson constructs his dialectics with the intention of making the reader see the mixed situations of the medley as natural and inevitable, and any ideological extreme as untenable. The primary, contending forces involved in the framing and core narratives of *The Princess* form three pairs: tradition and modernity, or the proper relationship between past and present; male and female, or the relative strength of each in shaping our identity; and the heroic and mock-heroic, or the power of generic conventions in shaping ideology. Tennyson makes these rigid dichotomies meaningful by showing how we engage eclectically with variety and that achieving synthesis must always involve compromise between like elements, not the exclusion of difference.

In the Prologue Tennyson establishes a complex dialectic between naïve eclecticism and the eclecticism that can be achieved only through an effort at selection and combination. Since volitional eclecticism usually constitutes an effort to cope with the burden of the historical inheritance, Tennyson's use of historical material in the framing story provides an index of his commitment to an eclectic outlook. The opening lines of the Prologue not only describe the setting, Vivian Park, but also invoke the tradition of the country house poem, which had been popular in English poetry during the Renaissance. While less explicitly a poem of praise than, say, Ben Jonson's "To Penshurst," the Prologue does present an exemplary scene of the times, commends the generosity of the host, surveys the riches of the house and its collections, and describes the joy of the common people who take advantage of a summer holiday on the park grounds. Combining the generic features of the country house poem with the memory of a feast of the Mechanics' Institute that he had witnessed at the Lushingtons' house in 1842, Tennyson brings the past forward into the present. In order to make the marriage between the tradition of country hospitality and social and scientific progress as natural as possible, Tennyson has to choose the elements of that union very carefully, so that a scene "Strange ... and smacking of the time" (l. 89) becomes reassuringly familiar.

The Prologue continually reinforces the poet's underlying eclecticism. Herbert F. Tucker has referred to the modern scene at Vivian-place as "a Crystal Palace without the walls" (354) and, though *The Princess* predates that quintessential Victorian edifice, this is an especially apt image of what Tennyson wants to accomplish. The reader is led from the lawn and the Mechanics' Institute into the house, where an apparently random collection of artifacts contributes to a distinctively modern harmony:

> Walter show'd the house,
> Greek, set with busts. From vases in the hall
> Flowers of all heavens, lovelier than their names,
> Grew side by side; and on the pavement lay
> Carved stones of the Abbey-ruin in the park,
> Huge Ammonites and the first bones of time;
> And on the tables every clime and age
> Jumbled together; celts and calumets,

> Claymore and snow-shoe, toys in lava, fans
> Of sandal, amber, ancient rosaries,
> Laborious orient ivory sphere in sphere,
> The cursed Malayan crease and battle-clubs
> From the isles of palm; and higher on the walls,
> Betwixt the monstrous horns of elk and deer,
> His own forefathers' arms and armour hung. (Prol.:10–24)

Eclecticism in art and architecture was meant to preserve the values attached to the different styles; the eclecticism of the collection operates in like manner. The Greek Revival house "set with busts" reaches back to a place remote from modern Britain both temporally and geographically, and contains the figures of great men whose ideas and actions have presumably influenced the evolution of Vivian Park. Here and throughout the Prologue, Tennyson links the long history of the family ("forefathers' arms and armour") and national traditions to an even more expansive geological time. Paired with the shell of an extinct mollusk, the ammonite, the ruins of the abbey are among "the first bones of time." In the collection, objects of "every clime and age" are "jumbled together," but instead of clashing they seem to open up and reveal each other. For example, softening the violence of the instruments of war (Celts, claymore, Malayan crease, battle-clubs) are the more peaceful objects in Sir Walter's collection (calumets, snowshoe, fans, rosaries, carved ivory). What would seem to be a collection without meaning, without a narrative—in other words, naïve eclecticism—becomes instead dialectical and expressive.

The effort to combine eclectically the values of past and present continues throughout the Prologue, culminating in the story of a princess who defies the spirit of her age, before reconciling with it. On his tour of the house and its collections, the poet-narrator picks up "a hoard of tales that dealt with knights / Half-legend, half-historic counts and kings..." (Prol.:29–30) and a woman warrior, figures all from the family's proud history. From the "half-legend, half-historic," the party moves to the half-modern scene of the summer holiday. Significantly, he "kept the book and had [his] finger in it— / Down thro' the park" (53–54), so that even as he looks upon the wondrous present, the poet holds open the door to the past. Instead of portraying the scientific displays as potentially disrupting the world of tradition invoked by the country house poem, the poet's figurative language brings the alien into the existing order:

> Strange was the sight to me;
> For all the sloping pasture murmur'd, sown

> With happy faces and with holiday.
> There moved the multitude, a thousand heads;
> The patient leaders of their Institute
> Taught them with facts. One rear'd a font of stone
> And drew, from butts of water on the slope,
> The fountain of the moment, playing, now
> A twisted snake, and now a rain of pearls,
> Or steep-up spout whereon the gilded ball
> Danced like a wisp; and somewhat lower down
> A man with knobs and wires and vials fired
> A cannon; Echo answer'd in her sleep
> From hollow fields; and here were telescopes
> For azure views; and there a group of girls
> In circle waited, whom the electric shock
> Dislink'd with shrieks and laughter; round the lake
> A little clock-work steamer paddling plied
> And shook the lilies; perch'd about the knolls
> A dozen angry models jetted steam;
> A petty railway ran; a fire-balloon
> Rose gem-like up before the dusky groves
> And dropt a fairy parachute and past;
> And there thro' twenty posts of telegraph
> They flash'd a saucy message to and fro
> Between the mimic stations; so that sport
> Went hand in hand with science; [. . .] (Prol.:54–80)

The poet-narrator offers up the strange sights that modern science has produced, but with the intention of seeing them integrated into the familiar cultural landscape, even of transforming science into a kind of fairy tale or myth ("rain of pearls," "gilded ball," "danced like a wisp," "Echo answer'd," and "a fire-balloon / Rose gem-like up before the dusky groves / And dropt a fairy parachute"). Young girls still giggle in shifting cliques, even if they have been moved by electricity rather than gossip. Children still play on the water with toy boats, though they might be powered by steam. Young men and women still flirt and court, even if the messages are not whispered into warm ears, but passed into the telegraph. Incorporating aspects of modern life into the most pleasing configuration of traditional social relations, Tennyson models in the Prologue on the level of society what he illustrates in the main tale on the level of the individual, namely that we will all be better off if we *blend* the diverse elements of which we are composed, rather than forcing them into conflict. Just as attendees of the Great Exhibition were meant to return to their homes feeling renewed optimism about the progress of their age, readers of *The Princess* were supposed to feel that the plenitude of the present could not be captured in any single style and that the generic and stylistic inclusiveness of the poem pointed the way to new possibilities for the art of poetry.

Throughout the Prologue the reader feels the shifting of temporal sands as the poet-narrator moves back and forth, as it seems, between past and present. After gazing long upon the modern scene, the group of friends, "satiated at length / Came to the ruins" (90–91). Quite deliberately, the poet-narrator frames a scene from within the ruins that blends past and present, creating the *juste milieu* that he has been seeking, neither past nor present but both together: "High-arch'd and ivy-claspt, / Of finest Gothic lighter than a fire, / Thro' one wide chasm of time and frost they gave / The park, the crowd, the house; but all within / The sward was trim as any garden lawn" (91–95). Within the theatrical space of the ruins, the host and his college friends, his sister, their Aunt Elizabeth, and various other ladies gather for a feast. Tennyson contrasts the liveliness of the young people with the serenity of the tomb where they will have their meal, as if to draw attention to the entirely commonplace idea of the persistence of human generation. Even when individual efforts fail and empires fall, the next generation waits to take their place; but the transfer of the life force does not travel in one direction only. Described as "Half child, half woman" (Prol.:101), Lilia, the host's sister—a key figure in the poem, drapes the broken statue of her ancestor Sir Ralph with an orange scarf, "That made the old warrior from his ivied nook / Glow like a sunbeam" (Prol.:104–5). In this poem, Tennyson often shows how the living restore life to the dead, and so does not commit the error Kingsley so detested, of "ignoring the Present to fall back on a cold and galvanised Medievalism" (250). Lilia's playfulness when she warms the statue with her scarf; the poet-narrator's finger in the ancient text; and the feast upon the tomb—all are gestures of restorative sympathy, a reaching out to the past, without surrendering to it. Following the pattern of the Prologue, the core narrative must strike a balance between admiration for what William Morris might have called the strong colors of the past and the necessity of living in the present:

> Heroic seems our princess as required—
> But something made to suit with time and place,
> A Gothic ruin and a Grecian house,
> A talk of college and of ladies' rights,
> A feudal knight in silken masquerade,
> And, yonder, shrieks and strange experiments

For which the good Sir Ralph had burnt them all—
This *were* a medley! (Prol.:223–30)

The present lends its own colors to old subjects and links ideas that gain in power from their juxtaposition. What makes eclecticism seem seductive to some and incoherent to others is its presumption that one can have, to paraphrase Voltaire, the best of all possible worlds. Rather than dismissing such idealism as naïve or ridiculous, Tennyson puts forward a vision of historical change as medley—evolution not revolution. Who would be happier to return to a time when they would be burnt for practicing science? Change should be welcomed, as long as it is tended like a garden—nurtured and loved, but clipped and pruned when required.

When the central narrative begins, we see that neither the Prince nor the Princess has learned to live with a medley of past and present. One of Tennyson's later revisions, the addition of the Prince's "weird seizures," underscores the attitude toward history displayed in the Prologue—one cannot begin to live until one lives in the present. Burdened by a hereditary malady, the Prince suffers from waking dreams, seems to walk among ghosts, and cannot tell truth from shadow. While the Prince's "fancies" keep him a prisoner in an insubstantial past, the Princess's fancies have more troubling consequences, for they concern the future. In attempting to bring about a Renaissance for women, the Princess selects from a largely mythical past. Any theory-driven picking and choosing seems doomed to failure; even the Princess acknowledges that she works in shadow, knowing only parts of the whole.

'. . . but we that are not all,
As parts, can see but parts, now this, now that,
And live, perforce, from thought to thought, and make
One act a phantom of succession. Thus
Our weakness somehow shapes the shadow, Time;
But in the shadow will we work, and mould
The woman to the fuller day.' (III:309–14)

As Tennyson must have learned from his Apostle friends, one had to test one's opinions, to discover their origins, and whether there was any truth in them. If one were surrounded only with flatterers and inferiors, it was unlikely that one would grow to maturity holding opinions that were mostly truthful; but instead, one would likely happen, by solitary reading and thinking, into opinions that were partly right and partly wrong. Encouraged by her theory-obsessed mentor Lady Blanche, and her fond friend Lady Psyche, Princess Ida was unlikely to weigh her convictions against any dissenting authorities—until she met the Prince.

The song "Tears, Idle Tears" and Princess Ida's response to it take up more explicitly the question of history's relevance in the present age. When a young woman sings of "Tears [that] from the depth of some divine despair / Rise in the heart, and gather to the eyes, / In looking on the happy autumn-fields, / And thinking of the days that are no more" (IV:22–25), Princess Ida answers this heartfelt song disdainfully:

> "If indeed there haunt
> About the moulder'd lodges of the past
> So sweet a voice and vague, fatal to men,
> Well needs it we should cram our ears with wool
> And so pace by. But thine are fancies hatch'd
> In silken-folded idleness; nor is it
> Wiser to weep a true occasion lost,
> But trim our sails, and let old bygones be,
> While down the streams that float us each and all
> To the issue, goes, like glittering bergs of ice,
> Throne after throne, and molten on the waste
> Becomes a cloud; for all things serve their time
> Toward that great year of equal mights and rights.
> Nor would I fight with iron laws, in the end
> Found golden. Let the past be past, let be
> Their cancell'd Babels; tho' rough kex break
> The starr'd mosaic, and the beard-blown goat
> Hang on the shaft, and the wild fig-tree split
> Their monstrous idols, care not while we hear
> A trumpet in the distance pealing news
> Of better, and Hope, a poised eagle, burns
> Above the unrisen morrow." (IV:44–65)

The attitude of the Princess to history represents an extreme that the poem is meant to overcome. As Carlyle wrote, the present is "the living sum-total of the whole Past" and so the past is always with us—that scene now muted, this now shining brightly. In the two decades preceding Tennyson's composition of *The Princess,* medieval and classical scenes obtruded regularly upon the public imagination, most notably the Eglinton Tournament of 1839. Tennyson would have heard of or witnessed such attempts to "bring the Middle Age forward" (as Kingsley put it), which rarely satisfied the nostalgia of the instigators and highlighted the futility of trying to recover medieval (or classical) vitality. These efforts struck many as "fancies hatch'd / In silken-folded idleness," but Tennyson's view is more moderate. The Princess is a theorist, who believes that she can resist the feelings engendered by history and "the days that are no more." But in becoming a fully developed human being, she cannot look exclusively toward the future, and she must do more than gather up those bits of the past that justify her powerful Hope (such as the list of great women in Psyche's history lesson).

In Part VII, when the Prince is recovering from his battle wounds, the Princess reads "to herself" the famous idyll "Come down, O maid, from yonder mountain height" (VII:177). She has been on the mountain, but she must now return to the valley, where love dwells. What good are her theories if not brought back to earth? What good the treasures of her college if not shared? As in the "Palace of Art," where the soul retires to a "cottage in the vale," Princess Ida abandons the mastering, panoramic view, and chooses the occluded and intimate view below. When the Prince finds love, he loses his doubts, and "all the past / Melts mist-like into this bright hour" (VII:334–35). In this mutual completion, Tennyson suggests that the soul grows richer not from mastery or possession, and certainly not from isolation, but from the many-sided development afforded by love, the true seeing.

Medley as "Symbolic Form"

Eileen Tess Johnston has written of the way that "medley," with its dual meaning of "mêlée" and "mixture," "gives symbolic form to the whole of *The Princess*" (568). Not only is the poem itself a literary medley, but it also promotes a concept of the individual as mixture within the mêlée of social life: "The entire central tale [. . .] presents the substitution of mêlées with medleys, of confusions with mixtures, of combats, literal and figurative, inward and outward, with creative interchange" (563). The two meanings of medley mirror the Janus-face of nineteenth-century eclecticism—the volitional and the naïve. The original meaning of medley, dating back to the fourteenth century, related exclusively to combat, especially "hand-to-hand fighting between two parties of combatants" (*OED*). We can demonstrate Tennyson's awareness of the archaic meaning of medley in his use of "mellay," a Middle English variant of medley (563; *OED*): "Down / From those two bulks at Arac's side, and down / From Arac's arm, as from a giant's flail, / The large blows rain'd, as here and everywhere / He rode the mellay, lord of the ringing lists" (V:491).[6] As medley's derivative meaning of "mixture" evolved, a "disparaging sense" soon attached to it. In this later sense, which became dominant as early as the seventeenth century, a medley was a "heterogeneous combination or mixture (of things)" or "a mixed company (of persons differing in rank, occupation, etc.)" (*OED*). Taken more broadly, as part of the symbolic structure of the entire work, Tennyson prompts his readers to consider the degree to which the heterogeneous elements of the poem (past and present, male and female, heroic and mock-heroic) remain in conflict or finally harmonize, leaving open the question of whether the poem performs the positive, now rarely used, meaning of medley, namely "A cloth woven with [. . .] different colours or shades" (*OED*).

As a prominent aspect of his philosophy of medley, Tennyson illustrates the Princess's journey from self-contained, one-dimensional individual to integrated, eclectic self. In promoting this idea of self as medley, he employs the motif of the lost child as a link throughout the entire poem.[7] Significantly, the necessity of losing the child is one of the principal arguments of the poem's feminist voices, a "theory" that must be undermined in order to achieve reconciliation between male and female. In Part I, when the Prince first wonders about the "fancies" (I:94) that make the Princess refuse to marry him, he hears from her father that Lady Psyche and Lady Blanche "fed her theories . . . Maintaining that with equal husbandry / The woman were an equal to the man" (I:129–30). Since women "had but been, she thought, / As children; they must lose the child, assume / The woman" (I: 135–37). Her fervor on this point leads her to produce "odes / About this losing of the child" (I:139–40). When the Prince arrives at the college disguised as a woman, paying compliments to the Princess, his "language proves [him] still the child" (II:44)—when men flatter women thus, they are treating them as either children or fools.

The seriousness of Princess Ida's argument against such degrading treatment is not entirely discounted by the poet-narrator, but the interpolated songs (sung by the women) do offer a counterpoint to the Princess's theories. The first song, "As thro' the land at eve we went," tells of a husband and wife who have quarreled without knowing why; the falling-out is a blessing in disguise when they "kiss again with tears" above the grave of the child "We lost in other years" (I:254, 256). The cause of separation is the thing forgotten, while the child and the shared memories of the past unite them. When Psyche recognizes her brother Florian in Part II, we see the same process unfold. At first Psyche maintains her separateness from him, declaring that she has "no country, none; / If any, this; but none, Whate'er I was / Disrooted, what I am is grafted here" (II:200–202). This denial of the past is a denial of the child and sister that she was, a requirement, she believes, of becoming a fully developed woman; but Tennyson means for us to see that Psyche has lost more than she has gained—disrooted, grafted, she is no more a whole person. (Later in the narrative, when she loses her baby, we see the psychic damage she sustains before recovering the child inside and outside herself.) Florian recalls her as "brother-sister Psyche, both in one" (II:236), intimating that the future Psyche prophesied in her lecture had already come to be: "everywhere / Two heads in council, two beside the hearth, Two in the tangled business of the world..." (II:155–57). As in the song, when the lovers "kiss again with tears," Psyche and Florian kiss and "betwixt them blossom'd up / From out a common vein of memory / Sweet household talk, and phrases of the hearth" (II:292–94). Their reunion prefigures the other unions of the poem, just as the mother in "Sweet and low, sweet and low," the song that follows Part II, promises her baby that its father will come home soon.

Much of the core narrative of *The Princess* concerns the means by which we develop an authentic self, whether it is by integrating our past and present selves, or by acknowledging the admixture of male and female in each of us. The prototype for Princess Ida comes from the past—a woman warrior larger than life—and the character that the seven male narrators create seems particularly inauthentic because she strives after greatness, wanting her deeds to live on into the future. Setting aside the question of whether Tennyson was sympathetic to feminist goals, it is still possible to consider the importance of the issue of authenticity in his underlying philosophy of medley—why can we not simply select the elements that we want to make up our personality? During one of his seizures, the Prince sees Ida as a "hollow show" and "Her college and her maidens empty masks" (III:169, 171); and in the same moment sees himself as "the shadow of a dream, / For all things were and were not" (III:172–73). When the college collapses following the battle between their two countries and the maidens rush to help the fallen soldiers, the narrator wants the reversion to seem inevitable. The Prince saw the maidens as empty masks, because they tried to conceal their true selves beneath the aspect of the scholar; but they could not simply choose to cut themselves off from their past selves or, Tennyson no doubt wants the reader to see, from their femininity. Ida's new persona is a hollow show and the girl she once was is her "dead self" (III:205); but neither does the Prince yet possess a stable identity, trapped as he is among the ghosts. When the wounded Prince kisses Ida, she glows, like the statue of Sir Ralph, coming to life again: "Her falser self split from her like a robe / And left her woman" (VII:146). Lest this resolution seem an utter denial of Ida's ambitions, and of a true dialectic within the poem, Tennyson has prepared the reader for a more nuanced handling of the hero and heroine's union. Defending the Princess before the battle, the

Prince makes the case to his father that women "have as many differences" as men (V:173) and must be accorded "More breadth of culture" (V:180). His father opposes change because he fears confusion between the sexes, the muddle of a middle:

> Man for the field and woman for the hearth;
> Man for the sword, and for the needle she;
> Man with the head, and woman with the heart;
> Man to command, and woman to obey;
> All else confusion. (V:437–41)

This is precisely the kind of extremist position that Tennyson's eclecticism is meant to overcome. At this moment, the Prince sees his father the king, the soldiers' camp, and the college all turned to hollow shows: "I seem'd to move in old memorial tilts, / And doing battle with forgotten ghosts, / To dream myself the shadow of a dream" (V:467–70). The repetition of his seizures at moments when the Princess and his father have been rigid, unyielding, and one-dimensional underscores the need for the happy medium of like in difference that is the goal of the poem:

> For woman is not undevelopt man,
> But diverse. Could we make her as the man,
> Sweet Love were slain; his dearest bond is this,
> Not like to like, but like in difference.
> Yet in the long years liker must they grow;
> The man be more of woman, she of man;
> He gain in sweetness and in moral height,
> Nor lose the wrestling thews that throw the world;
> She mental breadth, nor fail in childward care,
> Nor lose the childlike in the larger mind;
> Till at the last she set herself to man,
> Like perfect music unto noble words;
> And so these twain, upon the skirts of Time,
> Sit side by side, full-summ'd in all their powers,
> Dispensing harvest, sowing the to-be,
> Self-reverent each and reverencing each,
> Distinct in individualities,
> But like each other even as those who love. (VII:259–76)

It would be too easy to dismiss this passage as a clear articulation of a doctrine of separate spheres such as Ruskin sets out in "Of Queen's Gardens" (1865), seductive precisely because women seem powerful within their special sphere of, say, "childward care." That does not seem to be what Tennyson is after here. Instead he presents the culmination of the idea of the self as medley, a complex tune whose notes do not readily blend with another's music, but that will over time and with practice seamlessly interweave as each catches the other's melody. The woman and the man do not surrender individuality or distinctiveness, but reverence themselves and each other; they grow more like, more in harmony, as they love.

This sense of emergent harmony is what Tennyson wanted to hear in his own poem, and he struggled with a sense of failure—worried that *The Princess* was cacophony and unresolved conflict instead of interwoven harmonies. While most readers could accept the objectives of blending past and present, and male and female, it was much more difficult for them to admire Tennyson's generic mixture. The Princess and the Prince might have been heroic, but in making them "to suit with time and place," he injected a degree of mockery that made it hard to swallow the high-flown sentiments his characters expressed. For example, in Part IV, after the Princess has complained of men's mock-love and the mock-Hymen who sang of it, the poet-narrator describes several scenes in unmistakably comic fashion. When the Princess falls into the river, and the Prince pulls her to safety, he is "Oaring one arm, and bearing in my left / The weight of all the hopes of half the world" (IV:164–65). Looking out for the Amazon pursuit, the unmasked Florian hides "behind a Judith, [and] underneath / The head of Holofernes peep'd and saw..." (IV:207–8); while the Prince surrenders to the Goddess of Memory: "At last I hook'd my ankle in a vine / That claspt the feet of a Mnemosyne, / And falling on my face was caught and known" (IV:248–50). Taken before the Princess, the seriousness of her words makes the comedy that has just played out seem particularly sour. Women are the "laughing-stocks of Time, / Whose brains are in their hands and in their heels, / But fit to flaunt, to dress, to dance, to thrum, / To tramp, to scream, to burnish, and to scour, / For ever slaves at home and fools abroad" (IV:496–500). If the poet-narrator has been making light of the Princess's gravity, and poking fun at the idols of the women's college, then what are we to make of Ida's demand that women be taken seriously as the capable equals of men? Struck by another of his seizures, the Prince sees "The Princess with her monstrous woman-guard, / The jest and earnest working side by side" (IV:540–41), making the reader quite certain of the poet's self-conscious mixing of the heroic and the mock-heroic. In the Prologue, it was clear that the heroic would be associated with traditional form, but the reverence for tradition was to be coupled with the mock-heroic of the modern sensibility. It was no longer possible to have the purity of heroism, unmixed with a conviction that this nineteenth century was not a heroic age. To pretend otherwise would be fatal to Tennyson's purpose, which was not to present a sham Middle Ages, but rather to show the strands of the past woven into the present. When Ida moans that she has "made [her]self a queen of farce" (VII:228), Tennyson does not want us to take her for a fool, or to believe that her dreams were foolish, but to see that she did take herself too seriously. This was a kind of intellectual and emotional rigidity that had to be avoided. The poet-narrator acknowledges, finally, the problem with tone, that he had "wrestle[d] with the burlesque," sensing that the women "wish'd for something real" (Conc.:16, 18). Why, his critics ask, did he not make the Princess "true-heroic" and "true-sublime"? The framework of the poem made such purity impossible, and so he "moved as in a strange diagonal" between "the mockers and the realists" (VII:227, 224). Such a mixture was, however, typical of the mode of argument used by Cambridge Apostles. As Henry Sidgwick explained, "it was rather a point of the apostolic mind to understand how much suggestion and instruction may be derived from what is in form a jest—even in dealing with the gravest matters" (qtd. in Allen 6). For example, in the early 1830s when the political situation was at its most volatile, some of the Apostles helped to put out fires in the countryside near Cambridge and wrote a mock-heroic poem about rick-burning to commemorate their deeds; but as Peter Allen notes, they "pause in their comic treatment of these events to reveal their sympathy for the distressed and rebellious agricultural workers" (122). For the Apostles, the comic mode was available both as a means to defuse the tensions inherent in the situation, and to satirize the ideological extremes that had brought the nation to such an impasse.

An example of serious play not unlike the Apostles' poem "Swing, at Cambridge," *The Princess* tries the fit of various styles of "dress" *and* various poetic modes. Both formally and thematically, Tennyson creates a persuasive picture of inclusiveness. Instead of seeing such eclecticism as naïve, he makes it a requirement for human progress. His self-conscious structuring of the poem as medley, with its multiple significations of mixture, mêlée, and mélange, marks a significant attempt to formulate a poetics adequate to the nineteenth century, that is, a poetics of eclecticism.

The Critical Debate on Tennyson's Eclecticism

In the first half of this chapter, I have considered the extent to which eclecticism was abroad as an idea in the 1820s and how essential it was as a mode of thought among the Cambridge Apostles. I also examined the varieties of eclecticism in *The Princess,* particularly how Tennyson uses volitional eclecticism to avoid ideological extremes and achieve compromise—a mélange or medley. He models a theory of poetry based on the philosophical underpinnings of the idea of medley, which shares with philosophical eclecticism its sense of human knowledge and experience as a unified field. His effort represents, I believe, a conscious decision to make use of the medley form to create something quite original, a poetics that would represent the nineteenth century to itself. In the second half of this chapter, I want to analyze two reviews of the poem that bring into sharper focus what was at stake for Tennyson in making eclecticism a central issue in the poem as well as its creative inspiration.

Criticism of *The Princess* was sharply divided between those who discerned a unifying design in the poem—Tennyson was being deliberately eclectic—and those who could find no unity in the poem and saw in it only a grotesque reflection of perplexed modernity. In approaching Tennyson's poem *as medley,* C. P. Chretien and Aubrey De Vere reach opposite conclusions about the medley's effectiveness *as poetry.*[8] Chretien regards the poem's eclecticism as limiting its significance to the present only, whereas De Vere discerns in the poet's versatility a trait common to poetic genius throughout history. Sensitive to the peculiar character of the age, both reviewers acknowledge that Tennyson's genius is perhaps uniquely suited to represent and express it. For Chretien, however, this compatibility is no cause for rejoicing or for elevating Tennyson to the poetic pantheon: "The present is so exclusively his sphere that he cannot transcend it," and thus he can never become the "poet of our common humanity" (220). Unlike Kingsley, who praised Tennyson's grounding of the aspirations of the present on the foundation of all past and present times, Chretien asserts that Tennyson does *not* grasp that which is "permanent in human nature" (220) and, furthermore, that he lacks the power to synthesize the material of history: "He knows that age succeeds to age, blowing before it a noise of tongues and deeds, of creeds and systems. But he is never bold enough to hope that he has discovered the key which can open the mystery of the world, and detect order in its confusion" (220). As figures for the confusion he perceives in Tennyson's mind—a disorder that the poet, on some level, *allows* to persist—Chretien depends on tropes of architecture and design. In an ironic reflection of the Prologue of *The Princess* with its miscellaneous collection of persons and artifacts—"A Gothic ruin and a Grecian house"—he begins by comparing the mind of the poet to a cathedral, which, seen from the outside, "should impress us with the multiplicity of its parts" and, seen from the inside, "should be eminently *one*": "Here we should trace, in its full solemnity, that Form which all variety of detail must vary without concealing. Here, the diversity of individual taste is to be lost in the majesty of the mastermind. In that capacious area, all are instinctively to look one way, to think one thought, and wonder" (201).[9] Chretien imagines that a poet should have, like Christianity, a single great idea that he or she transmits to posterity. Even if the message is dispersed throughout many different poems, there should be an underlying unity—a "master mind"—that connects them all.

Because Tennyson's principal gesture in *The Princess* looks to Chretien like "fantastic playfulness" (202–3) and not like moral mastery, this long work reproduces the "faults and beauties" of Tennyson's shorter works, "an alteration in degree, but not in kind; an improvement, if any, which was not a development" (202). The improvement Chretien has in mind does not raise Tennyson above his old level among the poets, but only places him "in a larger and more ornate niche" (202). Tennyson's ornamentation in *The Princess,* since it does not augment the unity of the work, and, like many Victorian buildings, suffers from excessive heterogeneity, is taken as proof that the great poem promised by the early "fragments" would never come. Unlike the cathedrals whose walls show the accretion of history—"the noise of tongues and deeds, of creeds and systems"—*The Princess* fails to master its inheritance. Tennyson's work confirms Chretien in his belief that the "Tennysonians" have been persisting for too long under the delusion that the beautiful moments his poetry gave them would not simply burn out, but would feed poetry's eternal flame. Chretien asks his readers what this fantastic, disordered collection signifies beyond the individuality of its collector:

> Here was an antique statue glittering in the whiteness of its marble, and there a picture, somewhat Rubenesque, in a gold frame; on the one hand, Haroun Alraschid sat, in "merriment of kingly pride," under a canopy; on the other, a weather-beaten S. Simeon prayed, harangued, and soliloquized from the top of his pillar. Sometimes the poet's scroll displayed combinations of grave words—good, and beauty, and duty, and love, and so forth—which puzzled the metaphysician, who endeavoured to make their meaning definite; a turn of the leaf brought the reader to some lucubrations of a half profane, half maudlin tone, and a very vinous and questionable morality. What does it all mean? we asked; or rather, what does the author mean? Is he content that his mind, as reflected in his volumes, should rival an auction room, or an embryo museum, both in the multifariousness and confusion of its beauties? Are the pictures never to be hung up, the statues never to be placed in their niches? Shall the caliph, and the pillar saint, and the Will Waterproof, be crowded together in a capacious tent,

or picnic in common on the sward? Shall we never be shown how abstract philosophical speculation is made to bear on the beauties of nature, or cast a reflected light over dim pictures of imaginary ladies, some as sensuous, and all as sleepy, as any that Lely drew? (201)

Resembling nothing so much as a cabinet of curiosities (or "Palace of Art"), Tennyson's poetry has more in common with those "embryo museums" of the seventeenth and eighteenth centuries than it does with the modern, rational, didactic museum. The cabinet of curiosity lacks any organizing principle beyond the peculiar mind of the individual collector, while the collections of modern museums both result from and proceed according to a master narrative. In one of the most impressive instances of the tension between eclecticism and a merely eclectic world, the Victorians expended a great deal of effort in converting curiosities into ordered collections, even as the tide of miscellaneous goods threatened to overwhelm them. As Chretien's analysis suggests, Tennyson fails to be eclectic, and only reflects the eclectic confusion of modern life. Like many of his contemporaries, he seems to suffer from what Thomas Hardy would call, in his 1881 novel *A Laodicean*, "the malady of unlimited appreciativeness," a condition affecting those whose pleasure in the variety of the historical inheritance renders them incapable of ordering it, or selecting from it the necessary preliminaries to achieving a functional synthesis. Though Chretien acknowledges the distinct modernity of Tennyson's mental "auction room," he will not admit that the conditions producing Tennyson will prevail in the future, thus permitting unborn generations to appreciate "the poet of today." The "specimens of fossil beauty" (218) found throughout Tennyson's works have not been reanimated, and serve only to "adorn" the present; therefore, the "mine of conceits" (221) that is *The Princess* will itself one day be a curiosity, since, *as poetry,* it cannot speak to the future. Chretien picks up here on several important themes related to the critique of eclecticism: it is inauthentic, because it seeks to bring together things and ideas not organically related; it is the result of taste, rather than feeling, since passion is needed to reanimate the dead; it is merely picking and choosing from old styles, rather than synthesizing an authentic new style.

Alongside the critique of material eclecticism in the nineteenth century, there frequently appears a flanking attack on intellectual eclecticism and its analogous confusions. Anticipating one of the symptoms of modern poetry Kingsley scrutinizes in "The Prevailing Epidemic," and strengthening his claim that Tennyson's intricate beauties do not conceal any depth of meaning, Chretien also exposes Tennyson's dubious use of abstract, philosophical language. Far from casting illumination on the "multifarious" beauties of his poetry, Tennyson's philosophical dalliances compound the "confusion." The "combinations of grave words" only "puzzle[ ] the metaphysicians" without leading them to a single thought that would dissipate the Tennysonian fog. Chretien's irritation with Tennyson's "philosophical" digressions stems at least partly from the critic's perception that the poet is attempting to exceed his ability. Tennyson's reputation rests (as Chretien believes it should) on his facility with language, a talent that for Chretien is more a matter of mechanical skill than profound insight. If Tennyson possessed a great mind, then his "fluency" would signify "something far higher than a mere facility in using well-assorted words," and would "proceed[ ] from no skill in mechanical contrivance, but from an intellectual harmony" (205). The *mechanical* perfection of poetic language that Chretien observes in Tennyson had, of course, long been a cause for worry among those critics who believed that the best days of the art were past, and never to be recovered. Dryden's refinements of poetic language looked patently inferior to Macaulay, whose preference for Milton derived from the older poet's apparent isolation from the poetic fashions of his day. Peacock reckoned that the fashionable poets (the imitators, the refiners of language, the men of the Silver Age) had gained in mechanical skill what they had lost in passion. Tennyson, it would seem, could only amplify their perfection, or fall off from it. All his skill with the "instrument" avails him nothing without passion, which "like lightning, fuses and blends things most unlike with each other" (209). Chretien denounces Tennyson's introduction of antique and foreign expressions as one of the least successful attempts to blend old and new within *The Princess;* these Greek constructions might exhibit his erudition and provide a novel source of interest, but they chiefly highlight the lack of integration that on every level mars the poem. Even Tennyson's famous ability to render landscape realistically meets with Chretien's disapproval. Immediately after praising Tennyson for "tread[ing] in the very steps of nature," Chretien asserts that such "microscopic delineation is, to a great extent, artificial." He then sharpens his portrait of Tennyson as effeminate minstrel, a poet concerned only with the instrument, and never with the air: "These drawings with a fine point are necessarily wanting in power. They betray at every turn the labour of composition. No one could suspect Mr Tennyson of being a rapid writer, and throwing off his best passages without a sense of effort. This is one reason why he fails in his attempts to express strong emotion. He betrays none of the characteristic quickness of passion. However great his subject, he knows but one method of treating it. He sits down calmly before hero, saint, or villain, and draws his portrait, stroke by stroke, as a lady would paint a flower" (207). Eclecticism has been associated with the stylistic chaos of material culture, and with the strife of religious and philosophical dissent; now, after building a picture of Tennyson's mind as an "auction room" and his philosophy as multifarious and confused, Chretien asks his readers to judge the poet's fluency with language as yet another aspect of his modernity—*and* his eclecticism. Recalling Kingsley's preoccupation with the effeminacy of modern poets, evident, he thought, in their lack of affective power, and in their mental confusion, Chretien's denigration of Tennyson's skill as effeminate is revealing: Tennyson's effeminacy and his unfitness to create a poem that will be heard through the ages are symptoms of the same disease—"the prevailing epidemic" as Kingsley deems it—which produce the same negative result, a meaningless poem.

If C. P. Chretien traces Tennyson's weaknesses as a poet to his tendency to overpower a subject with the peculiarities of his own mind, Aubrey De Vere finds in the poetry of Tennyson the very model of genius at work. Rather than attributing the expression of modern sensibility found in Tennyson's works to transient features of the age, De Vere recognizes that Tennyson reveals more to us of future humanity than of past. He credits "the Versatility of [Tennyson's] imagination" (211) with holding together the "discordant materials" (209) of a poem whose design canvasses the entire scene of nineteenth-century life. A kind of "English Decameron" (205), the poem travels swiftly among scenes of science, classical and medieval history, education, art, politics, and the trials of modern love, by means of "imperceptible gradations and continual delicate variations of key" (Kingsley, "Tennyson" 250). De Vere concedes that only the genius of a Tennyson could successfully modulate such variety without becoming ridiculous: "Any but the most delicate execution in this respect would have produced a very coarse, not to say grotesque, effect. The humorous and the serious are, however, seldom here found antithetically opposed to each other; but blend rather, like the different shades of some fine material shifted in the light" (205). This positive evaluation of the poem's heterogeneity stands in sharp contrast to Chretien's, which emphasized Tennyson's failure to "blend" the old and the new, the comic and the tragic; De Vere rather commends the poem's ingenious combinations, which justify his high opinion of Tennyson. The versatility to which De Vere refers the success of *The Princess* places Tennyson, he argues, firmly within the great tradition of English poetry.

De Vere uses the opportunity of reviewing new editions of the works of Shelley and Keats alongside *The Princess* to position Tennyson in relation to "ideal" and "national" schools of poetry, and to predict that the greatest of living poets will eventually overtake the Romantics' lofty reputation. In his definition of versatility, De Vere is careful to delineate its positive and negative tendencies; and in this respect, his explanation of the strengths and weaknesses of the "versatile" imagination parallels descriptions of the "eclectic" imagination: "Versatility is sometimes indeed in poetry as in life, only the exercise of that imitative power which betrays a want of individuality, original conception, and tenacity of purpose. In such cases it proceeds from quick and volatile sympathies vividly open to external impressions, and from that clear unwrinkled mind, which, being all surface, apprehends and reflects all forms of thought, but is incapable of receiving a principle or resting in a conclusion. Poetry thus produced is the result neither of genius nor of high ability; but of that cleverness which bears often more resemblance to the former than to the latter" (212). If the poet is pliant before every impression, and resists no one and nothing, then the words flowing from his or her pen must be as superficial as the thoughts from which they spring. De Vere's "negative" versatility invites comparison to the philosophical eclecticism that comes under attack during roughly the same period. G. H. Lewes and Hippolyte Taine worried that Victor Cousin's genius for reflecting and imitating the precepts of various systems of thought would hasten the destruction of all philosophy, and all system. They contended that Cousin selected the best from others' philosophies because he had no original system of his own—no original genius, but only the semblance of it. To borrow De Vere's terms, Cousin "apprehends and reflects all forms of thought, but is incapable of receiving a principle or resting in a conclusion" (212); in fact, Cousin teaches that the eclectic can never rest in any conclusion, but must continually revise the truths he has discovered through contact with new ideas. The dialectic so central to Cousin's eclecticism, and certainly influenced by his long association with Hegel, is crucial both to De Vere's theory of poetic genius and to the structure of *The Princess*. Tennyson's detractors argued that he mirrored the perplexity of modern life without offering his readers any higher ground—to apprehend the character of the age, to erect a new philosophy, or to found a new school of poetry. These are the worries, too, of Kingsley in "The Prevailing Epidemic": the self-absorbed ramblings of too many modern poets betray the "want of individuality, original conception, and tenacity of purpose" that De Vere recognizes as the negative tendency of a versatile imagination. But versatility, De Vere argues, is also a "high poetic attribute" that Tennyson possesses in greater abundance than any other living poet: "It consists in mobility of temperament united to a large mind, and an imagination that diffuses or concentrates itself at will" (212). While Chretien might agree with De Vere as to Tennyson's versatility, he bases his case against Tennyson's place in literary history on his lack of mastery over his "multifarious" subjects. Versatility without a mastering gesture leads only to restless confusion.

De Vere interprets Tennyson's output (up through *The Princess*) in exactly opposite terms: Tennyson's "'various talents' are united with 'the single mind,' [giving him] 'moral might and mastery o'er mankind'" (212), *and* a coherent poetic vision. The versatility capable of achieving genuine synthesis, of "resting" in a conclusion, "enables the poet to apply his own experience, analogically and by imaginative induction, to regions unknown and forms of life untried,—at once passing into the being of others and retaining his own" (212). (Not coincidentally, this is precisely what Tennyson says in *The Princess* about men and women joined in love.) Being able to undergo the influence of diverse impressions, and still retain an inner core of self, seems essential both to an eclectic-critical method and to Tennyson's approach to poetry, as De Vere understands it. As proof of Tennyson's likely high position in the annals of his art, De Vere refers his readers to Tennyson's ability to create characters who combine "attributes of universality and individuality," appealing both to common humanity, which does not lose its essential contour over time, and to the peculiar character of the age. In other words, Tennyson eclectically combines those features of human nature that will endure, and explores the external features of the age alongside them, helping to determine what the nineteenth century will bequeath to posterity. De Vere emphasizes that having only the ability to portray realistically individual character does not make a poet great; equally, any attempt to exist solely upon the ambrosia of the universal leads to a "want of moral depth and tenacity." Poets who neglect the reality of their own time "remain for ever but imitators" (212); therefore, the poet who would speak to his fellows and to posterity must successfully navigate the unknown in the mundane vessel of his own time and place. Among recent poets Tennyson is unusual, De Vere believes, in his exploration of ordinary human "affections which depend not on instinct or imagination alone, but which, growing out of the heart, are modified by circumstance and association, and constitute the varied texture of social existence" (226). For De Vere, it is Tennyson's "versatility of heart" that makes him almost uniquely able to sympathize with persons caught up in the particular circumstances of life in the nineteenth century.

As Isobel Armstrong argues in *Victorian Scrutinies,* the "sympathy" so highly valued by De Vere is more than an expression; it forms part of a pragmatic critical vocabulary, which placed "emphasis [. . .] almost invariably on the human or social reference of the work of art, on its *effect on the reader,* and hence on the needs of the reader" (6). According to Armstrong, for Victorian critics sympathy was "the faculty of sharing and understanding the situation of another person by being able to change places with him in imagination" (9). In Tennyson this "faculty of sharing" was no doubt instinctive, but was also reinforced in his character by his interactions with the Apostles. The greatest poets of necessity possess the largest sympathies, and these sympathies derive from "versatility of heart." De Vere believes that all great poets, whenever and wherever they live, share this fundamental trait, a "vital power" common to "poetical periods" in history: "when men have ceased to be pressed down by the selfish wants of savage life, and not yet hardened and made selfish by the conventions of over civilization, the imagination has a versatility and sympathy, a vital power, which at other periods is quite unknown" (213). Like the historians Macaulay and Carlyle, De Vere links natural religion and natural poetry to periods when imaginative sympathy predominates; however, he asserts that, along with only a few other modern poets, Tennyson retains the capacity for sympathy that makes great poetry possible.

Confident that poetry will continue as long as the faculties producing it exist within at least one person, De Vere disagrees with those who believe that "modern England does not contain the materials of poetry": "those materials unquestionably are obscured by the rubbish that now overlays them; and to extricate and exhibit them requires [. . .] unusual poetic discernment" (227). Tennyson, of course, is unusually capable of "extricat[ing] and exhibit[ing]" the poetic aspects of modern life. While the youthful Tennyson's versatility might have been of a more pliable character, in maturity his gift shows itself in a widening sympathy with the circumstances of his age and country. De Vere considers the early eclectic phase as a necessary one in the evolution of Tennyson's poetic powers:

> The versatility of a very young poet is indeed but a part of his docility. He will listen, with the susceptive faith of youth, successively to each of the great masters of song; and the echo which remains in his ear will in some degree modulate his tone. He will trace every path in which the Muse has trod, in the hope of reaching that point from which they diverge; and it is well that he should try all things, provided he hold fast to that which is best. The infancy of the life poetic, like that of all life, learns much by unconscious imitation; but it can only so learn when the poet possesses those high faculties which seek, through imitation, only to work out their own development. True genius will soon cast aside whatever is alien to its individual nature; while, on the other hand, incorporating into its proper substance all poetic elements that are truly congenial, it will blend them also with each other, and stamp upon them a unity of its own. The poet will be original when he wields collectively the powers that were once his

only alternately; and versatility will then have been exalted into a higher
gift,—that of comprehensiveness. (213)

As a picture of artistic development, this passage hints at the central role of eclecticism in forming a personal style. Greater than the sum of one's education, and yet bearing some structural similarities to it, eclecticism enables an artist to develop an individual style; the artist must acquire an intimate knowledge of the traditions of his or her art, imitate its greatest masters, *and* possess the genius to withstand their influence. The artist of genius discards "whatever is alien" and incorporates whatever is "congenial," "blend[ing]" these elements in a unified creation—an idea of genius that was central in the Renaissance, but which became controversial in the eighteenth century with the shift to a Romantic conception of originality. De Vere conveys a powerful sense both of the artist's stature relative to history and the enlargement of the artist who "wields" its riches; he also suggests how comparatively rare must be the birth and maturation of a true artist, especially as history increases the number of potential stylistic models. Although most critics would have recognized that not all great works of art were immediately available for imitation, in the nineteenth century they were unlikely to cordon off any historical period as being irrelevant to contemporary artistic production; in fact, the greatest difficulty artists such as Tennyson confronted was the superabundance of history, that nothing would be excluded from speculation and appropriation. For De Vere, the nineteenth century shows its poetic versatility in its ceaseless effort to find new sources of poetic inspiration; the materials of poetry seemingly exhausted, the age invents a world of its own: "All regions of the earth have been ransacked for the materials of poetry—Persia, Arabia, Hindostan, Iceland: it has been the ambition of the poet to reproduce the forms and manners, if not the mind, of the remotest lands; and where the imagination has been content to tread on English soil, it has commonly taken refuge in some remote period of our history, and recounted the Saxon legend, the chivalrous exploit, or the feuds of border warfare" (214). Far from judging such eclectic form and content as symptomatic of the confusion of the age or, worse, as signaling the death of poetry, De Vere hails this romantic eclecticism as proof of the health of the art. Furthermore, a poet's choice of subject will depend not on the circumstances of the age, but primarily on his or her "moral nature, and the preponderance in it of a vivid sympathy with reality on the one hand, or on the other, of an ardent aspiration after the ideal" (214). De Vere's delineation of the "ideal" and "national" schools of poetry (the former concerned with embodying the abstract and the latter focused on reality) leads him to the crowning instance of Tennyson's supremacy: while at first he resembled his immediate precursors, Keats and Shelley, whose poetry seemed "distilled from poetry, rather than drawn from the living sources of life and truth" (227), Tennyson has progressed from ideal abstractions to "robust and characteristic" national sentiments.

In De Vere's view, Tennyson's greatness derives from his amplitude, his wider view and greater variety in representing the natural, moral, and intellectual spheres of human existence. Combining a thorough comprehension of timeless human nature with an acute recognition of the aspirations of his own age, Tennyson thus achieves the desired synthesis of antique and modern sentiment, ideal and national humanity. In evaluating the general thrust of De Vere's argument, it is evident that he did not need *The Princess* to convince him that Tennyson would ultimately have "taken his place among the true poets of his country" (227); but the particular features of this long poem did allow De Vere to demonstrate Tennyson's progress from youthful to mature "versatility," and, more specifically, the poet's masterful investigation of modern attitudes against the background of an eclectic historicism.

When Walter Pater wrote in 1888, "In this late day certainly, no critical process can be conducted reasonably without eclecticism," he had in mind as his "justifying example" the poetry of Tennyson: "How illustrative of monosyllabic effect, of sonorous Latin, of the phraseology of science, of metaphysic, of colloquialism even, are the writings of Tennyson; yet with what fine, fastidious scholarship throughout!" (*Appreciations* 17). Pater never doubted that Tennyson's versatility was a sign of his greatness. In his view literature was not the transcription of "mere fact, but of fact in its infinite variety, as modified by human preference in all its infinitely varied forms" (10). In *The Princess* Tennyson grasped the complexity of this "soul-fact" through his eclecticism. Despite the sincerity of the convictions that underlie Chretien's analysis of the poem, or perhaps because of them, he is unable to perceive that Tennyson's medley is more than a collection of unrelated facts—the mental "auction room" he thought an apt representation of the poet's mind—but rather reality modified by taste *and* feeling. The eclecticism that seemed to be picking and choosing, a "mine of conceits," is the foundation of Tennyson's originality; it is the source of his creativity. The very commonness of naïve eclecticism hints at the difficulty of the eclectic process, and the rarity of this form of genius. Although Tennyson did not intend to make the *form* of his poem an issue of contention, it was inevitable that his medley would provoke anxious discussion about the intellectual and material eclecticism of the age, particularly as it touched upon moral questions. Tennyson was keenly aware of the dangers of a solitary and solipsistic eclecticism, as we see in "The Palace of Art," and *The Princess* strains with the effort to find its *juste milieu*. Even in the present age, with our noted fondness for problem texts, no one would want to argue that *The Princess* is the great work of Tennyson's maturity; but because it is less than perfect, and betrays the poet's struggles with form, it gives us a template with which to approach a far greater work such as *In Memoriam,* which is no less eclectic than its precursor. It, too, canvasses dialectically "the state of current taste and thinking," before finally resting in synthesis. There, finally, Tennyson's eclecticism brings him to a religious compromise that would come to represent the spiritual aspiration of an entire generation, and to a poetic form that would give his generation its voice.

CHAPTER 5

Charles Kingsley
The Alexandrian Age

𝓘n an 1887 article for the popular monthly *Macmillan's Magazine,* the critic and biographer Mowbray Morris christened Victoria's reign the "Alexandrian Age," but Morris's appropriation of the idea of ancient Alexandria signaled a profound uneasiness about the present. Searching for the "precise note of [the] age, so as to fix and catalogue it for future use," Morris settles upon "Alexandrian," because Victorian culture, like its Hellenistic precursor, produced no "spontaneous and creative" literature, but only a vast quantity of writing that was "derived from that already existing" (28). In the first Alexandrian Age, Roman imperialism had spread the Greek language and Greek civilization everywhere, but "the free Greek life that had made that language what it was, and inspired that literature, was dead" (28). By the time Alexandria had become a center of learning, literary success was accomplished through discovering and obeying critical canons, making literature the prey of "mannerism and affectation." In the nineteenth century, an identical spirit of scholarly cosmopolitanism had infected literary production, giving birth to a highly stylized literature that could not, Morris argued, satisfy the "native manliness" of the English character: "the general tendency is to a minute, dissecting, curious mood, more given to pulling down than to building up" (31). To be Alexandrian, then, was to be ingenious, artificial, pedantic, effeminate, and decadent. The man largely responsible for shaping the idea of Alexandria upon which Morris establishes his analogy is Charles Kingsley, whose writings in the 1850s generated a disturbing and, ultimately, unflattering correspondence between past and present, between Roman Alexandria and Victorian Britain.[1]

Set in Alexandria, Egypt, Kingsley's 1853 novel *Hypatia; or, New Foes with an Old Face* is chiefly a sermon against two dangerous tendencies in nineteenth-century Christianity: the Oxford movement, powerfully represented by John Henry Newman; and what Kingsley calls "Anythingarianism," manifest in the teachings of American transcendentalist Ralph Waldo Emerson. The struggle to find a middle way between dogmatism and unbelief had already been played out in the religious conflicts of fifth-century Alexandria, a setting that would provide Kingsley with a safe cover for the exposition of his distinctive theology. Kingsley's *via media* would construct a religion that resonated with the spirit of the age, encompassing a democratic and "muscular Christianity," which regards as sacred all ordinary human relations and common duties of life, *and* the truth found in the competing doctrines of Judaism, Roman Catholicism, and spiritual philosophy.[2] The problem for the historian of ideas is to discern the extent to which Kingsley sees this eclecticism as a necessary precursor to the acceptance and renewal of Christianity, and the danger that excessive latitude poses to its institutional forms.

The historical novel *Hypatia* is therefore a crucial document in the history of the idea of eclecticism, and in the representation of Alexandria as the stage on which the drama of modernity is first enacted. The story of a fifth-century Neoplatonist philosopher is set within a city crowded with religious and philosophical notions; Christians, Greeks, Goths, Jews, and Romans vie for primacy in a city that has become the crossroads of ancient (and, in the repetition "New Foes with an Old Face," modern) thought. Like his teacher F. D. Maurice, Kingsley believed that the historical process involved the reconciliation of opposing forces in society. On the stage of cosmopolitan Alexandria in the year 413 Kingsley places the democratic creed of Christianity and aristocratic Neoplatonism; corrupt Eastern Christianity and healthy Western Christianity; Latin government and the Gothic, barbarian North. He opposes Alexandria and Rome; Rome and the Christian Church; Christianity and Judaism. In a tremendous struggle, from which no party can emerge unscathed, the Old World must give way to the New. But for Kingsley no form of belief ever disappears, but each instead is absorbed into new forms of belief, which better serve the Zeitgeist.

From the beginning two of the main characters are associated with rigid, doctrinaire positions—Philammon, the young ascetic monk, and

Hypatia, the Greek philosopher—and so neither is likely to achieve the *via media* that philosophy-torn Alexandria requires. Philammon remains a monk and Hypatia is brutally murdered by a Christian mob. The third of Kingsley's main characters, Raphael Aben-Ezra, a philosophical Jew who converts to Christianity, is the true hero of the novel and the representative of Kingsley's middle way.[3]

Hypatia and the Eclectic Philosophy

Gathered from various sources, the story of Hypatia, perhaps especially the prurient details attached to descriptions of her murder, inspired in Kingsley such an intense vision of the philosopher's final moments that he decided to write the novel that would cost him more intellectual labor than any of his other works, and which he hoped would secure his future literary reputation.[4] Still, the touching picture of Hypatia, cornered in a church and gazing at a portrait of Christ before being torn to shreds by the mob, could not overcome his basic lack of sympathy for the pagan philosopher, a failure of imagination that could account for the obscurity into which the novel has fallen. Kingsley does not tell Hypatia's story, or even Raphael's, so much as that of the city, in which the world-spirit was at that moment working out its destiny. Hypatia is introduced in chapter II, as the representative of the "dying world" who believes in the "old creeds, while every one else is dropping away from them," and though the gods no longer speak to their oracles, she will "show [herself] superior to the herd, by seeing the boundless depths of living glory in myths which have become dark and dead to them, [and] struggle to the last against the new and vulgar superstitions of a rotting age" (13). Kingsley introduces here the keynote of Hypatia's philosophy, namely its aristocratic exclusiveness. Her students are fashionable "loungers," gentlemen "fops" who flock to her lectures to admire Hypatia's beauty and to memorize the latest theories, which change, seemingly, with every season. (As the burly Goths proclaim, these philosophers cannot even be called men.) Hypatia's hatred of Christianity stems from its association with a "low-born" and "illiterate" deity, whose fanatical followers believe that the Son of God died for the beggar as much as for the noble, the beautiful, or the wise. In their pursuit of salvation, Christians are taught to disregard "learning, authority, antiquity, birth, rank, [and] the system of empire which has been growing up, fed by the accumulated wisdom of ages" (18). Hypatia shrinks from contact with anything dirty and vulgar and surrounds herself with books and statuary. Though her virtue and sincerity are never in question, Kingsley clearly sees Hypatia's sin as one of pride, especially the pride attached to rank and beauty: "she sits enshrined far above the noise and struggle of man and his work-day world" (125). Even when she "stoops to conquer" the young monk Philammon, newly arrived from the desert and clad in animal skins, she decides to teach him because she sees in his face and form a remnant of Greek beauty and masculinity that bespeaks his noble soul. Believing that the beautiful youth must be of patrician birth (in fact Philammon was born a slave), Hypatia declares to her father, "I have longed so to find one such man, among the effeminate selfish triflers who pretend to listen to me" (125). But Hypatia's admiration of Philammon's masculine beauty goes no further; indeed, her attitude of horror toward marriage strongly resembles the life-denying asceticism of her opponents.

Even Hypatia's renowned philosophizing appears to Kingsley to be merely a worship of appearances: Hypatia reveres the beauty of the ancient religion, but ignores its truths. Nonetheless, Cyril, the Patriarch of Alexandria, believes that while her lecturing continues, "and the great and powerful flock to it, to learn excuses for their own tyrannies and atheisms, so long will the kingdom of God be trampled underfoot in Alexandria" (23). Kingsley certainly exposes his eponymous heroine to the charge of sophistry. Hypatia regards books as she does men: "the soul is all with which our souls must deal; and the soul of the book is whatsoever beautiful, and true, and noble we can find in it" (99). Her eclectic method allows her to erase what is vulgar and ordinary in a poet such as Homer and to elaborate on the soul of the text, rejecting the notion that anyone could take Homer literally and leave his reputation intact: "Can they suppose that the divine soul of Homer could degrade itself to write of actual and physical feastings, and nuptials, and dances, actual nightly thefts of horses, actual fidelity of dogs and swineherds, actual intermarriages between deities and men, or that it is this seeming vulgarity which has won for him from the wisest of every age the title of the father of poetry? Degrading thought!" (99). Hypatia professes to open her heart to receive influences from all the great thinkers of the past, "from whencesoever they may have come," but the standard of selection—whatever is beautiful, true, and noble—lies in her immediate consciousness. She chooses what is "true" for her own use, which presupposes that she must carry in herself, as Zeller writes of eclectic philosophers generally, "the standard for decision between true and false, and that truth is directly given to man in his self-consciousness" (Zeller 17–18). Hypatia's approach to Homer makes the eclectic method look very dangerous. In dispensing with the senses, the body, and the round of ordinary human experiences, Hypatia strips literature of just those elements Kingsley placed at the center of all his work—

Kingsley sermonizes in order to teach people how to *live* as Christians. By contrast, Greek philosophy seemed "to distance its devotees from the common, 'unenlightened' human being" (Hawley 294). The starting point for Hypatia's Neoplatonism cannot be the world, because the world cannot be read literally: "Where is truth but in the soul itself, Facts, objects, are but phantoms matter-woven—ghosts of this earthly night, at which the soul, sleeping here in the mire and clay of matter, shudders and names its own vague tremors sense and perception" (98). Even as Hypatia proclaims that all individuals are part of the universal being, she rejects the notion that she should have any communion with her earthly yoke-fellows until she enters into "The Nothing, which is The All" (105). Hypatia's rapturous description of her "abysmal Deity" chills Philammon, who was raised on the notion of a personal God made man, a God made for the world.

Although Kingsley certainly understood the historical role of Neoplatonism in reconciling Christianity and pagan philosophy, he identified in Hypatia's teaching a spiritual and speculative confusion that was infecting intellectual Christians in his own time. The "unseen and indefinable" energy that Hypatia worshipped in the manifold forms of the Greek pantheon typifies for Kingsley a very modern dilemma. Hoping to satisfy their reason of the existence of God, many of his contemporaries sought refuge in vague definitions of a higher being, such as Hypatia offered her students, but in taking this route to faith, people consistently confuse the human and the divine, the first descent to "Pantheistic Infidelity" (294). Hypatia wonders why "men should be content to grovel, and be men, when they might rise to the rank of gods" (15) with her philosophy. Newman and the Tractarians traced this spiritual self-reliance back to the Protestant Reformation; even the Evangelical movement was a "house built upon [the] sands of inward assurance and private judgment" (Willey 77). By rejecting papal authority, the Reformation had subjected the Church to the State; by relying upon individual judgment, Protestantism had opened the way to sectarianism and ultimately to unbelief (77). Kingsley approached the problem somewhat differently than Newman. To his wife Fanny he wrote against the teaching that "leads back again to the Self[; . . .] when tempted to look inward, it is well to go immediately and work for others" (qtd. in Hawley 291). He feared the theological speculation and the scientific materialism that had produced an epidemic of doubt in the nineteenth century. Reviewing a stack of truly awful poetry in 1851, Kingsley derided the tendency of the modern poet to exalt himself as a God: "Older and cleverer men than you, with false prophet Emerson at their head, bandy about in their new Every-man-his-own-God-maker cant, the most holy and awful words, and apply unblushingly to man the attributes of Almighty God, little knowing how thin a paper-wall parts their Autotheism from sheer, blank, honest, manful Atheism,—honest and manful, because it wears no rouge, and has courage to look steadily at the reflection of its own skeleton-face" ("Epidemic" 498). Emerson was again the target of Kingsley's polemic in the 1852 dialogue *Phaethon: Loose Thoughts for Loose Thinkers*.[5] Kingsley wanted to expose the pitfalls of the American philosopher's "Anythingarianism," which was characterized by a "carelessness about induction from the normal phenomena, coupled with this hankering after theories built upon exceptional ones" (*Essays* 357). This "craving for signs and wonders" evident in pseudosciences such as phrenology and mesmerism always and everywhere accompanies, he felt, a decline of faith in God. In *Phaethon* the speaker's encounter with the American Professor Windrush reminds him of the Neoplatonists of Alexandria, and "their exactly similar course—downward from a spiritualism of notions and emotions, which in every term confessed its own materialism, to the fearful discovery that consciousness does not reveal God, not even matter, but only its own existence; and then onward, in desperate search after something external wherein to trust [. . .]" (358). This persistent learning without ever coming to the truth led many of Kingsley's contemporaries to give up believing altogether. Emerson did not embrace honest and manful atheism, but assisted in the reformation of Unitarianism, so that it became a religion of reason and, for Kingsley, an intellectual rather than a moral Christianity. Ironically, perhaps, the Unitarians supported Kingsley's position against the Tractarians, but their latitudinarianism went far beyond Kingsley's desire for an inclusive, simplified doctrine. American Transcendentalism was also associated with Eclecticism, via the French philosopher Victor Cousin, whose writings were widely translated in the United States during the 1830s and 1840s. Though Cousin never achieved a significant following in England, he was wildly popular in France and well received in the United States.[6] Cousin believed that the nineteenth century had recognized itself in eclecticism because it was essentially a philosophy of compromise and reconciliation. Ignoring the circular logic of his claims for eclecticism, Cousin argued that it provided a system for the judgment of systems, giving the individual a method for discriminating the portion of error that was mixed with the portion of truth in any system.

In the years immediately preceding the composition of *Hypatia*, Kingsley wrote frequently, in a variety of contexts, against the eclecticism that was pervading Victorian intellectual culture. Poetry had become eclectic, and each poet a little deity presiding over his wretched creation: the "Pseudo-Spiritualistic-Eclectico-Hypoplatonico-Pantheistico [. . .] Sentimentalism that is infecting the greater part of our bad poetry, and too much of our good, is an ugly sign of the 'unreality' [. . .] that is abroad in the world" ("Epidemic" 498). Echoing Carlyle, he urges poets to "get some definite and truthful meaning for your own words before you utter them," or, better yet, to stop writing and *do* something (499). When he took up his post as professor of English literature at Queen's College, London, in 1848, Kingsley designed a historical survey that would stop young women "wander[ing] up and down in all sorts of eclecticisms and dilettantisms" (*Essays* 247). He would retire the "Elegant Extracts" and "Select Beauties" typically given to female students, and let them feast on whole works. He would limit their contact with foreign literature, until they were secure in the literary history of their own nation. Without this firm foundation, "selfwill and irregular eclecticism are the natural results" (260). A woman must recognize the excellence of her own culture lest she by a "sudden revulsion [become] an equally prejudiced cosmopolite and eclectic" (263). In his review of Anna Jameson's study of Catholic art, Kingsley defines what it means to be an eclectic: "One who, in any branch of art or science, refuses to acknowledge Bacon's great law, 'that nature is only conquered by obeying her;' [*sic*] who will not take a full and reverent view of the whole mass of facts with which he has to deal, and from them deducing the fundamental laws of his subject, obey them whithersoever they may lead; but who picks and chooses out of them just so many as may be pleasant to his private taste, and then constructs a partial system which differs from the essential ideas of nature, in proportion to the number of facts which he has determined to discard" (216–17). In this instance Kingsley associates the Manicheanism of Byzantine and some early Italian painting with a deep "spiritual eclecticism" that constructs a fictitious "angelic nature" from "all which is negative in humanity, [because] they were prone to despise all by which man is brought into contact with this earth—the beauties of sex, of strength, of activity, of grandeur of form" (217). This Manichean art, for Kingsley, was not only spiritually eclectic but also effeminate and prudish. Spiritual expression for them was everything, but Kingsley cautions that it could never represent the whole of human experience. What is consistent in Kingsley's writing during this period is the constant association of eclecticism, effeminacy, and decadence; but his intellectual tendency certainly leans toward eclecticism as he praises Anna Jameson for bringing forward those lessons Protestants can learn from the "Romish" church, before Catholicism finishes on the rubbish heap of history.

Philammon and the Inhumanity of Ascetic Christianity

Kingsley opposes the sectarianism and dogmatism of the early Church because they embody a destructive, dissective tendency that threatens to destroy Christianity from within. An even greater threat to the health of religious and political life was asceticism, a rejection, Kingsley felt, of God's gift of our human nature. In his view monastic life constitutes a refusal to serve God, a religious imperative that can be satisfied only by serving others; the contemplative life is inherently selfish.[7] Though Kingsley reserves a sneaking admiration for the severe physical discipline under which the monks live, his notion of manhood must include sexual relations with women. However, his version of muscular Christianity and its frank celebration of "animal spirits" could be seen to promote male profligacy. Indeed, many condemned *Hypatia* as an obscene book on just these grounds.[8]

The peculiar emphases of Kingsley's picture of early Christianity are explicable when considered as a lifelong battle against Tractarian principles, which he associated with John Henry Newman. Susann Dorman argues that Newman intended his religious-historical novel *Callista* (1855) as a correction of the negative view of the early Church found in *Hypatia*. Previously, in "The Religion of the Day," Newman had characterized the Christianity of the nineteenth century as one-sided, retaining only the "brighter side of the Gospel,—its tidings of comfort, its precepts of love" (qtd. in Dorman 178). This was, Newman felt, "the religion *natural* to a civilized age, and well has Satan dressed and completed it into an idol of the Truth" (qtd. in Dorman 178). By leaving out the darker side of revelation, Christianity had developed a "wholly optimistic emphasis" that would have evolved anyway with the cultivation of reason and the refinement of taste and sentiment. Newman does not credit Christianity with directing the course of civilization, as Kingsley does, but regards the present emphasis in religion as "rational" picking and choosing, the recourse of "shallow men, in *every* age" (qtd. in Dorman 179). In *Callista* Newman sought to undermine Kingsley's humanist emphasis by associating liberal Anglicanism with the excessive refinement of eclecticism.

In *Hypatia* Kingsley explicitly condemns the gloomy asceticism of Newman and the Tractarian movement, which threatens "The very ideas of family and national life—those two divine roots of the Church, severed from which she is certain to wither away into that most godless and cruel of spectres, a religious world" (xiv). Kingsley clarifies his position yet again in an 1856 book review of *Hours with the Mystics:*

> As long as "the salvation of a man's own soul" is set forth in all pulpits as the first and last end and aim of mortal existence; as long as Christianity is dwelt on merely as influencing individuals apart—as "brands plucked, one here and another there, from the general burning"—so long will Mysticism,

in its highest form[,] be the refuge of the strongest spirits, and in its more base and diseased forms the refuge of the weak and sentimental spirits. They will say, each in his own way: "You confess that there can be a direct relation, communion, inspiration, from God to my soul, as I sit alone in my chamber. You do not think that there is such between God and what you call the world; between Him and nations as wholes—families, churches, schools of thought, as wholes; that He does not take a special interest, or exercise a special influence over the ways and works of men—over science, commerce, civilisation, colonisation, all which affect the earthly destinies of the race. All these you call secular; to admit His influence over them for their own sake (though of course He overrules them for the sake of His elect) savours of Pantheism. Is it so? Then we will give up the world. (*Essays* 328–39)[9]

For Kingsley, mysticism is too much akin to "selfish individualism" to do any good in the world it has abandoned. Newman, whom he calls "the one real mystic of any genius" writing and teaching in Britain (301), offers no message to compassionate the many, but preaches personal salvation at the expense of community and family life. The "true reason of mystical isolation" is despair of the world, a denial that "God's human world is sacred" (329). A corollary of Newman's position was its denial of the possibility of evolution in what he considered to be revealed dogma. Like other liberal Anglicans, Kingsley wanted to be self-conscious about the historical changes that were inevitable in every facet of every civilization. For the Tractarians this self-consciousness produced a rational, secular Christianity ever more removed from its divine origin.

The Oxford movement thus idealized the past and ignored the present, offering no solution to the "crisis of civilization, which for the Liberal Anglicans was first and foremost a national crisis" (Forbes, *Liberal Anglican* 102).[10] Perceiving similarities between the religious and political conflicts of nineteenth-century Britain and fifth-century Alexandria, Kingsley believed that he had identified both the nature of the crisis and its resolution. Kingsley puts his most naïve character, Philammon, a young ascetic monk, onto the treacherous stage of Alexandrian history without any knowledge of the world or of human nature outside his tiny desert monastic community. In the striking opening chapter, Philammon, comely as a Greek god and poised on the brink of manhood, stands gazing upon the forbidden pictures of an ancient Egyptian temple. As he contemplates the beauty of the women, he wonders if they are really all damned, both for being pagans and for appearing to take so much pleasure in their earthly existence. He has never seen a woman before and does not really know what a woman is. Perhaps he is led by curiosity, or by his restless youth, to seek his fortune in the city under the patronage of Cyril. Kingsley gives Philammon two guides, who show him apparently irreconcilable views of the city. The first, Eudaemon, a friendly philosophical porter, takes him to the harbor, ringed with palaces and towers, a grand panorama built by the "benighted heathens": "Did Christians make all this? Did Christians build that Pharos there on the left horn—wonder of the world? Did Christians raise that mile-long mole which runs towards the land with its two drawbridges, connecting the two ports? Did Christians build this esplanade, or this gate of the Sun above our heads?" (54). This is a valuable object lesson for the ignorant monk, but it is immediately balanced by an image of squalor that rivals Victorian London. "In squalid misery, filth, profligacy, ignorance, ferocity, discontent, neglected in body, house, and soul, by the civil authorities, proving their existence only in aimless and sanguinary riots, there they starved and rotted, heap on heap, the masses of the old Greek population, close to the great food-exporting harbour of the world" (62). The local parish priest who serves as the second guide exposes him also to the hypocrisy of the Christian Church in Alexandria, which has become bloated on the riches of the falsely pious. Both guides teach Philammon to use his eyes and to judge for himself.

Inspired by the Patriarch, he is overcome with a desire to convert Hypatia, to lead her captive in fetters before the church fathers. Hypatia converts Philammon instead, from a strapping young desert god into a pale, doubting student. His failure to confront her with his Christianity results at least in part from his disappointment in the character of the monks. They are uneducated and dirty, caring nothing for higher spiritual questions and wasting their time gossiping about the latest sectarian squabbles. When a gang of monks loots the Jewish quarter and drives its inhabitants from the city, Philammon is repelled by their random destructiveness: "a shudder of regret, he knew not why, passed through him, as he saw the mob tearing down pictures, and dashing statues to the ground. Heathen they were, doubtless; but still, the Nymphs and Venuses looked too lovely to be so brutally destroyed" (78). Philammon's thread in the novel might unravel the reader's faith: does Christianity represent progress, or is it the beginning of the end? What has this religion built to replace the grandeur and knowledge of ancient times? Perhaps taking his cue from Anna Jameson, Kingsley maintains throughout the narrative a steady appreciation for Greek, Roman, and Hebrew culture, always taking care to bring forward those elements that would best serve a healthy Christianity.

Philammon's teacher, the Abbot Pambo, preaches a doctrine of serving God through forming the most human bonds possible, a form of Christianity that demands the renunciation of neither love nor the world. When one of the desert monks guiltily confesses that he often longs to return to Rome, Pambo retorts that it is "Better to have something to love—even something to weep over—than to become in some lonely cavern thine own world,—perhaps, as more than one whom I have known, thine own God" (131). For Kingsley, mysticism in philosophy or in religion often leads one to the same bad place—to selfish individualism and self-deification. By serving humanity, Pambo argues, we keep God in view: "by fleeing into solitude a man cuts himself off from all which makes a Christian man; from law, obedience, fellow-help, self-sacrifice—from the communion of saints itself" (131). Philammon must learn that a thousand invisible ties, of variable thickness, connect him to every other living being. But in Alexandria the odds are against him making that discovery. Eudaemon observes that "the monks would exterminate the human race in a single generation, by a voluntary suicide" (53), but his philosophy does not stop him beating his Christian, black African wife. Hypatia, who will not marry or condescend to form familiar relationships, tangles Philammon in the web of her philosophy. The patriarch Cyril, in seeking to establish God's kingdom on earth, has forgotten its primary laws. Only the parish priest tries to teach Philammon how to live as a Christian. He does not learn this lesson fully until he discovers that he has a sister, Pelagia, who has been living as the concubine of the Goth Amalric. This is the "divine reality of kindred," the force that will deliver him from his very Victorian crisis of faith and identity. When Hypatia, who had set going the "earthquake-roll" in his soul that "jarred every belief, and hope, and memory" (110), has no word for the sinner Pelagia, Philammon realizes the emptiness of his idol's philosophy and smashes it to pieces. In his first Alexandrian dream, Philammon had a vision of Goths dancing, Hypatia with horns and cloven feet, riding three hippopotami around a theater, Cyril cursing and pelting him with flower-pots, and Pelagia as an angel with peacock's wings (62–63). This last image, the key to Philammon's story, is reminiscent of the first in a series of William Blake's proverbs in *The Marriage of Heaven and Hell:*

> The pride of the peacock is the glory of God.
> The lust of the goat is the bounty of God.
> The wrath of the lion is the wisdom of God.
> The nakedness of woman is the work of God.

Like his spiritual precursor Blake, Kingsley sought to undermine the prudishness of Christian doctrine. To accomplish this, he tried to balance the beauty of Greek art and culture and the civic and military life of Rome with the asceticism and mysticism of Christianity. But this "muscular Christianity" could be seen, as James Eli Adams has argued, as another, equally rigid form of self-discipline.[11] The portrait of Raphael Aben-Ezra would seem to support this claim; when he is driven from his home, he determines to spend his life wandering, a second Diogenes, not in search of a home, but in search of a man. He has given up his wealth, his friends, and his philosophy. In the clothing of a beggar, he crosses and re-crosses the Mediterranean, searching as much for an ideal of masculinity as for something to believe.

Raphael's *Via Media*

Early in his career, Kingsley came under the influence of the Cambridge Apostles, who "taught him that the truth could be approached from any number of avenues" (Hawley 289). His subsequent call for an Anglican *via media* outraged both dissenters and Tractarians. Though he too had once looked for the middle way, Newman, a convert to Roman Catholicism, came to believe that "to weaken a *part* of the dogmatic structure is to weaken the *whole*" (Willey 81). But "Newman's view of history was apocalyptic," while Kingsley's was progressive (81). For Kingsley, latitude made the historical process easier to bear, and, at least in his novel, history gave the victory to a Christianity founded on human nature. The hero of the *via media,* Raphael Aben-Ezra, is a Hellenized Jew whose mother was raped by barbarian invaders; he is a cosmopolitan and an eclectic, a man of taste and action, capable of ascetic discipline and filial love. Arriving at the brink of nihilistic skepticism, he blends the best features of the doctrines he has encountered in Alexandria within a conciliatory Christianity.

The truth of Kingsley's picture of the modern spiritual condition lies in his attention to the mixture of creeds that must exist within his conciliatory model of historical development. The late Hellenistic-Roman period in which Kingsley's novel is set provides him with just such a rich and potent mixture of peoples and their gods.[12] Rome had become the purveyor of syncretistic religion and of Christianity, which could itself be "the most complete example of ancient religious syncretism—in this case Hebraism combined with Hellenism" (Grant xv).[13] Kingsley wanted to show that Christianity prevailed at this moment in time, and would exist in some form for all time, because it was most adaptable to the needs of the human heart. An equally strong reason for its triumph over paganism was its capacity for assimilating other creeds and thus more easily reconciling converts to the loss of their native religions. Christianity was not only syncretistic but also cosmopolitan—a religion that could transcend its national origin.

When Raphael is thirty-three years old—the Christological age—he leaves Alexandria to become "the new Diogenes." Before Raphael decides to imitate the Greek Cynic and become a citizen of the world, he must first sever his ties with the Jewish community of Alexandria and give up the economic and political power he had wielded there, in his ironic and off-handed manner. Kingsley never leaves the reader in doubt, however, that Raphael holds immense powers in reserve. Philammon perceives this superiority in Raphael's "ease and grace, that courtesy and self-restraint" which seem to come not from rank but from "real strength" (79). Raphael has taste, self-possession, refinement, and good breeding—he is every inch the Victorian gentleman; but insisting on Raphael's self-control and independence, Kingsley more precisely invokes the gentleman in his role as head of family and promoter of the common weal. Raphael has all the advantages of a superior masculine type; Kingsley must next demonstrate the necessity of this man's conversion to Christianity. Hypatia recognizes in Raphael her only real student, "her superior in [. . .] moral earnestness and strength of will"; but she is "chilled by the disagreeable suspicion that he was only playing with her [. . .] while he reserved his real strength for some object more worthy of him" (96). Next to the "unfathomable Jew," other philosophers were mere "spinners of charming cobwebs [and . . .] builders of pretty houses," in which no one wanted live. Raphael is too smart and too skeptical to rest in Hypatia's Neoplatonism, which is no more habitable than the creeds of her rivals.

Arriving spiritually at "The Bottom of the Abyss," where his intellect has crippled his capacity for belief in anything in or of the earth, Raphael is moved by the simplicity of his dog Bran's instinct to protect her puppies, even when her master urges her to abandon them: "'You are right after all! Here are nine things come into the world; phantasms or not, there it is; I can't deny it. They are something, and you are something, old dog; or at least like enough to something to do instead of it; and you are not I, and as good as I, and they too, for aught I know, and have as good a right to live as I [. . .]'" (151). The dog's "mere common sense" encourages Raphael's belief in a tangible creation not of his own making, neither transcendent nor ineffable, but insistently alive. Soon after this "wonderful conversion" (261), Raphael encounters another example of filial devotion in the person of Victoria, a Roman Christian whose father has been wounded in battle and who is about to be sold as a slave. Still inclined toward fatalism, Raphael wants to leave them to their cruel destinies, but Bran "by no means agree[s] with his view of the case" and knocks one of the captors to the ground. Raphael follows the dog's lead, conceding, "You are at least a more practical teacher than ever Hypatia was" (155). Roused to action, Raphael frees Victoria by murdering the two men and reuniting her with her father, and thus emerges violently himself from the "slough" of philosophy. Though he has abandoned his nation, he begins to forge new ties, to acknowledge himself part of a network of relations and obligations. He can no more abandon his newfound family than Bran can desert her puppies. One thing only restrains him from converting to Christianity at this point: Victoria is destined for the convent. Raphael cannot accept any religion that promotes celibacy—that threatens to sever the ties of love that bind him to this woman.

Raphael's next teacher—after Bran—is Synesius, the "Squire-Bishop," a Christian priest who was a husband and father. As Susan Chitty has observed, Synesius "bears a striking resemblance to Kingsley himself" (154): "A man of magniloquent and flowery style, now without a vein of self-conceit; yet withal of overflowing kindliness, racy humour, and unflinching courage, both physical and moral; with a very clear practical faculty, and a very muddy speculative one [. . .]" (*Hypatia* 251). Kingsley winks at his reader here, acknowledging that Synesius's love of speculative philosophy, much like his own, has an element of self-delusion in it, but that will not stop his preaching "that eclectic farrago of his, which he calls philosophic Christianity" (95). No doubt Kingsley was sympathetic to Synesius's unorthodox belief system. Unwilling to anticipate the end of days or to leave off philosophizing in order to preserve theological dogma, Synesius was at best a reluctant instrument of the Church fathers (Davis 437). And having been taught by Hypatia, Synesius is well placed to mediate between Neoplatonic philosophy and Christian dogma (Davis 437). For Kingsley, therefore, Synesius belongs to the tradition of Christian eclecticism represented by Clemens of Alexandria (d. 215 C.E.). Clemens's ideal of the philosophical method was *eklektikon* (Donini 16), a process of preserving what was good and rejecting what was false in competing philosophical systems.

During the Victorian period, writers on Alexandrian Christianity singled out Clemens as the "peculiarly Christian philosopher" and representative theologian of that city, and the "head of the most learned Christian body of his day" (Tulloch 615; "Alexandrian Christianity" 408). But these two reviewers represent widely divergent views of how nineteenth-century Christians ought to regard a Christian tradition of eclectic thought. The 1855 reviewer of Kingsley's *Alexandria and Her Schools* objects to the idea that a "world-philosophy," which is embodied in Clemens's eclecticism, can account for all phenomena or incorporate all the diverse thought that has been: "To the Jews he had given the law; to the Greeks philosophy; and Clemen[s] seemed to have imagined some analogous preparatory dispensation to the Magian and the Brahmin; and each had served as a schoolmaster to lead them to Him, and His last crowning dispensation, which completed and superseded all" ("Alexandrian" 413). While the reviewer does not deny that the Alexandrian Christians thus "aimed to include all mankind in the scheme of God," he feels with some of his contemporaries that millions of souls *were* destined to die without salvation, just as millions of seeds in nature were never fertilized. Like Synesius, Clemens did not accept this principle of waste in nature; indeed, he believed that God had "lighted" every person at birth, and "every man lived continually under a dispensation from him," carrying a portion of the world-philosophy from which all would benefit.

Taken from Tennyson's *In Memoriam,* the epigraph to Kingsley's volume represents well the ambivalence of Christian eclecticism:

Our little systems have their day;
They have their day and cease to be;
They are but broken lights of thee,
And thou, O Lord, art more than they. (11. 17–20)

John Tulloch, in "Alexandria and Its Christian School," is much more sympathetic than Kingsley's 1855 reviewer to a tradition of thought that acknowledges how Christianity is caught up in the historical process—that it is not necessarily the "crowning dispensation." Clemens claims our respect, Tulloch argues, because "in circumstances so different from ours, and amidst a complication of moral and speculative difficulties, which at least rival ours, [he] maintained so steadfastly the great principles of the faith" (616). If one does not attend to the implications of the parallel between Alexandrian and Victorian Christianity, then, Tulloch asserts, "The very meaning of the present life around him must be hid from him as he gazes with a stolid dogmatism on its varied expressions. Still more will the past and its lessons be shut to him—a blind gallery hung round with expressive portraits and great scenes, not one of which he can see, through the dimness of superstition or the mists of bigotry with which he invests them" (616). If "Alexandrian Christianity" comes to mean heresy in the nineteenth century, there will be little opportunity to benefit from it. Systems do have their day and they do change, but as "broken lights" of God, they must be reverently preserved and studied.

A wanderer before settling in Alexandria, Clemens had studied with teachers from at least six countries, which makes him an apt prototype also for Raphael, a cosmopolitan who finds his spiritual home in Christianity.[14] Just as Raphael has learned to believe in what he sees, he learns to read sacred text as the historical record of the thoughts and actions of human beings who once were alive; for example, the *Song of Songs,* he discovers, is about physical love, not a mystification of the divine. He also has to become skeptical of skepticism, before he can rest in Christianity. Eclectic vacillation is, as Eduard Zeller argues, the unrest of skepticism, which for most thinkers precedes "positive conviction" (20). Such a model accords with Kingsley's philosophy of history, which allows for periods of *unrest,* such as the fifth century and the nineteenth century, during which systems of thought are in flux. The spirit of the age is with Raphael—not with the eponymous heroine, who is slow to realize her world is dying. Her philosophy has entered a period of decline, in which it becomes eclectic, but she struggles still for lost certainty and purity. A Greek who worships the old gods, Hypatia cannot believe in progress, only in perpetual decadence. Raphael's faith in the future is reflected in his love for Victoria, whom he "saves" in marriage. And although Kingsley makes a point of telling us that Raphael and his child are killed in war, that knowledge does not detract from his assertion that we have to participate in the world, that we have to act for good. Not only does Kingsley allow the reader to know the fates of individuals, but as a historian he must also admit that the institutions of the Eastern Church did not produce a *final* reconciliation, a true world-philosophy, but "absorbed into the sphere of Christianity all which was most valuable in the philosophies of Greece and Egypt, and in the social organization of Rome, as an heir-loom for nations yet unborn; and laid in foreign lands, by unconscious agents, the foundations of all European thought and Ethics" (*Hypatia* xi). No other philosophical system was capable of providing a point of union that might unite the disparate peoples of Alexandria, who retained their separate national identities while inhabiting a cosmopolitan city. Cosmopolitanism provided not the solution to the crisis, but rather a broad-based religious unity founded on the model of family life. Although it was Kingsley's intention to defend the Broad-Church, latitudinarian position in *Hypatia,* he principally succeeded in making "Alexandria" the byword for a decadent society. His claims for the *via media* were obscured for contemporary readers by an ugly picture of the early Church and his inability to distinguish the middle way from the haphazard eclecticism that pervaded Alexandrian *and* Victorian thought.

Chapter 5: Charles Kingsley

Eclecticism and Empire

In an 1870 article provocatively titled "Eclecticism and Brahmoism," Robert Milman, the bishop of Calcutta, provides, after Kingsley, the most extended exploration of Alexandria as an analogue of Victorian Britain, including, however, a decisive rejection of the reconciliation between faiths that might be expected to flow from the incorporation of territories. Milman identifies Alexandria as the birthplace of the eclecticism that was threatening the integrity and, ultimately, the survival of Christianity; and, by linking the compromise philosophy with Britain's empire in India, he indicates the source of the present danger. The cosmopolitanism engendered by empire is, for Milman, the source of its weakness.

Intending to disgust the upper-middle-class, High-Church readers of *Good Words,* Milman describes Roman Alexandria, with its "mingled [and] eclectic population," as "cosmopolitan." Like the man who gave the city its name, Alexandria provided a temporary point of contact and center of union among the empire's varied dominions (793), but it failed to create an enduring confederation among peoples "vain, fickle, and shifting with every breath of popular opinion" and following "but one god, [. . .] gain" (793). But it is Alexandria's intellectual capital—a wasteful extravagance of knowledge for its own sake—that draws the bishop's censure. Surrounded by "its menagerie, its botanical gardens, its halls of science, its schools of art, its studious cells" (793), the city's great museum stands, for the bishop of Calcutta, as the symbol of the Alexandrians' way. The mixed Greek, Roman, and Egyptian architecture of the museum, its varied collections, and its international school exert a profound influence on the character of the philosophy produced there. In their effort to explain the mysteries of the universe, the Alexandrian scholars communed not only with the "accumulated treasures of the poetry, the history, [and] the philosophy of past ages" (793) but also with distant regions beyond the empire, such as Persia and India. Rather than choosing between the philosophies then "in vogue at Rome," the Alexandrians used their Neoplatonism to "forc[e] those systems which seemed even antagonistic into a curious and unnatural union with it" (794). Unwilling to accept the authority of a single author or a single system, the Eclectics joined in "unnatural union" elements of any system that pleased them, "like a clever piece of mosaic" (794). Only cleverness of this reckless type could unite "Theism and Pantheism" and "look with affected or real impartiality on all the various philosophies and religions which came within the scope of their attention" (795). Condemned for their impartiality and clever reasoning by all true believers, the Eclectics won few converts. With no guide but one's own mind among the tangled web of past and present philosophies, eclecticism would never be a reliable path to the truth.

Observing the similarities between the Roman and the British empires, Milman implied that this second great historical encounter between East and West was likely to be as dangerous, and uncertain of outcome, as the first; indeed, as imperialism assimilated other cultures, Christianity came increasingly under threat. Milman believed that the Indian scholars of the Brahmo Somaj—the "modern Eclectic school" in India—were promoting an "unnatural union" of opposites like that produced in doomed Alexandria. He explained the unwillingness of the Brahmo scholars to accept Christianity as the consequence of "superficial knowledge" rather than admit that their dilemma might result from the contradictions and inconsistencies of the Christian religion itself confronted with Hinduism and other philosophies. That the Brahmoists might detect the incipient collapse of a system of belief based on the willful ignorance of competing systems does not occur to the bishop; blindness is "moral courage" and credulity is "manly resolution" (799). To acknowledge value in the learning of disparate cultures—as the Brahmoists willingly did—was to admit some truth and some error in each, and, in Milman's view, to risk the precipice of unbelief.[15]

Milman sought to provide his readers with a stronger foundation for their Christian faith by exposing the weaknesses inherent in eclectic thinking. The Alexandrian Eclectics were, in his view, little more than very diligent explorers of curiosities who accumulated vast quantities of knowledge, which they turned to little account (792)—that is, they did not find reasonable proof of a higher being. In stark contrast to Kingsley, who freely admitted the mixed heritage of Christian theology, Milman ignored the contributions of Christian eclectics such as Clemens and Synesius who adapted Alexandria to their religion and their religion to Alexandria. Indeed, the bishop's negative judgment of the Eclectic school seems to rest on its "aristocratic elevation of knowledge," "over-refinement," "conceit in intellect," "fastidiousness," and "picking and choosing" (799, 796)—just those tendencies that he saw reappearing in the intellectual and artistic culture of Europe in 1870. Kingsley had also condemned the aristocratic exclusiveness of dogmatic religion in the Oxford movement *and* the sectarian and speculative debates of nineteenth-century Christianity—these were his "new foes" with old Alexandrian faces. But Milman's hysterical reaction to "all the various expressions of opinion and belief, or unbelief, with which Europe [was] fermenting" showed that the crisis would not easily be resolved (798). Weakly echoing Kingsley's exhortation to preserve intuitive belief as the bulwark against doubt, Milman could only recommend the dignity of submission to the higher authority of the Church. Whereas Kingsley had been most concerned with promoting a Christianity activist in spirit and simplified in doctrine, Milman was poised to repeat the errors of the Church fathers and the scholastics in order to secure Western Christianity against the waves of foreign influence that British imperialism had already put into motion.

Implicit in Mowbray Morris's characterization of Victoria's reign as "an Alexandrian Age" was a question on which he refused to speculate: "When is the great division of Empire to be?" If Hellenistic Alexandria and Victorian Britain were indeed parallel in their cultural, political, and religious development, then British imperialism would of necessity reach an end as complicated—and as inevitable—as the literary culture it had produced.[16] Curiously, Morris had nothing to say about the bombardment of Alexandria by British imperial forces that had taken place only a few years earlier, in 1882, apparently in retaliation for an Egyptian nationalist attack on the city's foreign population. Like most of his contemporaries, Morris had little interest in nineteenth-century Alexandria, except for its location, after 1869, on the trade route to India. In a sketch of "Alexandria Old and New," one visitor recorded a sentiment typical of European travelers to Egypt in the nineteenth century—that the greatness of its ancient civilization had been thoroughly degraded by its Arab inhabitants: "we reached the excavations which are gradually laying bare the site of the great city, the rival of Rome, with her temples, and her palaces, and her vast necropolis, where, by a strange contradiction, the resting-places and remains of the dead are in a far more perfect and recognisable condition than the most magnificent dwellings and resorts of the living" (229). For this traveler, the Arabs who carried off "blocks of granite and red porphyry, the portions of fluted columns, the capitals of acanthus-crowned pillars, to build their miserable huts" were motivated by "greed," whereas the English "desire" was only to "secure [the fragments] for some collection, public or private" (229). The idea that the relics of Alexandria's glorious past were more valuable than the living inhabitants of a muted nineteenth-century city fueled Europe's proprietary interest in the forgotten capital.

In 1858 it was possible for a confident imperialist to assert, without a sideways glance at the Egyptian population of Alexandria, "The East, having no politics of its own, has been and is still made the arena for the politics of the West" ("Egypt and Syria" 154). Alexandria, he argues, could not sustain its own commerce without British intervention. If Britain were to abandon Egypt, where the "West meets the East, and predominates" (151),

Alexandria "would soon shrivel up into a fourth of its present dimensions" (163). Blaming the Muslims for a "savage intolerance" that prohibits commercial development and historical progress, the writer takes up the image of ancient Alexandria popularized by Kingsley in order to justify imperial expansion. In this tradition Alexandria lives only when the eyes of Europe are upon her, gaining thereby a galvanic vitality—"Nothing of internal, or at least innate life, yet appears in the East. It is all derived, and of course fitful, as well as unnatural and unhealthy" (173). Even through the writer's bold assertions of the desirability of Britain's imperial presence in Egypt, it is possible to perceive his anxiety about the birth of another Frankenstein's monster from the contact between East and West. Having early declared himself a believer in the "science of nations," as it came to be known in the nineteenth century, the writer fears what James Martineau calls "the violence done to *nationalities*" (299).[17] Kingsley had written with apparent delight of the collapse of the Roman empire: "Everywhere the mangled limbs of the Old World were seething in the Medea's caldron, to come forth whole, and young, and strong" (*Hypatia* xiii). The "exhausted" races of the Mediterranean gained more than they lost, in Kingsley's view, by their union with the "Gothic races" of the North—national differences were valuable only as they contributed to vigorous hybrid offspring. However, as Kingsley's critics complained, if the analogy between Roman Alexandria and Victorian Britain holds, then "he seems to anticipate for Europe a social dissolution like that of the lower empire" (Martineau 296), in which the purity of Christian Europe is lost.[18]

Kingsley's vision of cosmopolitan Alexandria had provoked a reassessment of the dialogue between East and West. Whereas writers such as Milman and Martineau wanted to administer a spiritual inoculation against the influence of foreigners, Kingsley had always tried to recognize the Zeitgeist, wherever it could be found, and to nurture that vitality, which he perceived as the working out of God's will in the world. While Kingsley was never explicit in anticipating the disintegration of the British Empire, the decline of Alexandria cautioned Britons to expect a similar fate: "I have shown you New Foes under an Old Face—your own likenesses in toga and tunic, instead of coat and bonnet. One word before we part. The same devil who tempted these old Egyptians tempts you. The same God who would have saved these old Egyptians if they had willed, will save you, if you will. Their sins are yours, their errors yours, their doom yours, their deliverance yours. There is nothing new under the sun. The thing which has been, it is that which shall be" (*Hypatia* 389). Raphael's deliverance had depended on compromise and combination, on a religion of action that would revive the "divine roots of the Church"—family and national life.

Now that they knew their sins and their doom, where could Kingsley's countrymen seek their deliverance? In the "contact zones" of East and West. In writing that now seems prophetic, Kingsley considered the fate of Alexandria, and the world, after the Muslim conquest, and arrived at a very different judgment than did his contemporaries. The Crusaders, he felt, had been wrong to try to stamp out the "peculiar life and character" of Egypt, an endeavor in which they necessarily failed—a failure that allowed the learning of Islam and its commerce to flow into Christendom. He imagines that the Crusaders were changed by their encounter with the East: "They learnt wider, juster views of man and virtue, which I cannot help believing must have had great effect in weakening in their minds their old, exclusive, and bigoted notions, and in paving the way for the great outburst of free thought, and the great assertion of the dignity of humanity, which the fifteenth century beheld" (*Alexandria and Her Schools* 167–68). And looking to the future, Kingsley imagines that Alexandria might again become a "point of fusion" where the "young and buoyant vigour of the new-born nations may at once teach, and learn from, the prudence, the experience, the traditional wisdom of the ancient Europeans" (170). But for this to occur there would have to be another historical reconciliation, this time between "the Crescent and the Cross."

CHAPTER 6

Matthew Arnold
The Second Best Life

It might seem perverse to make Matthew Arnold, that high priest of the highest of culture, into a representative for a literary middle way; but that is precisely how Arnold saw himself. In an 1869 letter to his mother, Mary Arnold, he claims that his "poems represent the main movement of mind of the last quarter of a century" and that they "will probably have their day as people become conscious to themselves of what that movement of mind is, and interested in the literary productions which reflect it" (*Selected Letters* [hereafter *SL*] 217). I have tried to suggest that the "main movement of mind" in the nineteenth century was toward eclectic synthesis—of competing philosophies, histories, and literary and artistic styles; and that it is impossible to separate these developments from the coming to power of the middle classes or from the process of cultural globalization. The eclecticism apparent in so many aspects of nineteenth-century British culture is no less prominent in the work of the man who became its self-appointed critic and prophet. Indeed, Arnold goes on to explain to his mother that though he has "less poetical sentiment than Tennyson and less intellectual vigour and abundance than Browning," he manages to combine the best characteristics of each, and to "[apply] that fusion to the main line of modern development" (*SL* 217). More profound even than the peculiar combination of sentiment and intellect that Arnold perceives as his poetic legacy is his "translation" of a variety of histories and styles into a modern poetic idiom. Far from lacking "sympathy with the wants of the present generation" (as the Anglican cleric G. D. Boyle uncharitably suggested in an 1853 review [70]), Arnold directs his poetic and critical efforts toward overcoming the modern condition of being "between two worlds," as he famously expressed it in "Stanzas from the Grande Chartreuse." At one moment, this liminal figure is a foreigner, who, "Thinking of his own Gods, [. . .] / In pity and mournful awe might stand / Before some fallen Runic stone—." Ideas that once seemed as permanent as the stone on which they were etched have been abandoned: time spares no one. In another moment Arnold's liminal narrator steps outside the time stream, refusing to cast off his mourning and join in the clamor of progress triumphant: "Fenced early in this cloistral round / Of reverie, of shade, of prayer, / How should we grow in other ground? / How can we flower in foreign air?" Few poems convey so vividly the sense of unending loss that runs all through Victorian literature, with its fatal, historical awareness. The present was necessarily derivative, a secondary creation; but did it have to be always a contraction of what came before? Was it always a falling away from the best that nature intended?

In one of his lesser-known poems, "The Second Best," Arnold again characterizes the present as transitional, but holds out hope that he is moving toward the future's enduring form. The eclectic principle he imbibes from Victor Cousin and other French thinkers creates a temporary order in the present moment, and opens a door into a world untroubled by doubt, diversity, or division. Although he might have seen himself as "second best," after Tennyson and Browning, Arnold tries to blend "the best that has been thought and known in the world" into the in-between self, thereby mastering the rudderless eclecticism of modern life. Increasingly, however, the study of "excellent models" leads Arnold away from poetry. He resigns himself to the production of criticism, and to its secondary level of creation. Throughout the 1860s, in his second career as a literary critic, Arnold uses eclecticism as a tool for reforming middle-class taste. By the end of the decade, in *Culture and Anarchy,* Arnold's criticism pivots on the contrast between two forms of eclecticism—the naïve, middle-class eclecticism of "doing as one likes" and the volitional eclecticism of finding the "best that has been thought and known." On this pivot point turns the future of literature.

Becoming Eclectic

As a young man Arnold emulated French manners, read widely in French literature, and later counted the critic Sainte-Beuve (a disciple of Victor

Cousin) as one of the four men from whom he was "conscious of having learnt" (*SL* 233). Arnold commenced his career as a critic long after the star of Cousin had faded from view, but Cousin's writings on eclecticism almost certainly influenced the evolution of Arnold's critical principles, both directly and indirectly through his reading of other French writers. The earliest extant reading lists (1845–47) reveal the centrality of Cousin's philosophical works in Arnold's intellectual development.[1] In September 1845 Arnold recorded his reading of Cousin's *Introduction à l'histoire de la philosophie*—the published version of the famous 1828 Sorbonne lectures that set out the theory of eclecticism. Later in the same year, he read Cousin's *Cours de l'histoire de la philosophie du xviiie siècle,* which continued the 1828 lectures and illustrated the practice of eclecticism in the history of philosophy. During the next two years, Arnold seems to have relied on Cousin's guidance in determining the direction of his further reading in philosophy. The eleventh lecture of the *Introduction* probably led Arnold to Vico, Herder (the *Metakritik zur Kritik der reinen Vernunft* appears on reading list IV), and Creuzer (the *Symbolik und Mythologie der alten Völker, besonders der Griechen* of 1810–12 appears on the same 1846 list). Lecture VI of the *Cours* contains a long discussion of the *Bhagavad Gita* (that would directly influence Arnold's 1848 poem "The World and the Quietist" with its concept of holy work) and praises Humboldt's analysis of the sacred text (which appears on the third reading list as "Humboldt. uber die B. G." and recurs on lists IV and V as well). Allott theorizes that Cousin's mention of Glanvill in the twelfth lecture of the *Cours* probably encouraged Arnold to read *The Vanity of Dogmatizing* (a 1661 text that Arnold bought in 1844, "but did not read until he found [it] mentioned in Cousin" [260]).[2] The same lecture by Cousin inspired Arnold to include Cudworth's *The True Intellectual System of the Universe* (1678) on the same reading list of December 1845. In reading the earlier dialogues of Plato during these years, Allott suspects that Arnold used Cousin's translation, "for the sake of the 'Arguments philosophiques' prefixed to the dialogues" (261), a claim supported by the transcriptions we find in Arnold's *Note-books* of Plato in the French of Cousin (150, 166). Finally, Cousin's discussion of Plotinus (Lecture VIII of the *Cours*) might have led Arnold to read the *Enneads* (List IV). On the fifth reading list, Arnold includes one of Cousin's critics, Abbé V. Gioberti; if he in fact read Gioberti, Arnold would have found a scathing attack on Cousin's "panthéisme." While Cousin's name does not appear again on any of Arnold's reading lists (not, I think, in consequence of his reading of Gioberti), many of those whom Cousin influenced do—Michelet, Sainte-Beuve, Stendhal, Guizot, Renan, and Jules Simon, among others. Also recorded are the scores of philosophical and religious works to which Cousin had introduced him.[3]

Allott therefore logically characterizes Cousin as Arnold's "mentor" during the 1840s (266), suggesting that Cousin's eclecticism was useful in providing the young poet with "a lively guide to a comparatively mysterious field of knowledge" and with "a source of ideas which [could] be transferred to a literary or more popular context" (259–60). Like most modern critics, Allott dismisses Cousin as a "feeble" and unoriginal thinker, perhaps capable of stimulating a superior mind such as Arnold's, but unlikely to leave any significant imprint on the age. In any event, it is impossible to disregard the eclecticism that is a leading feature of Arnold's scholarship during the period in which he read Cousin, and that afterwards appears so prominently in his poetry and criticism.[4] When Arnold met Cousin in 1859, however, he seems to have been more interested in the old philosopher's role as education minister than in his forgotten fame as the promulgator of modern eclecticism, an omission that must qualify any claim of "influence."[5] Yet an admixture of this predisposition to a French style of thought and the pessimism Arnold felt about the progress of poetry led him to become, after Cousin, the most influential eclectic thinker of the nineteenth century. The fundamental truth that drives the eclectic ceaselessly through the wilderness of ideas, namely that no one system can lay claim to all parts of the truth, also drove Arnold 1) to resist the literary tendencies of his age and to theorize a new direction for poetry; 2) to compare critically the literatures of the world, past and present, and provide the tools with which the literature of the future might be written; and 3) to diagnose the intellectual confusion of the middle classes and to pursue eclecticism as its remedy.

Arnold concedes the necessity of eclecticism when he writes in the 1853 preface to *Poems* that, in the "confusion of the present times," the young writer needs "a hand to guide him through the confusion" (48). In a striking statement of surrender to the spirit of the age, Arnold lays the foundation for the theory of eclecticism that will be most fully articulated in "The Function of Criticism at the Present Time": "If we must be *dilettanti:* if it is impossible for us, under the circumstances amidst which we live, to think clearly, to feel nobly, and to delineate firmly: if we cannot attain to the mastery of the great artists;—let us, at least, have so much respect for our art as to prefer it to ourselves. Let us not bewilder our successors; let us transmit to them the practice of poetry, with its boundaries and wholesome regulative laws, under which excellent works may again, perhaps, at some future time, be produced, not yet fallen into oblivion through our neglect, not yet condemned and cancelled by the influence of their eternal enemy, caprice" (*Complete Prose Works* I:15). The guiding "hand," which Arnold has found and which he earnestly recommends to his fellow poets, is the small number of "excellent models" that exhibit the "boundaries and wholesome regulative laws" of the art. Even if the young poet cannot be original and produce what is excellent without the guiding hand, he can at least imitate the classics, and thus preserve the *art* of poetry so as to make possible the production of future great works. The preface exhibits a characteristically eclectic approach to artistic production by recognizing that artists of the nineteenth century "must be *dilettanti*"—they are, as Winckelmann would have said, *Nachahmer.* Living in an unpoetic age, they must "respect the art more" than themselves and, in a historical project strongly reminiscent of Cousin's eclecticism, endeavor to "transmit the practice of poetry" to future generations.

The charge of dilettantism that Arnold levels against the artists of his generation derives from Goethe's delineation of the two types of dilettantes who write poetry: the one "neglects the indispensable mechanical part, and thinks he has done enough if he shows spirituality and feeling; and [the other] seeks to arrive at poetry merely by mechanism, in which he can acquire an artisan's readiness, and is without soul and matter" (I:15). In this judgment Arnold echoes both Kingsley's diagnosis of "The Prevailing Epidemic" in modern poetry, namely that poets have forgotten their art and produce poems merely out of vanity, and Carlyle's argument in "Signs of the Times" that the acute self-consciousness and "machine spirit" of the age have brought about the destruction of art. As Goethe argues in his brief 1799 essay, both kinds of dilettantism are harmful to art, so much so that it is better to "adhere to accepted models and imitate the good that exists rather than strive for originality" (216). In surrendering the goal of originality, Arnold repudiates the Romantics and sides with the unpopular eclectics and academicians whose faith in traditional institutions as arbiters of taste seemed counterintuitive in an age of democracy. For Goethe, however, obedience to standards and rules was necessary *for dilettantes only,* who, as "plagiarists," "undermine and destroy all natural beauty in language and thought by mimicking and aping it in order to cover up their own vacuity" (216). Arnold, by contrast, does not regard imitation as shameful plagiarism or eclecticism as dull mimicry, preferring to work for the future rather than yielding to a moment of despair. Even in this earliest piece of critical writing, aimed ostensibly at the reform of poetry, Arnold attacks the intellectual confusion and aesthetic laissez-faire of the middle classes—the real sources of poetry's decline. When he urges that we collect and preserve the rules of poetry, to protect them from "neglect" and "caprice," Arnold sounds a lot like Macaulay (a writer for whom he had little respect) in "Dryden" when Macaulay argues "that the creative faculty, and the critical faculty, cannot exist together in their highest perfection," or in the review of poetaster Robert Montgomery when Macaulay sets out to give readers a lesson in what makes good poetry. Arnold shares with Macaulay and Carlyle a powerful sense of historical determinism informing his judgment that poetry cannot be great in an unpoetic age; unlike many of his contemporaries, however, Arnold believes that history itself will provide the subject matter that allows poetry to go forward.

As do so many of Arnold's essays, the 1853 preface responds directly to various critics of his work, including his friend and fellow poet Arthur Hugh Clough. A review of new poetry—Arnold's own and that of a Glasgow mechanic named Alexander Smith—had given Clough the opportunity to consider more broadly the proper subject of poetry in the nineteenth century. To explain Alexander Smith's greater achievement, Clough employed a powerful architectural metaphor: "The novelist does try to build us a real house to be lived in; and this common builder, with no notion of the orders, is more to our purpose than the student of ancient art who proposes to lodge us under an Ionic portico. We are, unhappily, not gods, nor even marble statues. While the poets, like the architects, are—a good thing enough in its way—studying ancient art, comparing, thinking, theorizing, the common novelist tells a plain tale, often trivial enough, about this, that, and the other, and obtains one reading at any rate; is thrown away indeed tomorrow, but is devoured to-day" (145). Clough suggests that the more ancient arts of poetry and architecture are too preoccupied with cataloguing their own histories to "tell a plain tale," meaningful to an ordinary reader. According to Clough, Alexander Smith's volume of poetry shares with contemporary novels this ability to "build us a real house to be lived in." Though they are as disposable as modern architecture, modern novels provide immediate shelter, immediate relief, immediate lessons. It is no longer practical to lodge beneath an Ionic portico, and while it might form a fascinating entry in the history of architecture or an attractive setting for a cold hard statue, the ancient styles and ancient stories will not warm the heart of a living being. When he says that the common builder has "no notion of the orders," or history, of his art, he intends to question whether Arnold's "More refined, [. . .] and more highly educated sensibilities, [are] too delicate [. . .] for common service" (153). Like the eclectic architects, poets too concerned with the glories of past styles miss the opportunity to communicate and connect with modern subjects, and to create for their art a style appropriate to the age.[6]

In the preface Arnold answers charges of aesthetic refinement by pointing out the difference in poetic terms between simplicity and excessive ornamentation. If poets follow the example of Shakespeare, Keats, or even Tennyson, then they run the risk of attending too much to "ingenuity of expression" and too little to the selection of an action. Following Goethe, Arnold asserts that what distinguishes a genuine artist from an amateur is the sense of *Architectonicè,* "that power of execution, which creates, forms, and constitutes: not the profoundness of single thoughts, not the richness of imagery, not the abundance of illustration" (I:9). The problem is that these superficial features are "more easily seized than the spirit of the whole," and young poets frequently write poems "for the sake of single lines and passages; not for the sake of producing any total impression" (I:9, I:7). Arnold recognizes the danger of the age's haphazard eclecticism in these immature and untalented poets. The problem is not, as Clough would have it, an incorrect choice of subject, but the crude appropriation of the superficial points of style.

Although the distinction between design and ornamentation was architecturally and poetically significant, Clough had good reason to link his friend's poetic efforts with those of contemporary architects. Nineteenth-century architecture was beset by a crisis of invention. The only good architecture of the period, William Morris would conclude in 1888, had been laboriously eclectic. Architects depended on past styles to give meaning to buildings raised for modern purposes, but the meanings thus conveyed were often wildly inappropriate. For critics such as Pugin and Ruskin, the incongruity between historical styles and their contemporary applications drew attention to the nineteenth century's loss of faith in the principles that underlay the great architecture of the past. Similarly, Clough viewed Arnold's eclectic subject matter as a melancholy ramble through the ruins of history, as the enervated effort of a scholar: "There is something certainly of an over-educated weakness of purpose in Western Europe [. . .]. There is a disposition to press too far the finer and subtler intellectual and moral susceptibilities [. . .]" (163). This tendency to criticize high Victorian culture for its "weakness of purpose" must be connected to the perception that it was eclectically "over-educated" and therefore incapable of satisfying the expressive needs of modern sensibilities. To respond to this modern dilemma, as Arnold does, with a poetics based on scholarship and imitation—in other words, with a more rigorous form of eclecticism—appeared to his critics to be a kind of artistic suicide. As long as art expressed little more than the greatness of the past, then it would be relegated, ever more quickly, to the margins of contemporary life.

At an emotional crossroads in the review of "Recent English Poetry," Clough asks himself whether he can reconcile these "totally different, repugnant, and hostile theories of life" (162)—or whether he needs to make a choice. He feels the dilemma of being equally "at home" in Smith's "real house" and beneath Arnold's Ionic portico. Clough recognizes the technical superiority of "A.'s" poems, but sees his mission in the review as "going forth to battle in the armor of a righteous purpose, [. . .] with Alexander Smith" (161). As an artist-imitator, Arnold represents "ascetic and timid self-culture," the opposite of Alexander Smith's "unquestioning, unhesitating confidence" (163). In a revealing moment, Clough admits that he has "been inclined to yield to a preference for the picture of simple, strong, and certain, rather than of subtle, shifting, and dubious feelings" (165)—exactly what so many of Arnold's poems will not do. The moral restlessness of the poet gives no rest to the reader. A poetics of subtlety and doubt rarely produces the certainty that confident action requires. In his sympathetic reading of both poets, Clough understands the impulses that produced each, but he wants to choose the poems that help him to live in the present. Implicitly, Clough fears Arnold's moral eclecticism. As if in danger of following Arnold into the abyss, Clough backs away from the better poet to grasp the hand of the stronger man.

The Eclectic Compromise in Arnold's Poetry

The first volume of poetry, *The Strayed Reveller, and Other Poems* (1849), represents, as many critics have noted, Arnold's effort "to reconcile two modes of poetry": "Romantic introspection and a classical ideal of detached lucidity" (Machann 19–20). Canvassing Arnold's sources, however, it is apparent that he was trying to attach meanings to his work much more varied than those belonging to Classic and Romantic. There is no doubt that the early poetry grew out of his eclectic reading. In addition to those sources gleaned from his reading of Cousin, Arnold found inspiration for "Mycerinus" in Herodotus, for "The New Sirens" in George Sand's *Lélia* (1833), for "Written in Butler's Sermons" in Joseph Butler's *Fifteen Sermons* (1726), for "In Utrumque Paratus" in the *Enneads* of Plotinus and in Coleridge's *Biographia Literaria,* for "The Forsaken Merman" in the Danish folk ballad "Agnes and the Merman," for "The Strayed Reveller" in Book X of the *Odyssey,* for "The Sick King in Bokhara" in Alexander Burnes's *Travels in Bokhara* (1834), and for several others in Spinoza, Emerson, Cruikshank, Goethe, and Sophocles.[7] Such a diverse array of textual sources is not unusual in Victorian poetic practice; what is distinctive about Arnold's eclecticism is his effort toward synthesis, to detect in the multitudinous voices of history the consistent articulation of eternal verities.

Arnold desires an eclectic unity of expression within the "Time Stream" that necessitates stepping outside of it.

Many of the 1849 poems imagine circumstances under which an individual might transcend the limits of time. For example, "Mycerinus," "Fragment of an 'Antigone,'" and "The Sick King in Bokhara" represent actions that free the actor from transient concerns—"A goal which, gain'd, may give repose" ("Resignation: To Fausta"), while "Shakespeare," "The Strayed Reveller," "To My Friends," and "The World and the Quietist" depict ways of seeing that get beyond the "narrow margin" put up by the "Mountains of Necessity" ("To a Republican Friend, Continued"). An oracle reveals to King Mycerinus that "when six years are measured," he dies, but the young king turns night into day and lives instead for twelve, no more the "Slave [. . .] of a tyrannous necessity" (11. 18, 42). When she "dares / To self-selected good / Prefer obedience to the primal law, / Which consecrates the ties of blood" (11. 28–31), Antigone chooses the timeless bond of family over the briefer links we forge with strangers. When the young king tells his old vizier that he will bury a commoner in his own royal tomb, he does so in the full knowledge that fame and glory are fleeting, but that tending another man's honor after death is within reach.

> Even the great honour which I have,
> When I am dead, will soon grow still.
> So have I neither joy, nor fame.
> But what I can do, that I will. (11. 217–20)

Against the vizier's seeming wisdom—no man can take on the world's sorrows—the king comes closer to Allah in his care for the least of these. While proper acting can bring repose, and peace, that "secret of life" ("Resignation"), peculiar seeing makes the poet:

> *In the day's life, whose iron round*
> *Hems us all in, he is not bound.*
> *He leaves his kind, o'erleaps their pen,*
> *And flees the common life of men.*
>   *He escapes thence, but we abide.*
>   *Not deep the Poet sees, but wide.* (italics in original; "Resignation" 11. 209–14)

Shakespeare's breadth of vision depends on his freedom from the Zeitgeist: he is "Self-schooled, self-scanned, self-honoured, self-secure" (1. 10) and "Didst walk on earth unguessed at" (1. 11). Though ordinary mortals "ask and ask," Shakespeare smiles and is "still / Out-topping knowledge" (ll. 2–3). "All pains," "All weakness," and "all griefs" find their voice in Shakespeare. Possessing this comprehensive soul and relieved of the necessity of painful doubting, Shakespeare achieves immortality. In "The Strayed Reveller" Arnold presents a conflict between two poetic visions, that of the bards who are capable of seeing life in its totality, but must suffer with humanity; and that of the youth who watches life from Circe's palace, outside the time stream, intoxicated by "the wild, thronging train, / The bright procession / Of eddying forms, / [that] Sweep through [his] soul!" (ll. 294–97). The narrator of "To My Friends" battles his "master," Time, with poetic remembrance:

>   Time's current strong
> Leaves us true to nothing long.
> Yet, if little stays with man,
> Ah! retain we all we can
> If the clear impression dies,
> Ah! the dim remembrance prize
>   Ere the parting hour go by,
>   Quick, thy tablets, Memory! (ll. 57–64)

The poet of "mournful rhymes" in "The World and the Quietist" sees that "the world hath set its heart to live" (l. 11); but in its turning of "life's mighty wheel" (l. 13), the world forgets time and death. In a surprising turn, Arnold makes remembrance of death the key to immortality. The laborer at the wheel hears "adverse voices" (l. 19), and comprehends his omnipotence, and knows that he is more than matter. Like the adverse voice of the servant to Darius the king, reminding him every evening of the power of Greece to defeat him, the poet speaks liberation.[8]

Many of Arnold's readers did not want to hear the message of liberation that he tried to bring them, and too often the moral tendency of his poems was unclear. Indeed, Clough's 1853 review is typical of the reception of the early poetry: the poet has squandered his talent in building up an effete intellectualism. Arnold himself occasionally expressed dissatisfaction with being the poet of ideas. In May 1853 he confessed to Clough, "I feel immensely—more and more clearly—what I *want*—what I have (I believe) lost and choked by my treatment of myself and the studies to which I have addicted myself" (*SL* 86). Kenneth Allott interprets "studies" here as the philosophical and related studies of the six early reading lists, pursuits inspired by his "mentor" Cousin (264). While these studies might or might not have harmed Arnold as a poet, Allott stresses that "the motive for them is easily grasped" (264). The intellectual confusion of the age required Arnold to master disparate fields of knowledge—science, religion, philosophy, and literature—to attempt to synthesize them, and thus to find their direction and meaning, if he were to contribute anything. When Charles Kingsley asked, "To what purpose all the self-culture through which the author must have passed ere this volume [*The Strayed Reveller*] could be written" (Review 42), Arnold would have liked the answer to be more apparent: he wanted to make sense of tradition *and* the Zeitgeist.

Kingsley's objection to Arnold's early poetry formed part of the chorus of reviewers who maintained that poetry should speak to the needs of the age—or remain silent: "What does the age want with fragments of an Antigone? or with certain 'New Sirens?'—little certainly with these last seeing that the purport of them is undiscoverable (as is, alas! a great deal more of the volume)" (43). Kingsley blames the incomprehensibility of modern poetry on the poets' inward turn. They are fiddling, he says, while Rome is burning, and should instead be "taking [...] active part in God's work" (45). In one of his more Carlylean moments, he warns Arnold that "If he chooses to trifle with the public by versifying dreamy, transcendental excuses for laziness, for the want of an earnest purpose and a fixed creed, let him know that the day is at hand when he that will not work neither shall he eat" (45). Implicit in Kingsley's argument is the notion that poetry has "work" to do on behalf of the age. A peculiar kind of laborer, the poet observes from the margins of active life (and here one must think of Ford Madox Brown's quintessential portrait of the mid-nineteenth century, *Work*), yet he participates in that life by representing it. If his poems "transcend" this essential reality, then they are not doing their proper work of making meaning. Opposing Arnold's presumed "laziness" to the implied demand for real work, Kingsley hints that the poet refuses to touch real life for fear of contagion or out of intellectual snobbery. Furthermore, when Kingsley equates "earnest purpose" and "fixed creed," he clearly believes that one cannot have the former without the latter. He perceives that Arnold is searching for meaning over the broadest possible field of knowledge, because his creed is not yet fixed; but to put into print the evidence of an eclectic process will only confuse his readers. Kingsley sees Arnold's eclecticism as working against the age, rather than in harmony with it. In his very earnest novel *Alton Locke* (1850), Kingsley has Sandy Mackaye lecture the young tailor-poet, who is trying to write verses about a roving missionary who encounters naked island girls in the South Pacific: "What do ye ken anent the Pacific? Which is maist to your business?—the bare-backed hizzies that play the harlot o' the other side o' the world, or these—these thousands o' bare-backed hizzies that play the harlot o' your ain side—made out o' your ain flesh and blude? You a poet! True poetry, like true charity, my laddie, begins at hame" (88). Sandy's object lesson continues with a visit to a group of impoverished seamstresses, who embody the notion of "classic tragedy [. . .], man conquered by circumstance" (89). After encountering these pathetic and noble souls, Alton is converted to the view that "Fact is grander" than fiction and chooses to write of that "dark, noisy, thunderous element, that London life" (94). More troubling for Kingsley than Arnold's use of historical material in *The Strayed Reveller and Other Poems* is the poet's apparent neglect of the most pressing social issues of the time. After all, Kingsley would go on to write historical novels, and he approved of Tennyson's handling of contemporary issues within the historical framework of *The Princess* (1847); it would therefore be unreasonable to make him the spokesman for poetic presentism. But like many other writers, he felt that the orientation of modern literature toward the long ago and far away was often a symptom of its intellectual confusion and false principles. A poet who wanted to step outside the time stream might be trying to get a clearer picture of his historical moment; or, he might simply be trying to escape it.

Kingsley's sense that the author of *The Strayed Reveller* wrote against the age, rather than with it or for it, is surely confirmed by many of Arnold's statements about contemporary poetry. In a revealing letter to Clough written in November 1848, Arnold expresses his irritation with the favorable reception of his friend's poem *The Bothie of Toper-na-Fousich,* which seems too ready to cater to popular taste: "I have been at Oxford the last two days and hearing Sellar and the rest of that clique who know neither life nor themselves rave about your poem gave me a strong almost bitter feeling with respect to them, the age, the poem, even you. Yes I said to myself something tells me I can, if need be, at last dispose with them all, even with him: better that, than be sucked for an hour even into the Time Stream in which they and he plunge and bellow. I became calm in spirit, but uncompromising, almost stern. More English than European, I said finally, more American than English: and took up Obermann, and refuged myself with him in his forest against your Zeit Geist" (*SL* 49). In a swiftly developed line of association from the *Bothie,* to the Oxford clique, to an English, and finally American, Zeitgeist, Arnold articulates two ideas that will be repeated often in his later criticism. First, the sentiments of popular taste are transient, so that poetry catering exclusively to the fashion of the moment is poetry that will be forgotten; and, second, Anglo-American culture suffers from the crippling narrowness of excessive attention to the present and to the individual. Like Arnold, Clough is a classical scholar; but unlike Arnold, Clough allows himself to "be sucked [. . .] into the Time Stream" when he produces a poem of momentary, and not of eternal, interest. As we have seen, in the preface Arnold places himself in the curious position of defending an eclectic solution (hewing to superior models in writing poetry) in an eclectic age, but this position is carefully vetted in his letters to Clough of the late 1840s. Since modern writers such as "Keats Tennyson et id genus omne" only confuse writers of the "foot soldier" variety, he believes that those who cannot read the best examples (the Greeks) "sh[ou]ld read nothing but Milton & parts of Wordsworth" (*SL* 50). These writers have less in their works of a transient character, and more of "those elementary feelings which subsist permanently in the race, and which are independent of time" (I:4). He believes that he and Clough are living in "damned times" when "everything is against one—the height to which knowledge is come, the spread of luxury, our physical enervation, the absence of great *natures,* the unavoidable contact with millions of small ones, newspapers, cities, light profligate friends, moral desperadoes like Carlyle, our own selves, and the sickening consciousness of our difficulties" (*SL* 59). While he never argues that modern middle-class life is devoid of poetic interest, Arnold does imply here that the rise of democratic institutions has hindered the development of great natures and that the din of the popular press has diminished the power of great voices. How will the *best* emerge from the crowd? How will the work of genius be heard in the cacophony?

Throughout his poetry of the late 1840s and early 1850s, Arnold imagines characters who stand outside the mainstream, and yet still overlook society, finding there the quiet space in which an adverse voice might be heard. In *Empedocles on Etna,* Arnold makes the calmness of spirit that he invoked against Clough and the Zeitgeist into an enduring critical position—disinterestedness. Like Arnold's hero, Obermann, Empedocles turns against the Zeitgeist, but in choosing exile he does not occlude the needs of society; on the contrary, he recognizes that the spirit of the age is for heedless progress, but he cannot ignore the suffering that progress brings with it. As most readers of Arnold are aware, the dramatic poem *Empedocles on Etna* holds an uneasy position in his poetic oeuvre. Expelled from his collection of *Poems* in 1853, it represented a crisis, famously characterized as the "dialogue of the mind with itself," which, while true, even in its proper historical moment, could in no way "infuse delight" and thereby justify its literary existence. Setting aside Arnold's *mea culpa* and the overwrought poetics that followed upon it, we have in *Empedocles* a particularly lucid expression of the difficulty of preserving the core self apart from the spirit of the age, neither following the crowd nor standing in futile opposition to it.

The frequent exhortation to "know thyself" found here and everywhere in Arnold's poetry gains a deeper relevance when considered as an aspect of his eclecticism. When critics of the eclectic method point to the core problem of determining the principles of selection, they are really asking what makes any particular individual capable of rigorous eclecticism. As Arnold's critical outlook becomes more overtly eclectic, he justifies his own capacity for selection in three ways: he gains a panoramic or comprehensive vision of human knowledge and affairs by imagining a viewpoint outside or above the time stream, he avoids partisan entanglements by canvassing the widest possible range of opinions, *and* he knows his own mind, as much as anyone can. But how does one get to know one's mind without some standards external to oneself? Empedocles' awareness of this dilemma is signaled early in the poem when he describes the human soul as a wind-tossed mirror, glancing fragments of some larger truth in its surface:

> Hither and thither spins
> The wind-borne, mirroring soul,
> A thousand glimpses wins,
>   And never sees a whole;
> Looks once, and drives elsewhere, and leaves its last
>   employ. (I,2:82–85)

Possessing never more than partial knowledge of the conditions of existence, most people rely on each other or on tradition, rather than seeking for the truth within—but "Man gets no other light, / Search he a thousand years" (I,2:144–45). Most people never find their best internal resources, Empedocles warns, because they too often mistake will for intelligence. He advises his medical friend Pausanias that this is the root cause of man's mental unease: "'Tis that he makes this *will* / The measure of his *rights,* / And believes Nature outraged if his will's gainsaid" (I,2:154–56). This tendency to make will the measurement for all good in life must be resisted, if we are to become capable of intelligent self-reflection. Once this error is uprooted, we come closer to accepting the limits of our existence—"Limits we did not set / Condition all we do; / Born into life we are, and life must be our mould" (I,2:184–86). Nature is the soil, and our ancestors the roots and stem from which we grow. As Empedocles says, we must keep time to tunes we did not make.

In the Stoic tradition that Arnold draws upon here, conformity to nature and the moderation of desire are the first steps to happiness *and* to knowing one's own mind; but accepting limits does not make a human being an amoeba. We can have both immoderate "bliss" and vast knowledge. To back off from either goal makes us less than we could be. In particular, Empedocles despises the limits we place on our knowledge of nature—calling it a sin to investigate the workings of the universe, giving up in despair because certain answers seem out of reach, and concluding that they must be the province of the gods alone: "Fools! That in man's brief term / He cannot all things view, / Affords no ground to affirm that there are gods who do; / Nor does being weary prove that he has where to rest" (I,2:347–51). This admonition against rest when there is work to do might seem to contradict the drift of Empedocles' Stoicism, but it constitutes an important defense of eclecticism. Opponents might contend that an eclectic viewpoint is an artificial construct only, depending on an impossibly vast erudition; but Arnold repeatedly offers models of the "internal eye" (as Cousin termed it) that make eclecticism seem not only possible, but a moral responsibility. Eclecticism is the only method available to human beings for dealing with the burden of the past and the vastness of the universe. Knowledge is gained piecemeal and we must spend our lives piecing it together, not "looking once" and turning away.

Throughout the philosophical chant, Empedocles seems continually to iterate negative truths about human existence—we will never see things in their wholeness, we will never achieve the fulfillment of all our desires, and we will never find answers to all the questions we ask; in short, we have to remember that we are not gods, but instead something second best, human beings who can imagine a godlike perspective. Kenneth Allott notes the resemblance between these lines—

> But still, as we proceed
> The mass swells more and more
> Of volumes yet to read,
>   Of secrets to explore.
> Our hair grows grey, our eyes are dimmed, our heat is
>   tamed; . . . (I,2:332–36)

—and lines found in Arnold's early poem, "The Second Best." While Act II of *Empedocles* lays out the philosophical principles that shape the harmonious and productive life, including those of eclecticism, the few lines quoted above hint at the pitfalls awaiting the ardent eclectic—the more books one reads, the further the horizon of contentment recedes from view. "The Second Best" thus echoes many of the themes found in early-nineteenth-century writing about the "sea of knowledge" and the loss of intellectual authority that followed the rapid expansion of literacy in the period. The speaker is a scholar who, like Arnold, feels obligated to pursue an array of studies, even though he recognizes that he is straining and "overfeeding... his wit with reading" (11. 14–15). In the word "yet" that introduces these lines, however, the poet qualifies the experience: "yet,... No small profit that man earns" (11. 13, 16). He shapes his reading, rather than allowing himself to be consumed by it:

> No small profit that man earns,
>
> Who through all he meets can steer him,
> Can reject what cannot clear him,
> Cling to what can truly cheer him;
>   Who each day more surely learns
>
> That an impulse, from the distance
> Of his deepest, best existence,
> To the words, 'Hope, Light, Persistence,'
>   Strongly sets and truly burns. (11. 16–24)

Having no alternative but to confront the swelling "mass" of books, the scholar sets himself toward the best. Though he might not gain "his deepest, best existence," reading eclectically gives him at least the "second best" life. Contact with the best minds gives him the principles that "steer him." He reaps the profits of greater clarity, sharpening his capacity for judging and ordering knowledge. He learns to "cling to what can truly cheer him" and to discard what only diminishes life.

The muted hopefulness of "The Second Best" is found everywhere in Arnold's writings, but it is a difficult mood to sustain, particularly when he or his characters feel that they are in conflict with the spirit of the age. From the heroism of a scholarly Prometheus, one easily descends into the excessive introspection and despair of Empedocles. In the dramatic form of *Empedocles on Etna,* Arnold creates not only a dialogue between Pausanias and Empedocles, with a counterpoint in Callicles' songs, but also a dialogue within the mind of the philosopher-hero. While in the first act Empedocles counseled self-reliance, in the second act we see that inner strength "impaired" by "some secret and unfollowed vein of woe." Unable to live with others or with himself any longer, Empedocles chooses self-destruction, and termination of the "dialogue of the mind with itself." Most readers recognize that, for Empedocles, suicide is salvation. But what has happened to that second best life of contemplation and scholarly pursuits? For Arnold, Empedocles' suicide was an expression of a diseased self-consciousness that could no longer be disinterested. More a disease of loneliness than of eclecticism, or scholarly "overfeeding," Empedocles' despair stems from his sense that the world has turned against him by misunderstanding him: "Their thoughts, their ways, their wishes, are not thine" (II,1. 19). Even as men exult him and look to him for magical cures for all their ills, they "rid him of the presence of himself" (II,1. 223), driving him into solitude. Like the narrator of "Stanzas from the Grande Chartreuse," who characterizes the modern condition so succinctly as being "between two worlds," Empedocles also feels himself "miserably bandied to and fro / like a sea-wave, betwixt the world and thee [nature]" (II,11. 230–31). The leap into Etna's crater is finally an expression of faith, because Empedocles fears the continuance of the mind after death, particularly reincarnation, where "each succeeding age in which we are born / Will have more peril for us than the last" (II,11. 377–78). Successive rebirths would only drive Empedocles, a refugee from present times, deeper, and more impossibly, into the past. Implicit in his last thoughts before death is the notion that the future will continue to be a falling-off from glorious beginnings. The echo here of feelings Arnold expressed in numerous other poems and in letters to Clough is unmistakable; and though he removed the poem in 1853 because of its untimely modernity rather than its ancient setting, *Empedocles on Etna* embodies a nostalgia that might be said to have originated with history itself.

In the art and literature of the nineteenth century, such nostalgia was pervasive, and a few writers felt that the feelings it engendered and the eclecticism it encouraged ought to be resisted. Elizabeth Barrett Browning acknowledges the force of Arnold's arguments in the poems and Preface of the 1850s by devoting much of the pivotal central section of *Aurora Leigh* (1856) to answering them.

> Ay, but every age
> Appears to souls who live in't (ask Carlyle)
> Most unheroic. Ours, for instance, ours:
> The thinkers scout it, and the poets abound
> Who scorn to touch it with a finger-tip:
> A pewter age—mixed metal, silver-washed;
> An age of scum, spooned off the richer past,
> An age of patches for old gaberdines,
> An age of mere transition, meaning nought

Except that what succeeds must shame it quite
If God please. That's wrong thinking, to my mind,
And wrong thoughts make poor poems. (Book V:154–65)

Like many of Arnold's early reviewers, Browning is annoyed by Arnold's apparent reluctance to "touch [the age] with a finger-tip"—for her it is a question of whether the poet should remain on the margins or dive into the mainstream of life. In order to overcome the confusion of the present times, Arnold believes that he must stand apart—only then can he separate what has meaning and endures from what is meaningless and transient. Browning, however, spends much of the novel-in-verse arguing that artists are not always, romantically, social outsiders, but are sometimes those who define the character of an age and shape the nation's future. In the guise of her eponymous heroine, Browning also speculates on one of the most commonly vetted problems of the period, the perception (real or imagined) of the decline of art. She lends modern resonance to images of decline familiar since ancient times that have been continually invoked to describe the Victorians' sense of their own historical position ("A pewter age—mixed metal, silver-washed"); she also utilizes more homely and ironically eclectic images to emphasize the poet's plight: "An age of scum, spooned off the richer past, / An age of patches for old gaberdines." It seemed to many, including Arnold, that the age was an unpropitious one for the production of great works of art. Eclecticism, which seemed to skim off the riches of the past, or to be passing off old clothes as new, would naturally come under fire as a symptom of enervation and decadence. Echoing Carlyle in *On Heroes and Hero-Worship,* Browning denies that the present age is without its heroes. In her view, "All actual heroes are essential men, / And all men possible heroes: every age, / Heroic in proportions, [. . .]" (V:151–53). Letting go of the notion that the nineteenth century is without heroes allows the poet to represent the "great actions" (as Arnold would say) and the "essential men" of her own time (precisely what Browning attempts in *Aurora Leigh*). In what reads like a direct response to Arnold's 1853 Preface, she contends that regarding the age as one "of mere transition, meaning nought / Except that what succeeds might shame it quite" is "wrong thinking" that will not necessarily produce great poetry *in* the future. In claiming that a poet's "sole work is to represent the age" (V:208), Browning nevertheless looks unflinchingly ahead. The poet's concern about the future should be limited to this question: will the generations to come feel the beating heart of the nineteenth century if she does not produce a "living art, / Which thus presents and thus records true life" (V:221–22)? Browning shares with Arnold what E. D. H. Johnson calls a "double awareness" typical of Victorian writing: they agree that poetry needs to speak to the needs of the present, even as it "transcend[s] topicality" (ix). While Arnold believes that representing the present in its specificity will make a poem unreadable in the future, Browning relies on readers of the future to feel sympathy, as the Victorians certainly did, with their past, a sympathy that will be possible only if they record "true life."

As he would later write in a letter to his mother, Arnold believed that his poetry would evoke such sympathy, representing as it did "the main movement of mind in the nineteenth century." Eclecticism did not produce an artificial culture with which it was impossible to have sympathy; on the contrary, it could represent a breadth of experience unmatched by an exclusive focus on the present moment. Arnold's poetry ranged over an exceptionally diverse historical and geographical landscape, without seeking to exclude Britain or the nineteenth century, which turned up everywhere in his lyrical poems. What he resisted most emphatically, however, was the model of evolution that was always opposed to the model of synthesis. Antagonistic to the outlook of eclecticism, the theory of "incarnate history" (about which George Eliot wrote in her review "The Natural History of German Life") had a fatalistic appeal uncongenial to Arnold's primary mode of thought. If a people's historical development was written in their genes, so to speak, then they were freed from the responsibility of commanding it. A true eclectic such as Arnold could never surrender his influence over development, and resisted its often pseudoscientific rationalization.

Not surprisingly, Arnold's ideas about history played a central role in the formation of his critical eclecticism. His belief in the possibility of freedom from the Zeitgeist runs directly counter to the positivists' faith in the evolution of humankind through necessary stages (indeed, Auguste Comte may be one Frenchman from whom Arnold did not wish to learn). Arnold does not believe, however, with Clough, Kingsley, Barrett Browning, or *The Spectator,* that "'the poet who would really fix the public attention must leave the exhausted past, and draw his subjects from matters of present import, and *therefore* both of interest and novelty'" (I:3).[9] Underscoring his opinion that relevant poetry need not have a "modern" subject, Arnold based many of the new 1853 poems on history, myth, and legend: "Sohrab and Rustum" derives from the Persian *Shah Nameh of Firdousi* (via Sainte-Beuve's "Le Livre des Rois, par Firdousi" [1850] and Sir John Malcolm's *History of Persia* [1815]); the source for "The Church of Brou" is Edgar Quinet's essay "Des Arts de la Renaissance et de l'Église de Brou" (1839); "The Neckan" derives, as does its earlier companion piece, "The Forsaken Merman," from Scandinavian folklore; "Philomela," the story of a woman who was raped and mutilated by her sister's husband, the King of Thrace, has its origin in Greek mythology; and "Balder Dead" drew upon a contemporary translation of the *Prose Edda of Snorri Snurlson* and, like "Sohrab and Rustum," was an imitation of classical epic having a mythological source. Even an apparently modern poem, "The Scholar-Gypsy," derives from Glanvill's seventeenth-century philosophical treatise and stays close to it in spirit. As in the Glanvill version, Arnold writes of a man who searches for a solution to living among society's outcasts, and recasts the dominant theme of so many of his earlier poems:

> O born in days when wits were fresh and clear,
>   And life ran gaily as the sparkling Thames;
>   Before this strange disease of modern life,
>   With its sick hurry, its divided aims,
>   Its heads o'ertaxed, its palsied hearts, was rife— (201–5)

For Arnold, of course, "modern life" refers to the nineteenth century, and its "strange disease," an intellectual confusion for which the cure is exile. But already in *The Vanity of Dogmatizing,* Glanvill had recognized that "The Disease of our Intellectuals is too great, not to be its own Diagnostick: [. . .]. The weakness of humane understanding, all will confess: yet the confidence of most in their own reasonings, practically disowns it: And 'tis easier to perswade them it [is] from other lapses then [*sic*] their own; so that while all complain of our Ignorance and Error, every one exempts himself" (62–63).[10] By Arnold's time this disease affected a much greater portion of society—virtually anyone who could read. Ruth apRoberts has argued that "Glanville's [*sic*] whole book was important in shaping Arnold's thought, and the Scholar-Gipsy himself becomes a symbol for the [. . .] anti-dogmatic philosophy of the *seeker*" (145). As Arnold surely learned from Cousin, in every incarnation of eclectic philosophy the eclectic begins as a seeker, with a method; and Arnold manages to practice a form of eclecticism that never verges into system, by keeping himself detached from the time stream, like the scholar-gypsy.

Confused by Arnold's declaration in favor of the Greek and Roman models, many contemporary reviewers of the 1853 volume ignored its stylistic range and varied subject matter, and the degree to which Arnold vividly bodied forth the complex, hybrid nineteenth century. However, the difficulty with becoming the eclectic scholar-gypsy was that Arnold could not really overcome, in this way, "the dialogue of the mind with itself." Although Arnold was concerned with the suffering that "finds no vent in action," his famous characterization of modern suffering finds its counterpart in Cousin's "internal eye," the position from which he would judge what was true and what was false in the history of philosophical, educational, and political systems. While G. H. Lewes and others judged Cousin's imagined detachment and objectivity as absurd, Cousin needed this objectivity to practice the history of philosophy as an eclectic, and to find truth wherever it existed. But in relying solely on the powers of his mind to juxtapose systems and discern the truth within each, Cousin ran the risk of being merely provincial. The erudition needed to put into practice either Cousin's eclecticism or Arnold's objective poetics was practically impossible for any one person. Cousin's nonpsychological formulation for historical study sounds rather more plausible and probably influenced Arnold in the 1840s: "eclecticism must be the basis of the new history of philosophy because an infallible law requires that every philosophy, which in its turn becomes predominant, after having finished its theoretical developement [*sic*], must look back towards former ages, must interrogate them in its own spirit, and terminate in an history of philosophy conformable to itself" (*Introduction to the History of Philosophy* 428). The best historicist writing of the nineteenth century always built a bridge from past subject to present need. Arnold's efforts at translation in the 1849, 1852, and 1853 volumes (including *Empedocles on Etna*—the poem that Arnold later considered too modern, in the worst sense) were always directed toward interrogating the past in the spirit of the present, if not from the present of Kingsley, Clough, or Browning, then from his own unified self. Eventually, however, even this would not be enough for the poet who was increasingly becoming a critic, a role that afforded a much more secure position from which to observe the world and raise his "adverse voice." In a letter to his sister Jane dated 6 September 1858, he confesses that to "submit voluntarily to the exhaustion of the best poetical productions" would entail giving up too much. It is unnatural, he writes, in the present unpoetical age, to attempt poetry at all; he cannot do it "without an overwhelming and in some degree morbid effort" (*SL* 111). Arnold finds the solution to living in the present age—and writing for it—somewhere between being a fanatic and being "chalf blown by the wind" (*SL* 59); he will be neither dogmatic nor excessively latitudinarian, but will instead be eclectic in relation to the Zeitgeist. The middle class will find itself capable of living only when it recognizes that it has the freedom to shape its destiny, and is willing to listen to the "adverse voice" of Arnold.

The critical exclusiveness of Arnold's poetry—its scholarly quality, its expression of faith in the past, its detachment from the time stream—was meant to preserve his contemporaries from making bad choices by being aware of the choices they had to make. In that context eclecticism gave Arnold a way of coping with history and the problem of producing original art that would, at least obliquely, reflect the age. As a volitional eclectic, Arnold favored synthesis over development, seeking to live in synchronic rather than diachronic time—outside the time stream. In translating cultural material, Arnold created the potential for change. In promoting the ideal of Goethe, he eschewed nationalism and organic historicism: "Let us conceive of the whole group of civilised nations as being, for intellectual and spiritual purposes, one great confederation, bound to a joint action and working towards a common result; a confederation whose members have a due knowledge both of the past, out of which they all proceed, and of one another" (IX:38). When writing poetry in the styles of the past became too strenuous, Arnold decided to write for the future. In abandoning the writing of poetry for the writing of highly polemical criticism, he confirmed his membership in what we might term "the prophetic school" of literary criticism, where his controversial style would have a more profound and lasting effect. With the publication in 1865 of the *Essays in Criticism,* Arnold puts the eclectic principles worked out in his poetry into practice in his prose.

In his preface to the collection, Arnold begins by declaring his allegiance with his audience, "The English middle class, of which I am myself a feeble unit" (III:288), so that he might argue more effectively against their present way of doing things. He is especially worried that the English middle class seem content with the philosophy of Benthamism and do not perceive the slightest reason to question its ascendancy. Arnold implies that his work will do just the opposite; namely, he will cause his readers to question every received opinion and to rest in none of them: "To try and approach truth on one side after another, not to strive or cry, nor to persist in pressing forward, on any one side, with violence and self-will—it is only thus, it seems to me, that mortals may hope to gain any vision of the mysterious Goddess, whom we shall never see except in outline, but only thus even in outline. He who will do nothing but fight impetuously towards her on his own, one, favourite, particular line, is inevitably destined to run his head into the folds of the black robe in which she is wrapped" (III:286). Arnold brings eclecticism to do battle with middle-class complacency. As an eclectic, he has learned to approach the truth from many sides, and in his ideal of detachment, not to argue violently for any particular side. In his style of argument Arnold will often seem to be ducking and weaving like a boxer—he wants to pummel the reader, but he throws his punches only to the place where his reader most resists. In ventriloquizing the philosophy of Empedocles, Arnold asserts that we must accept the fragmentary vision of eternal things, as if our souls were mirrors blown by the wind. To fight for one favorite view of the truth inevitably misses a hundred others equally persuasive at different moments. For Arnold the "epoch of transformation" is not finished, and never will be finished, because we mortals never grasp more than a limited or momentary glimpse of what is true. Arnold thus sets out the need for eclecticism as a critical method, and will put this method into practice in his own work. In three of these essays, "The Function of Criticism at the Present Time," "The Literary Influence of Academies," and "Heinrich Heine," Arnold argues that criticism must have a key role in the present if literature is to have any future at all.

Arnold as Comparatist

If Arnold had only used the term "eclecticism," his brilliant essay on "The Function of Criticism at the Present Time" might have come down to us as the manifesto of eclectic criticism. In it he uses for the first time the phrase that would forever be associated with Arnold—"the best that is known and thought in the world" (III:283)—a clear expression of his eclecticism. The starting point of Arnold's argument (a reminder of certain points from his controversial Homer lectures) probably did not endear him to his English readers: "almost the last thing for which one would come to English literature is just that very thing which now Europe most desires,—criticism" (III:258). The "power and value" of English literature thus "impaired," Arnold makes a case for the development of critical principles in the most untheoretical of nations. Unlike the Germans and the French, whose critical efforts have all been directed toward seeing the "object as in itself it really is," the English let their fondness for custom and a proud literary tradition obscure their judgment. Certainly, Arnold concedes, the critical faculty "is of lower rank than the creative"; but if we look unflinchingly at history it will be plain to see that "the production of great works of literature or art [. . .] is not at all epochs and under all conditions possible" (III:260). Arnold stays close to the tradition of eclectic thought when he argues that criticism constitutes a transitive effort, namely getting from one creative period to the next. However, he goes a step further toward acknowledging the permanent need for eclecticism when he suggests, "The grand work of literary genius is a work of synthesis and exposition, not of analysis and discovery; its gift lies in the faculty of being happily inspired by a certain intellectual and spiritual atmosphere, by a certain order of ideas, when it finds itself in them; of dealing divinely with these ideas, presenting them in the most effective and attractive combinations,—making beautiful works with them, in short" (III:261). The artist, apparently, is always doing something "eclectic" with the materials of the age; he or she does not discover new ideas—Arnold believes that is the work of the philosopher—but only achieves new combinations. Since the English fail to see the object as in itself it really is, their artists do not have the materials necessary to produce effective combinations of ideas—in other words, great art. Criticism, however, has more control over the materials it synthesizes; it makes them usable by seeing "in all branches of knowledge, theology, philosophy, history, art, science" the object as in itself it really is. This tends at last, Arnold believes, "to make an intellectual situation of which the creative power can avail itself. It tends to establish an order of ideas, if not absolutely true, yet true by comparison with that which it displaces; to make the best ideas prevail" (III:261).

Arnold's faith in the power of criticism to be creative, to create epochs in which the creative spirit is in ascendance, derives from his historical outlook. Some critics argue that Arnold accepts a cyclical model of history derived from Giambattista Vico's *The New Science* (1744), while others claim that Carlyle and the German Romantic philosophers were stronger influences on the formation of Arnold's historicism.[11] As an eclectic who wanted to approach the truth from as many sides as possible, Arnold allowed himself to be influenced by a variety of sources; but as in so many arenas of his intellectual life, the profound and lasting influence came from France. Arnold and the French historian Ernest Renan (1823–92) were near contemporaries, but Renan's influence on Arnold is easily traced to 112 entries in the *Note-Books,* references to Renan in twelve different essays or books, and the essay on Renan in *Essays in Criticism, Third Series* (Bachem 229).[12] Like Arnold, Renan loses his faith as a young man and searches for "une philosophie vitale et compréhensive" that will let him "harmonize within himself the divergent skills and insights of scholar, critic, philosopher, and poet" and will let him "'grasp the whole from every point of view'" (qtd. in Chadbourne 40). Richard Chadbourne concedes that to Victor Cousin, "Renan probably owes most of his terminology and ideas concerning synthesis" (41). From Cousin he borrows the notion of the three ages of humanity (which Cousin had distilled from various Enlightenment and Romantic sources): in the first stage of history, the "syncretic," we exist in an instinctive and poetic union with the world outside ourselves; in the second age, the "analytical," we separate ourselves from nature; and in the third age, the "synthetic," we achieve "true wisdom" when we integrate reason with religion (Chadbourne 42). If we were following Vico's schema, then this third stage would actually represent the beginning of a decadence and collapse, wherein society returns to its origins to be reborn. For Renan the third age is not decadent, but eclectic; that is, it incorporates what was best in each of the other ages. Renan, influenced by Cousin, sees eclecticism as a historical inevitability, although it defies the model of organic development that he found so appealing in other respects. Cousin had written in the *Introduction à l'histoire de la philosophie* of the need to accept changes that had come since the Revolution: "the irresistible march of time will by degrees unite the minds and hearts of all in the intelligence and in the love of the constitution, which contains at once the throne and the country, monarchy and democracy, order and liberty, aristocracy and equality, all the elements of history, of thought, and of things" (439). With everything around it being so "mixed, complex, and mingled, is it possible that philosophy can avoid being eclectic" (440)? In his *Studies of Religious History,* Renan calls eclecticism the "obligatory method of our age," suited to the present intellectual temperament of France and its desire for compromise. Although he is wary of traveling the road from eclecticism to relativism and nihilism, he believes that "it is impossible for an enlightened man to shut himself up in one [school] exclusively" (35). The points of contact between Arnold's thought and Renan's are clear, as is the significance of the early influence of Cousin. Both men were disposed to be eclectic and both believed that their eclectic criticism would shape the age to come.

Flavia Alaya has written that Arnold and Renan "both had been led, by way of their explorations of the roots of modern institutions, to the axiomatic truth that societies are not so much altered by the ideas of single men as by the impress of such ideas upon mass opinion" (555). Both would have to become "popularizers" if they were to prepare for the "direction of social transformation [. . .] in advance" (555). In "The Function of Criticism at the Present Time," we see Arnold breathing the fire of ideas into the "epoch of expansion [that] seems to be opening" (*Complete Prose Works* III:269). This fire is fueled by criticism. In no other way can the epoch of concentration be exploded. The worship of tradition, the blind observance of customary forms, and the resistance to new ideas hold society in this concentrated phase. In opposing these alternating epochs Arnold accepts, as Renan did, an eclectic philosophy of history. By way of example, Arnold refers frequently to the Renaissance as "a great hybrid movement," which was a fusion of the Hebraic and the Hellenic, of the Middle Ages and antiquity (Culler 143). Synthesis usually occurs after a period in which there has been intense competition between ideas, and finds a way to bring the opposing sides into harmony. The expansion that Arnold has in mind for the nineteenth century is similar to that of the Renaissance, in that criticism will carry forward the best ideas and create the foundations on which the new age will be built. Criticism depends on the "free play of the mind," obeying an instinct to know the best that has been thought and known in the world. Its only rule, Arnold proclaims, is its disinterestedness. Any prejudice, any "absorption" into politics would, like the casting of a vast net, restrict the free play of ideas. Arnold admits that England has its critics, but they are too involved in practice, are "too polemical and controversial," to lead the masses toward perfection. Although Arnold might have difficulty avoiding controversy himself, he has no trouble following the last of his dictates: since "much of the best that has been thought and known in the world cannot be of English growth," the English critic "must dwell much on foreign thought" (III:282–83)—and this is just what most English critics will not do. Criticism, he concludes, must regard Europe as being "one great confederation, bound to a joint action and working to a common result" (III:284). If the intellectual boundaries of England are expanded, creative activity will again become possible. However, expansion is not the only way to serve the future of literature; Arnold also imagines that centralization, in the form of an academy, can produce the criticism that the age so desperately needs.

Throughout this history of the idea of eclecticism, I have exhibited the resistance to academies and academicians as one symptom of the general resistance to eclecticism. Taking up this important question of the value of institutions in regulating taste and establishing standards for the arts, Arnold remains true to his eclectic principles. While "The Function of Criticism at the Present Time" argues for the vital role of the critic in preparing the way for future literature, "The Literary Influence of Academies" asserts the need for an institution that will guide their activities. In this essay Arnold again looks to the example of France: he praises the work of the French Academy and decries the lack of any comparable institution in England. Taking his cue from Renan, Arnold contends that without a literary academy in England, "inferior" literature will eventually gain the upper hand. In chapter 3 we saw how anxiously writers such as Coleridge, Southey, and Mill watched the rise of the popular press and worried that the number of voices competing to be heard would overwhelm those of real value. For them this development represented the advent of a variety of eclecticism, random and indiscriminate in nature. Thomas Love Peacock realized that there were two types of eclecticism, the first the accident of a late and democratic period in history, and the second the result of a disciplined process of selection and synthesis. For Arnold academies belong in this second category; at the same time, they are useful in overcoming the naïve eclecticism of the first category. This is because the academy has the capacity for "creating a form of intellectual culture *which shall impose itself on all around*" (Renan qtd. in Arnold III:235). However, it is this very imposition to which Englishmen most object. Arnold devotes much of the essay to denouncing the English complacency that hinders the establishment of an academy, which would regulate English taste and prevent Englishmen from always "going their own way." It might at first seem paradoxical that Arnold opposes "going one's own way" to "openness of mind," a quality of which the English are in too short a supply. Going one's own way or "doing as one likes" usually means following after the crowd or traveling in the ruts of custom and convenience. The English do not go their own way as individuals, approaching the truth from all sides at once; rather, they go their own way collectively, as a nation, not bothering to ask whether what their grandparents or neighbors believed to be true continues to be so. The French, by contrast, have the "Openness of mind and flexibility of intelligence [that] were the signal characteristics of the Athenian people in ancient times" (III:237). The good qualities of the English people—energy and honesty—seem to resist the fixed standards and centralized authorities of academies: "By this [the English nation] certainly escapes certain real inconveniences and dangers, and it can, at the same time, as we have seen, reach undeniably splendid heights in poetry and science. On the other hand, some of these requisites of intellectual work are specially the affair of quickness of mind and flexibility of intelligence. The form, the method of evolution, the precision, the proportions, the relation of the parts to the whole, in an intellectual work, depend mainly upon them" (III:238). Arnold is getting at the same prickly problem of the age that he confronted in "The Function of Criticism at the Present Time": the English might be superior in every way that matters in creative endeavors such as poetry and science, but they are inferior when it comes to prose, and critical prose is what is most needed at the moment. To write good prose one must have a flexible intelligence that sees how the parts relate to the whole, and sees the object as in itself it really is. Fortunately, Arnold believes, "quickness of mind and flexibility of intelligence" can be learned, unlike the "free activity of genius" (III:238). The academy "consecrates and maintains" these qualities, engendering genius in the long term, and thus advancing the cause of the "human spirit."

Without intelligence, English literature is susceptible to "hap-hazard, crudeness, provincialism, eccentricity, violence, blundering" and will therefore have less influence over the public and be a less effective agent for change (III:241). For Arnold, the chief fault here is English provincialism. Lacking the "center and rallying point" that an academy would provide, English letters suffers from provincial fragmentation, so that its divided efforts lead to "ignorance and charlatanism" rather than to progress (III:242). Arnold means that English intellectuals, without the checks of their contemporaries upon them, are subject to "vagaries" and "intellectual eccentricity of all kinds" (III:243). We might take George Eliot's Casaubon as the very type of the English intellectual who, isolated from his peers, does not realize that his "Key to all Mythologies" duplicates the decades-old work of German philologists. His life's work is meaningless, except as a private exercise, because he has taken no account of developments in the field, particularly abroad; and he has had no body of peers to referee his scholarship. Casaubon's case is an extreme one, as Eliot intended, but his faults are exactly those that Arnold ascribes to English criticism: his work is too provincial and too eccentric, relying too much on individual genius and ignoring the larger context within which one must always work.[13] What will cure the English of their provinciality?—only its opposite, "urbanity," which can be achieved via the "intellectual metropolis" of an academy: "for it brings us on to the platform where alone the best and highest intellectual work can be said fairly to begin. Work done after men have reached this platform is *classical;* and that is the only work which, in the long run, can stand. All the *scoriae* in the work of men of great genius who have not lived on this platform are due to their not having lived on it. Genius raises them to it by moments, and the portions of their work that are immortal are done at these moments; but more of it would have been immortal if they had not reached this platform at moments only, if they had had the culture which makes men live there" (III:245). To "get rid of provinciality" the English need a broader vision of culture. Arnold imagines that they will attain this wider view by ascending a kind of historical plateau, a "certain stage of culture" (III:245). When they are upon the platform, they are "classical," "immortal," and urbane. When they fall back into history, into the time stream, they are again prejudiced, transitory, and provincial. Arnold makes a very similar argument in "On the Modern Element in Literature," his inaugural lecture as Professor of Poetry at Oxford, when he claims that ancient Greek literature is, in fact, modern because it "adequately comprehended, [and] adequately represented" its own age (I:21). Having before them the spectacle of a "copious and complex present" and behind them the spectacle of a "copious and complex past," the English must eclectically "compare the works of other ages with those of our own age and country" and preserve those literatures that "solved for *their* ages the problem which occupies ours" (I:21). Having again reached a "highly developed, culminating epoch," Arnold believes that it is again necessary to ascend the platform and to try to comprehend the whole.

Arnold's opponents often found his reverence for foreign writers and institutions excessive and even disloyal. In calling on "foreign witnesses" to judge English culture, Arnold follows the lead of Heinrich Heine, who exemplifies the urbane spirit, the "tone of the city," that will ultimately deliver the English from their provinciality, *and* their Philistinism. To this end, the cosmopolitan Heine was, in his own words, "a brave soldier in the Liberation War of humanity" (III:107). He is a "Liberator" because he is uniquely capable of feeling the force of modern ideas: "Modern times find themselves with an immense system of institutions, established facts, accredited dogmas, customs, rules, which have come to them from times not modern. In this system their life has to be carried forward; yet they have a sense that this system is not of their own creation, that it by no means corresponds exactly with the wants of their actual life, that, for them, it is customary, not rational. The awakening of this sense is the awakening of the modern spirit" (III:109). If Goethe began the work of dissolving "the old European system of dominant ideas and facts," then Heine continues it. Unlike his German Romantic contemporaries, "[Heine] is not conquered by the Middle Age"; instead, he wages his war against the Philistines from the "intellectual metropolis" of modernity, Paris. Heine believes that "the French, as a people, have shown more accessibility to ideas than any other people," and he despises their opposite, "the *genuine British narrowness*" (III:112). While the French perceive a lack of correspondence between old institutions and present needs, the English want nothing more than to patch up the old systems, and to hang on to the old ideas as long as possible. Instead of referring to "general principles," the English proceed "by the rule of thumb" and have become "of all people the most inaccessible to ideas and the most impatient of them" (III:113). In escaping from the narrowness of his own country, Heine did not, however, become merely a Francophile; rather, in locating himself between two cultures, the German and the French, "he found something new" (III:120). No doubt Arnold admired Heine for his embracing of modern ideas, but he emphasizes that Heine was not "an acrid dissolvent" of the old. Heine belongs to "the main current of the literature of modern epochs" because he applied "modern ideas to life" (III:122), not because he abandoned the past. His great contribution was in using French ideas to air out German attics. His country already had a wealth of ideas but needed a rational intelligence to order them and make them serve the present. Heine accepted the in-betweenness of modern life and exploited it to produce original art. Like Heine, Arnold wants his people to have a wider view of the present, in all its complex relations, and the *Essays in Criticism* as a whole attempt to build the "intellectual metropolis" out of the best ideas that have been thought and known in all the world. He also wants to give the English a new language to speak. In modern times there is no longer the division between the language of scholarship and the language of the people; there is only the vernacular. Like Heine, Arnold wants to make the vernacular cosmopolitan. Arnold's "intellectual metropolis" requires a language as diverse as history itself.

While the *Essays on Criticism* provided his English readers with examples of the greatness of European literature and culture, his next critical work, *On the Study of Celtic Literature,* brought home the implications of his critical method. Following the lead of Renan, who had published a study of the poetry of the Celtic races about ten years earlier, Arnold recommends the study of Celtic literature as a way to correct some of the faults of the English character. Probably nothing would have been more galling to his readers than this particular piece of advice: the English ought to look to the Irish and the Welsh for culture. (Critics today not directly interested in Celtic language and literature have tended to shy away from Arnold's 1867 work as altogether embarrassing, because underlying his discussion of the literature are disconcerting assumptions about race, language, and national identity.) In 1865 he explained to his mother how Celtic studies would fit into his overall critical enterprise (Machann 66): "I hate all over-preponderance of single elements, and all my efforts are directed to enlarge and complete us by bringing in as much as possible of Greek, Latin, Celtic cultures; more and more I see hopes of fruit by steadily working in this direction" (*SL* 168). The "fruit" would seem to be those fresh combinations of the materials of the age that produce great art. Imitating Renan, Arnold begins his study of Celtic literature with a visit to Celtic territory, to Wales. He even attends a festival of Welsh literature and language, which he judges a dull affair; but he is nonetheless inspired to witness the enthusiasm of common people there for poetry and history, something entirely lacking in the dull Anglo-Saxon.

At first glance Arnold's efforts seem entirely noble. He only wants his contemporaries to acknowledge and to make use of the richness of a native tradition that has been ignored for centuries. Emphasizing that English culture contains a mixture of Celtic, Norman, and Teutonic elements, Arnold wants to refute the popular notion that "it is vain to seek after Norman or Celtic elements in any modern Englishman" (*Complete Prose Works* III:336) because these populations were entirely absorbed. Why does Arnold want to revive these old tribal and national differences? One recent biographer has noted that he seems to be describing aspects of himself. Certainly, he is not unpatriotic in the assertion of mixture over purity, because he believes (with Renan) that mixed nationalities are stronger and, in much of his work, he seems to advocate a kind of literary husbandry. If he cultivates the strengths of each racial element, then he will "complete" the English character, bringing it to its highest perfection. In order for this eclectic project to go forward, he also has to defeat those philologists who want to dismiss the imaginative literature of the Celts as "evidence of the existence of a common stock of ideas, variously developed according to the formative pressure of external circumstances. The materials of these tales are not peculiar to the Welsh" (III:325). Arnold, by contrast, wants to argue for a unique tradition linked to racial and national identity. This is a key moment in the history of the idea of multiculturalism: do we say that people should read something because it is universally and timelessly important, or do we say that people should read something "foreign" because it will reveal something of the uniqueness of another race or group of people? Arnold comes down at first on the side of difference and variety. He contends that the discovery of commonalty is "one of the most interesting discoveries of modern science; but modern science is equally interested in knowing how the genius of each people has differentiated, so to speak, this common property of theirs; in tracking out, in each case, that special 'variety of development,' which [. . .] 'the formative pressure of external circumstances' has occasioned; and not the formative pressure from without only, but also the formative pressure from within. It is this which he who deals with the Welsh remains in a philosophic spirit wants to know" (III:325). Arnold does not seem to want true multiculturalism, the coexistence of many cultures within one, because he is too insistent on the need for the Welsh to give up their language, that which most constitutes their separateness: "The fusion of all the inhabitants of these islands into one homogeneous, English-speaking whole, the breaking down of barriers between us, the swallowing up of separate provincial nationalities, is a consummation to which the natural course of things irresistibly tends; it is a necessity of what is called modern civilisation, and modern civilisation is a real, legitimate force; the change must come, and its accomplishment is a mere affair of time" (III:296–97). For Arnold, history tends to bring about homogeneity, but also strength and completeness, if managed properly. Instead of multiculturalism, this is eclecticism moving toward synthesis, federation, and the spirit of a nation in Renan's terms (and a nation always demands sacrifice, forgetting): "In the first place, Europe tends constantly to become more and more one community, and we tend to become Europeans instead of merely Englishmen, Frenchmen, Germans, Italians; so whatever aptitude or felicity one people imparts into spiritual work, gets imitated by the others, and thus tends to become the common property of all. Therefore anything so beautiful and attractive as the natural magic I am speaking of, is sure, now-a-days, if it appears in the productions of the Celts, or of the English, or of the French, to appear in the productions of the Italians; but there will be a stamp of perfectness and inimitableness about it in the literatures where it is native, which it will not have in the literatures where it is not native" (Arnold III:376). Blending races will always mean some loss, because the perfectness of a blended race's original constitution and mode of expression will be gone. Perhaps unconsciously, Arnold's readers feared hybridity, feared his eclectic method, because it would lead ultimately to the loss of singularity, of English national identity. Though keenly aware of the values of difference and variety, Arnold found that comparison, union, fusion, and mixture would be of more benefit to the future of literature. His own work, so indebted to diverse European sources, might have lost something of the power of the original, but it brought new color and new strength to English literature.

From Heine, Arnold derived one of his most fruitful oppositions, that of the two Renaissances of the sixteenth century: the Hellenic and the Hebrew. Within the German Romantic poet, these two forces coexisted, but Arnold sensed they were out of balance, the Greek side being, perhaps, too dominant. In "Pagan and Medieval Religious Sentiment," another of the *Essays* of 1865, Arnold acknowledges that Heine could keep himself alive by "colossal irony" and "sinister mockery," but the moral dimension required by the millions is absent (III:229). Arnold's most famous work of social criticism, *Culture and Anarchy,* is often read as an argument for privileging the classical, high culture to which many of his middle-class contemporaries lacked access or for making poetry into a new religion. While there is certainly a pervasive sense of anxiety about "low" cultures in Arnold's 1869 work, he is in fact charting the course for a middle way appropriate to a democratic, middle-class-dominated society. Above all, it is a call for balance and moderation, for the perfection of a "many-sided development" (V:239). Arnold's strategy for guaranteeing the future of literature rested mainly on preservation of and regular contact with the great minds of the past. This mandate was directed not only, nor even principally, toward future academicians, but toward the general educated reader on whose shoulders would fall the burden of selection. Part of dealing with the condition of being "between two worlds" is finding what they have in common and creating a meaningful synthesis. In both the poetry and the criticism, Arnold developed a trans-historical styles discourse, aimed at the discovery of a new style appropriate to the age. By listening to the adverse voices of history, Arnold found a way to live in adversity and with diversity. By approaching the truth from all sides at once, Arnold found, at least, his own intellectual deliverance.

CHAPTER 7

Walter Pater and Thomas Hardy
"Triumph in Mutability"

It is appropriate to conclude the history of the age of eclecticism with a writer for whom eclecticism became the necessary foundation of all his literary and critical efforts: "In this late day certainly, no critical process can be conducted reasonably without eclecticism" (*Appreciations* 16). Walter Pater seems to relish living late in history. He makes no effort to dissociate eclecticism from a perception of decline or belatedness. His "critical process" is one of "winnowing" and "searching," and of becoming "conscious of the words he would select in a systematic reading of a dictionary, and still more of the words he would reject" (15). The elements of language "change along with the changing thoughts of living people"; the resources of literature increase rather than diminish; the accumulation of knowledge—of precursors—over time enriches rather than impoverishes. Logically, then, Pater feels none of that pessimism about the future of poetry that many Romantic and post-Romantic writers did. In his criticism Pater is always seeking beauty of mixed parentage, what I would term, thinking of Tennyson, the beauty of the medley. In all his work, but most deliberately in his novel *Marius the Epicurean* (1885), Pater carries on the work that Tennyson began in *The Princess,* that is, the conscious effort to formulate a poetics of eclecticism, and to write the eclectic self.

223

A familiar marker of eclecticism is its preference for mixtures, combinations, and medleys over all exclusive doctrines and devotions. In an 1868 review of the poetry of William Morris, Pater begins to develop an aesthetic that depends on the fulfillment of this eclectic principle. His admiration for Morris's poetry stems from its perfect representation not of any particular moment in history, but of "an artificial or 'earthly paradise' [...] a finer ideal, extracted from what in relation to any actual world is already an ideal" ("Poems by William Morris" 144). In Pater's view Morris thus exceeds the limitations of the nineteenth-century historical revivals: "This poetry is neither a mere reproduction of Greek or mediaeval life or poetry, nor a disguised reflex of modern sentiment" (144). Morris's handling of historical material never becomes antiquarianism, which would constitute "a waste of the poet's power" (146), nor does it become allegory or *roman à clef*. Rather Morris throws into relief the Greek or medieval life in a way that illuminates our relation to it or even our desire for it; he gives meaning to the past by making the reader feel the vitality of the past within the present: "The composite experience of all the ages is part of each one of us; to deduct from that experience, to obliterate any part of it, to come face to face with the people of a past age, as if the middle age, the Renaissance, the eighteenth century had not been, is as impossible as to become a little child, or enter again into the womb and be born. But though it is not possible to repress a single phase of that humanity, which, because we live and move and have our being in the life of humanity, makes us what we are; it is possible to isolate such a phase, to throw it into relief, to be divided against ourselves in zeal for it, as we may hark back to some choice space of our own individual life. We cannot conceive the age; we can conceive the element it has contributed to our culture; [...]" (146–47). In this important passage from Pater's early criticism, a key element of his volitional eclecticism is already present: neither can we develop beyond any age or phase of our history nor can we cease moving through time to settle into only one: "the choice life of the human spirit is always under mixed lights, and in mixed situations" (147). At these moments, the spirit is expectant, ready to leap forward to "the promise." Pater highlights those mixed elements of Morris's poetry, where he senses that division of self, where distinct influences or "sentiments" create a mixed situation. The Arthurian legends of *The Defence of Guenevere* (1858) yield their "sweetness" only in a "Christian atmosphere" (144); the simpler passions of *The Life and Death of Jason* (1867) come as a Renaissance in Morris's poetry, "explain[ing] through him a transition which, under many forms, is one law of the life of the human spirit" (146); and again, "It is precisely this effect, this grace of Hellenism relieved against the sorrow of the middle age, which forms the chief motive of *The Earthly Paradise* [1868], with an exquisite dexterity the two threads of sentiment are here interwoven and contrasted" (147). Morris and his characters live in medley, through the contradictions of accumulated history, revealing the nature of self in a late age. The conclusion to Pater's review of Morris (later revised as the conclusion to *The Renaissance*) celebrates the ability of the best poets to enlarge and enrich our experience, something Morris accomplishes by throwing into relief those elements of history that have contributed to our culture and are seen to be still at work within it.

Thomas Hardy's 1881 novel, *A Laodicean,* which has been the (sometimes hidden) keystone of this account of the age of eclecticism, might seem like an uneasy playfellow for Pater's great works, *Studies in the History of the Renaissance* and *Marius the Epicurean.* Critics have rarely considered these contemporaries together, and when they do, as Uttara Natarajan has noted, it is only in passing (849).[1] Natarajan herself goes much further in making the case for Pater's importance in shaping Hardy's idea of modernity (in *The Return of the Native*)—something that interests me as well, but in the context of their engagement with volitional eclecticism. Eclecticism was for Hardy, as for Pater, an inescapable condition of (literary) modernity. In *A Laodicean* Hardy takes two characters who have a practical, rather than intellectual, relationship with (and within) their own very mixed conditions, and demonstrates by the conclusion of the romance that their survival and their progress as human beings depend on their choosing to be eclectic. It is a heroic struggle, tinged with humor, an updating of romance (and Gothic) to suit the time and place.

Romance in *Marius the Epicurean* and *A Laodicean* is the generic equivalent of the historical mixed situation that Pater found in Morris's poetry. Diane Elam theorizes romance in much the same way that Pater theorizes Renaissance. It is a mode that always exists, and the mode of romance has always been postmodern, "a counter-discourse on history and the real" (3). Romance never really sees history as past (unlike realism, she says, which narrates history only in order to put it aside): "the postmodern romance re-members the past, re-situates its temporality, in order to make the past impossible to forget" (15). Like eclecticism, romance plays fast and loose with history, preferring the anachronistic to the diachronic; but this anachronism is always a point of integration and blending, a mélange— or medley—of past and present. In romance, it does not matter that history is unraveled and re-sewn on a new pattern, because romance wants to remake the world in its own image through subversion and play.[2] As Fredric Jameson puts it in "Magical Narratives: Romance as Genre," it is "that struggle between two worlds which characterizes the romance as a genre" (145). If Matthew Arnold's lines "Wandering between two worlds, one dead / The other powerless to be born" may be made to stand, as they often have, for the Victorian Zeitgeist, then it is not surprising that so many writers, Hardy and Pater among them, should return to romance by the end of the century to represent that struggle. For Jameson, "Romance as a form thus expresses a transitional moment, yet one of a very special type: its contemporaries must feel their society torn between past and future in such a way that the alternatives are grasped as hostile but somehow unrelated worlds" (158). Hardy dramatizes a Battle of the Styles in *A Laodicean*—Gothic versus Greek, tradition versus modernity—in such a way that it becomes a debate on what it would mean to choose eclecticism instead of any one style. Elam's theorizing of romance as postmodern, anachronistic, and playful helps me to read the fictions of Hardy and Pater as repudiations of organic historicism. They choose revolution over evolution—they choose to return. History is still an object of desire, but it is no longer a distant one, because eclecticism brings the past closer to the present, and validates the activity of romance in picking up the pieces.

Eclecticism as Renaissance

Pater's flexible use of the term "Renaissance" in the review of Morris to describe a phase in the life of a poet hints at both further refinement and further expansion of the idea. In *The Renaissance: Studies in Art and Poetry* (originally published as *Studies in the History of the Renaissance* [1873]), Pater attends to a series of "mixed situations" that create the opportunity for what he defines broadly as rebirth or Renaissance. In each of the nine studies, he attempts to distinguish the particular enabling mixture of characteristics and circumstances in the lives and works of artists who lived between the late Middle Ages and the eighteenth century. Pater's principle of selection, if it might be called that, depends on locating those moments of Renaissance that emerge when the artist casts the peculiar or "mixed" light of his personality over his creation. As Pater tells his readers in the preface, he aims "to distinguish, to analyse, and separate from its adjuncts, the virtue by which a picture, a landscape, a fair personality in life or in a book, produces this special impression of beauty or pleasure, to indicate what the source of that impression is, and under what conditions it is experienced" (xx–xxi). Emphasizing, with a quote from Sainte-Beuve, that this can be accomplished only by contact with works at first hand, the passage recalls the process by which the early-nineteenth-century eclectic philosopher Victor Cousin hoped to recover and synthesize the truth from all the various systems of thought that had existed throughout time—but with a crucial difference that makes Pater a new kind of eclectic. Instead of attempting a totalizing eclecticism that would encompass the best thoughts and aspirations of humanity (such as Cousin or Arnold might have done), Pater abandons that line of inquiry for a personal eclecticism, asking, what is this work of art to me? Instead of relying on Cousin's "internal eye" to map an external truth, the aesthetic critic analyzes his own impressions for what they mean, first of all, in relation to himself. Eclecticism remains for Pater what it was for Cousin and Arnold, a method of study and discovery, but it quickly transmutes into something else, a method of creation. Nevertheless, Pater's eclecticism has more in common with the praxis of nineteenth-century culture than with any effort to establish a criterion of truth by which one might judge the productions of the past. In the character of the dilettante, he makes a claim on our attention, as perhaps having found the way forward in the arts. While Cousin and Arnold hoped that progress, both social and aesthetic, could be achieved through volitional eclecticism, Pater assumes it. He compares his own eclectic operation to that of the chemist who, discovering an element, makes a note of its properties for himself and others, and so presumes to build on humanistic knowledge and aesthetic experience the way that scientists have always done. As the critic learns to recognize the types and varieties of influence that works of art have on him, he becomes more susceptible to beauty in all its diversity. In this way he overcomes at once the dilemma of style and the anxiety of being eclectic: "What is important, then, is not that the critic should possess a correct abstract definition of beauty for the intellect, but a certain kind of temperament, the power of being deeply moved by the presence of beautiful objects. He will remember always that beauty exists in many forms. To him all periods, types, schools of taste, are in themselves equal. In all ages there have been some excellent workmen, and some excellent work done. The question he asks is always:—In whom did the stir, the genius, the sentiment of the period find itself? where was the receptacle of its refinement, its elevation, its taste?" (xxi). The temperament of the critic is paramount, because Pater does not believe there are any objective criteria by which the works of history can be arranged, compared, and judged. Neither will tradition be a guide, since all judgments established by habit or custom are to be avoided. At once cut adrift from history and totally immersed in it, the aesthetic critic responds to beauty as to a physical rather than an intellectual force—seeing and feeling rather than thinking and judging. Eclecticism—selecting the best that has been thought and known—now becomes a matter of personal conviction. The extreme relativity of this position is not disconcerting, a cause for anxiety or pessimism about the future, because each age, as each critic and artist, will view the past in its own mixed light.

Much of the preface to *The Renaissance* reads like an answer to Arnold's "The Function of Criticism at the Present Time." Beginning the essay by setting out the goal of aesthetic criticism, Pater slyly concedes, "'To see the object as in itself it really is,' has been justly said to be the aim of all true criticism whatever"; but he then proceeds to refigure Arnold's objectivist (outside-the-time-stream) criticism as an entirely subjective project: "in aesthetic criticism the first step towards seeing one's object as it really is, is to know one's own impression as it really is, to discriminate it, to realise it distinctly" (xix).[3] As Geoffrey Tillotson suggests, the disinterested criticism that Arnold advocated "was, and is, impossible in practice" (92–93). The problem with seeing the object as in itself it really is could be traced back to history; Arnold wanted to pretend he could step outside the time-stream, to proceed as though "unaware that the date of a mind mattered" (Tillotson 94). No one, as far as Pater was concerned, could step outside of time; as he wrote of Morris, every individual is a composite of all the ages that came before. The object could not be independent of history any more than the spectator or reader could be. In absorbing Arnold's criticism, Pater simply took what he could use and transformed it according to his different understanding of history. Another significant difference between Arnold and Pater is in their principle of selection (of the "best"). While Arnold searches for those works that are "modern" in the sense of being adequate to comprehend and represent the age in which they were produced (Arnold dips into history only to extract objects from it), Pater uncovers the "virtue" or "active principle" in a work, "the action of [its] unique, incommunicable faculty" (xxii). In emphasizing the individual virtue of a work of art, Pater does not neglect its place in history: "The various forms of intellectual activity which together make up the culture of an age, move for the most part from different starting-points, and by unconnected roads. As products of the same generation they partake of a common character, and unconsciously illustrate each other; but of the producers themselves, each group is solitary, gaining what advantage or disadvantage there may be in intellectual isolation" (xxiii–xxiv). In *The Renaissance* Pater wants to account for culture, not a culture that has come and gone, but culture that continues to shape the present. By contrast, Arnold wants to reform and improve the culture of the present on a model extracted from the past. At the end of the preface, Pater is again thinking of Arnold when he says that certain eras do provide more favorable conditions for the mutual impacting of art, poetry, philosophy, and religion. The Renaissance was just such a "many-sided, centralised, complete" age, in which each producer participated "in the best thoughts which that age produced" (xxiv). Pater believes this, but it is not the structuring principle of the work; the movement of the Renaissance is not centripetal, but centrifugal—outward through space and time. In his studies the importance of Renaissance derives not only from the discovery of "old and forgotten sources" of imaginative pleasure but also from the "divination of fresh sources thereof—new experiences, new subjects of poetry, new forms of art" (2), which give new resources to the present and the future.

The preface to *The Renaissance* provides only the first instance of Pater's coming to terms with the personal, even private, nature of criticism. Deeply influenced as Arnold was by French literature and criticism, Pater, too, looked to the eclectic examples of Renan and Sainte-Beuve in particular, to reach some of his most enduring conclusions about the means and ends of criticism. In her exhaustive, two-volume study *Walter Pater's Reading,* Billie Inman cites "Renan's eclectic mode of thought" as one of the three major influences on Pater by 1866 (xi).[4] Renan's thesis in "The Religions of Antiquity" underlies "Pater's idea that the modern mind is eclectic" (98). It is the same source from which Arnold would have imbibed Renan's eclectic principles. Unlike Arnold, Pater does not regard eclecticism as a cure for the naïve eclecticism of the period, because he is not interested in the age as a particularly eclectic one. Like renaissance, eclecticism as a concept is not fixed historically or geographically. Eclecticism is instead most persuasive, and most fruitful for Pater, as an explanation of the peculiar operations of his own mind. Inman, who has most carefully traced Pater's unscholarly borrowings, translations, transformations, and misquotations, puts it this way: "Pater developed a remarkable originality through self-confident judgment, selective imitation, bold modification, and a gift for expressive phrasing. With a great mass of material to work upon, he was able to select, shape, and define ideas—indeed to form an authorial identity for himself" (ix). His eclectic reading, conducted apparently without system, permitted him to explore the relation of each text to his own mind, to read "responsively."

Pater's style of criticism derives from his style of reading, which can be characterized by its unusual receptivity. Not surprisingly, then, one of the traits of the Renaissance that attracts Pater is its openness to new ideas. As a "student" of the period, Pater has an advantage, he feels, over the student of the Reformation or French Revolution, because "he is not beset at every turn by the inflexibilities and antagonisms of some well-recognised controversy, with rigidly defined opposites, exhausting the intelligence and limiting one's sympathies" (20). Like the French Romantics who saw eclecticism as a way beyond ideological polarization, Pater sees the Renaissance as a model for overcoming the false dilemma posed by the historical inheritance: "Here there are no fixed parties, no exclusions: all breathes of that unity of culture in which 'whatsoever things are comely' are reconciled, for the elevation and adorning of our spirits" (20–21). Pater probably owes something of this catholic attitude to Sainte-Beuve, whose work (like Renan's) stands behind so much of *The Renaissance*. In his famous essay "What Is a Classic?" Sainte-Beuve argues against the old, narrow definition of the term.[5] In France the Academy determined which authors were classics or models, "established *rules* for composition and style, *strict rules* to which one must *conform*" (86). A largely reactionary effort meant to beat back the advance of romanticism, the restriction of the meaning of the term "classic" did little to nurture "classic" literature. Sainte-Beuve, in attempting to redefine as classic "an author who has enriched the human spirit," emphasizes that a classic can be born in any time and place: "The important thing today, it seems to me, is to maintain the conception and creed, while at the same time broadening it" (92). Sainte-Beuve, who had a difficult relationship with the French philosopher of eclecticism, Victor Cousin, is nonetheless echoing his teacher by acknowledging the need for selection without dogmatism. Rather than contracting the size of the literary canon, Sainte-Beuve would give it more generous proportions: "Moreover, there is really no question of sacrificing or disparaging anything. The Temple of Taste, I think, needs to be rebuilt; but in rebuilding it we have only to enlarge it, that it may become the Pantheon of mankind's best, of all those who have made a notable and lasting contribution to the store of the spirit's treasures and delights" (93).[6] Sainte-Beuve also probably influenced Pater's personal approach to criticism. After listing those authors whom he would invite to his remodeled Temple of Taste, Sainte-Beuve gestures toward an infinite process of selection and revision: "The imagination of each reader will enable him to complete the sketch and even to choose the group he prefers. For choose one must, because the primary condition of good taste, after all has been understood, is to cease from endless voyaging and finally settle somewhere and take a stand" (96).[7] With the comfortable, solid example of French eclecticism before him, Pater can proceed with confidence to judge and classify the literature of the past, to give it an order that, while entirely his own, will nonetheless guide others toward a revised understanding of their own and past cultures.

As part of a general effort to see all ages and tastes as equal (in the sense of what they have to offer to the student of culture), Pater continually bears witness in *The Renaissance* to those moments in which historical oppositions are overcome or held in balance within the works of exceptional artists, precisely the mixed situations he prefers in Morris's poetry.

A few examples will demonstrate the eclectic pattern of Pater's judgments. In general, Pater conceives of the Renaissance as the period when "the rude strength of the middle age turns to sweetness; and the taste for sweetness generated there becomes the seed of the classical revival in it" (2). Pater considers the poetry of Provence, with its "earthly passion, with its intimacy, its freedom, its variety" to represent a starting point for a medieval Renaissance (3). The poetic expression of liberty he finds there marks the beginning of a new phase of human experience, "the free play of the human intelligence around all subjects presented to it" (3). The literature of the medieval Renaissance, described in "Two Early French Stories," is the product of mixed parentage: the "outbreak of reason and the imagination" within the intense atmosphere of the Christian ideal. Much of the essay concerns the form taken by the era's "antinomianism," especially the "search after the pleasures of the senses and the imagination" (18–19). The one-sidedness of Christianity gives rise to these desires, a conclusion that strongly echoes Arnold's in the "Hebrew and Hellene" chapter of *Culture and Anarchy*. Not surprisingly, like Arnold, Pater wants to suggest that a balance, or mixture, is more likely to produce great art.

Pater also pursues this theme in "Sandro Botticelli" where he identifies the peculiar appeal of the painter's work as having its source in a "middle world." Preoccupied neither with Heaven nor with Hell as were so many of his contemporaries, Botticelli wanted to paint "men and women, in their mixed and uncertain condition" (43). Pater even theorizes that Botticelli subscribed to a heresy of the time, that human beings were actually fallen angels, who had taken no side in the war for Heaven. This uncertain, in-between condition evokes the painter's sympathy, causing him to paint his figures with a shadow of this knowledge upon them, of a great chance not taken. The mixture Pater perceives in Botticelli's subjects was evident in his practice as well. In language reminiscent of Reynolds's *Discourses,* and the post-Renaissance academic tradition more generally, Pater describes Botticelli's genius as eclectic: "the genius of which Botticelli is the type usurps the data before it as the exponent of ideas, moods, visions of its own; in this interest it plays fast and loose with those data, rejecting some and isolating others, and always combining them anew" (42). While Donald Hill cites William Blake's (largely negative) annotations of Reynolds as an influence on Pater's preface to *The Renaissance* (and by extension on his aesthetic criticism), the Botticelli essay points to a different way of interpreting Blake's aphorism "Ages are all equal, but genius is always above its age" (xxi; qtd. in Hill 299). What the geniuses of the Renaissance shared, in Pater's reckoning, was the capacity to usurp and combine data they are given, to make it their own. Blake is typically figured as a proponent of uninstructed, native genius (in the same vein as Edward Young's *Conjectures on Original Composition*) when he derides Reynolds's educational methods (master the tradition first, and then create something new); but Pater clearly makes Blake his own when he makes Botticelli's genius—his membership in the broader Renaissance—dependent on his eclecticism.

For the sculptors Pater takes up in "Luca della Robbia," membership in the Renaissance is again the result of a transitional historical situation and an eclectic method. In Pater's account, the fifteenth-century Tuscan sculptors lie somewhere between the universalizing practice of the Greeks (meant to express the perfect type of the individual, free of accidents) and the incompleteness of Michelangelo (meant to express individuality and intensity). They "unite to an intense and individual expression by a system of conventionalism as skilful and subtle as that of the Greeks" "elements of tranquillity, of repose" (54). Reynolds would have approved. They mastered convention, and brought to it their particular individuality. In "The Poetry of Michelangelo," Pater elaborates on his judgment that the genius of Michelangelo had been "spiritualised by the reverie of the middle age, penetrated by its spirit of inwardness and introspection" (52), blending a "lovely strangeness" with classical form, "sweetness" with strength (58). The fifteenth century into which both Leonardo and Michelangelo were born presents the historian with a "two-fold" movement, "partly the Renaissance, partly also the coming of what is called the 'modern spirit,' with its realism, its appeal to experience" (86). The Renaissance is modern because it is backward-looking—and both nature and antiquity are compassed in its view. In Leonardo's painting Pater sees the same "peculiar atmosphere and mixed lights" (86) that define his revolutionary modernity; there is, for example, in Leonardo's *Saint John the Baptist* a "strange likeness to the *Bacchus* which hangs near it, and which set Théophile Gautier thinking of Heine's notion of decayed gods, who, to maintain themselves, after the fall of paganism, took employment in the new religion" (93). The invocation here is not fanciful. Pater regards the blending as a "symbolical invention" that will be used "as the starting point of a train of sentiment, subtle and vague as a piece of music" (93). One gets the sense in reading *The Renaissance* that this is the music Pater has been hearing all along. When he comes to the description of "La Gioconda," the reader knows it is the climax of his quest. The historical blending recurs, but on a huge scale, with Pater seeing all the "thoughts and experience of the world" in her face (98). In this justifiably famous passage, he seems to follow the woman, who has been dead many times, through the graveyards and "deep seas" of history. She is a singular being, but she is also the pictorial embodiment of the eclectic, "modern idea," the representative of collective human experience.

The essays on the arts of the Renaissance, along with the preface and conclusion, were certainly the most important for determining the shape of literary modernism in Britain, but they do not reveal as clearly the terms of the Victorian debate on eclecticism, as does Pater's one essay on a fellow scholar. In "Pico della Mirandola," Pater exposes one of the peculiar passions of the Renaissance, the desire to reconcile the Christian religion with that of ancient Greece. Pater responds to Pico's effort with both fascination and uneasiness, much as a contemporary might have done. In the first instance, Pater recognizes the impulse as a "generous" one: "To reconcile forms of sentiment which at first sight seem incompatible, to adjust the various products of the human mind to one another in one many-sided type of intellectual culture, to give humanity, for heart and imagination to feed upon, as much as it could possibly receive, belonged to the generous instinct of that age" (23).[8] Pico himself, while embodying the "picturesque union of contrasts" (37) present in so much Renaissance art, yet failed to discover the perfect order that would explain all differences and resolve them. As J. B. Bullen has argued, the process of Renaissance at work here allows us to access the "composite experience" of all past ages (*Myth* 282)— what Pater saw and felt in *La Gioconda*. The uneasiness Pico's contemporaries felt, and which Pater's probably felt, derives from their anxiety that having access to rival traditions would ultimately displace Christianity. And though Pater admires Pico's effort, he finally concedes that the "reconciliation" between Christianity and paganism can be only an "imaginative" one, achievable exclusively through art.

Pater responds to the efforts of Pico as to a precursor who attempted the same experiment under similar conditions. As a working model of aesthetic criticism, the imaginative reconciliation of opposing forces becomes the keynote in all of Pater's writings; but even he was not immune to the powerful sense of failure provoked by the eclecticism of his age, a failure always marked by intellectual confusion (arguably of the kind represented by Pico). His attitude toward Pico's effort to resolve the differences between Christianity and paganism is complicated by Pater's acceptance of a developmental historical model, derived from Hegel and Lessing, among others. Countering the instinct that drives Pico and others like him, Pater writes that a "modern scholar" would remember that "all religions may be regarded as natural products," organically related to the age in which they were born (25). By contrast, the scholars of the fifteenth century "lacked the very rudiments of the historic sense, which, by an imaginative act, throws itself back into a world unlike one's own, and estimates every intellectual creation in its connection with the age from which it proceeded" (26). In essence, Pater brings historicism to bear on the question of eclecticism; the strength of nineteenth-century historicism gave birth to eclecticism and its attendant crises, but it also appeared to be the surest means of arresting the eclectic tendency. Passages on the subject in *Plato and Platonism,* generally considered to be his mature pronouncement on these competing critical methods, are especially revealing in this respect.[9] Commencing his account of Platonic philosophy with a brief sketch of the intellectual situation of the period, Pater shows us a world not so different from the late nineteenth century: "the world Plato had entered into was already almost weary of philosophical debate, bewildered by the oppositions of sects, the claims of rival schools. Language and the processes of thought were already become sophisticated, the very air he breathed sickly with off-cast speculative atoms" (*Plato and Platonism* 6). Demonstrating that every age experiences the burden of history, Plato has to become, at least in the *Timaeus,* "an eclectic critic of older [theories]" offering "a sort of storehouse of all physical theories" (6–7). These older thinkers are "everywhere" in Plato's philosophy, "not as the stray carved corner of some older edifice, to be found here or there amid the new, but rather like minute relics of earlier organic life in the very stones he builds with" (7). This image, perhaps more than any other in Pater's writings, portrays the natural eclecticism of intellectual work. He does not represent Plato's intellectual architecture as naïvely eclectic, with tacked-on ornamentation, but neither is it volitionally eclectic; rather he invokes a third term, a kind of organic eclecticism, best represented by the image of fossils in stone. The image also suggests the necessity of excavation, and the operation in the present, of the historic method. There is nothing new in Plato, "or rather, as in many other very original products of human genius, the seemingly new is old also, a palimpsest, a tapestry of which the actual threads have served before" (8). When Pater on the very next page rejects eclectic criticism in favor of that historic method that will allow him to excavate Plato's philosophy, he does so, I believe, not in consequence of the obsolescence of eclecticism, but because it is not the proper tool with which to criticize "speculative opinion" (8). Pater calls eclecticism "the method which has prevailed in periods of large reading but with little inceptive force of their own" (9). Its defect, he claims, is its "tendency to misrepresent the true character of the doctrine it professes to explain, that it may harmonise thus the better with the other elements of a pre-conceived system" (9). Rather than view Pater's judgment on eclecticism as his final word on the subject, I want to look carefully at his characterization of Plato's philosophizing. Plato had to become eclectic to cope with the mass of existing theories, but his own strong personality shaped these "relics of earlier organic life" into a new dwelling of his own creation.[10] Unlike many earlier critics of eclecticism (especially G. H. Lewes), Pater does not view eclecticism as the study method of an apprentice. In fact, he views eclecticism as having too powerful a creative tendency; it misrepresents others' ideas (as Pater so often does) in order to harmonize them with an inner vision. Nevertheless, Pater is keenly aware that, in his own century, the "historic method" has discredited the "generous, eclectic or synthetic method" in criticism, because eclecticism colors one's object of study too vividly (9). The products of history are really only intelligible, Pater concedes, at their own date and in their own environment. This claim, while seeming to go against his own scholarly and critical method, can only have been intended as a starting point to the study of history, but never the goal of the (imaginative) historians he admired, such as Winckelmann or Michelet, who transcribed not mere fact, but "fact in its infinite variety, as modified by human preference in all its infinitely varied forms" (*Appreciations* 10–11). Indeed, it is not even the result of his study of Platonic thought, since Pater is always returning to the notion that Plato is modern because he was a relativist, unwilling to rest in any conclusion. Like eclecticism, Platonism cultivates the "habit ... of tentative thinking and suspended judgment" (*Plato and Platonism* 195). It is not surprising, then, that the American classics scholar Paul Shorey, after reading Pater, made Plato "the true spiritual father of the long and illustrious line of sceptics and eclectics," in which he also numbers Victor Cousin and Matthew Arnold (261).

Bullen and many others have observed that Pater's "studies" are largely about the discovery of selfhood, precisely what made his contemporaries so uneasy about the work.[11] Indeed, Pater's final essay has often been read as the key to his project and Winckelmann as the precursor who, like Pater, remade the world according to his own peculiar vision of a moment in history. Winckelmann acknowledged that great art would be both imitative and original, and he lived his life in much the same way; in his lifestyle he emulated, as he thought, a Greek existence and, through this discipline, became in his own time thoroughly original. In Winckelmann's life and writings, Pater discovers the same pattern of Renaissance—a "mixed situation," and rebirth through combination: "The basis of all artistic genius lies in the power of conceiving humanity in a new and striking way, of putting a happy world of its own creation in place of the meaner world of our common days, generating around itself an atmosphere with a novel power of refraction, selecting, transforming, recombining the images it transmits, according to the choice of the imaginative intellect" (*Renaissance* 170). In his reconstruction of Winckelmann's life, Pater focuses his attention on just these effects of artistic genius. When he moves to Rome, eats only bread and drinks only wine, and creates friendships with "brilliant youths," Winckelmann puts "a happy world of [his] own creation in place of the meaner world of our common days." Coming into contact with the antique, first in Dresden and then in Rome, the antiquarian "escape[s] from abstract theory to intuition, to the exercise of sight and touch" (147); he generates around himself "an atmosphere with a novel power of refraction, selecting, transforming, recombining the images it transmits, according to the choice of the imaginative intellect." As Hegel famously testified, Winckelmann opened a new organ for the human spirit through this critical effort. But it was not distant, disembodied criticism that could accomplish the revival of the Greek spirit in art; rather it was Winckelmann's bodily immersion in the past that allowed for the transformation of the present. Only the revival of the (albeit imagined) Greek style of life could make their art viable again.

That powerful sense of historical development evident in all of his writing made Winckelmann the first modern historian of art; and perhaps, too, his comprehension of a historical situation bounded by loss and mitigated by irreversible decline gave subsequent writers and artists a perspective from which to criticize their own culture. Even as he recognized that "Greek art was determined by its particular environment: the climatic, social, and political conditions [...] made it unique" (*Reflections* xix), he saw past this determining moment to a "period of beginning [...] an age when man came slowly to realize it was not some superhistorical force or authority but he himself who determined the course of his destiny" (xxi). This acceptance of historical development in conjunction with its opposite, the loosing of the trammels of history at the moment of self-awareness, gave birth to the enlightened eclecticism of the nineteenth century (and of Pater in particular), an eclecticism whose modus operandi was the resuscitation of styles of life (in order to revive whatever particular element of that lifestyle seemed desirable, whether art, architecture, social organization, or literature). Winckelmann himself escapes the taint of naïve eclecticism because his system of imitation appeared to be internally coherent. James Eli Adams makes a compelling argument for the influence of Winckelmann's anachronisms on the development of Pater's critical persona. Characterizing Winckelmann himself as "a relic of classical antiquity," Pater "associates the critic's life with previous discoveries of the physical relics of Greek art, events that confirm and extend the authority of 'the Hellenic tradition'" (Adams 158). Adams further argues that "Pater recasts that identity [the instinctive, anachronistic pagan] as a tradition in which his own reception of Winckelmann participates. [...] Pater's essay takes its place in a series of critical encounters that constitute the authority of the Greek ideal as a tradition renewed and extended with each discovery of a 'relic' of Greek culture" (158). Viewed as an entry in a series of recurrent Renaissances, Pater's recovery of Winckelmann perpetuates, I think, the kind of eclecticism that Winckelmann himself attributed to the Carracci. As *Nachahmer* (artist-imitators), they had no choice but to come to terms with the historical inheritance. In order to become inimitable themselves they had to imitate ancient art. Winckelmann imitated Greek culture, and in imitating Winckelmann, Pater too becomes completely original and inimitable.

Eclecticism as Romance

Until the end of the nineteenth century the romance of architecture was literature's privileged interlocutor for conversations about the proper mixture of past and present, and romance and realism in modern life. And as J. B. Bullen has observed in connection with Hardy in *A Laodicean*, "the choice of architectural styles [. . .] is but a symptom of a multiplicity of other choices" (*The Expressive Eye* 122). When the architect-hero of *A Laodicean* makes his first appearance, he is sketching a medieval church. At the time Hardy published this novel, in 1881, George Somerset's pastime would have been a respectable one, even a middle-class cliché—but with a difference. The Gothic Revival in architecture is in decline, and Somerset has only just become enthusiastic. During his formative years, while Gothic was in ascendance, he favored the classical styles; about to embark on his professional life, he believes that it would be profitable to have more than a passing acquaintance with medieval architecture. While in the vicinity of De Stancy Castle, he comes upon a Baptist church where he witnesses a young woman, Paula Power, refuse to go through with her baptism into the community. The minister, Mr. Woodwell, delivers a scorching sermon on her lack of commitment to her father's faith, introducing into the novel the theme of the "Laodicean." He draws attention to these words in the Book of Revelation: "*I know thy works, that thou are neither cold nor hot: I would thou wert cold or hot. So then because thou art lukewarm, and neither cold nor hot, I will spue thee out of my mouth. . . . Thou sayest, I am rich, and increased with goods, and have need of nothing; and knowest not that thou art wretched, and miserable, and poor, and blind, and naked*" (14). Originally directed at the Christians of a wealthy trading community in a Roman province of Asia Minor, the designation "Laodicean" came to mean any person who was half-hearted in religion or politics, and in this novel, in the choice of a style. Hardy has already informed us that Somerset, too, is a Laodicean: he vacillates on the question of style; although he is highly educated and even talented, he remains unformed by his still-limited experiences and uncommitted to any particular aesthetic doctrine or more conventional faith. Hardy describes him as having "more of the beauty—if beauty it ought to be called—of the future human type than of the past" (4). An aspect of this future life will be—is—*indecision* resulting from excessive introspection: George Somerset "had suffered from the modern malady of unlimited appreciativeness as much as any living man of his own age" (7). To be modern, perhaps, means seeing—and enjoying—too much, because one has too much *access* to everything: sights and ideas, past and future.

Paula and George share the same dilemma, the same contradictory impulses and perceptions, which Hardy concentrates in the Gothic castle that brings them together. The young and beautiful heiress to a railway fortune inherits her father's profound modernity and the castle, representing history and all that her father could not give her—traceable genealogy, a portrait gallery exhibiting family physiognomy, a place in the nation's history, and so on. The castle provokes a crisis; even as George demonstrates to Paula that he is capable of undertaking a sensitive expansion and restoration of the dilapidated buildings, Paula—"A mixed young lady" (30)—anachronistically wants to construct a Greek court in its center. She confesses to George that she is not a medievalist, but an eclectic who longs for the romance of history (78). She wants to manufacture Greek pottery in a town that she will build herself, a utopian community of artisans. She exercises in a special gymnasium. Her castle room is cluttered with books and periodicals from America and the Continent: "These things [George observes], ensconced amid so much of the old and hoary, were as if a stray hour of the nineteenth century had wandered like a butterfly into the thirteenth, and lost itself there" (31). George associates Paula with "the march of mind—the steamship, and the railway, and the thoughts that shake mankind" (79), but the young architect witnesses the shifting of her allegiance toward the Gothic. When she is condemned in the newspaper as a barbarian outsider who threatens to destroy the castle, instead of holding it in trust for the public, Paula abandons her eclectic plan. Further, the spell of everything associated with the De Stancy family affects her deeply, so much so that Mr. Woodwell fears she is losing her faith under the influence of medieval Catholicism: "Sometimes I think those Stancy towers and lands will be a curse to her. The spirit of old papistical times still lingers in the nooks of those silent walls, like a bad odour in a still atmosphere, dulling the iconoclastic emotions of the Puritan" (54). Although George had "inclined to each denomination as it presented itself" and "had travelled through a great many beliefs and doctrines without feeling himself much better than when he set out" (48), he too is repelled by Paula's threatened return to the national religion. By giving up her Dissenting inheritance and restoring her castle to a "pure" Gothic, Paula moves one step closer toward a dangerous mistake: marriage with Captain De Stancy. This melodramatic turn in the plot is precipitated by the novel's villain, De Stancy's son William Dare, a cosmopolite photographer who specializes in creating illusions. He perceives Paula's weakness, her artistic predilection for "a well-known line of ancestors" (96), her desire to be "romantic and historical" (95). As George falls in love with Paula, his own artistic principles loosen to the extent that he adopts an eclectic point of view against Paula's dangerously exclusive Gothic outlook. When Paula first poses the question "Do you think it a thing more to be proud of that one's father should have made a great tunnel and railway like that, than that one's remote ancestor should have built a great castle like this?" (79), George still favors the castle. After examining the great railway tunnel and observing its integration within the landscape, Somerset and Hardy seem to offer a contrary response, or at least an eclectic one. Hardy's architect hero begins to recognize that medieval architecture is dead, while modern constructions such as the elder De Stancy's suburban villa and the ugly Baptist chapel are vital and vibrant.

As the melodramatic plot unfolds against the backdrop of a realistic novel, and Paula first accepts Captain De Stancy's offer of marriage—he wins her heart when he poses before a De Stancy portrait wearing armor and asking "Is the resemblance strong?"—and then rejects him when Dare's plot to gain her fortune and discredit Somerset is uncovered. Paula then literally goes on a quest to win the love of Somerset, following him on a journey through Europe. This final reversal of the conventions of romance had been anticipated earlier in the story when Paula rescued Somerset from a castle tower where he had been entrapped. In the end, when Paula has found the object of her desire, she accepts Mr. Woodwell's designation for her: "What I really am, as far as I know, is one of that body to whom lukewarmth is not an accident but a provisional necessity, till they see a little more clearly" (376). As if to maintain her inconsistency to the end, Hardy has Paula wish that her castle had not burnt down and that her lover were a De Stancy (379), even as George is planning to "build a new house from the ground, eclectic in style" (378). The castle will truly be, what it should already have been, a ruin whose original faith and significance were irretrievably lost long before the nineteenth century. Hardy's fiction articulates well the despair of contemporaries such as William

Morris over the possibility of a Gothic Revival, and also the dilemma of his heroine as she tries to separate herself from the Gothic influence, to find out what she will become herself.

The question of exactly how to do this was a vital one, both for those working in the architectural profession, and for those simply caught up in its romance. Hardy answers decisively in favor of eclecticism, by making architecture the figure for all the other choices one has to make in the nineteenth century, when all the old authorities have gone the way of Stancy Castle, and by foregrounding the desire for romance. Twice during Captain De Stancy's courtship of Paula Power, the narration comments on the desire that is driving the heroine's story. The first time it is the narrator who defines her romanticism as natural, even healthy: "Human nature is at bottom romantic rather than ascetic, and the local habitation which accident had provided for Paula was perhaps acting as a solvent of the hard, morbidly introspective views thrust upon her in early life" (188). Even though the castle leads Paula astray, in one sense, it does allow her to forge a connection with the past that has been missing from her previous experience. That might be a good thing, the narrator tells us, for making her views less dogmatic and narrow. When she asserts at the novel's end that it is right to be lukewarm until she sees a little more clearly, she might be making a broader claim for the age, and for human beings in general. Is it not better to be a Laodicean than to be resolutely, even passionately wrong? (One thinks here of William Butler Yeats's memorable lines from "The Second Coming," which refer to the events of the Russian Revolution, "The best lack all conviction, while the worst / Are full of passionate intensity" [7–8].) The second time the narration comments on romantic human nature, it is focalized through Somerset: "But romanticism, which will exist in every human breast as long as human nature itself exists, had asserted itself in her. Veneration for things old, not because of any merit in them, but because of their long continuance, had developed in her; and her modern spirit was taking to itself wings and flying away" (242). For Somerset the old thing lacking merit is first of all the De Stancy line, which has enchanted the woman he loves; but the claim here has far-reaching implications for the dilemma of style Hardy represents. If Paula's "modern spirit" takes wings and flies away, if she tries to put the castle back the way it was, ignoring all of the intervening centuries, then she is being untrue to herself and to the present age. The eclectic does not time-travel. She does not put herself into the past; rather, she brings the past forward. In Elam's terms, this is what romance has always done. It "re-members" the past in order to make it "unforgettable." The Gothic Revivalists who tried not to be eclectic had to fail, because they were neglecting the modern spirit.

As Hardy and Morris recognized in their SPAB (Society for the Protection of Ancient Buildings) activities, restoration that stripped away the accumulated layers of history was a crime against the history the restorers pretended to honor. Only in the blending of the layered past with the multifarious present is history actually preserved. When Paula finally rejects De Stancy, she says that she does not "care one atom for artistic completeness and a splendid whole" (309). Paula does not stop longing for romance, but she will have it through eclecticism.

As a romance, *Marius the Epicurean* probably has more in common with the aestheticism and dreamlike narratives of George MacDonald's *Phantastes* (1858) or his later *Lillith* (1895) than it does with Hardy's *A Laodicean,* and yet it is the closer kin of Hardy's mixed work because it foregrounds the problem of eclecticism in the formation of the self. In it Pater largely repeats Winckelmann's effort to recombine images according to the author's (and character's) peculiar sense of fact, but it also represents Pater's supreme effort to "reconcile" competing styles of life—just as Hardy has Paula Power do. Pater would have been attracted to the second century A.D., where he sets the action, for much the same reason he was intrigued by the Renaissance. As a period in history that allowed for the simultaneous existence of various literatures, philosophies, religions, and ritual practices, it would have been rich with the alloys created by their amalgamation. Marius enters this complex world from one bound by the traditions of home and the ancient religion of Numa. Very early in the narrative, Marius lets go of his exclusive devotion, so "that that early, much cherished religion of the villa might come to count with him as but one form of poetic beauty, or of the ideal, in things; as but one voice, in a world where there were many voices it would be moral weakness not to listen to" (I:43–44). The initial rival to the religion of home is simply a new phase of life, rich with new opportunities. He begins to think that he has spent too much time in contemplation of the past (one of the tendencies of his traditional form of worship), observing that when the modern world turns toward or absorbs something of the past, "for the purpose of a fastidious self-correction, in matters of art, literature, and even, as we have seen, of religion, at least it improved, by a shade or two of more scrupulous finish, on the old pattern" (I:48). These observations are in accord with Pater's usual attitude regarding the quarrel of the ancients and moderns; modernity offers incremental improvement on the past, because of the accretion of all past times. Pater even manages to avoid any prolonged note of nostalgia in the early chapters, by this turn of Marius's toward the present and the future. Marius begins to see that neither individuals nor societies are impoverished by time, but rather are made richer by its perpetual motion.

As he turns decisively toward the future, Marius encounters the character who will voice some of Pater's most enduring views on language and literature (that will be reiterated and extended in *Appreciations*). Together with Flavian, a young poet, Marius reads the "Golden Book" of the day, Apuleius's *The Golden Ass*. From describing the external appearance of the precious book, the narrator turns to what is inside, prefiguring as he does something of Pater's description of Tennyson's language in "Style": "And the inside was something not less dainty and fine, full of the archaisms and curious felicities in which that generation delighted, quaint terms and images, picked fresh from the early dramatists, the lifelike phrases of some lost poet preserved by an old grammarian, racy morsels of the vernacular and studied prettinesses:—all alike, mere playthings for the genuine power and natural eloquence of the erudite artist, unsuppressed by his erudition, which, however, made some people angry, chiefly less well 'got-up' people, and especially those who were untidy from indolence" (I:56). Pater's admiration for the mixed languages of contemporary authors such as Newman, Carlyle, and Tennyson is translated, here, into Marius's appreciation of certain ancient writers, who were equally affected by a mixed situation. Most of Pater's readers would not instinctively have grouped the "classics" with such authors of their own day whose literary languages were personal and complex, thinking perhaps that ancient writers were pure, fresh, and unburdened by precursors. The narrator, whose temporal location is coterminous with Pater's, as the references to Swift and Gautier in this chapter indicate, declares emphatically, "No! it was certainly not that old-fashioned ease of the early literature, which could never come again" (I:56). By acknowledging the problem of self-consciousness here, Pater rejects an entire tradition of literary criticism (operative for more than three centuries) that bemoaned the loss of originality, freshness, naïveté, purity, an unconditioned self—whatever ideal condition was held against the self-consciousness of the belated artist. Pater is more interested in showing his readers an ancient literature that shares certain key elements, even a sensibility, with the literature of his own, eclectic age. His generation delights in "archaisms," such as those to be found in Morris's poetry; they take pleasure in the "racy morsels of the vernacular" that might be uncovered in Browning; and they recognize the "natural eloquence of the erudite artist" in someone such as Arnold, who indeed made them angry enough to cry for more of Alexander Smith! Apuleius, too, wrote in the vernacular, and like the literary languages developed by Morris, Browning, Arnold, and Pater himself, it was written "with all the care of a learned language" (I:57).

The chapter on "Euphuism" that follows the boys' reading of Apuleius sets out some of the elements of eclecticism that Pater repeats three years later in "Style." The narrator tells us that Flavian himself possessed "a fine instinctive sentiment of the exact value and power of words," and he designs for himself a "literary programme" that distinctly resembles Pater's own, at least as he represented it in "Style": "He would make of it a serious study, weighing the precise power of every phrase and word, as though it were precious metal, disentangling the later associations and going back to the original and native sense of each,—restoring to full significance all its wealth of latent figurative expression, reviving or replacing its outworn or tarnished images. Latin literature and the Latin tongue were dying of routine and languor; and what was necessary, first of all, was to re-establish the natural and direct relationship between thought and expression, between the sensation and the term, and restore to words their primitive power" (I:96). The young man is both ambitious, seeking to become a leader among men by increasing the power of his words, and patriotic, wishing to rehabilitate "the mother-tongue, then fallen so tarnished and languid" (I:94). Flavian envisions an improved, vernacular literary language, a combination of the "increasingly artificial" and "barbarously pedantic" classical Latin with the "colloquial idiom" and its "thousand chance-tost gems of racy or picturesque expression" (I:95). This combination is what Pater discovered in "Joachim Du Bellay" and the Pleiad school of poets in sixteenth-century France: "Du Bellay's object [was] to adjust the existing French culture to the rediscovered classical culture" (*The Renaissance* 128). This project was based, like Flavian's, on the writer's faith in the vernacular. Great literature comes from a language that is free, and alive. Du Bellay wanted to learn from the classics, but to bring the strength of antique words and images into French, rather than to borrow Greek and Latin, to put another's words into his mouth. The passage in *Marius* also echoes the familiar pronouncements of Vico, Wordsworth, or Carlyle on the necessity of returning to origins ("primitive power") in order to reinvigorate a dying language. Pater recommends a similar operation in "Style," in which the writer uses eclecticism to find his own original vocabulary: "A writer, full of a matter he is before all things anxious to express, may think of those laws, the limitations of vocabulary, structure, and the like, as a restriction, but if a real artist will find in them an opportunity. His punctilious observance of the proprieties of his medium will diffuse through all he writes a general air of sensibility, of refined usage" (12–13). Though Pater admits that some writers might fall into "mannerisms" and "fopperies," a great writer, "braced by those restraints," will discover "his own true manner" (14). A "real artist" finds opportunity in restriction, and a treasure house in the burden of the past. Pater's argument here should sound familiar, not only because it runs all through his work, but because it is identical to the claims made by eclectics from Winckelmann and Reynolds to Cousin and Arnold. For Pater, then, Euphuism is not mere affectation; rather it is care of language, care of the instrument with which the artist creates. He answers the question of why a writer cannot say a thing simply, like the old writers of Greece, with a spirited defense of Euphuism: "Certainly, the most wonderful, the unique, point, about the Greek genius, in literature as in everything else, was the entire absence of imitation in its productions. How had the burden of precedent, laid upon every artist, increased since then! It was all around one:—that smoothly built world of old classical taste, an accomplished fact, with overwhelming authority on every detail of the conduct of one's work. With no fardel on its own back, yet so imperious towards those who came labouring after it, *Hellas,* in its early freshness, looked as distant from [Flavian] even then as it does from ourselves. There might seem to be no place left for novelty or originality,—place only for a patient, an infinite, faultlessness" (*Marius* I:99–100). Neither Flavian nor Pater retreats from "the burden of precedent," feeling instead what Harold Bloom named, in Pater's honor, "the intoxication of belatedness." Pater reiterates here what he wrote in *The Renaissance,* that there are neither poetical nor unpoetical ages. Poetic beauty was not "a thing ever one and the same," but "changing with the soul of time itself" (I:100). As the soul accumulates experience, it becomes more complex, yielding greater riches to the artist. Pater has Flavian wonder whether future ages would look back on his time and think it ideal in comparison to their own, underscoring the essential continuity of the conditions of creation throughout history.

The central problem of the romance is not literary but religious, although Pater clearly sees parallels between them. After Flavian's death from the plague (brought, not insignificantly, by the imperial armies of Marcus Aurelius, the philosopher-emperor), Marius tries out various approaches to life, but is unable to rest in poetry, mysticism, or Greek philosophy. In finding a resolution to Marius's philosophical dilemma in "complete education" or Cyrenaicism, Pater defers the religious question. The practical goal of his philosophy and his life (apart from the idealistic one of experiencing as many sensations as possible) would be to understand "the various forms of ancient art and thought, the various forms of actual human feeling" (I:152) with impartiality; to accomplish this end he would become, of necessity, a critic because, "in a world, confessedly so opulent in what was old, the work, even of genius, must necessarily consist very much in criticism" (I:153). As an interpreter "of the beautiful house of art and thought which was the inheritance of the age" (I:153), Marius would have to live much in reminiscence, turning inward, achieving intimacy with his impressions.

In Marius's subsequent adventures, the narrator reveals some of the dangers involved in the hero's endeavor. As he encounters competing systems of thought, most significantly that embodied by the Stoic emperor, Marcus Aurelius, he risks the loss of his own system. We follow in chapters such as "Second Thoughts" and "A Conversation Not Imaginary" Marius's dialectic, the process by which he tests and ultimately secures his own beliefs. The gravest challenges to Heraclitus, Epicurus, and Aristuppus of Cyrene come from the emperor and from Christianity, the emperor representing "the strange medley of superstition, that centuries' growth, layer upon layer, of the curiosities of religion" that was the Roman empire in the second century, and Christianity embodying a somewhat different selection of the old religions. The key point, I think, is that both challenges to Marius's already eclectic philosophy come from varieties of religious syncretism. In Rome, "A blending of all the religions of the ancient world had been accomplished" (I:184). Far from disdaining the "medley of superstitions" held by his people, the Stoic emperor (perhaps enlivening his own bleak outlook) entered into all their rituals. But Marius cannot accept either Marcus Aurelius's religiosity or his Stoicism once he has seen the spectacle of animal sacrifice. The emperor and the general mass of his followers reject no practices, no rituals, no beliefs at all, and therefore, in their naïve form of eclecticism, seem to confound true religion entirely. Even in Cyrenaicism, there had to be distinctions, such as that between good and evil. In sharp contrast to the semiofficial naïve eclecticism of the empire, Christianity offers an attractive blending of the art, philosophy, and literature of various faiths, which Marius sees for the first time in the "church" in Cecilia's house. Like Kingsley in his early Christian novel, *Hypatia,* Pater wants to show how Christianity grew up eclectically around a set of core beliefs. Within this paradigm, Christianity's wisdom is found in its eclecticism: "'Wisdom' was dealing, as with the dust of creeds and philosophies, so also with the dust of outworn religious usage, like the very spirit of life itself, organizing soul and body out of the lime and clay of the earth. In a generous eclecticism, within the bounds of her liberty, and as by some providential power within her, she gathers and serviceably adopts, as in others matters, so in ritual, one thing here, another there, from various sources—Gnostic, Jewish, Pagan—to adorn and beautify the greatest act of worship the world has seen" (II:126–27). When Marius is moved to sincere admiration of Christianity's "generous eclecticism," he enters the final phase of his romance, where he is able, finally, to reconcile the moral and the aesthetic; but the conclusion of *Marius the Epicurean* is not definitive. It is a triumph of the sort that is characteristic of modern literature, what Ruskin called "triumph in mutability." Rather than placing Christianity teleologically at the end point of the romance, as the fulfillment of the narrative, Pater carefully makes the hero's conversion and martyrdom ambiguous, a sacrifice more for a feeling (hope) than a purpose (friendship). Eclecticism is described here as operating in accord with "the very spirit of life itself" when it organizes "soul and body out [. . .] of the earth." When the "dust" of the "outworn" returns to the "lime and clay," eclecticism molds it into a new form, in harmony with the self and the age. Eclecticism is generous, because it is inclusive; but it is also moral, because it works "within the bounds of [. . .] liberty." And, finally, it is aesthetic, because it takes for the adornment of Christian worship all that was beautiful in the Gnostic, the Jewish, and the Pagan. Nothing that was beautiful is ever really lost, so long as the eclectic "gathers" and "adopts."

Pater, more than any other nineteenth-century writer, explores the natural eclecticism of the human mind—the fossils in the stones, or the dust in the clay—and in particular, the eclecticism of the modern self, thereby dispelling the anxiety that had perplexed his immediate precursors, who feared there would never be a style to represent the age. As he contends in the "Postscript" to *Appreciations,* the nineteenth century has its style, and it is "an eclectic one": "Appealing, as he may, to precedent in this matter, the scholar will remember that if 'the style is the man' it is also the age: that the nineteenth century too will be found to have had its style, justified by necessity [. . .] an intellectually rich age such as ours being necessarily an eclectic one, we may well cultivate some of the excellences of literary types so different as those: that in literature as in other matters it is well to unite as many diverse elements as may be: that the individual writer or artist, certainly, is to be estimated by the number of graces he combines, and his power of interpenetrating them in a given work" (261). In order to function at all, he seems to tell us, we must live with this complexity, and in order to create, we must learn to be conscientiously eclectic. Neither our language, nor our art, nor our religion can ever be simple; we can recover primitive language at times as a "corrective," but our real style—our best style—will always be mixed. In his early essay on "Coleridge" (1865, rev. 1880) he wrote of the "sickly thought" that struggled against the spirit of the age, and "saddened [Coleridge's] mind, and limited the operation of his unique poetic gift" (*Appreciations* 69). Modern thought, Pater recognized, cultivates the relative in place of the absolute, but Coleridge went on seeking absolutes. Pater speculates that Coleridge would have gained much by pursuing "the relative spirit"; but instead there is his failure, and "endless regret, the chords of which ring all through our modern literature" (104). As a critic Pater is sensitive enough to recognize the interconnectedness of the sickness (relativism) and the cure (eclecticism). Though Pater refines and extends his philosophical and literary eclecticism in the essays that make up *Appreciations,* he has already written his true apologia in *Marius,* with its mingling of triumph and regret. It is usually read as an explanation of a philosophical position that was misunderstood in the conclusion to *The Renaissance;* but it is equally important, in literary-historical terms, to read the work as an apology for eclecticism, and as the coda for an eclectic age.

AFTERWORD

When I began to write this study of nineteenth-century eclecticism, I was still looking at the problem from the perspective of its critics. I had in my mind an image of the "Citizen of the Nineteenth Century Strolling in the Ruins of History." I would reveal this intrepid tourist for the tomb raider he was, plundering ruins (and regularly looting exotic cultures) for the raw materials of his derivative, exhausted creations. But almost from the beginning, I found myself in sympathy with this individual whose historical belatedness provoked such intense, intellectual anguish. The eclecticism of the nineteenth century was, in large part, an answer to the dilemma of style—in what style should we build, paint, write?—but it was also a deliberate, philosophical turn of mind—balm on the deep wound of unbelief. In art, it was an effort to combine the best of "history's diverse beauties"; in philosophy, eclecticism meant that one could be skeptical and still believe in something, namely one's own ability to sort through various systems of thought and come out with a fair amount of cold, hard truth. At some point I realized that my research was becoming a performance of my own intellectual predicament. Driven by an awareness of the superabundance of history, eclecticism, comparative literature, and, most recently, multicultural literary studies have all shared the common aim of rebuilding the humanities according to an integrative social and political model. But I saw that comparative literature, like eclecticism, tried to comprehend too large a field of knowledge within the scope of an impossible erudition. The project has been haunted by two related questions: first, is eclecticism a viable approach to the study of the humanities? And, second, to what extent does eclecticism already describe the current state of literary studies, both its "crisis" and the efforts to resolve that dilemma of purpose?

In trying to ascertain whether our own "crisis" is a continuation of the crisis of the nineteenth century, it is important to map the historical relationship between eclecticism and three aspects of the current dilemma: translation, comparison, and cosmopolitanism. Each of these terms carries a heavy burden of significance for the present purpose and future survival within the university of the humanities in general, and literary study in particular. To test the relevance of the concept of "eclecticism" within the field of literary studies, I was drawn into dialogue with three critics whose writings on translation, comparison, and cosmopolitanism have been influential in shaping my understanding of the new terrain in which most of us will (and many already do) work: Wolfgang Iser, Charles Bernheimer, and Bruce Robbins. In "The Emergence of a Cross-Cultural Discourse: Thomas Carlyle's *Sartor Resartus*," his essay for the collection *The Translatability of Cultures*, Iser suggests that the rift opened up by the quarrel between the ancients and the moderns in the eighteenth century would provoke Carlyle's effort to renegotiate the relationship between past and present, foreign and domestic cultures. The theory of translatability that emerges from *Sartor Resartus* in effect "manages" the crisis and, in doing so, might have some bearing on the crisis provoked in our own time by the burgeoning of world literatures. For comparatists, the vexing question of translation will thus become more insistent as we try to telescope ever more "distant" objects of study within our fields of expertise. In his introduction to the collection *Comparative Literature in the Age of Multiculturalism* (for which the 1993 ACLA report, "Comparative Literature at the Turn of the Century," provides the occasion), Charles Bernheimer reflects on the anxiety that "comparison," generally speaking, has always produced, and he speculates on the future direction of a "discipline" that once defined itself both as exclusive (in its membership) and all-inclusive (in its scope). Upsetting the more traditional notion of cosmopolitanism considered by some of the contributors to Bernheimer's volume, Bruce Robbins throws into doubt the efficacy of any model of cosmopolitanism that relies on detachment, universality, and transcendence to achieve its aims. Instead, he proposes that our "Actually Existing Cosmopolitanisms" are made up of messy particularities, of the multiple linkages created by technology, religion, profession, diaspora, "race," language, and, yes, even old-fashioned nationality.

The cultural situation that provoked Thomas Carlyle to write in 1833 "Am I a botched mass of tailors' and cobblers' shreds, then; or a tightly-articulated, homogeneous little Figure, automatic, nay alive?" (*Sartor Resartus* 45) (and to affirm that a man and his clothes are two separate creations) might best be explained as the confrontation between a new cultural situation and the old understanding of identity. As Iser points out in the essay on *Sartor Resartus,* this relationship among cultures (of contact and mutual influence) did not pose a problem as long as the "interconnection of traditions—whether in terms of receiving an inheritance or of recasting a heritage—was taken for granted" (245). During the eighteenth century, however, the notion of culture underwent important shifts: not only was the distance between the ancients and the moderns recognized and accepted, but the gulf between national cultures also widened: "by discovering difference as the dividing line between cultures, history as a cross-cultural discourse emerged" (246). Partly as a consequence of imperialist endeavors and partly in response to a globalizing economy, nineteenth-century thinkers such as Carlyle either constructed "theories" for coping with newly discovered difference or they constructed ever more rigid versions of national identity. Iser suggests that Carlyle's paradigm for cultural translation works on two levels. It revitalizes the "amputated past by turning it into a mirror in which the present is refracted" (247)—precisely what Carlyle achieves in *Past and Present.* Only by "mutual mirroring" do we get "mutual interpenetration," since the differences between the two cultures can never be effaced. Therefore, Iser writes, "[cultural pathology] can be counteracted not just by taking over features and attitudes from different cultures, but first and foremost by instilling a self-reflexivity into the stricken culture, thus providing a scope for self-monitoring" (248). At best, Iser argues, this is a kind of therapy for cultures in crisis. The old ways of coping with the incursion of competing traditions, pragmatic assimilation or appropriation, no longer alleviate the crisis. Translatability allows for the "mutual impacting" of cultures upon one another.

Iser and the other contributors to the collection were developing a concept of translation and translatability that resonated with the Victorian idea of eclecticism, although they never used the word or invoked the history of eclecticism in philosophy that stands behind Carlyle. Extending the efforts of the eclectic philosophers in France, Carlyle in *Sartor Resartus* was attempting to reconcile German idealism and British empiricism or, more proximately, Scottish common sense. The work (of eclecticism) is necessarily self-reflexive for Carlyle. In the persona of the Editor, he continually reflects upon the labor of selection and construction required to set out Herr Teufelsdröckh's Philosophy of Clothes for an English-speaking audience. In allowing for "mutual impacting," the narrative of experience (Teufelsdröckh's life-story) is frequently "punctured" by expositions of transcendental philosophy (both assembled from the bags of notes and fragments that the Editor received from Germany). The constant interchange between narrative and argument allows for "mutual interpenetration" of the two cultures. The narrative of experience makes the philosophical speculation accessible, while the exposition of transcendentalism becomes a means of "exceeding the familiar" (Iser 249). The juxtaposition brings out "something" in the British readers of which they had never been aware. What this is, exactly, Iser does not say. Perhaps he does not need to because *his* essay on *Sartor* clearly exhibits the "something" that Carlyle manifests for him. Iser takes up the metaphor of a "Philosophy of Clothes"—the ostensible subject of *Sartor Resartus,* remember—in his effort to explain Carlyle's theory of cultural translation and to propose one of his own.

The autobiographical materials discovered by the nameless Editor of *Sartor Resartus* tell the story of a man whose life has no shape until he hits upon the philosophy of clothes. At the moment when Teufelsdröckh resolves his life-endangering crisis with the sartorial philosophy, he lays the foundation of a theory of translatability. Iser explains: "[The] self-inspecting autobiographer turns more and more into a tailor, who constantly designs new clothes, or refashions garments inherited from the past. The autobiographer becomes a philosopher of clothes because he is unable to capture himself. Such a space-between can be 'bridged' only by 'clothing,' that is, by giving it a shape" (249–50). Failing in the project to know others as they really are, and failing to know ourselves as we really are, we turn to the study of clothing, that is, the shape they and we are given by what Carlyle calls the "Garments of Thought." In metaphorically linking the forms of language and thought to fashion, Carlyle emphasizes that differences in style are translatable. *Sartor Resartus* poses as a translation from the German of Teufelsdröckh's philosophy of clothes; in reality, it is Carlyle's translation of German Romantic philosophy into a British style of thought. Similarly, in *Past and Present* Carlyle identifies language as the carrier of cultural identity and attempts to prove that cast-off Garments of Thought, such as those belonging to twelfth-century monasticism, may be recovered and repaired, clothing the impoverished languages of the present.

Carlyle's theory of cross-cultural discourse imagines a possible, evolved nineteenth-century language that would be informed both by primitive or ancient sources and by infusions from other cultures. From this confluence of languages he proposes that we make and remake the world as "crises" dictate. To try to purify language (or thought) or resist the mongrelization of culture is to falsify communication and to become trapped in the lie of whole-cloth identity. Carlyle has contributed, in Iser's view, the outline of cross-cultural praxis. How will the garments of foreign styles of thought gradually replace or interweave with our own? What will be the role of world literatures within an evolving canon? The Philosophy of Clothes—Iser's cross-cultural discourse—"anatomizes the process of translatability itself which, more often than not, is glossed over when imitation or depiction is the overriding concern of representation" (255). For Iser and Carlyle, translation can take place only metaphorically, as something that gives a shape to the unknown, the "space-between." By making Carlyle's Philosophy of Clothes into a theory of cultural translation, Iser has provided one eclectic model for coping with the "crisis" of multiculturalism. However, the resistance by some critics today to models of translation predicts a new retreat, even in this "age of multiculturalism," behind national and disciplinary boundaries. Rather than surrendering to our fear of disintegration and mongrelization, we ought to view eclectic translation as a way to retailor ourselves as cosmopolitan citizens of the world. This does not mean that we will become "botched masses of cobblers' and tailors' shreds," but that we will be changed by the mutual mirroring that takes place when we attempt translation. Carlyle's contribution to the theory of cultural translation bears reconsideration in light of recent debates on multiculturalism, and the eclecticism of that vision just might guide us through the wilderness of our superabundant diversity.

And yet comparatists have long been uneasy about the instrumentality of translation. In the ACLA Reports of 1965 and 1975, and to a lesser degree in the 1993 Report, there is a persistent theme of textual translation as debasement. According to the authors, translation debases the values on which the discipline is founded—the distinctly elite values of the old notion of cosmopolitanism, Eurocentrism, and scholarly asceticism. Translation betrays the author. Translation can never give a reader insight into a foreign text or the tradition from which it emerges. Claiming knowledge of an author, text, or national literature via translation is the trick of the dilettante; the true comparatist must always do better, must underwrite faith in origins, in the original, in originality by claiming ownership at the source. Translation is therefore shameful. It is merely a service provided for those who will never have access to the cultural real. What is the relationship between textual translation, so reviled by "authentic" comparatists, and the cultural translation represented by Carlyle and theorized by Iser? As Charles Bernheimer has written, comparative literature is the most "anxiogenic" of disciplines. In order to uphold the "values" of the post–World War II European founders of the discipline, we think we have to—think we are doing—more than our colleagues in modern languages, and yet we often have a hard time explaining the nature of our special contribution. The multifacetedness of comparative literature is often taken as the proof of its dilettantism, since the object of study is no longer clear. At the risk of sounding as omnivorous as some of our predecessors in the field, I want to suggest that the crisis of comparative literature has become everyone's crisis, that issues of comparison and translation are now as endemic in English studies, French studies, and German studies as they are in the discipline that was supposed to take care of all that.

Beginning graduate school in the early nineties, when the dominance of theory gave way, as Bernheimer emphasizes, to the "study of the 'extrinsic' relations of literature, its placements within psychological, historical or sociological contexts" (5), I became anxious about context. What was the good of avoiding translations, when my cross-cultural studies were making it impossible to know any one culture really well? Reading in the nineties meant taking into account race, gender, class, sexual orientation, history, politics, location, *and* language. For me, "narrowing" my field of study to British literature and culture within a European context was a calculated effort to become a better reader, in the new sense. However, with the diversification of the canon in all the modern languages, one cannot simply escape from the problem of translation, or comparison; any method of literary study depends on translation. With the advent of multiculturalism, it is impossible to be comfortable within even a single literary tradition. In English, we must take into account English-speaking literatures around the world, and, most importantly for our students, the multiethnic literary traditions of North America. Now, more than ever before, literary scholars might be accused of dilettantism (of being naïvely eclectic), as we try to encompass more and more material within our range of expertise. What can we learn from comparative literature, the discipline known for persisting within a perpetual state of anxiety? As Bernheimer suggests, comparative literature is valuable because it teaches us to be self-critical as we live with instability. And so we must be cautious, as Rey Chow warns in her contribution to Bernheimer's volume, about substituting for European masterpieces another canon of non-European works. She argues that the entire multiculturalist model is "flawed by its tendency to essentialize other cultures, attributing to them far more unity, regularity, and stability than they actually have" (Bernheimer "Introduction," 8). The cross-cultural discourse Iser sees emerging from the nineteenth century provides a partial answer to this dilemma; new varieties of cosmopolitanism force us to acknowledge the partialness of our understanding, even as cosmopolitanism enables the development of ever more complex cross-cultural discourses.

Contributors to the 1998 collection *Cosmopolitics: Thinking and Feeling beyond the Nation* describe "actually existing cosmopolitanism" (not the old notion of a universal humanity as "a style of practical consciousness") (Robbins 2; Cheah 21). Rather than an expansive feeling of connectedness, we experience a feeling of narrowness, of the limits of our understanding. A growing awareness of particularities, and of permanent differences, does not necessarily lead, in his view, to wagon-circling and border patrols. Robbins sees actually existing cosmopolitanism as a series of variably intense connections "both within and beyond the nation" (12). The "cosmopolitics" Robbins wants to formulate depends on that very Victorian notion of "sympathy," on "defin[ing] collectivities of belonging and responsibility in the absence of that long history of face-to-face interaction that [. . .] was necessary to community" (9). It is vital, then, that the cosmopolitan get beyond "mere aesthetic spectatorship" and "privileged and irresponsible detachment" (4). Coping with the loss of authenticity, originality, and community, "*critical* cosmopolitanism" could change (and is already changing) comparative literature and multicultural literary studies by keeping its own historical and geographical origins firmly in view. According to this model, we still need humanistic criticism, but of a kind that strives toward "mutual translatability" without ever expecting to find "humanity."

Translation occurs metaphorically and continuously as we attempt to understand the other in new terms of relation, around the space occupied by our differences. Eclecticism, a very old style of cross-cultural discourse, constitutes the conceptual opposite of something like deconstruction because it implies belief within a framework of skepticism. Under the rubric of eclecticism, comparison leads not to indifference, but to affirmation. If we think about cultural translation eclectically, keeping in mind that no system could lay claim to the whole truth, and if we pursue rigorously dialectic reading, we might find "something" *in ourselves* that we'd never been aware of before. I am reminded of Walter Pater's claim that eclecticism is the vernacular of sophisticated societies. Whether we want it or no, our language evolves to accommodate incursions from "outside," styles of thought that alter our own. If we have no choice about being eclectic, then we must speak and write conscientiously as Eclectics: this is the lesson of the nineteenth century. Emerging from a literary reaction against the materialism of the eighteenth century, eclecticism gave humanists a concept of "progress" that had been lacking—but on a very different historical model. Operating metaphorically and comparatively, eclecticism allows for synthesis, for incremental changes, not for rapid development and not in one direction only. Eclecticism promotes a cosmopolitan attitude of mind. From seeing Europe as a single confederation whose cultures were mutually interpenetrated, it was not long (historically speaking) until Europeans recognized, after the million contacts of colonization, forms of connection and mutual mirroring with cultures that seemed ever more diverse. How many colonials must have felt this way, when the comfortable boundaries of their world were forever changed by contact? We used to imagine that contact went only one way, changed only those who did not invite the change; but now, as we learn to speak a cosmopolitan vernacular, we understand that the only possible form of cross-cultural discourse is this mutual mirroring or comparison or eclecticism that finally makes exchange possible.

NOTES

Introduction

1. I borrow the distinction between "The Two Modernities" from Matei Calinescu's classic study, *Five Faces of Modernity*, pp. 41–46.

Chapter 1

1. In his 1934 essay "What Is Baroque?," Erwin Panofsky makes a strong case for the Carracci being at the center of a late-sixteenth-century movement toward synthesis, though by this time the negative term "eclectic" is simply omitted. Annibale Carracci, he writes, "began with a deliberate effort to synthesize the plastic values of classical antiquity and classical High Renaissance art with such purely pictorial tendencies as had survived the manneristic intermezzo, namely the Venetian colorism and the Correggesque 'sfumato'" (38). Furthermore, Panofsky affirms the role of the Bolognese school as artistic reformers who wished to restore the "good old traditions" (36).

2. In the 1959 foreword to his 1924 book *Idea: A Concept in Art Theory*, Erwin Panofsky qualifies the original priority he gave to Bellori's 1672 "classicistic interpretation" of art and traces the concepts of the *Idea del pittore, dello schultore, e dell' architetto* back to Giovanni Battista Agucchi, whose manuscript papers clearly show that ideas about the Carracci's resolution of the conflict between "unnatural" Mannerism and "raw" Naturalism were already in circulation between 1607 and 1615 (vii). Despite this revision of Panofsky's original genealogy, his contribution to the history of *Idea* is still valuable. It is particularly interesting how he distinguishes the Mannerists' Neopla-

tonic understanding of *Idea* from that of the Carracci (and Agucchi/Bellori). Neither the Mannerists nor the Naturalists were on the right path. If Idea has a metaphysical origin, then the artist can ignore sensory reality. Bellori argued that Idea originates from sensory perception, and comes into being through the *selection* of natural beauties, especially from art: "The infallible measure of this *juste milieu* was obviously the art of antiquity, which was honored not as a 'naturalistic' art but—precisely because of its limitation to a 'purified' or 'ennobled' reality—as a truly 'natural' art" (Panofsky, *Idea,* 105). Thus classical art theory is born from an eclectic process, of which the Carracci may be considered the originators.

3. According to Mahon, "eclectic" designates neither a period in the history of art nor a recognizable visual style, and cannot be recovered as a value-free critical term, since it "is unable to divest itself of its inherent qualitative connotation (which entails the confusing injection of aesthetic judgment into the argument): because of its obvious etymological origin and subsequent history it does not lend itself, as Gothic and Baroque have done, to gradual metamorphosis into qualitative neutrality" (228).

4. Commentators on the Carracci experienced some semantic difficulty after Mahon banned the use of "eclectic." Donald Posner, in his two-volume monograph, concedes Mahon's point: since "Annibale's analytical and selective stylistic experiments were mainly confined to the period before 1600, [. . .] the attempt of later critics to see the whole of Annibale's Roman art as broadly and programmatically 'eclectic' was an unjustified exaggeration" (116). Posner concedes this point only to disagree with Mahon at the back door: "to suggest that Annibale's art was in any way naïvely formed in a simple response to new influences would be equally unjustified. Annibale's analytical deliberation in creating his style—his selection of Raphael as his main source, his investigation of Correggio within the context of his new style, his introduction of elements from Michelangelo and the Antique, the preservation of pictorial qualities from his Bolognese style—made him the first critically retrospective artist in the history of art and an example for artists and theorists for the next three centuries" (118). In 1977 Charles Dempsey acknowledges that Denis Mahon played a vital role in making a critical re-evaluation of the Carracci possible, that he had effected "a revolution in taste" (1). But he goes on to write of Annibale's confrontation with the "central intellectual issue which faced all artists of his time—the bringing together of Theory and Practice, both in the painting of his own pictures and in the training of young artists" (3). Like Posner, Dempsey credits the Carracci with "uniting Tuscan *disegno* and Lombard *colore* through mastering the theoretical basis of both in natural observation and analysis"; he adds, "in doing so [they] rose above the mere eclecticism of combining the natural perfections already expressed in the various manners of others" (43). In 1988 another Carracci historian, Carl Goldstein, feels obliged to come to terms with Mahon's and Dempsey's diametrically opposed readings of the Carracci, and produces a book chiefly concerned with reexamining the relationship between theory and practice, with a special emphasis on contemporary understandings of the theory and history of painting. He describes the Carracci (without using the word eclectic) "as thoughtful artists who consciously chose from among the artistic options available to them, developing a particular aesthetic stance and pictorial styles as a result of their assessment of past and recent art," but whose achievements were misrepresented by well-meaning literati (*Visual Fact* 6). Margaretha Rossholm Lagerlöf, in her study of classical landscape painting, agrees with Mahon "that the wording employed by the theorists has simplified or concealed important aspects of these paintings"; but she goes on to admit, "It cannot be

denied, however, that the Carracci school won the high regard of the classicists, of the advocates of selection according to the principles of beauty together with subjects and a style derived from the repertoire of antiquity, and a mode of expression resembling that of Raphael" (42). This prompts Lagerlöf to ask, "What was it in the Carracci paintings that could satisfy this type of taste and yet be regarded as innovative, a conquest of new artistic territory?," to which I would answer: a successful eclectic synthesis of their study of past art and of nature.

5. Despite Dempsey's appreciation for Mahon's contribution to the study of Baroque painting, he strongly disagrees with Mahon's attempt to throw out the theoretical interpretation with "the bathwater of eclecticism" (54). In defending the Carracci against critics who underrated the Carracci by subscribing to a critical notion of eclecticism, Mahon ignored the very reliable historical sources such as Agucchi who testified to the Carracci's effort to reform painting through imitation of various masters (56).

6. The original Italian text is given by Denis Mahon in his discussion of its correct attribution:

Sonetto in lode di Nicolò Bolognese.
Chi farsi vn bon pittor cerca, e desia
    Il disegno di Roma habbia alla mano,
    La mossa, coll'ombrar Veneziano,
    E il degno colorir di Lombardia.
Di Michel'Angiol la terribil via,
    Il vero natural di Tiziano,
Del Coreggio lo stil puro, e sourano,
    E di vn Rafel la giusta simetria.
Del Tibaldi il decoro, e il fondamento,
    Del dotto Primaticcio l'inuentare,
    E vn pò di gratia del Parmigianino.
Ma senza tanti studi, e tanto stento,
    Si ponga solo l'opre ad imitare,
    Che quì lascioci il nostro Nicolino. (208)

7. Mahon believes that Malvasia is responsible for these verses, whether they were actually written by a mourner at Abate's funeral or invented later for his *Felsina Pittrice* (1678).

8. Fuseli's early argument against eclecticism resonates well into the nineteenth century. In "The Nature of Gothic" John Ruskin will value "imperfection" in art over mechanistic perfection and launch the entire reformation of nineteenth-century arts and crafts.

9. It would be intriguing to interpret Blanc's assessment of the Carracci in light of a recent study of Blanc's own eclecticism by Misook Song. She claims that "Blanc's eclecticism, although it appears strongly hybrid in nature, can be reduced to his purist belief in the all-embracing universal notion of 'eternal geometry' whose pedigree ultimately goes back to Plato" (105). The line Song traces from Blanc back to Plato would certainly have to include the Neoplatonists of the sixteenth and seventeenth centuries who propagated many of the theories the Carracci found so congenial.

10. In his comprehensive study *Teaching Art,* Carl Goldstein affirms that "The visual evidence [. . .] shows that the Carracci did indeed mine the works of the masters of the Renaissance, regarding such works as sources of images at least equal to nature, which

is to say that their practice was demonstrably 'eclectic,' and eclecticism is a doctrine residing in the innermost sanctum of the academic tradition" (36). However, Goldstein believes that Carracci eclecticism was based on the Renaissance notion of "imitation" and that their practice involved a higher degree of improvisation than such an institutionalized system might allow. Assuredly, Goldstein says, they were not systematically eclectic in their teaching. But he admits "That later academies may have been influenced by reports of Carracci 'eclecticism'" (36).

11. Academic prestige might have fallen off in the first half of the nineteenth century, but the academies remained for artists the primary route to public success. Thus, I do not wish to overemphasize the importance of Romanticism, since Carl Goldstein, in his comprehensive study *Teaching Art,* has shown that the two revolutions of the late eighteenth century, the political and the cultural, did not substantially affect teaching methods in the academies (58–61). More substantial reforms, described by Albert Boime in "The Teaching Reforms of 1863 and the Origins of Modernism in France," would come later, but even these, Goldstein argues, were primarily "external" (having to do with admissions and the awarding of prizes and with overcoming the prejudice against craft) (61); that is, the academic teaching methods based on eclecticism remained.

12. While the academic tradition might have originated in Italy and reached its pinnacle of prestige and organization in France, Goldstein points out that nowhere "did doctrine take so strong a hold or play so central a role as it did in the Royal Academy officially established in London in 1768" (*Teaching Art* 54). Founded to establish an academy of design and to hold annual exhibitions, it incorporated the best of the Italian and French academies. He also notes that Reynolds's series of *Discourses* would largely be supported by his successors, which "testif[ies] to a consensus in the Royal Academy, as though the members had entered into a pact as to the means and ends of visual art" (58).

13. Albert Boime's *Thomas Couture and the Eclectic Vision* is by far the most comprehensive account of eclecticism in painting. He provides not only a history of its sources in the philosophy of Cousin and his contemporaries, but also a detailed study of the art and teaching of Thomas Couture—the genesis of his eclectic style, his search for "the *juste milieu* expression," and "the iconography of the *juste milieu.*" Couture and other eclectic artists wanted to mediate between the "extremes of romanticism and classicism in the fine arts" (29). Boime points out that even those artists whom we consider most "Romantic" were deeply affected by Cousin's teachings. Eugène Delacroix believed that eclecticism had its source in national identity: "One might say that eclecticism is, par excellence, the French banner for the arts of drawing and music. In their art, the Germans and the Italians have marked qualities some of which are often antipathetic to others: the French seem to have striven since time immemorial to reconcile these extremes by attenuating whatever seemed to be disharmonious therein" (qtd. in Boime 29). As Boime points out, it is not contradictory to associate romanticism with eclecticism. Both represented the aspirations of the middle classes; both wished to expand political and cultural frontiers; and both "emphasized the individual's consciousness as the ultimate test of experience" (30). Boime's work on eclecticism effectively reminds us of how dominant it was as a way of thinking in all artistic and cultural movements of the nineteenth century.

Patricia Mainardi is another critic whose work attends to the intersections between high art and popular culture. In her 1987 book *Art and Politics of the Second Empire: The Universal Expositions of 1855 and 1867,* Mainardi explores the impact of eclectic theory on academic painting and international exhibitions. The 1855 Exposition Universelle des Beaux-Arts allowed ordinary French people to see art from around the world for the first time, to compare the art of different countries, and to "form their own opinions" (66). Actually, Mainardi argues, the critic became more important than ever in helping the visitor to understand the dizzying range of works of art. In accordance with the "government dictum of eclecticism," artists representing twenty-eight countries were honored at the exhibit. Eclecticism thus attempted "to find a structure, a theory, which could encompass in coherent fashion the varied art" on display (69). The second mandate of eclecticism, that of "combining the qualities of different schools into a harmonious ensemble," was admirably fulfilled by the French artists themselves for whom eclecticism became a national aesthetic. Even an art critic such as Théophile Gautier was satisfied with this formulation, proposing that English art represented the idea of individuality, Belgian art the idea of facility, German art the idea of intellect, and French art the idea of eclecticism (70).

14. For Reynolds the prestige of poetry derived from its independence of the accidents of nature. In "Ut Poesis Pictura: Reynolds on Imitation and Imagination," Harvey D. Goldstein asserts that Reynolds consistently opposes the two arts, because poetry "applies itself directly to the imagination 'without the intervention of any kind of imitation.' The 'poetry of painting' locates, for him, the imaginative effect of the art divorced from the subject which is that art's language" (227). Nevertheless, Goldstein concedes, the painter must follow the ways belonging to art—the "study of authentic models of excellence"—to *learn how* an object strikes the imagination (227).

15. Despite Ruskin's powerful critique of the academic method Reynolds advocated, there is strong evidence to suggest that Reynolds ultimately won the war. Prominent academicians of the later nineteenth century, such as John Everett Millais, Lord Leighton, G. F. Watts, and Sir Lawrence Alma-Tadema, not only were trained using traditional academic methods but also led the revival of typical academic subjects (history and mythology) and lent them a new post-Romantic prestige. Ample proof of the eclecticism of later-nineteenth-century art can be found in Andrew Bolton Marvick's 1994 dissertation, "The Art of John William Waterhouse: Eclecticism in Late Nineteenth-Century British Painting." In his conclusion, Marvick affirms the notion on which this study is based, namely that Waterhouse's "eclectic program [. . .] suggests the possible existence of parallel examples of eclecticism in the art of Waterhouse's era and social milieu" (abstract). Marvick arrives at this conclusion after a careful examination of "[t]hree predominant historical situations [. . .]: first, that an environment suitable for the emergence of a consistent eclectic—as it were, a consistently inconsistent—figurative art within the Royal Academy existed at the time of Waterhouse's studentship; second, that Waterhouse responded, with an extraordinary degree of variety, to that stimulus to create any number of eclectic inventions while maintaining his links with the Academy; third, that his work was, in more or less degree, recognized by his contemporaries as primarily an eclectic art, an art of style" (270). Marvick's study of Waterhouse thus lends support to my claim that academic eclecticism dominated nineteenth-century art.

16. In what follows, I affirm the importance of Scott's literary example to the touristic pursuit of history and argue that Scott contributed to the growth of an eclectic-historical outlook in architecture. Scott's place in the genealogy of eclecticism is more complex and far-reaching. Most notably, Scott's reception in France by Stendhal, Balzac, and Hippolyte Taine is significant in light of the fact that they were all influenced by the arch-eclectic philosopher Victor Cousin (the subject of chapter 2). Balzac in

particular seems to have recognized Scott's eclecticism as his genius: "certain rounded and completed beings, certain *bifron* intellects, embracing all, want lyric and action, drama and ode, believing that perfection requires a sense of the total. This school, which must be named that of *literary eclecticism,* demands a representation of the world as it is: images and ideas; the idea in the image, or the image in the idea, movement, and reverie. Walter Scott satisfied completely these eclectic natures" (Balzac 127). In this passage, Balzac seems to describe the exemplary form of the novel, a genre which was born, through Cervantes, a hybrid creature. Not surprisingly, he includes himself in the eclectic school, determining that only such an all-embracing vision would be adequate to represent such a complex age.

17. Ruskin was wrong about Scott's Presbyterianism, at least according to recent biographer John Sutherland. Scott attended Episcopalian services with his mother, and then with his wife, though he read the Scottish prayer book at home. As Sutherland puts it, "Scott seems not to have put much importance on the mere forms of religious devotion" (72). But Ruskin's broader sense about Scott's religion is correct—it is not a serious matter with him, and is probably therefore an accurate measure of the writer's modernity, and his eclecticism.

18. There is plenty of evidence to suggest that Scott was a volitional eclectic. Ian Duncan puts it this way: "Scott composed *Ivanhoe* out of the quarry of his extensive reading in English literature from the Middle-English romances and old ballads to Shakespeare and the King James Bible" ("Editor's Notes" 525). The image of a compositional quarry is an apt one for Scott, and could illustrate his writing process from *The Lady of the Lake* (1810) through to the end of his career. In the "Dedicatory Epistle" that accompanied the first edition of *Ivanhoe* (1819), Scott makes it clear that he is mixing history and romance, and "intermingling fiction with truth" (17), and, though the completion of Abbotsford is a few years off, he makes a prophetic (and typically self-deprecatory) comparison with trends in architecture: "it is extremely probable that I may have introduced, during the reign of Richard the First, circumstances appropriate to a period either considerably earlier, or a good deal later than that era. It is my comfort, that errors of this kind will escape the general class of readers, and that I may share in the ill-deserved applause of those architects who, in their modern Gothic, do not hesitate to introduce, without rule or method, ornaments proper to different styles and to different periods of the art" (21). The letter is signed by the fictitious Laurence Templeton and is addressed to his friend, the equally fictitious Dr. Dryasdust, suggesting that Scott regarded as silly the preoccupation with antiquarian details of modern Gothic. Scott was an obviously self-conscious practitioner of literary eclecticism, and given the allusion here to contemporary architecture, it is safe to assume that he was equally aware of the mixture of styles employed at Abbotsford.

19. In his study *Architecture and Utopia: Design and Capitalist Development,* architectural historian Manfredo Tafuri points to awareness of urban eclecticism early in the nineteenth century when he cites this passage from F. Milizia's *Principi di architettura civile* (3rd ed., 1813): "The plan of the city should be distributed in such a way that the magnificence of the whole is subdivided in an infinity of individual beauties, all so different one from the other that the same object is never encountered twice, and moving from one end to the other one finds in each quarter something new, unique, and surprising. Order must reign, but in a kind of confusion... and from a multitude of regular parts the whole must give a certain idea of irregularity and chaos, which is so fitting to great cities" (qtd. 21).

20. I have written elsewhere of picturesqueness as the dominant aesthetic of eclecticism, specifically in the design of Bedford Park (see Bolus-Reichert, "Everyday Eclecticism," 162–96). Established in London in 1875, the early garden suburb of Bedford Park represented the best effort of architects and designers to live up to the ideals of the Aesthetic Movement. In most contemporary accounts, visitors remark on the picturesqueness, variety, and novelty of the Queen Anne architecture, in stark contrast to the drab monotony they would find in the ordinary middle-class housing estate. William Morris visited the suburb in 1879 and soon after began writing of the historical dilemma provoked by the Queen Anne style, which captured the qualities of the picturesque only by eclectic imitation. Morris's revision of the idea of the picturesque and the writing of his utopia *News from Nowhere* emerge in dialogue with the aesthetic and communitarian principles of Bedford Park. The picturesque eclecticism of Bedford Park remains as a persuasive image of the road not taken in twentieth-century domestic architecture, a failure of vision more easily explained by Morris's socialist critique of the picturesque aesthetic.

Chapter 2

1. George Boas's 1925 history, *French Philosophies of the Romantic Period* (1964) is still the best account in English. Valuable contemporary histories include Charles Adam's *La Philosophie en France (première moitié du XIXe siècle)* (1894) and Félix Ravaisson's *La Philosophie en France au XIXe siècle* (1868). Paul Bénichou's *Le Temps des prophètes: Doctrines de l'âge romantique* (1977) is probably the most influential recent study of the period. During the 1990s there was a spate of studies on Cousin's legacy in France. Notable among them are Éric Fauquet's edited collection *Victor Cousin: Homo Theologico-Politicus: Philologie, philosophie, histoire littéraire* (1996), Jean-Pierre Cotten's *Autour de Victor Cousin: Une politique de la philosophie* (1992), and Patrice Vermeren's *Victor Cousin: Le jeu de la philosophie et de l'état* (1995). Donald R. Kelley gives the best recent account in English of the varieties of philosophical eclecticism *before* Cousin in "Eclecticism and the History of Ideas," pointing out that although eclecticism was neither a school nor a real tradition, it was given new life (and a history) in early modern times (580). The appearance of several books and articles in the *Journal of the History of Ideas* in recent years seems to indicate that the history of eclecticism is being written once more, lending credence to Martin Mulsow's claim that "in a 'multi-option society' eclecticism is a virtue which is necessary for life" because, like our Enlightenment precursors, "we are faced [. . .] with a breadth of choice before which the making of a considered judgment becomes a farce, for it can lead only to paralysis" (476). Eclectic thinking has once again become a necessity. In his review of German scholar Michael Albrecht's monumental history of eclecticism, *Eklektik. Eine Begriffsgeschichte mit Hinweisen auf die Philosophie- und Wissenschaftsgeschichte* (1994), Ulrich Schneider agrees, "eclecticism has lost its traditional bad reputation and seems increasingly attractive to late twentieth-century thought in search of non-dogmatic and nonsystematic forms of philosophizing" (173).

2. Cousin had originally published his early lectures in five volumes as the *Cours de l'histoire de la philosophie moderne* in 1841. He selected what he considered the key elements of his philosophy and republished the extracts in one volume as *Du Vrai, du Beau et du Bien* in 1853. They were translated into English the same year as *Lectures*

on the True, the Beautiful, and the Good. All citations refer to the 1872 American edition.

3. Cousin does not speculate whether that synthesis had been achieved in Christianity, although some later writers do. For example, Charles Kingsley's novel *Hypatia* (1852–53), set in fifth-century Alexandria, deals with exactly the period of transition that Cousin describes, but he sees Christianity as fulfilling and indeed exceeding the promise of Hellenistic eclecticism.

4. Though Cousin does not here give his philosophy the name "spiritualism," by 1853, when he is writing the preface to *Lectures on the True, the Beautiful, and the Good,* he says "Our true doctrine, our true flag is spiritualism" (9). After decades of attacks on eclecticism, he seems to find safe harbor in spiritualism and gives it a respectable lineage, including Socrates, Plato, the Gospel, Descartes, Royer-Collard, Chateaubriand, and Madame de Staël. He still calls eclecticism "dear to us, for it is in our eyes the light of the history of philosophy," but now it is an "application of the philosophy which we teach, but it is not its principle" (9).

5. In the best recent account of the "eclectic" interregnum, John Dillon and Anthony Long try to shed the negative judgment that these unaffiliated philosophers were mere "indiscriminate assemblers of other thinkers' doctrines" (vii).

6. Both Donini and Dillon and Long want to overthrow the long-standing influence of Zeller's account of eclecticism in Greek philosophy, arguing that his account was reductive and frequently uninformed about the actual contributions of philosophers to whom he attached the negative epithet. Donini canvasses the variety of meanings that can be attached to eclecticism in this period, arguing finally for great caution in applying the term at all, which seems to have only limited usefulness. See "The History of the Concept of Eclecticism," especially pp. 31–33.

7. Donini points out that most of Diderot's definition is "derived from, or almost translated from, [Jakob] Brucker" (19). Neither Brucker nor Diderot originated the ideas presented in the *Encyclopédie,* however, as a positive orientation toward eclecticism in philosophy had been building since the late Renaissance (20).

8. Along with Casini and Donini, several other historians of philosophy have detected in Diderot, and the Enlightenment more generally, a powerful strand of eclectic thought. Petr Lom looks at the element of skepticism in Diderot's thought, which he traces back to ancient skepticism and the Pyrrhonists, arguing that Diderot intentionally rejects the destructiveness of their doubt in favor of the constructiveness of eclecticism: "The eclectic free thinker [. . .] is to walk side by side with the sceptic, in order to pick up everything that his companion 'has not reduced to dust by the severity of his inquiries'" (9). Although skepticism was an element of his thought, Diderot believed that "'no philosopher [was] mad enough not to discern some element of the truth'" (qtd. in Lom 10)—there had to be a point where the doubting stopped. Wilhelm Schmidt-Biggemann regards eclecticism, with rationalism, as one of the two mainstreams of the German *Aufklärung:* "They were both optimistic theories, they were both interested in the freedom of mankind: eclecticism in a practical way, rationalism in a theoretical way, a way which had to discover the possibility of freedom" (550).

9. A professor of philosophy and Vico specialist, Joseph Ferrari, launched one of the most serious attacks on Cousin's teachings in 1849 with *Les philosophes salariés.* Although he believes eclecticism to be a false philosophy riddled with errors, he does not specifically take issue with Cousin's appropriation of Vico; rather Ferrari is more concerned to explore the links between the state and its quasi-official philosophy.

10. Sainte-Beuve's relationship to Cousin was complicated throughout his life by his reliance on the prominent philosopher's patronage. Literally saving Sainte-Beuve from a poverty that "kept his youth in chains," Cousin, as Minister of Education, appointed him director of the Mazarine Library in 1840, but the 4,000 francs per annum constituted perhaps a new form of bondage. Sainte-Beuve's respect for Cousin must have been sorely tested in the 1840s when the philosopher made use of some unpublished material on Pascal and Madame de Longueville that Sainte-Beuve had brought to light. Enraged, he wrote a vicious letter to Cousin berating him for taking the food from his plate, but did not send it, remembering that he still needed a sponsor at the French Academy. Once elected in 1844 Sainte-Beuve no longer had to restrain criticism of his patron. When Villemain and Cousin resigned their government appointments in protest against restrictions that would be imposed by Louis Napoleon, Sainte-Beuve attacked them both publicly. His abuse of the liberals and their cause had the effect of alienating many of his former associates. Proust later contended that Sainte-Beuve's criticism of Cousin never really hit its mark; to say that the philosopher's egoism had got in the way revealed nothing of importance. See Harold Nicolson, *Sainte-Beuve* (1957).

11. John Brooks offers an excellent account of the influence of Cousin's eclectic spiritualism on the development of psychology and sociology in nineteenth-century France. Whereas Brooks convincingly recovers the suppressed history of eclecticism in the "human sciences," I want to trace the influence of Cousin and a broader eclecticism on the literary history of the period.

12. Taine blames the influence of German philosophy, imported by de Staël and Cousin, for much of the vagueness of eclecticism and for the collapse of philosophical inquiry in nineteenth-century France: "Les horribles substantifs allemands, les mots longs d'une toise, noyèrent la prose nette de d'Alembert et de Voltaire, et il sembla que Berlin émigré fût tombé de tout son poids sur Paris" (298) ["The horrible German substantives, the long words of a measuring apparatus, were embedded in the clear prose of d'Alembert and Voltaire, and it seemed that Berlin had fallen with all its weight on Paris" (my translation).]

13. The art historian Albert Boime has written the most lucid account to date of the tremendous importance Cousin's eclecticism had for the development of French Romanticism in all its aspects. In his view, all the major writers and artists of the first half of the nineteenth century were affected by Cousin including (in addition to those I discuss) Hugo, Vigny, Sand, Flaubert, and Merimée. See *Thomas Couture and the Eclectic Vision*, pp. 3–22.

14. In *Racine et Shakespeare*, Stendhal credits Cousin with converting the youth of France to Romanticism: "Mais, monsieur, l'immense majorité des jeunes gens de la société a été convertie au romantisme par l'éloquence de M. Cousin . . ." (151). He goes on to say that if Cousin were still permitted to teach (in 1824 he was in exile), he would convert any who remained unconvinced.

15. At the time of his attack on Cousin, Hamilton occupied "an underpaid and undemanding Chair in Civil History" at Edinburgh, having been refused the post of the Chair of Moral Philosophy, which he had desired (Ryan xv). The article on Cousin was Hamilton's first for the *Edinburgh Review* and made his name in intellectual circles, where he was previously unknown. As Ryan relates, it was "an editor's nightmare, being late in arrival, much too long, and completely beyond the grasp of most readers of the *Review*. But it was a great success with Cousin himself, and it served notice on the outside world that someone in the British Isles was abreast of European philosophy"

(xv). It is the earliest review of Cousin that I have discovered in any British periodical, which accounts for the attention it receives here.

16. While the reception of Cousin's writings by the British public was largely negative, and I do tend to focus on those writers who best articulate the opposition to eclecticism, it was not entirely so. J. D. Morell provides a critical defense of Cousin's career in his review of a five-volume collection of the philosopher's works in 1851. For example, he answers the charge of pantheism leveled against Cousin: "Indeed pantheism has always been the child of over-wrought speculation, the refuge of the recluse, when worn out with pondering over the mysteries of existence and the insoluble problems of human destiny; while the whole tendency of our author's eclecticism is to depreciate mere individual speculation, to appeal to the sentiments of mankind at large, and to consider that no philosophical dogma has any authority whatever, until it is shown to be based upon and sustained by the massive foundations of common sense" (227). In conclusion, Morell declares that Cousin had presided over "a remarkable era in the literary history of France" (228). Reviewing the works of Cousin's biographers in 1890, John Owen agrees with them that Cousin was "the master critic of modern France" (459), talks of "his sturdy mental independence" (487), and believes, in spite of the failure of eclecticism, that "the spirit—the *vis viva*—of Cousin's work still survives [. . .]. He still remains the greatest philosopher, the most eminent systematizer of philosophical and cultured thought, in the France of the nineteenth century" (487).

17. Ryan reminds us that in the first half of the nineteenth century, philosophy and psychology had not yet attained their current meanings. "But whereas we now tend to draw a sharp distinction between the empirical inquiry into the mind and its powers which we call psychology, and the non-empirical inquiry into the possibility of knowledge or into the intelligibility of knowledge-claims which we now call philosophy, no such distinction appears in [Mill's] *Examination*" (ix), and nor did it in Cousin's *Cours de philosophie* or Hamilton's review of it.

18. The phrase is Henry Calderwood's. In *The Philosophy of the Infinite* (1854), he objected to Hamilton's proposition that we can have no notion of an Infinite Being and actually sided with Cousin on this issue. Belief, he said, "rises above things of matter" and the mind looks upon a finite world and realizes that its powers are limited. Nonetheless, the mind is conscious of the belief that the Infinite Being exists without limits. He agrees with Kant that our practical reason gives us the knowledge of "God as a necessary postulate for proper moral action." Calderwood acknowledges that the "balance of truth" is Cousin's, but he makes it clear "that in upholding the French philosopher, we do so only to a limited extent, and that merely in reference to this individual doctrine, and not in reference to the relation which this doctrine holds in his system. [. . .] We admire the great central truth in the philosophy of M. Cousin, but we regard the various points of Eclecticism, which he has made to cluster around it, as so many outposts, worse than useless, which ought to fall to atoms, and which have so fallen under the effective assaults of the Scottish metaphysician" (14–15). Calderwood differentiates between being conscious of the Infinite (here used as synonymous with Absolute, as in Cousin) and being able to mimic its powers—assuming the position of God. Interestingly, J. S. Mill, in his complete demolition of Hamilton's philosophy, agreed with Hamilton that we have no direct knowledge of God. Whatever we know of God is by inference only (*Examination* 36). However, he uses Hamilton's essay on Cousin to assert that "the most unquestionable of all logical maxims, [is] that the meaning of the abstract must be sought for in the concrete, and not conversely" (34).

19. One of the sciences that Lewes saw as having potential for practical application and verifiability was phrenology, also a favorite of Comte's (see Lewes, *Biographical History of Philosophy* 749–68, and Simon, "Two Cultures" 48).

20. Lewes also tells a hair-raising story about Cousin's exploitation of Hegel (372–74). It is hard to overlook in Lewes's vicious critique at least some degree of personal animosity he must have felt over Cousin's treatment of Comte. The quarrel between the two philosophers was well known at the time. Born only six years apart in the final decade of the eighteenth century, Cousin and Comte yet seemed a generation apart in their professional success and cultural values. When Cousin was already teaching at the Sorbonne and the École Normale, Comte was still a student at the École Polytechnique; fifteen years later Cousin, the "idol of Parisian academic youth," was appointed to an educational post in the new government, while Comte still held only a minor teaching post and began writing his *Cours de philosophie positive* in total obscurity. Cousin became director of the École Normale, wrote a syllabus for philosophical instruction that was adopted for use throughout the secondary system of the Université, and was the founder of the official philosophy, eclecticism, while Comte still pestered the government to create a Chair for him in the History of Science. When he was refused by Cousin's friend, Guizot, then Minister of Education, Comte turned against the government and the entire educational establishment (Simon, "Two Cultures" 46).

Chapter 3

1. Coleridge's career parallels Cousin's rather remarkably: both men were attracted to eclectic styles of thought; both men wanted to rescue forgotten thinkers; both traveled to Germany and studied philosophy; both espoused a vague spiritualism and both were condemned for pantheism; both were great talkers who seemed unable to fulfill their promise by publishing a magnum opus; both were addicted to reading and quotation and both were accused of plagiarism; both valued poetry as the highest form of expression; both gained numerous, enthusiastic followers; and both were liberals with pragmatic conservative leanings accused of apostasy later in life.

2. Coleridge is drawing upon Leibniz's *Trois Lettres à M. Remond de Montmort* (1714) and *Éclaircissement de difficultés que M. Bayle a trouvées [...]* as they are quoted and translated in the German of F. H. Jacobi, *Über die Lehre des Spinoza* (1789). Leask points out the appropriateness of this heavily mediated paragraph (French text quoted and translated in German text translated into English and, at the end, back into French), the subject of which is philosophical syncretism (Leask 402). Engell and Bate in their note on the same passage say that it should not be taken as Coleridge's approval of eclecticism (*Works* 7.1: 245–46).

3. Leask translates Leibniz: "I have found that most [philosophical] sects are right in a good part of what they assert, but not in what they deny" (403).

4. A great number of publications billing themselves "eclectic" appeared in the first half of the nineteenth century as a means of collecting disparate areas of knowledge for easier consumption. The *Eclectic Review* was published in London from 1805 to 1868, but the vast majority of eclectic journals issued from American publishers: the *American Eclectic, or Selections from the Periodical Literature of All Foreign Countries,* and the *Museum of Foreign Literature, Science and Art,* which joined to become the *Eclectic Museum* and the *Eclectic Magazine,* was published in Boston. This journal continued under

various titles through the turn of the century. Also in the United States, a number of eclectic medical publications appeared, including the *Eclectic Medical Journal* out of Cincinnati and the *Eclectic Journal of Medicine* from Philadelphia. Perhaps the best-remembered eclectic publication today is the McGuffey's series of "Eclectic Readers."

5. Mill praises the efforts of the Society for the Diffusion of Useful Knowledge as marking an important first attempt in combination. He imagines that ultimately, "authors, as a collective guild, must be their own patrons and their own booksellers" (106).

6. Perhaps the greatest proof of the link between eclecticism and democracy can be seen in the wider acceptance of Cousin's teachings in America. Not only did most of the translations into English of Cousin's works come from American publishers, but Transcendentalism, the most important philosophical system in the United States during the first half of the nineteenth century, was "eclectic in nature" and also "represented a phase of idealistic reaction" as French eclecticism had done. Following a survey of the sixty-six references to French philosophy in American periodicals between 1828 and 1848, Georges Joyaux concludes that "Cousin's doctrine was widely known in America and generally well received" and that "Much of the interest devoted to Cousin originated in the transcendentalist *milieu*, [and] most of it paralleled closely the rise and development of transcendentalism" (336–37).

7. Vico's 1744 *New Science* probably reached England by around 1827 via the French translation of Michelet. Cousin actually encouraged Michelet—who then counted himself among Cousin's followers—to undertake the translation, no doubt as part of Cousin's effort to bring to light the greatest works in all fields of knowledge. Vico's work influenced Michelet's own historiography, and thus the entire historiographical effort of the later nineteenth century.

8. Two modern studies of the idea of literary decline cover the major, pre-Romantic figures: Judith A. Plotz, *Ideas of the Decline of Poetry*, and W. Jackson Bate, *The Burden of the Past and the English Poet*. David J. DeLaura outlines the genealogy from Hazlitt to Carlyle, for which I am indebted in this section. See DeLaura, "The Future of Poetry," pp. 148–80.

9. Similarly, Peacock places Milton between the modern ages of gold and silver, "combining the excellencies of both" (13), and Dryden in the modern Silver Age, with its poetry of civilized life, authority, and the "exquisite and fastidious selection of words" (9).

10. Moving beyond the battle of the Ancients and the Moderns, Dryden praised Milton in much the same terms as the Carracci painters had been praised in the early seventeenth century for their eclectic combinations of the best attributes of their precursors:

> Three poets, in three distant ages born,
> Greece, Italy, and England did adorn.
> The first in loftiness of thought surpassed,
> The next in majesty, in both the last:
> The force of Nature could no farther go;
> To make a third, she joined the former two. ("Epigram on Milton" 1688)

Chapter 4

1. Edgar Finley Shannon, Jr., tracks the early critical reception of *The Princess* in his *Tennyson and the Reviewers: A Study of His Literary Reputation and of the Influence of the*

Critics upon His Poetry, 1827–1851 (1952). In his chapter on *The Princess,* Shannon is at pains to debunk the notion that early reviewers misunderstood the genius of the poem and that only later critics read it rightly. On the contrary, he shows that the early reviews were generally positive and that by 1851, when *The Princess* reached its fourth edition, critical opinion had reached another high point. During these four years, however, negative reviews appeared with regularity, prompting Tennyson to make many changes to his work, primarily in the interest of improving the unity of the whole (Shannon 97–140).

2. Christopher Ricks downplays the significance of the Cambridge Apostles in shaping Tennyson's worldview, noting that "Tennyson's participation in the group was to be generally torpid—so torpid as to lead to his formal resignation when he failed to deliver his paper on 'Ghosts'" (29). But as Ricks acknowledges, most of Tennyson's close friends, including Arthur Henry Hallam, were also Apostles.

3. In a brief survey of four "Cambridge poems"—the prize-winning "Timbuctoo," "A Character," "Lines on Cambridge of 1830," and "The Palace of Art"—John Coyle and Richard Cronin characterize Tennyson's engagement with the Apostles as part of a sustained effort to chart a poetic territory in which he can write about his age, but remain detached from it. They have suggested that "it was the point of transition that held Tennyson's poetic interest," that he was "fascinated by the process of waking" (114).

4. In the *Memoir* Tennyson's notes on *The Princess* record that "the 'Tale from mouth to mouth' was a game which I have more than once played when I was at Trinity College, Cambridge, with my brother undergraduates" (*Memoir* I:253.) Nonetheless, this "game" of storytelling has much in common with debating, as each orator must be careful to take up points made by the previous speaker in order to advance his own interpretation of the material.

5. In her recent *Victorian Poetry* article, Alisa Clapp-Itnyre argues that the interpolated songs are genuinely providing counterpoint, or antithesis, to the main verse-narrative: "they tell the story that Ida might have told if the women had controlled her story: a more realistic portrait of Victorian women's social roles and creative energies to counter the narrators' parody of women's social and creative aspirations" (230). While I do not make a strong distinction between the male and female voices that are telling the story of Princess Ida, except as they are involved in the broader dialectical effort of the poem, I do take Clapp-Itnyre's point that these lyrics are integral to her story, particularly as they suggest the importance of finding the lost child in order to develop her complete womanhood and her creative power.

6. For Johnston this usage of "mellay" or medley to describe the conflict between Arac and the Prince underscores the contest between Ida and the Prince, specifically war as "the unproductive convention of a superannuated social code" against which the Princess protests when she refuses to marry the Prince or anyone else (Johnston 563).

7. Some of Tennyson's remarks on the *Princess,* including this one, had originally appeared in a letter to and had been published by Canadian critic S. E. Dawson: "The child is the link thro' the parts as shown in the songs which are the best interpreters of the poem" (*Memoir* I:254). When "the public did not see the drift" after publication of the first edition, Tennyson decided to include interpolated songs explaining it.

8. Considering the readership and orientation of the periodicals in which these two reviews appeared, the divergence of opinion is not surprising. The *Christian Remembrancer* was, according to Alvar Ellegard, a quarterly "exponent of conservatively orthodox High Church views, [and] appealed chiefly to the High Church clergy" (30).

In 1860 its circulation was about 2,000. As a reviewer, however, Charles Peter Chretien was prominent enough to attract Tennyson's attention: he denounces Chretien's review in a letter to De Vere of October 1849, because of the claim that Tennyson always represents the sea "dead asleep," "which is a lie" (*Letters* I:305). Nevertheless, Chretien's review offers a valuable counterpoint to De Vere's inasmuch as religious beliefs often shaped responses to eclecticism—an element that is missing from De Vere's analysis.

The *Edinburgh Review*, also a quarterly and available at Mudie's, was of course the chief organ of the Whig-Liberals. At its peak in 1818, it boasted a circulation of 13,500 though by 1860 it had slipped to around 7,000 (Ellegard 27). In the contemporary press, it was generally considered second only to the *Quarterly Review* in importance. Naturally, this would have given Aubrey De Vere a much bigger readership than Chretien could have hoped for, even with library circulation figured in. It is also important to recognize that Aubrey De Vere was a friend and admirer of Tennyson. In his diary De Vere records that he heard portions of the *Princess* in manuscript as early as April 1845. In May of the same year, Tennyson and De Vere again talked about his "University of Women," and "discussed poetry, denouncing exotics, and saying that a poem should reflect the time and place" (*Letters* I:237–38). De Vere not only is responding to early negative reviews of the *Princess*, but is trying to work out a new direction for poetry of which Tennyson's work is the harbinger.

9. As Isobel Armstrong notes, Chretien borrows this extended metaphor from Wordsworth. In the preface to *The Excursion,* Wordsworth wrote that "all his work was essentially a whole," that *The Excursion* was related to the unpublished *Prelude*, as the antechapel to the body of a gothic church, and "his minor Pieces will be found by the attentive Reader to have such connections with the main Work as do the little cells, oratories, and sepulchral recesses, ordinarily included in these edifices" (qtd. in Armstrong 200).

Chapter 5

1. Morris and certainly Kingsley were also likely to have been influenced by Shakespeare's representations of Rome and Alexandria in *Antony and Cleopatra* (1606, 1607). Other possible influences on the Victorian idea of Alexandria covering the same material as Shakespeare include John Dryden's *All for Love* (1678) and G. F. Handel's *Giulio Cesare* (1724).

2. The *OED* quotes James Fitzjames Stephen's 1858 review of Thomas Hughes's *Tom Brown's Schooldays* (1857) in defining "muscular Christianity": "The principal character of the writer whose works earned this burlesque through expressive description, are his deep sense of the sacredness of all ordinary relations and the common duties of life, and the vigour with which he contends . . . for the great importance and value of animal spirits, physical strength, and hearty enjoyment of all the pursuits and accomplishments connected with them" (qtd. in Adams 108). As James Eli Adams notes, this "regimen marks a revival of aristocratic norms of manhood, and as such seems to have appealed to middle-class men (and boys) anxious to align themselves with more traditional sources of masculine identity" (108). This alliance between aristocratic ideals and middle-class manhood complicates Kingsley's rejection of the aristocratic exclusiveness of Hypatia's philosophy.

3. John C. Hawley's account of Kingsley's Anglican *via media* has strongly influenced my interpretation of *Hypatia,* particularly his characterization of the struggle in Alexandria as a contest between atheism and dogmatism.

4. *Hypatia* was first published serially in *Fraser's Magazine* from 1852 to 1853 and as a book in the summer of 1853 (Baldwin 126). Kingsley's biographer Susan Chitty locates the practical inspiration for *Hypatia* in a trip Kingsley made to Roman ruins in Germany in 1851, where "he imagined all the hellish scenes of agony and cruelty that the place had witnessed" (151); yet, for at least two years, Kingsley had been reading the early Church fathers and "contemplating a book about Alexandria after the sack of Rome, depicting the clashes between Christians, Jews, Greeks and barbarians in that dissension-rent city" (152). Kingsley probably first encountered the tragic story of Hypatia in chapter 47 of *The Decline and Fall of the Roman Empire,* though he disagreed with Gibbon's representation of fifth-century Alexandria: "And thus an age, which, to the shallow insight of a sneerer like Gibbon, seems only a rotting and aimless chaos of sensuality and anarchy, fanaticism and hypocrisy, produced a Clemens and an Athanase, a Chrysostom and an Augustine" (*Hypatia* xi).

5. Chitty also views this work as a crucial precursor of *Hypatia.* It was Kingsley's first "practical sortie into the past," and the two works share a common plan, wherein each of the major characters was to represent a school of thought (152); however, in *Phaethon* the intention was to demolish Neoplatonic Anythingarianism, and in *Hypatia* the goal is to forge from the combination of elements a Christian *via media*.

6. In an exhaustive study of American periodicals published before 1850, Georges J. Joyaux has investigated the vexed question of the influence of French Eclecticism on American Transcendentalism. Many scholars would prefer that Emerson were indebted only to the German idealists and not at all to the "rational, urbane, compromise philosophy" of eclecticism. As Joyaux admits, however, "the two systems are both philosophically eclectic in nature, and that, furthermore, both represented a phase of idealistic reaction" (327). Joyaux concludes that Cousin, whose works were "widely known and generally well received" (336) in the United States, especially as the explicator of German philosophy, must at least have provided a catalyst to the study of metaphysics.

7. Kingsley had taken this position some years earlier in *The Saint's Tragedy; or, The True Story of Elizabeth of Hungary* (1848). The focus of the play is on the "agonising contradiction" in the mind of Elizabeth, a pure *and* married woman who has been taught "the Manichean contempt with which a celibate clergy would have all men regard the names of husband, wife, and parent" (Project Gutenberg text, p. 6).

8. Susann Dorman recounts the story of how Edward Pusey used *Hypatia* as grounds for derailing the Prince of Wales's nomination of Kingsley for an honorary Oxford doctorate (192).

9. Dorman points out that Kingsley borrows some of Newman's own phrases in this passage (192).

10. For further comparison and analysis see Duncan Forbes, *The Liberal Anglican Idea of History,* chapter 4, "Practical History," especially pp. 102–11.

11. See chapter 3, "Imagining the Science of Renunciation: Manhood and Abasement in Kingsley and Tennyson," pp. 105–47. Although Adams does not deal with *Hypatia,* his judgment that Kingsley's novels betray "a powerfully masochistic impulse [. . .] where his heroes typically experience an unusually violent oscillation of desire and restraint" (110) could well apply to Kingsley's representation of fifth-century Alexandria as a contest between two undesirable extremes, abstinence and sensuality.

12. As Frederick Grant has argued, the "main characteristic feature of Hellenistic religion was syncretism: the tendency to identify the deities of various peoples and to combine their cults" (xiii).

13. In tracing the fortunes of the concept of eclecticism throughout history, Pierluigi Donini distinguishes, as seventeenth-century eclectics also did, between syncretism and eclecticism. It is important to note that Kingsley wavered between a stance that might be described as syncretistic and one that might legitimately be designated eclectic. Eclecticism is a method for choosing doctrines and seeking the truth; it is most frequently opposed to dogmatism and sectarianism. Thus, "anyone who becomes a faithful disciple of an eclectic philosophy loses by this very fact the right of being considered eclectic" (Donini 20). A syncretist "aimed to *reconcile* widely different opinions and [. . .] succeeded only in producing a 'heap' [or] 'large shapeless mass'" (Donini 21). The religious historian Brian Hatcher agrees that syncretism is distinguished from eclecticism by "the additional feature of reconciliation. That is, it is not sufficient, when speaking of syncretism, to refer only to the process of encounter and appropriation; one must also speak of merging, accommodation, or amalgamation" (8). Donini does not see, however, that the distinction has any currency in philosophy, although syncretism is still used as "a technical term" in the history of religion. Indeed, in philosophy, the two terms are now used interchangeably.

14. Both Victorian writers acknowledge Philo of Alexandria's probable influence on Clemens and the first school of Christian theology. Another eclectic thinker, Philo, as a Jew, might well be another model for Raphael. Kingsley devotes a long chapter to Philo in *Alexandria and Her Schools*.

15. Some years after Robert Milman published his article on Indian Brahmoism, John Murdoch published in the series "Papers on Indian Reform" a pamphlet titled "The Brahma Samaj and Other Modern Indian Eclectic Systems of Religion in India: Religious Reform, Part IV." In introducing his readers to the Indian eclectic school, Murdoch paints them as reformers in religious matters: "The adherents of the new eclectic systems in India are far more enlightened than the greatest Hindu philosophers in former times. They have much clearer ideas of God than the authors of the Vedic hymns" (1). Furthermore, Murdoch writes, "The members of the Brahma Samaj are monotheists, and hold a pure system of morality. As protesters against idolatry and advocates of social reform, they are doing excellent service" (2). Murdoch attributes this reformist tendency to the influence of Christianity.

16. In his guide to the city, E. M. Forster does not attempt to draw any parallel between Alexandria (ancient or modern) and Britain, which perhaps signals the diminished importance of the comparison by 1922. However, as Forster puts it, Alexandria had still "nourished imperial dreams" during the nineteenth century (91) and "Life flowed back into her" when "The eyes of Europe were again directed to the deserted shore" (93). James Stevens Curl's fascinating study of the *Egyptomania* of the nineteenth century confirms that, for Europeans, interest in Egypt revived with the "imperial dreams" of Napoleon, Nelson's victory at Aboukir Bay, and the building of the Suez Canal from 1859 to 1869. The mania for Egyptian design motifs and artifacts endured throughout the century. Curl observes that "eclecticism involving Egyptianising themes was one of the richest of tendencies in a century already rich in invention" (206). See chapter 9, "Aspects of the Egyptian Revival in the Later Part of the Nineteenth Century," pp. 187–206.

17. A product of European Romanticism and German historicism, the "science of nations" offered a pseudoscientific justification for Europe's domination over the native

peoples of Asia, Africa, and the Americas. The writer's expression of this view is typical of Romantic nationalism: "The life and habits of a people are, to a large extent, moulded by their climate and the peculiarities of their land. Orientalisms and Occidentalisms are not altogether capricious and arbitrary. Many of them are the offspring of the sky and soil. Certain features must always be peculiar to certain nations, not merely because of their ancestry, but because of their physical distinctions; and though, to some extent, there may be a fusion of these, an interchange of peculiarities, yet there are certain great ridges or outlines which must remain unobliterated and almost unsoftened" ("Egypt and Syria" 150). Kingsley, too, relied on such essentialist views of cultures and peoples. In the preface to *Hypatia*, he had judged the "races of Egypt and Syria" in ancient times to be "effeminate, over-civilized, exhausted by centuries during which no infusion of fresh blood had come to renew the stock. Morbid, self-conscious, physically indolent, incapable then, as now, of personal or political freedom, they afforded material out of which fanatics might easily be made, but not citizens of the kingdom of God" (xiv).

18. In his review of *Alexandria and Her Schools* (1854), James Martineau accepts the "parallelism [. . .] in the broad features of the two ages": "The decline of ancient faith without mature successor to take the vacant throne; the attempt of metaphysics to fit the soul with a religion; the pretensions of intuition and ecstasy; the sudden birth, from the very eggs of a high-flown spiritualism, of mystagogues and mesmerists, as larvae are born of butterflies; the growth of world-cities and world-science, with their public libraries and institutes, their botanic and zoölogic gardens, their cheap baths and open parks; the joint diffusion of taste and demoralization, of asceticism and intemperance; the increase of a proletary class amid the growing humanity of society and the laws; the frequency of frightful epidemics; the combination of gigantic enterprises and immense commerce with decay at the heart of private life" (295). Martineau refuses to accept, however, the analogy between "declining empire" and the "intellectual tendencies of the present age," because "the cosmopolitanism of modern times is altogether different" (298). Roman cosmopolitanism had led to the almost universal adoption of one or two languages; whatever was specialized became provincial and eventually servile: "All that was indigenous and characteristic was smoothed away; and over the wooded uplands and sequestered meadows of history, the paved roads of universal empire pushed their level way" (297). By contrast, modern cosmopolitanism arises from a "universal faith" that acknowledges "the common law and common kindred of the human race, in all the highest relations" (298). Like most of Kingsley's contemporaries, Martineau believes that the spirit of world history is fulfilled in Christianity. While he praises the coexistence of different languages, he is unconcerned at the loss of diversity in religion.

Chapter 6

1. In 1959 *Victorian Studies* published these early reading lists with commentary by Kenneth Allott. In establishing the importance of Cousin's thought for Arnold's intellectual development, I rely on Allott's discussion of his reading during this period. Although monographs by Iris Sells and F. J. W. Harding treat Arnold's relationship to French literature and culture in great detail, neither mentions Arnold's reading of Cousin. Sells's book appeared in 1935, before the early reading lists were published, but Harding's 1964 *Matthew Arnold the Critic and France* should have taken Allott's work into account.

2. Allott argues, therefore, that "Cousin seems to deserve a little of the credit for 'The Scholar Gypsy'" (260), since Glanvill is the source of the scholar-gypsy legend.

3. In his diary entry for 9 April 1851, Arnold does record his reading of Cousin's article on revolutions: "Des Principes de la révolution française et du gouvernement représentatif," published in the *Revue des deux mondes* 10 (1851): 5–46 (*Letters* 202n14).

4. Clinton Machann notes that Arnold was "eclectic in his reading of George Sand (whose liberal idealism appealed to him and whose version of feminine sentimentality may have reminded him of his mother), Goethe (who had largely displaced his earlier interest in Byron), the French poet Beranger (who reinforced his affectation of French culture), and the Hindu classic *Bhagavad Gita* (where he found a discipline of resignation congenial with his developing stoicism): he typically balanced his studies of Kant, Lucretius, Descartes, and the Epicureans and Stoics with critical refutations of their positions, following the dialogic impulse that would lead him to his later work as critic" (18). Allott remarks that "Arnold's assent to the eclectic variety of Stoic ethics preached to Pausanias as practical wisdom in the second scene of 'Empedocles on Etna' was always more intellectual than emotional while he was still capable of writing poetry" (86). While both these critics perceive Arnold as eclectic, generally speaking, neither investigates the deeper significance of his eclecticism.

5. While traveling in France as school inspector, Arnold met many of the leading intellectuals of the day including Barthélemy St. Hilaire, Mignet, Villemain, Guizot, Thiers, Sainte-Beuve, and Renan (*SL* 118–31). He first met Cousin in March 1859, at dinner and then at the Sorbonne ("Cousin well worth seeing.") and he wanted to meet him again, though it is not clear that he ever did so: "My great inducement in going back [to Paris] would be to see and talk to Cousin who has himself had a Report to make much like that on which I am engaged" (*Letters* 426; *SL* 130). The report to which Arnold refers was completed in 1860 and published as *The Popular Education of France with Notices of that of Holland and Switzerland* (1861). During the 1830s Cousin had published reports on the state of elementary education in Holland, Prussia, and Germany; during the 1840s he focused his attention on France, coming out with the definitive report *Instruction publique* in 1850.

6. Clough was not the only one to see the limits of Arnold's imitations, architectonic though they might be, of past styles and subjects of poetry. G. H. Lewes (among others) wrote reviews decrying Arnold's new poetics. In directing young poets to study the classics and to "beware of the syren-charms which enervate the Moderns," Arnold is recommending imitation (Lewes, "Schools of Poetry," 82). As a positivist, Lewes condemns imitation: "the retention in our organism of the elements which *have lived* is in itself fatal as a source of destruction, poisoning the very life these elements once served, so in the onward progression of Humanity the old elements must pass away, transmitting to successors the work they had to perform" (78). To imitate, apparently, is to eat the dead, and be poisoned unto death.

7. For the eclectic sources of Arnold's poetry, I am relying on Kenneth Allott and Miriam Allott's edition of *The Poems of Matthew Arnold*.

8. In his reading of "The World and the Quietist," George Forbes relates how in the *Bhagavad Gita,* Krishna tells the warrior Arjuna that he is "all-grasping death" and "Time, the destroyer of mankind" (157). Forbes sees Arnold's "adverse voices" as reminders of Krishna and of death to human beings who have "their hearts set on the goals of their frantic and futile activity" (157). Krishna is Time and death, but he is also "generation and dissolution; the place where all things are reposited, and the

inexhaustible seed of nature" (159). Arnold would undoubtedly have found these images of incorporation in the body of time most appealing as a solution to the problem of the divided self, and to the dilemma of style.

9. Sidney Coulling, in the best account of the development of the 1853 preface, identifies the writer of these words, the editor of *The Spectator,* Robert Stephen Rintoul, in a review of the poetry of Edwin Arnold, as Matthew Arnold's immediate target. Arnold disagreed with the whole premise of *The Spectator*'s literary criticism, that "poetry must be both modern and moralistic." The quoted comment is thus "typical of the criticism of the age—a specious criticism designed to confuse the reader and mislead the poet" (Coulling 235).

10. In his 1956 monograph on Glanvill, Jackson Cope examines the sources of the eclecticism of the Cambridge Platonists. In tracing the sources of their eclecticism, Cope discovers traces of Skepticism, Stoicism, and Aristotelianism, mixed up with Platonism (139). It would be useful to trace Arnold's eclecticism back from Cousin to Leibniz and the German Eclectics and to Glanvill and the Cambridge Platonists.

11. In "Arnold and the Cambridge Platonists," Ruth apRoberts traces the "Viconian" influence back from Michelet and Herder (both influenced by the Italian philosopher of history), thus allowing for a French point of departure in his thinking, which I deem appropriate. She argues that Arnold imbibed Vico's *New Science* from his father and from Rugby, where Vico's "The Social Progress of States" was a textbook (139). She points to the odd periodization in texts such as the preface to *Poems* of 1853 (where Arnold speaks of the age of the Greeks, and then of the moderns, Shakespeare and Goethe) as evidence of his "belaboring the three Viconian ages." ApRoberts claims that Arnold sees "the dialogue of the mind with itself" as "an obverse side of Renaissance culture." Again, in "On the Modern Element in Literature," he posits recurrent modern ages, in keeping with Vico's theory of historical cycles. In his excellent *The Victorian Critic and the Idea of History,* Peter Allan Dale also explores the connection between Arnold's thought and Vico's, emphasizing that Arnold shares with Vico "his high opinion of the healthy, fully developed modern age as a stage in the cycle" (94). Dale also explores Arnold's assimilation of Carlyle and the German philosophers, particularly the concept of Zeitgeist; but in Arnold it is a radically different concept than it is in Hegel (128). In *The Victorian Mirror of History,* Dwight Culler entirely dismisses the role of Vico and traces Arnold's thinking about the Zeitgeist and the Time-Stream to "the Philosophy of Clothes in Carlyle's *Sartor Resartus*" (139). Arnold agrees with Carlyle that changes are initially spiritual, and that the forms of society—the Clothes—are continually lagging behind (138); nevertheless, as David DeLaura has written in "Arnold and Carlyle," Arnold would ultimately reject the example of the older writer as insufficiently disinterested.

12. Lewis Mott, F. J. W. Harding, Flavia M. Alaya, and Stephen Prickett have all offered persuasive arguments for the French historian Ernest Renan's key role in the development of Arnold's critical principles. The parallels between Arnold's career and that of Renan are indeed remarkable. Alaya and Prickett observe the similarities in their writings on the Celts and on religion, in particular their emphasis on the need for both the Hellenic and Hebraic principles. Not all critics who have examined the Arnold-Renan relationship agree on its importance in Arnold's work. Sidney Coulling contends that the claims of influence have been exaggerated, providing evidence that Arnold had written about such key ideas as "disinterestedness" before he had read Renan. Coulling would rather talk of resemblances. Rose Bachem, in her comparison of

the two writers' views on perfection, also downplays the question of influence, agreeing with Saintsbury's 1902 assessment: "Mr. Arnold needed no teaching from Mr. Renan" (229).

13. In fact, so many of Victor Cousin's English critics reacted violently against his eclecticism because they felt there would be no check on the individual eclectic's determination of what was true and what was false. But of course, Cousin worked within the context of the French Academy and followed developments in philosophy and the history of philosophy around the world.

Chapter 7

1. Hardy met Pater in London in 1886 (Donoghue 13), after the publication of the works I am considering here; but as Natarajan points out, he was well acquainted with Pater's work by 1878 (849).

2. Diane Elam takes up the question of the politics of romance from Fredric Jameson and Northrop Frye. All three critics see a revolutionary potential in romance that depends largely on its willingness to remake the world on a new pattern: "romance contains a transformative potential which allows the articulation of marginalized desire" (20). See Elam, pp. 19–25; Frye, pp. 161–88; Jameson, pp. 157–62.

3. Billie Inman points out that this idea—"the first step towards seeing one's object as it really is, is to know one's own impression as it really is"—derives from Hegel's *Aesthetik* (Inman xiv, 56–57).

4. The other influences cited by Inman are 1) Hegel's and Schiller's ideas on aesthetics, and 2) Quinet's and Michelet's orientation in history. She points out that Pater had "command of a general range of reference—classical, German, French, and English, quite astounding to one who realizes that it was primarily the fruit of only six years" (xi-xii). He had not, however, mastered whole subjects. As Inman puts it, "He was a highly literate dilettante" (xii). Furthermore, by 1869 "Pater's mind was formed," which makes it "inadvisable to speak of major influences from his readings after that time" (xii).

5. In his notes to *The Renaissance,* Donald L. Hill identifies the echo of Sainte-Beuve's essay in "Two Early French Stories" (319).

6. "Au reste, il ne s'agit véritablement de rien sacrifier, de rien déprécier. Le Temple du goût, je le crois, est à refaire; mais, en le rebâtissant, il s'agit simplement de l'agrandir, et qu'il devienne le Panthéon de tous les nobles humains, de tous ceux qui ont accru pour une part notable et durable la somme des jouissances et des titres de l'esprit" (*Causeries du lundi* 50).

7. "Voilà nos classiques; l'imagination de chacun peut achever le dessin et même choisir son groupe préféré. Car il faut choisir, et la première condition du goût, après avoir tout compris, est de ne pas voyager sans cesse, mais de s'asseoir une fois et de se fixer" (*Causeries du lundi* 53).

8. Instead of seeing here a choice between the historic method and the eclectic method, Carolyn Williams perceives a "graphic contrast between the historical method and the allegorical method" (*Transfigured World* 105). In Williams's view, Pater is drawing a distinction between "temporal and spatial modes of 'reconciliation'" (105). "Allegorical juxtaposition imitates 'agreement'" in space, while the historical method would give priority to temporal differences. While I believe that Williams's distinction is an

important one, I do not wish to take up the relationship between the allegorical and the eclectic in this study. For the moment, it is sufficient to acknowledge Pater's own characterization of Pico's allegorical approach.

9. Donald Hill's notes on the Pico essay (322–23) led me to the relevant passages in *Plato and Platonism*. John Conlon also deals with the *Plato and Platonism* passages and comes up against the inconsistency in Pater's thought regarding critical practices "somewhat allied to 'impressionism,' the 'dogmatic,' the 'eclectic,' and 'the historic method'" (*Walter Pater and the French Tradition* 148). Conlon notes that Pater is "by no means free" from eclecticism, "especially in his pursuit of the Romantic spirit from ancient Greek culture to the nineteenth century" (149), an assessment with which I heartily agree.

10. In this account of Plato's creation of an original philosophy, Pater makes it clear that all creation incorporates the ideas, images, and aspirations of others. This could account for that homesickness that so many of Pater's critics have observed in him. Bullen claims that these "translations" of other cultures bring us back into contact with a world we've lost, "counteracting the homesickness of the modern condition" (279).

11. Gerald Monsman's 1980 study *Walter Pater's Art of Autobiography* is probably the most thoroughgoing account of the creation of selfhood in all of Pater's writings. He sees the shaping of self in these works as an ongoing dialectic "between the autobiographer shaping his life and the emergent work which reflects and enhances that identity" (36). The unity that emerges is a provisional one, since the "center is always in movement away from the present toward layers deeper within or frames further outside" (36). Monsman's characterization of Pater's writing of self rings true, particularly since Pater so often wrote of the creations of others as involving a dialectic, or mixed, situation.

WORKS CITED

Adam, Charles. *La Philosophie en France (première moitié du XIXe siècle)*. Paris: Félix Alcan, 1894.
Adams, James Eli. *Dandies and Desert Saints: Styles of Victorian Masculinity*. Ithaca, NY: Cornell University Press, 1995.
Alaya, Flavia M. "Arnold and Renan on the Popular Uses of History." *Journal of the History of Ideas* 28 (1967): 551–74.
Aldrich, Megan. *Gothic Revival*. London: Phaidon Press, 1994.
"Alexandria Old and New." *All the Year Round* 8 (1862–63): 228–32.
"Alexandrian Christianity." *North British Review* 23 (1855): 393–421.
Allen, Peter. *The Cambridge Apostles: The Early Years*. Cambridge: Cambridge University Press, 1978.
Allott, Kenneth. "A Background for 'Empedocles on Etna.'" *Essays and Studies* 21 (1968): 80–100.
———. "Matthew Arnold's Reading-Lists in Three Early Diaries." *Victorian Studies* 2 (1959): 254–66.
apRoberts, Ruth. "Arnold and the Cambridge Platonists." *Clio* 17 (1988): 139–50.
Archer, John. *The Literature of British Domestic Architecture*. Cambridge, MA: MIT Press, 1985.
Armstrong, Isobel. *Victorian Scrutinies: Reviews of Poetry 1830–1870*. London: The Athlone Press, 1972.
Arnold, Matthew. *The Complete Prose Works of Matthew Arnold*. 11 vols. Edited by R. H. Super. Ann Arbor: University of Michigan Press, 1960–78.
———. *The Letters of Matthew Arnold*. Edited by Cecil Y. Lang. Vol. 1, *1829–1859*. Charlottesville: University Press of Virginia, 1996.

———. *The Note-Books of Matthew Arnold.* Edited by Howard Foster Lowry, Karl Young, and Waldo Hilary Dunn. London: Geoffrey Cumberlege, Oxford University Press, 1952.

———. *The Poems of Matthew Arnold.* 2nd ed. Edited by Kenneth Allott and Miriam Allott. London: Longman, 1965.

———. *Selected Letters of Matthew Arnold.* Edited by Clinton Machann and Forrest D. Burt. Ann Arbor: University of Michigan Press, 1993.

Bachelard, Gaston. *The Poetics of Space.* Translated by Maria Jolas. Boston: Beacon Press, 1962.

Bachem, Rose. "Arnold's and Renan's Views on Perfection." *Revue de littérature comparée* 41 (1967): 228–37.

Baldwin, Stanley. *Charles Kingsley.* Ithaca, NY: Cornell University Press, 1934.

Balzac, Honoré de. *Personal Opinions.* Edited and translated by Katharine Prescott Wormeley. Boston: Hardy, Pratt, and Company, 1904.

Barrell, John. "The Public Prospect and the Private View: The Politics of Taste in Eighteenth-Century Britain." In *Landscape, Natural Beauty, and the Arts,* edited by Salim Kemal and Ivan Gaskell. Cambridge: Cambridge University Press, 1993. 81–102.

Bate, W. Jackson. *The Burden of the Past and the English Poet.* Cambridge, MA: Harvard University Press, 1970.

Bell, Quentin. *The Schools of Design.* London: Routledge & Kegan Paul, 1963.

Bellori, Giovanni Pietro. *The Lives of Annibale and Agostino Carracci.* 1672. Translated by Catherine Enggass. Foreword by Robert Enggass. University Park: Pennsylvania State University Press, 1968.

Bénichou, Paul. *The Consecration of the Writer, 1750–1830.* Translated by Mark K. Jensen. Lincoln: University of Nebraska Press, 1999.

———. *Le Temps des prophètes: Doctrines de l'âge romantique.* Paris: Gallimard, 1977.

Beresford Hope, A. J. *The Common Sense of Art: A Lecture Delivered in Behalf of the Architectural Museum.* London: John Murray, 1858.

Bernheimer, Charles. "Introduction: The Anxieties of Comparison." In *Comparative Literature in the Age of Multiculturalism,* edited by Charles Bernheimer. Baltimore: Johns Hopkins University Press, 1995. 1–17.

Bernheimer, Charles et al. "Comparative Literature at the Turn of the Century." In *Comparative Literature in the Age of Multiculturalism*, edited by Charles Bernheimer. Baltimore: Johns Hopkins University Press, 1995. 39–48.

Betjeman, John. *Ghastly Good Taste; or, A Depressing Story of the Rise and Fall of English Architecture.* 1933. London: Anthony Blond, 1970.

Blanc, Charles. *Histoire des peintres de toutes les écoles.* Paris: J. Renouard, 1865–77.

Bloom, Harold. "Walter Pater: The Intoxication of Belatedness." *Yale French Studies* 50 (1974): 163–89.

Boas, George. *French Philosophies of the Romantic Period.* 1925. New York: Russell and Russell, 1964.

Boime, Albert. "The Teaching Reforms of 1863 and the Origins of Modernism in France." *Art Quarterly* 1 (1977): 1–39.

———. *Thomas Couture and the Eclectic Vision.* New Haven, CT: Yale University Press, 1980.

Bolus-Reichert, Christine. "Everyday Eclecticism: William Morris and the Suburban Picturesque." *Nineteenth Century Prose* 29, no. 2 (2002): 162–96.

Boyle, G. D. Review of Matthew Arnold, *Empedocles on Etna. North British Review*

9 (1853): 209–14. Reprinted in *Matthew Arnold, The Poetry: The Critical Heritage*, edited by Carl Dawson. London: Routledge & Kegan Paul, 1973. 67–70.

Brooks, John I. *The Eclectic Legacy: Academic Philosophy and the Human Sciences in Nineteenth-Century France*. Newark: University of Delaware Press, 1998.

Brooks, Michael W. *John Ruskin and Victorian Architecture*. New Brunswick, NJ: Rutgers University Press, 1987.

Browning, Elizabeth Barrett. *Aurora Leigh*. 1856. New York: Oxford University Press, 1993.

Bullen, J. B. *The Expressive Eye: Fiction and Perception in the Work of Thomas Hardy*. Oxford: Clarendon Press, 1986.

———. *The Myth of the Renaissance in Nineteenth Century Writing*. Oxford: Clarendon Press, 1994.

Cafritz, Robert C. "Classical Revision of the Pastoral Landscape." In *Places of Delight: The Pastoral Landscape*, by Robert C. Cafritz, Lawrence Gowing, and David Rosand. London: Weidenfeld and Nicolson; Washington, DC: The Phillips Collection in assoc. with the National Gallery of Art, 1988. 82–111.

Calderwood, Henry. *The Philosophy of the Infinite; with Special Reference to the Theories of Sir William Hamilton and M. Cousin*. Edinburgh: Thomas Constable and Co., 1854.

Calinescu, Matei. *Five Faces of Modernity: Modernism, Avant-Garde, Decadence, Kitsch, Postmodernism*. Durham, NC: Duke University Press, 1987.

Carlyle, Thomas. "Characteristics." *Edinburgh Review* 54 (1831): 351–83. Reprinted in *The Emergence of Victorian Consciousness: The Spirit of the Age*, edited by George Levine. New York: The Free Press, 1967. 39–68.

———. *Past and Present*. 1843. Edited by Richard D. Altick. New York: New York University Press, 1965.

———. *Sartor Resartus*. 1833–34. Edited by Kerry McSweeney and Peter Sabor. Oxford, UK: Oxford University Press, 1987.

———. "Signs of the Times." In *Thomas Carlyle: Selected Writings*, edited by Alan Shelston. New York: Penguin Books, 1971. 61–85.

Casini, Paolo. "Diderot et le portrait du philosophe éclectique." *Revue Internationale de Philosophie* 38 (1994): 35–45.

Chadbourne, Richard M. *Ernest Renan*. New York: Twayne Publishers, Inc., 1968.

Cheah, Pheng. "Introduction Part II: The Cosmopolitical—Today." In *Cosmopolitics: Thinking and Feeling beyond the Nation*, edited by Pheng Cheah and Bruce Robbins. Minneapolis: University of Minnesota Press, 1998. 20–41.

Chitty, Susan. *The Beast and the Monk: A Life of Charles Kingsley*. London: Hodder and Stoughton, 1974.

Chow, Rey. "In the Name of Comparative Literature." In *Comparative Literature in the Age of Multiculturalism*, edited by Charles Bernheimer. Baltimore: Johns Hopkins University Press, 1995. 107–16.

Chretien, C. P. "The Princess." *Christian Remembrancer* 17 (1849): 381–401. Reprinted in *Victorian Scrutinies: Reviews of Poetry 1830–1870*, edited by Isobel Armstrong. London: The Athlone Press, 1972. 200–222.

Clapp-Itnyre, Alisa. "Marginalized Musical Interludes: Tennyson's Critique of Conventionality in *The Princess*." *Victorian Poetry* 38 (2000): 227–48.

Clark, Kenneth. *The Gothic Revival: An Essay in the History of Taste*. 1928. London: John Murray, 1995.

Clough, Arthur Hugh. "Recent English Poetry: A Review of Several Volumes of Poems by Alexander Smith, Matthew Arnold, and Others." 1853. Reprinted in *Selected Prose Works of Arthur Hugh Clough,* edited by Buckner B. Trawick. Tuscaloosa: University of Alabama Press, 1964. 143–71.

Coleridge, Samuel Taylor. *Biographia Literaria.* Edited by Nigel Leask. London: Everyman, 1997.

———. *The Collected Works of Samuel Taylor Coleridge.* 15 vols. Edited by James Engell and W. Jackson Bate. London: Routledge & Kegan Paul, 1983.

Colquhoun, Alan. "Three Kinds of Historicism." In *Modernity and the Classical Tradition: Architectural Essays, 1980–1987.* Cambridge, MA: MIT Press, 1991. 3–18.

Conlon, John J. *Walter Pater and the French Tradition.* Lewisburg, PA: Bucknell University Press, 1982.

Cope, Jackson I. *Joseph Glanvill, Anglican Apologist.* St. Louis: Washington University Studies, 1956.

Cotten, Jean-Pierre. *Autour de Victor Cousin: Une politique de la philosophie.* Paris: Diffusion les Belles Lettres, 1992.

Coulling, Sidney M. B. "Matthew Arnold's 1853 Preface: Its Origin and Aftermath." *Victorian Studies* 7 (1964): 233–63.

———. "Renan's Influence on Arnold's Literary and Social Criticism." *Florida State University Studies* 5 (1952): 95–112.

Cousin, Victor. "Exposition of Eclecticism." 1833. In *Philosophical Miscellanies, Translated from the French of Cousin, Jouffroy, and B. Constant.* Translated and edited by George Ripley. Vol. 1. Boston: Hilliard, Gray, and Company, 1838. 55–157.

———. *Introduction to the History of Philosophy.* Translated by Henning Gotfried Linberg. Boston: Hilliard, Gray, Little, and Wilkins, 1832.

———. *Lectures on the True, the Beautiful, and the Good.* 1853. Translated by O. W. Wight. New York: D. Appleton and Company, 1872.

———. "On the Destiny of Modern Philosophy." 1829. In *Philosophical Miscellanies, Translated from the French of Cousin, Jouffroy, and B. Constant.* Translated and edited by George Ripley. Vol. 1. Boston: Hilliard, Gray, and Company, 1838. 45–54.

Coyle, John, and Richard Cronin. "Tennyson and the Apostles." In *Rethinking Victorian Culture,* edited by Juliet John and Alice Jenkins. New York: St. Martin's Press, 2000. 114–25.

Crook, J. Mordaunt. *The Dilemma of Style: Architectural Ideas from the Picturesque to the Post-modern.* Chicago: University of Chicago Press, 1987.

Culler, A. Dwight. *The Victorian Mirror of History.* New Haven, CT: Yale University Press, 1985.

Curl, James Stevens. *Egyptomania: A Recurring Theme in the History of Taste.* Manchester: Manchester University Press, 1994.

Daiches, David. *Sir Walter Scott and His World.* London: Thames and Hudson, 1971.

Dale, Peter Allan. *The Victorian Critic and the Idea of History: Carlyle, Arnold, Pater.* Cambridge, MA: Harvard University Press, 1977.

Davis, Harold T. *Alexandria, The Golden City.* Vol. 2, *Cleopatra's City.* Evanston: The Principia Press of Illinois, Inc., 1957.

DeLaura, David J. "Arnold and Carlyle." *PMLA* 79 (1964): 104–29.

———. "The Future of Poetry: A Context for Carlyle and Arnold." In *Carlyle and His Contemporaries: Essays in Honor of Charles Richard Sanders,* edited by John Clubbe. Durham, NC: Duke University Press, 1976. 148–80.

Dempsey, Charles. *Annibale Carracci and the Beginnings of Baroque Style*. Glückstadt, Germany: Augustin, 1977.
De Quincey, Thomas. "Superficial Knowledge." In *The Collected Writings of Thomas De Quincey,* edited by David Masson. Vol. 10, *Notes from the Pocket-Book of a Late Opium-Eater.* Edinburgh: Adam and Charles Black, 1890. Reprint, New York: AMS Press, 1968. 449–54.
De Vere, Aubrey. "Modern Poetry and Poets." *Edinburgh Review* 90 (October 1849): 204–27.
Dillon, John M., and A. A. Long. Preface and Introduction to *The Question of "Eclecticism": Studies in Later Greek Philosophy,* edited by John M. Dillon and A. A. Long. Berkeley: University of California Press, 1988. vii–viii; 1–13.
Donini, Pierluigi. "The History of the Concept of Eclecticism." In *The Question of "Eclecticism": Studies in Later Greek Philosophy,* edited by John M. Dillon and A. A. Long. Berkeley: University of California Press, 1988. 15–33.
Donoghue, Denis. *Walter Pater: Lover of Strange Souls*. New York: Alfred A. Knopf, 1995.
Dorman, Susann. "*Hypatia* and *Callista:* The Initial Skirmish between Kingsley and Newman." *Nineteenth-Century Fiction* 34 (1979): 173–93.
Drabble, Margaret. *A Writer's Britain: Landscape in Literature*. London: Thames and Hudson, 1979.
Dryden, John. "Epigram on Milton." In Vol. 1 of *The Norton Anthology of English Literature.* 7th ed. Edited by M. H. Abrams and Stephen Greenblatt. New York: W. W. Norton & Company, 2000. 2108–9.
Duncan, Ian. Editor's Notes to *Ivanhoe*. Oxford: Oxford University Press, 1996. 525–81.
Eagleton, Terry. *The Ideology of the Aesthetic.* Oxford: Blackwell, 1990.
Eastlake, Charles L. *A History of the Gothic Revival.* 1872. Introduction by Alan Gowans. Watkins Glen, NY: American Life Foundation, 1975.
"Egypt and Syria: Western Influence." *North British Review* 29 (1858): 149–76.
Elam, Diane. *Romancing the Postmodern.* London: Routledge, 1992.
Eliot, George. "The Natural History of German Life." In *Selected Essays, Poems, and Other Writings,* edited by A. S. Byatt and Nicholas Warren. New York: Penguin Books, 1990. 107–39.
Ellegard, Alvar. *The Readership of the Periodical Press in Mid-Victorian Britain.* Stockholm: Göteborg, 1957.
Enggass, Robert. Foreword to *The Lives of Annibale and Agostino Carracci,* translated by Catherine Enggass. University Park: Pennsylvania State University Press, 1968. vii–xix.
Fauquet, Éric, ed. *Victor Cousin: Homo Theologico-Politicus: Philologie, philosophie, histoire littéraire.* Paris: Éditions Kimé, 1997.
Fergusson, James. *History of the Modern Styles of Architecture.* 3rd ed. Edited by Robert Kerr. New York: Dodd, Mead, 1891.
Ferrari, Joseph. *Les philosophes salariés.* 1849. Introduction by Stéphane Douailler and Patrice Vermeren. Paris: Payot, 1983.
Forbes, Duncan. *The Liberal Anglican Idea of History.* Cambridge: Cambridge University Press, 1952.
Forbes, George. "Arnold's 'The World and the Quietist' and the *Bhagavad Gita.*" *Comparative Literature* 25 (1973): 153–60.
Forster, E. M. *Alexandria: A History and a Guide.* New ed. Gloucester, MA: Peter Smith, 1968.

Fried, Michael. "Antiquity Now: Reading Winckelmann on Imitation." *October* 37 (1986): 87–97.
Frye, Northrop. *The Secular Scripture: A Study of the Structure of Romance*. Cambridge, MA: Harvard University Press, 1976.
Fuseli, Henry. *The Life and Writings of Henry Fuseli*. 3 vols. Introduction and edited by John Knowles. London: Henry Colburn and Richard Bentley, 1831.
Glanvill, Joseph. *The Vanity of Dogmatizing: The Three "Versions."* Introduction by Stephen Medcalf. Hove, Sussex: The Harvester Press, 1970.
Goethe. "On Dilettantism." 1789. *Essays on Art and Literature*. Edited by John Gearey. Princeton, NJ: Princeton University Press, 1994. 213–16.
Goldstein, Carl. *Teaching Art: Academies and Schools from Vasari to Albers*. Cambridge: Cambridge University Press, 1996.
———. *Visual Fact over Verbal Fiction: A Study of the Carracci and the Criticism, Theory, and Practice of Art in Renaissance and Baroque Italy*. Cambridge: Cambridge University Press, 1988.
Goldstein, Harvey D. "Ut Poesis Pictura: Reynolds on Imitation and Imagination." *Eighteenth Century Studies* 1 (1967): 213–35.
Grant, Frederick. "Introduction." In *Hellenistic Religions: The Age of Syncretism*, edited by Frederick Grant. Indianapolis, IN: Bobbs-Merrill Educational Publishing, 1953. xi–xxxix.
Hamilton, William. "M. Cousin's *Course of Philosophy*." *Edinburgh Review* 50 (1830): 194–221.
Harding, F. J. W. *Matthew Arnold the Critic and France*. Geneva: Droz, 1964.
Hardy, Thomas. *A Laodicean*. 1881. London: Penguin Books, 1997.
Hatcher, Brian A. *Eclecticism and Modern Hindu Discourse*. New York: Oxford University Press, 1999.
Hawley, John C., S.J. "Charles Kingsley and the *Via Media*." *Thought* 67 (1992): 287–300.
Hazlitt, William. "On Certain Inconsistencies in Sir Joshua Reynolds's Discourses." In *Table Talk, or Original Essays*. London: J. M. Dent and Sons, 1908. 122–68.
———. "Why the Arts Are Not Progressive?—A Fragment." 1814. In *The Selected Writings of William Hazlitt*, edited by Duncan Wu. Vol. 2, *The Round Table/Lectures on English Poets*. London: Pickering and Chatto, 1998. 158–62.
Hill, Donald L. Critical and Explanatory Notes to *The Renaissance: Studies in Art and Poetry. The 1893 Text*, edited by Donald L. Hill. Berkeley: University of California Press, 1980. 277–463.
Holt, Elizabeth Gilmore, ed. *A Documentary History of Art*. Vol. 2, *Michelangelo and the Mannerists, The Baroque and the Eighteenth Century*. Princeton, NJ: Princeton University Press, 1982.
Inman, Billie Andrew. *Walter Pater's Reading: A Bibliography of His Library Borrowings and Literary References, 1858–1873*. New York: Garland Publishing, 1981.
Iser, Wolfgang. "The Emergence of a Cross-Cultural Discourse: Thomas Carlyle's *Sartor Resartus*." In *The Translatability of Cultures: Figurations of the Space Between*, edited by Sanford Budick and Wolfgang Iser. Stanford, CA: Stanford University Press, 1996. 245–64.
Jameson, Fredric. "Magical Narratives: Romance as Genre." *New Literary History* 7 (1975): 135–63.
Johnson, E. D. H. *The Alien Vision of Victorian Poetry: Sources of the Poetic Imagination in Tennyson, Browning, and Arnold*. Princeton, NJ: Princeton University Press, 1952.

Johnston, Eileen Tess. "'This Were a Medley': Tennyson's *The Princess*." *ELH* 51 (1984): 549–74.

Joyaux, Georges J. "Victor Cousin and American Transcendentalism." *French Review* 29 (1955): 117–30. Reprinted in *Critical Essays on American Transcendentalism*, edited by Philip J. Gura and Joel Myerson. Boston: G. K. Hall & Co., 1982. 326–38.

Kelley, Donald R. "Eclecticism and the History of Ideas." *JHI* 62 (2001): 577–92.

Kerr, Robert. "English Architecture Thirty Years Hence." 1884. In *Some Architectural Writers of the Nineteenth Century*, by Nikolaus Pevsner. Oxford: Clarendon Press, 1972. 291–314.

Killham, John. *Tennyson and* The Princess: *Reflections of an Age*. London: University of London, The Athlone Press, 1958.

Kingsley, Charles. *Alexandria and Her Schools: Four Lectures*. Cambridge: Macmillan and Co., 1854.

———. *Alton Locke, Tailor and Poet: An Autobiography*. 1850. New York: Oxford University Press, 1983.

———. *Hypatia; or, New Foes with an Old Face*. 1853. Kila, MT: Kessinger Publishing Company, 1997.

———. *Literary and General Lectures and Essays*. London: Macmillan and Co., 1890.

———. "The Prevailing Epidemic." *Fraser's Magazine* 43 (1851): 492–509.

———. *The Saint's Tragedy; or, The True Story of Elizabeth of Hungary*. 1848. Project Gutenberg. 27 August 2008. http://www.gutenberg.org/etext/11346.

———. "Tennyson." *Fraser's Magazine* 42 (1850): 245–55.

———. Review (unsigned) of *The Strayed Reveller, and Other Poems*, by A. *Fraser's Magazine* 29 (May 1849): 575–80. Reprinted in *Matthew Arnold, the Poetry: The Critical Heritage*, edited by Carl Dawson. London: Routledge & Kegan Paul, 1973. 41–46.

Klein, Norman M. *The 1828–1829 Lecture Series of Victor Cousin and Abel Villemain: Aspects of the Relationship between the University and the Intellectual Life at the End of the Restoration*. Master's thesis, University of Minnesota, 1968.

Knight, William Angus. *Studies in Philosophy and Literature*. London: C. Kegan Paul & Co., 1879.

Kugler, Franz. *Handbook of Painting: The Italian Schools*. Edited by Sir Charles Eastlake. 3rd ed. London: John Murray, 1855.

Lagerlöf, Margaretha Rossholm. *Ideal Landscape: Annibale Carracci, Nicolas Poussin and Claude Lorrain*. New Haven, CT: Yale University Press, 1990.

Latour, Bruno. *We Have Never Been Modern*. Translated by Catherine Porter. Cambridge, MA: Harvard University Press, 1993.

Leask, Nigel. Introduction to *Biographia Literaria*. Edited by Nigel Leask. London: Everyman, 1997. xvii–liii.

Lee, Rensselaer W. Review of D. Mahon, *Studies in Seicento Art and Theory*. *The Art Bulletin* 33 (1951): 204–12.

Lewes, George Henry. *The Biographical History of Philosophy from Its Origin in Greece Down to the Present Day*. New York: D. Appleton and Company, 1857.

———. *The Letters of George Henry Lewes*. Vol. 1. Edited by William Baker. Victoria, BC: English Literary Studies, University of Victoria, 1995.

———. "The Modern Metaphysics and Moral Philosophy of France." *British and Foreign Review* 15 (1843): 353–406.

———. "Schools of Poetry, Arnold's Poems." *Leader* 4 (26 Nov. and 3 Dec. 1853): 1146–47; 1169–71. Reprinted in *Matthew Arnold, the Poetry: The Critical Heritage*, edited by Carl Dawson. London: Routledge & Kegan Paul, 1973. 77–84.

Lom, Petr. *Scepticism, Eclecticism and the Enlightenment: An Inquiry into the Political Philosophy of Denis Diderot.* Florence: European University Institute, 1998.

Loudon, John Claudius. *Encyclopedia of Cottage, Farm, and Villa Architecture.* 1833. Rev. ed. New York: R. Worthington, 1883.

Lukács, Georg. *The Historical Novel.* Introduction by Fredric Jameson. Translated by Hannah and Stanley Mitchell. Lincoln: University of Nebraska Press, 1983.

Macaulay, Thomas Babington. "Dryden." *The Edinburgh Review* 47 (1828): 1–36.

———. "Milton." In *The Works of Lord Macaulay,* edited by Lady Trevelyan. Vol. 5, *Critical and Historical Essays.* London: Longmans, Green, and Co., 1879. 1–45.

———. "Mr. Robert Montgomery's Poems." In *The Works of Lord Macaulay,* edited by Lady Trevelyan. Vol. 5, *Critical and Historical Essays.* London: Longmans, Green, and Co., 1879. 369–87.

Machann, Clinton. *Matthew Arnold: A Literary Life.* New York: St. Martin's Press, 1998.

Mahon, Denis. "Art Theory and Artistic Practice in the Early Seicento: Some Clarifications." *The Art Bulletin* 35 (1953): 226–32.

———. "Eclecticism and the Carracci: Further Reflections on the Validity of a Label." *Journal of the Warburg and Courtauld Institutes* 16 (1953): 303–41.

———. *Studies in Seicento Art and Theory.* London: The Warburg Institute, University of London, 1947.

Mainardi, Patricia. *Art and Politics of the Second Empire: The Universal Expositions of 1855 and 1867.* New Haven, CT: Yale University Press, 1987.

Marcus, Sharon. "Same Difference? Transnationalism, Comparative Literature, and Victorian Studies." *Victorian Studies* 45 (2003): 677–86.

Martineau, James. "Alexandria and Her Schools." 1854. *Essays, Philosophical and Theological.* Vol. 2. New York: Henry Holt and Company, 1883. 293–317.

Marvick, Andrew Bolton. "The Art of John William Waterhouse: Eclecticism in Late Nineteenth-Century British Painting." PhD Diss., Columbia University, 1994.

Mather, Frank Jewett. *A History of Italian Painting.* New York: Henry Holt and Company, 1923.

Mill, John Stuart. "Civilization: Signs of the Times." *Westminster Review* 25 (1836): 1–28. Reprinted in *The Emergence of Victorian Consciousness: The Spirit of the Age,* edited by George Levine. New York: The Free Press, 1967. 87–111.

———. *An Examination of Sir William Hamilton's Philosophy.* Vol. 9 of *Collected Works of John Stuart Mill,* edited by J. M. Robson. Toronto: University of Toronto Press, 1963.

———. "The Spirit of the Age." In *Mill,* edited by Alan Ryan. New York: W. W. Norton & Company, 1997. 1–40.

———. "Tocqueville on Democracy in America (Vol. II)." 1840. In *Essays on Politics and Culture,* edited by Gertrude Himmelfarb. Garden City, NY: Doubleday, 1962. 214–67.

Milman, Robert. "Eclecticism and Brahmoism." *Good Words* 11 (1870): 792–99.

Monsman, Gerald. *Walter Pater's Art of Autobiography.* New Haven, CT: Yale University Press, 1980.

Morell, J. D. "Cousin." *Edinburgh Review* 93 (1851): 219–32.

Morris, Mowbray. "An Alexandrian Age." *Macmillan's Magazine* 55 (1886–87): 27–35.

Morris, William. "The Revival of Architecture." 1888. In *Some Architectural Writers of the Nineteenth Century,* by Nikolaus Pevsner. Oxford: Clarendon Press, 1972. 315–24.

Mott, Lewis F. "Renan and Matthew Arnold." *Modern Language Notes* 33 (1918): 65–73.
Mulsow, Martin. "Eclecticism or Skepticism? A Problem of the Early Enlightenment." *JHI* 58 (1997): 465–77.
Murdoch, John. *The Brahma Samaj and Other Modern Eclectic Systems of Religion in India.* Papers on Indian Reform Series. Madras: The Christian Literature Society, 1893.
Natarajan, Uttara. "Pater and the Genealogy of Hardy's Modernity." *SEL* 46 (2006): 849–61.
Newman, Gerald. "Anti-French Propaganda and British Liberal Nationalism in the Early Nineteenth Century: Suggestions toward a General Interpretation." *Victorian Studies* 18 (1975): 385–418.
Nicolson, Harold. *Sainte-Beuve.* Garden City, NY: Doubleday & Company, Inc., 1957.
Ousby, Ian. *Literary Britain and Ireland.* New York: W. W. Norton & Company, 1990.
Owen, John. "Victor Cousin." *Edinburgh Review* 172 (1890): 454–90.
Panofsky, Erwin. 1924. *Idea: A Concept in Art Theory.* Translated by Joseph J. S. Peake. New York: Harper and Row, 1960.
———. "What Is Baroque?" 1934. In *Three Essays on Style,* edited by Irving Lavin. Cambridge, MA: MIT Press, 1995. 19–88.
Pater, Walter. *Appreciations, with an Essay on Style.* 1889. London: Macmillan and Co., 1910.
———. *Marius the Epicurean.* 2 vols. 1885. London: Macmillan and Co., 1910.
———. *Plato and Platonism: A Series of Lectures.* 1893. London: Macmillan and Co., 1910.
———. "Poems by William Morris." *Westminster Review* 90 (1868): 144–49.
———. *The Renaissance: Studies in Art and Poetry. The 1893 Text.* Edited by Donald L. Hill. Berkeley: University of California Press, 1980.
Patmore, Coventry. "Glimpses of Poetry." *North British Review* 19 (1853): 209–18.
———. Review (unsigned) of *Poems* by Matthew Arnold. *North British Review* 21 (Aug. 1854): 493–504. Reprinted in *Matthew Arnold, the Poetry: The Critical Heritage,* edited by Carl Dawson. London: Routledge & Kegan Paul, 1973. 114–24.
Peacock, Thomas Love. "The Four Ages of Poetry." In *A Defence of Poetry and the Four Ages of Poetry,* edited by John E. Jordan. Indianapolis, IN: Bobbs-Merrill, 1965. 3–21.
Plotz, Judith A. *Ideas of the Decline of Poetry: A Study in English Criticism from 1700 to 1830.* New York: Garland Publishing, 1987.
Posner, Donald. "The Roman Style of Annibale Carracci and His School." PhD Diss., New York University, 1962.
Prickett, Stephen. "Matthew Arnold and Ernest Renan." *Franco-British Studies* 16 (1993): 1–11.
Pugin, A. W. N. *Contrasts, or a Parallel between the Architecture of the Fifteenth and Nineteenth Centuries.* 2nd ed. London: Charles Dolman, 1841.
Ravaisson, Félix. *La Philosophie en France au XIXe siècle.* Paris: Librairie Hachette, 1868.
Renan, Ernest. *Studies in Religious History.* London: William Heinemann, 1893.
Reynolds, Sir Joshua. *Discourses.* 1798. Edited by Pat Rogers. London: Penguin, 1992.
Ricks, Christopher. *Tennyson.* 2nd ed. Berkeley: University of California Press, 1989.
Robbins, Bruce. "Introduction Part I: Actually Existing Cosmopolitanism." In *Cosmo-*

politics: Thinking and Feeling beyond the Nation, edited by Pheng Cheah and Bruce Robbins. Minneapolis: University of Minnesota Press, 1998. 1–19.

Rothschild, Lincoln. *Style in Art: The Dynamics of Art as Cultural Expression.* New York: Thomas Yoseloff, 1960.

Ruskin, John. *The Works of John Ruskin.* 39 vols. Edited by E. T. Cook and Alexander Wedderburn. London: George Allen, 1903–12.

Ryan, Alan. Introduction to Mill, *An Examination of Sir William Hamilton's Philosophy,* edited by J. M. Robson. Toronto: University of Toronto Press, 1963. vii–lxvii.

Sainte-Beuve, Charles-Augustin. "Qu'est-ce qu'un classique?" 1850. *Causeries du lundi.* Vol. 3. 3rd ed. Paris: Garnier Frères, 1857–1862. 38–55.

———. "Victor Cousin." 1847. *Portraits littéraires.* Edited by Gérald Antoine. Paris: Robert Laffont, 1993. 1019–26.

———. "Villemain comparé à Guizot et Cousin." In *Profils et jugements littéraires. Tome III.* Paris: Bibliothèque Larousse, 1927. 161–62.

———. "What Is a Classic?" In *Literary Criticism of Sainte-Beuve.* Translated and edited by Emerson R. Marks. Lincoln: University of Nebraska Press, 1971. 82–97.

Schmidt-Biggemann, Wilhelm. "The Two Philosophical Mainstreams of the German *Aufklärung:* Rationalism and Eclecticism." *Studies on Voltaire and the Eighteenth Century* 263 (1989): 544–50.

Schneider, Ulrich Johannes. "Eclecticism Rediscovered." *JHI* 59 (1998): 173–82.

Scott, George Gilbert. *Remarks on Secular and Domestic Architecture, Present and Future.* London: J. Murray, 1857.

Scott, Sir Walter. *Ivanhoe.* 1819. Edited by Ian Duncan. Oxford: Oxford University Press, 1996.

Sells, Iris. *Matthew Arnold and France: The Poet.* Cambridge: Cambridge University Press, 1935.

Shannon, Edgar Finley, Jr. *Tennyson and the Reviewers: A Study of His Literary Reputation and of the Influence of the Critics upon His Poetry, 1827–1851.* Cambridge, MA: Harvard University Press, 1952.

Shorey, Paul. Review of *Plato and Platonism* by Walter Pater. *Dial* 14 (1 April 1893): 211–14. Reprinted in *Walter Pater: The Critical Heritage,* edited by R. M. Seiler. London: Routledge and Kegan Paul, 1980. 256–63.

Simo, Melanie Louise. *Loudon and the Landscape: From Country Seat to Metropolis.* New Haven, CT: Yale University Press, 1988.

Simon, Jules. *Victor Cousin.* Translated by Gustave Masson. London: George Routledge and Sons, 1888.

Simon, W. M. "The 'Two Cultures' in Nineteenth-Century France: Victor Cousin and Auguste Comte." *Journal of the History of Ideas* 26 (1965): 45–58.

Song, Misook. *Art Theories of Charles Blanc, 1813–1882.* Ann Arbor, MI: UMI Research Press, 1984.

Southey, Robert. "State and Prospects of the Country." *Quarterly Review* 39 (1829): 475–520. Reprinted in *The Emergence of Victorian Consciousness: The Spirit of the Age,* edited by George Levine. New York: The Free Press, 1967. 112–26.

Stendhal. *Racine et Shakespeare.* 1823, 1825. Utrecht: Jean-Jacques Pauvert, 1965.

———. "Sur Victor Cousin." *Mélanges II: Journalisme. Oeuvres complètes. Tome 46.* Paris: Slatkine Reprints, 1986. 203–10.

Strachey, Lytton. *Eminent Victorians.* 1918. Introduction by Michael Holroyd. London: Penguin, 1986.

Summerson, John. "The Evaluation of Victorian Architecture: The Problem of Failure." In *Victorian Architecture: Four Studies in Evaluation*. New York: Columbia University Press, 1970. 1–18.

———. "Viollet-le-Duc and the Rational Point of View." In *Heavenly Mansions and Other Essays on Architecture*. New York: W. W. Norton & Company, 1963. 135–58.

Sutherland, John. *The Life of Walter Scott*. London: Blackwell, 1995.

Tafuri, Manfredo. *Architecture and Utopia: Design and Capitalist Development*. Cambridge, MA: MIT Press, 1976.

Taine, Hippolyte. *Les Philosophes classiques du XIXe siècle en France*. 1857. 13th ed. Paris: Librairie Hachette, 1929.

Tennyson, Alfred. *The Letters of Alfred Lord Tennyson*. Vol. 1. Edited by Cecil Y. Lang and Edgar F. Shannon, Jr. Cambridge, MA: Harvard University Press, 1981.

———. "The Palace of Art." 1832 (1842, 1853). In *Tennyson's Poetry*. 2nd ed. Edited by Robert W. Hill, Jr. New York: W. W. Norton & Company, 1999. 55–63.

———. *The Princess*. 1847; 1849–51. In *Tennyson's Poetry*. 2nd ed. Edited by Robert W. Hill, Jr. New York: W. W. Norton & Company, 1999. 129–203.

Tennyson, Hallam. *Alfred Lord Tennyson: A Memoir*. 2 vols. London: Macmillan, 1897.

Tillotson, Geoffrey. "Arnold and Pater: Critics Historical, Aesthetic and Unlabelled." In *Criticism and the Nineteenth Century*. London: The Athlone Press, 1951. 92–123.

Tucker, Herbert F. *Tennyson and the Doom of Romanticism*. Cambridge, MA: Harvard University Press, 1988.

Tucker, Irene. "International Whiggery." *Victorian Studies* 45 (2003): 687–97.

Tulloch, John. "Alexandria and Its Christian School." *Good Words* 2 (1861): 613–16.

Vermeren, Patrice. *Victor Cousin: Le jeu de la philosophie et de l'état*. Paris: Éditions L'Harmattan, 1995.

Vico, Giambattista. *The New Science*. 1744. Translated by Thomas Goddard Bergin and Max Harold Fisch. Ithaca, NY: Cornell University Press, 1968.

Viollet-le-Duc, Eugène. *The Architectural Theory of Viollet-le-Duc: Readings and Commentary*. Edited by M. F. Hearn. Cambridge, MA: MIT Press, 1990.

Wightwick, George. *The Palace of Architecture: A Romance of Art and History*. London: James Fraser, 1840.

Willey, Basil. *Nineteenth Century Studies: Coleridge to Matthew Arnold*. New York: Columbia University Press, 1949.

Williams, Carolyn. *Transfigured World: Walter Pater's Aesthetic Historicism*. Ithaca, NY: Cornell University Press, 1989.

Winckelmann, Johann Joachim. "Essay on the Beautiful in Art." [*Abhandlung von der Fähigkeit der Empfindung des Schönen in der Kunst, und dem Unterrichte in Derselben*, 1763.] Translated by Susan Powell. In *Winckelmann: Writings on Art*, edited by David Irwin. London: Phaidon Press, 1972. 89–103.

———. *The History of Ancient Art*. [*Geschichte der Kunst des Alterthums*, 1764.] Translated by G. Henry Lodge. Boston: Houghton Mifflin, 1872.

———. *Reflections on the Imitation of Greek Works in Painting and Sculpture*. 1756 German text with English translation by Elfriede Heyer and Roger C. Norton. La Salle, IL: Open Court Publishing Co., 1987.

Wittkower, Rudolf. "Imitation, Eclecticism, and Genius." In *Aspects of the Eighteenth Century*, edited by Earl R. Wasserman. Baltimore: Johns Hopkins University Press, 1965. 143–61.

Zeller, Eduard. *A History of Eclecticism in Greek Philosophy*. Translated by Sarah F. Alleyne. London: Longmans, Green, and Co., 1883.

INDEX

Abbotsford, 12, 43–50, 60, 62, 262n18
Accademia degli Incaminati (Bologna), 22
Adams, Charles, 263n1
Adams, James Eli, 180, 236–37, 270n2, 271n11
Addison, Joseph, 123
Agucchi, Giovanni Battista, 20, 22, 257n2, 258n2, 259n5
Alaya, Flavia, 214, 275n12
Albrecht, Michael, 263n1
Aldrich, Megan, 44
Alexandria, Egypt, 15, 68, 169–71, 174, 177–89, 271n3, 271n4, 271n11, 272n16
Alexandria and Her Schools (Kingsley), 182, 189, 272n14, 273n18
Alighieri, Dante, 47, 122
Allen, Peter, 143–44, 157
Allott, Kenneth, 192–93, 199, 204, 273n1, 274n2, 274n4, 274n7
Allott, Miriam, 274n7
Alma-Tadema, Sir Lawrence, 261n15
Alton Locke (Kingsley), 200–201
anachronism, 225–26, 236

Appreciations, with an Essay on Style (Pater), 6, 223, 235, 242–43, 246–47
apRoberts, Ruth, 209, 275n11
Apuleius, 242
Archer, John, 61
Aristippus of Cyrene, 245
Aristophanes, 48
Aristotelianism, 275n10
Armstrong, Isobel, 164–65, 270n9
Arnold, Mary, 190
Arnold, Matthew, 9–10, 14–15, 113, 141, 190–222, 226–29, 231, 235, 242, 244, 273n1, 274n3, 274n4, 274n5, 274n6, 274n7, 274–75n8, 275n9, 275n10, 275n11, 275–76n12. See also *Culture and Anarchy; Empedocles on Etna;* "The Function of Criticism at the Present Time"; "Heinrich Heine"; "The Literary Influence of Academies"; "On the Modern Element in Literature"; *On the Study of Celtic Literature;* "Preface to *Poems*"; "The Scholar-Gypsy"; "The Second Best"; "Stanzas from the Grande Chartreuse";

The Strayed Reveller, and Other Poems; "The World and the Quietist" asceticism, 175–80
Aurora Leigh (Browning), 206–7

Bachelard, Gaston, 62
Bachem, Rose, 213, 275n12
Baldwin, Stanley, 271n4
Balzac, Honoré de, 90, 261–62n16
Baroque classicism, 19–20, 23, 26, 30, 32, 37, 258n3, 259n5
Barrell, John, 38–39
Barthélemy St. Hilaire, Jules, 274n5
Bate, Walter Jackson, 114, 120, 122, 267n2, 268n8
Battle of the Styles, 42, 52–57, 226. *See also* classicism; Gothic Revival; medievalism
Bautain, Abbé, 67
Beckford, William, 45. *See also* Fonhill Abbey; *Vathek*
Bedford Park, 64, 263n20
Bell, Quentin, 33, 37
Bellori, Giovanni Pietro, 20, 22, 24, 28–29, 257n2, 258n2
Bénichou, Paul, 79, 263n1
Bentham, Jeremy, 56, 211
Béranger, Pierre Jean de, 274n4
Beresford Hope, A. J., 58–59, 63
Bernheimer, Charles, 249, 252–53
Betjeman, John, 63–64
Bhagavad Gita, 192, 274n4, 274n8
Biographia Literaria (Coleridge), 14, 104–10, 197
Blake, William, 33, 179, 231–32
Blanc, Charles, 25, 29–30, 259n9
Bloom, Harold, 244
Boas, George, 67, 263n1
Boime, Albert, 56, 90, 260n11, 260n13, 265n13
Bolus-Reichert, Christine, 263n20
Botticelli, Sandro, 231–32
Boyle, G. D., 191
Brooks, John, 265n11
Brooks, Michael, 46
Brown, Ford Madox, 200
Browning, Elizabeth Barrett, 206–8, 210. See also *Aurora Leigh*
Browning, Robert, 190–91, 242

Brucker, Jakob, 72, 264n7
Bullen, J. B., 233, 235, 237, 277n10
Bulwer Lytton, Edward, 133–34
Burckhardt, Jacob, 28
Burke, Edmund, 38
Burnes, Alexander, 197
Butler, Joseph, 197
Byron, Lord, 116, 124–25, 274n4

Cafritz, Robert, 31
Calderwood, Henry, 266n18
Calinescu, Matei, 257n1
Calvert, Denis, 22
Cambridge Apostles, 143–45, 150, 157, 165, 180, 269n2, 269n3
Cambridge Platonists, 275n10
Campagnola, Domenico, 31
capitalism, 7, 10, 20, 42
Caravaggio, 24
Carlyle, Jane, 144
Carlyle, Thomas, 5, 14, 113, 125–31, 133–34, 141, 144, 151, 165, 175, 194–95, 202, 207, 213, 242–43, 249–51, 268n8, 275n11. *See also* "Characteristics"; *Past and Present; Sartor Resartus;* "Signs of the Times"
Carracci, the (Agostino, Annibale, and/or Ludovico), 11–12, 19–26, 28–30, 32, 34, 41, 123, 127, 237, 257n2, 258n2, 258–59n4, 259n5, 259n9, 259–60n10, 268n10. *See also individual names*
Carracci, Agostino, 26, 259n6
Carracci, Annibale, 22, 24, 26–27, 30–31, 38, 257n1, 258n4
Carracci, Ludovico, 22, 29, 34
Casini, Paolo, 75, 264n8
Cassels, W. R., 131–32, 134
Castle of Otranto, The (Walpole), 45
Cervantes, Miguel de, 262n16
Chadbourne, Richard M., 213–14
"Characteristics" (Carlyle), 127–30
Chateaubriand, 85, 264n4
Cheah, Pheng, 254
Chitty, Susan, 182, 271n4, 271n5
Chow, Rey, 253
Chrétien, C. P., 14, 140, 142, 158–63, 167, 270n8, 270n9

Christianity, 15, 50, 53, 85, 106, 170–71, 176–81, 186, 246: Alexandrian, 182–84; muscular, 176, 180, 270n2; as *via media,* 15, 170–71, 180–84, 271n3, 271n5
Clapp-Itnyre, Alisa, 269n5
Clark, Kenneth, 43–44, 63–64
classical theory (in painting), 20, 258n2
classicism, 23, 42, 54–56, 64, 83, 260n13
Clemens of Alexandria, 182–84, 186, 272n14
Clough, Arthur Hugh, 195–97, 199, 201–2, 208, 210, 274n6
Coleridge, Samuel Taylor, 14, 45, 90, 104–10, 116, 134, 144, 197, 215, 246, 267n1, 267n2. See also *Biographia Literaria*
Colquhoun, Alan, 45
Comte, Auguste, 67, 93–96, 98, 208, 267n19, 267n20
concordia discors, 40
Conlon, John, 277n9
conservatism, 20, 106
Constable, John, 41
Contrasts (Pugin), 50–52
Cooper, James Fenimore, 90
Cope, Jackson, 275n10
Correggio, 22, 257n1, 258n4
cosmopolitanism, 10, 77, 104, 108, 169, 180, 184–86, 249, 252–55, 273n18
cottage ornée, 60–62
Cotten, Jean-Pierre, 263n1
Coulling, Sidney, 275n9, 275n12
Cousin, Victor, 4–5, 13, 15, 65–108, 111–12, 130, 142–45, 163, 191–94, 197, 199, 204, 209–10, 213–14, 226–27, 230, 235, 244, 260n13, 261n16, 263n1, 263n2, 264n3, 264n4, 264n9, 265n10, 265n11, 265n12, 265n13, 265n14, 265n15, 266n16, 266n17, 266n18, 267n20, 267n1, 268n6, 268n7, 271n6, 273n1, 274n2, 274n3, 274n5, 275n10, 276n13
Couture, Thomas, 56, 260n13
Cowley, Abraham, 123
Coyle, John, 269n3
Creuzer, Georg Friedrich, 192
Cronin, Richard, 269n3
Crook, J. Mordaunt, 42

Cruikshank, George, 197
Crystal Palace, 59, 146
Cudworth, Ralph, 192
Culler, A. Dwight, 214, 275n11
Culture and Anarchy (Arnold), 9, 191, 221, 231
Curl, James Stevens, 272n16

da Vinci, Leonardo, 232
Daiches, David, 45
Dale, Peter Allan, 275n11
Davis, Harold T., 182
Dawson, S. E., 269n7
De Quincey, Thomas, 14, 112–13
De Vere, Aubrey, 14, 139–40, 142, 158, 162–67, 270n8
Delacroix, Eugène, 260n13
DeLaura, David J., 268n8, 275n11
della Robbia, Luca, 232
Dempsey, Charles, 258n4, 259n5
Descartes, René, 72, 79, 95, 97, 264n4, 274n4
Diderot, Denis, 72, 74–76, 264n7, 264n8
Dillon, John M., 25, 264n5, 264n6
Diogenes, 180–81
Discourses (Reynolds), 12, 32–40, 231, 260n12
Donini, Pierluigi, 75, 182, 264n6, 264n7, 264n8, 272n13
Donne, John, 123
Donoghue, Denis, 276n1
Dorman, Susann, 176, 271n8, 271n9
Drabble, Margaret, 44
Dryden, John, 14, 99, 119–24, 127, 161, 195, 268n9, 268n10, 270n1
du Bellay, Joachim, 243
Duncan, Ian, 262n18
Dutch School, 35, 37, 39, 41

Eagleton, Terry, 63
Eastlake, Charles, 43–44
Eclectic Review and other eclectic magazines, journals, and readers, 267n4
eclecticism: in architecture, 7–8, 11–12, 41–64, 140, 143, 147; and the burden of the past, 3, 6, 10, 14, 16, 113–25; and collecting, 147; compared to romanticism, 4;

compared to postmodernism, 4;
and comparative literature, 212–22,
248–55; and decadence, 3, 5, 10, 15,
19, 104, 106; in education, 7, 11, 30,
32–41, 74, 108, 111–13, 175; and
imperialism, 7, 15, 185–89; and the
literary marketplace, 108–11; and
the middle classes, 7, 12, 56, 60, 64,
66, 221, 260n13; and multiculturalism, 248–55; naïve, 7–10, 14–16,
76, 229, 234, 236, 245; opposed to
organic development, 8, 10, 15,
211; in painting, 11, 19–41, 143; in
philosophy, 5, 13, 65–101; in poetry,
127–68, 174–75, 197–212; in religion, 8, 15, 48, 50, 52–53, 126, 129,
134, 144, 169–89; as renaissance,
226–37; as romance, 237–47; and
self-consciousness, 14, 64, 125–35,
242; and synthesis, 3, 5–7, 10–11,
15, 42, 63, 211; volitional or rigorous, 8–11, 15–16, 30, 43, 76, 191,
211, 224–25, 227, 234, 262n18
Eglinton Tournament, 44, 151
Egyptomania, 272n16
Elam, Diane, 225–26, 240, 276n2
Eliot, George, 208
Ellegard, Alvar, 269–70n8
Emerson, Ralph Waldo, 141, 170,
173–74, 197, 271n6
Empedocles on Etna (Arnold), 202–6,
210, 212, 274n4
Engell, James, 267n2
Enggass, Robert, 22
Epicureanism, 73, 245, 274n4
Euston Station, 64

Fauquet, Éric, 263n1
Fergusson, James, 55
Ferrari, Joseph, 264n9
Fichte, Johann Gottlieb, 91, 133
FitzGerald, Edward, 141
Flaubert, Gustave, 67, 265n13
Fonthill Abbey, 45
Forbes, Duncan, 177, 271n10
Forbes, George, 274n8
Forster, E. M., 272n16
Four Ages of Poetry, The (Peacock),
116–18, 120

Fried, Michael, 24
Frye, Northrop, 276n2
"The Function of Criticism at the
Present Time" (Arnold), 193,
212–16, 228
Fuseli, Henry, 24–25, 27–28, 30, 34,
125, 127, 259n8

Gainsborough, Thomas, 39
Gallic stereotype, 103–4
Gautier, Théophile, 232, 242, 261n13
Gibbon, Edward, 271n4
Gioberti, Vincenzo, 192
Glanvill, Joseph, 192, 209, 274n2,
275n10
Goethe, Johann Wolfgang von, 194,
196–97, 211, 218, 274n4
Goldstein, Carl, 29, 258n4, 259–60n10,
260n11, 260n12
Goldstein, Harvey D., 261n14
Gothic Revival, 7, 42–59, 63–64, 106,
135, 240, 258n3, 262n18. *See also*
Battle of the Styles; medievalism
Grand Style, 34, 38, 40–41, 43
Grand Tour, 36
Grant, Frederick, 180, 272n12
Great Exhibition, 58, 149
Great Reform Bill, 5, 56
Guizot, François, 192, 267n20, 274n5

Hadrian's villa (Tivoli), 58
Hallam, Arthur Henry, 269n2
Hamilton, Sir William, 13, 90–95,
105–6, 143, 265n15, 266n17, 266n18
Handel, G. F., 270n1
Harding, F. J. W., 273n1, 275n12
Hardy, Thomas, 6, 8, 11, 14, 16, 55,
160, 225–26, 237–41, 276n1
Hatcher, Brian, 272n13
Hawley, John, 173, 180, 271n3
Hazlitt, William, 14, 38, 104, 114–16,
118, 268n8
Hegel, G. W. F., 75–77, 95–96, 163, 233,
236, 275n11, 276n3, 276n4
Heine, Heinrich, 212, 218–19, 221, 232
"Heinrich Heine" (Arnold), 212,
218–19, 221
Heraclitus, 245
Herder, Johann Gottfried, 192, 275n11

Herodotus, 197
Hill, Donald, 231, 276n5, 277n9
historicism, 8–9, 11, 13, 45, 73, 76, 87, 94, 130, 211, 213, 226, 234, 272n17
Holt, David, 133
Homer, 47, 122, 125, 172, 197
Hughes, Thomas, 270n2
Hugo, Victor, 265n13
Hypatia (Kingsley), 15, 169–84, 245, 264n3, 271n3, 271n4, 271n5, 273n17

Idea vs. *fantasia*, 22
imitation vs. copying, 24
Inman, Billie, 229, 276n3, 276n4
In Memoriam (Tennyson), 168, 183
Iser, Wolfgang, 10, 12, 249–53
Ivanhoe (Scott), 44, 46, 262n18

Jameson, Anna, 175, 178
Jameson, Fredric, 225–26, 276n2
Johnson, E. D. H., 207
Johnston, Eileen Tess, 152, 269n6
Jonson, Ben, 146
Jouffroy, Théodore, 94, 96–97, 101
Joyaux, Georges, 268n6, 271n6
juste milieu, 5, 56, 62, 79, 85, 103, 143–44, 149, 168, 258n2, 260n13

Kant, Immanuel, 73, 91, 95–96, 117, 266n18, 274n4
Keats, John, 162, 167, 196, 202
Kelley, Donald R., 263n1
Kerr, Robert, 99
Killham, John, 142
Kingsley, Charles, 14–15, 130–35, 139, 151, 158, 160, 162–63, 169–89, 194, 200, 208, 210, 245, 264n3, 270n1, 270n2, 271n3, 271n4, 271n5, 271n7, 271n8, 271n9, 271n11, 272n13, 272n14, 273n17, 273n18. See also *Alexandria and Her Schools; Alton Locke; Hypatia;* "The Prevailing Epidemic"
Klein, Norman, 67
Knight, William Angus, 98–100, 105
Kugler, Franz, 25, 28–30

Lady of the Lake, The (Scott), 44, 262n18

Lagerlöf, Margaretha Rossholm, 31, 258–59n4
Lamartine, Alphonse de, 90
landscape painting, 30–31, 38–41, 47
Laodicean, A (Hardy), 6–7, 16, 160, 225–26, 237–41
latitudinarianism, 43, 59, 102, 108, 111, 123, 143, 174, 184, 210
Latour, Bruno, 45
Leask, Nigel, 267n2, 267n3
Lee, Rensselaer, 22–25, 30
Leibniz, Gottfried Wilhelm, 73, 107–8, 267n2, 267n3, 275n10
Leighton, Lord, 261n15
Lerminier, Eugène, 67
Lessing, Gotthold Ephraim, 233
Lewes, G. H., 13, 67, 93–98, 100–101, 105, 134, 143, 163, 210, 235, 267n19, 267n20, 274n6
liberalism, 6–7, 63, 106, 143
"The Literary Influence of Academies" (Arnold), 212, 215–17
Locke, John, 73
Locker-Lampson, Frederick, 141
Lom, Petr, 264n8
Long, A. A., 25, 75, 264n5, 264n6
Longueville, Mme de, 265n10
Lorrain, Claude, 39
Loudon, John Claudius, 46, 56–57, 63
Lucretius, 274n4
Lukács, Georg, 48
Lutyens, Edwin, 63

Macaulay, Thomas Babington, 14, 99, 101, 118–25, 127, 134, 161, 165, 194–95
MacDonald, George, 241
Machann, Clinton, 197, 219, 274n4
Mahon, Denis, 11, 19–25, 29–31, 258n3, 258n4, 259n5, 259n6, 259n7
Mainardi, Patricia, 260–61n13
Malvasia, Carlo Cesare, 22, 26, 28, 259n7
Manicheanism, 175
Mannerism, 21–22, 24, 29, 35, 257n1, 257n2, 258n2
Marcus, Sharon, 4
Marcus Aurelius, 245
Marius the Epicurean (Pater), 15–16, 223, 225, 241–47

Index

Martineau, James, 188, 273n18
Mather, Frank, 22–23
Maurice, F. D., 143–44, 170
medievalism, 12–13, 43–45
Melrose Abbey, 44, 49
Merimée, Prosper, 265n13
Michelangelo, 22–23, 34–35, 125, 232, 258n4
Michelet, Jules, 76, 192, 235, 268n7, 275n11, 276n4
Mignet, François, 274n5
Mill, John Stuart, 14, 103, 110–13, 215, 266n17, 266n18, 268n5
Millais, John Everett, 261n15
Milman, Robert, 185–87, 272n15
Milton, John, 14, 101, 118–20, 123, 129, 161, 202, 268n9, 268n10
modernism, 3, 11, 43, 63–64, 233
Modern Painters (Ruskin), 12, 38, 40, 47, 49
Monsman, Gerald, 277n11
Montgomery, Robert, 124–25, 127, 195
Morell, J. D., 266n16
Morris, Mowbray, 169–70, 187
Morris, William, 54–55, 149, 196, 224–26, 228, 230, 240–42, 263n20, 270n1
Mott, Lewis, 275n12
Mozart, 125
Mulsow, Martin, 263n1
multiculturalism, 4, 220, 252–54
Murdoch, John, 272n15

Natarajan, Uttara, 225, 276n1
nationalism, 11, 77, 211
naturalism, 257n2, 258n2
neoclassicism, 37, 50, 55
Neoplatonism, 73–74, 170, 173–74, 181, 257–58n2, 259n9, 271n5
Newman, Gerald, 104
Newman, John Henry, 144, 170, 173, 176–77, 180, 242, 271n9
Newton, Sir Isaac, 97
Niccolò dell'Abate, 26, 31

"On the Modern Element in Literature" (Arnold), 217–18, 275n11
On the Study of Celtic Literature (Arnold), 219–20

originality, 8–9, 11–12, 26, 30
Ousby, Ian, 44
Owen, John, 266n16
Oxford Movement, 170, 177, 186. *See also* Tractarians

"Palace of Art, The" (Tennyson), 145, 152, 160, 168
Panofsky, Erwin, 257n1, 257n2
Pascal, Blaise, 265n10
Past and Present (Carlyle), 250–51
pastiche, 36
Pater, Walter, 6, 9–10, 14–16, 23, 89, 167, 223–37, 241–47, 254, 276n1, 276n4, 276–77n8, 277n9, 277n10, 277n11. *See also Appreciations; Marius the Epicurean; Plato and Platonism; The Renaissance*
Peacock, Thomas Love, 14, 116–18, 120, 161, 215, 268n9. *See also The Four Ages of Poetry*
Perugino, Pietro, 35
Philo of Alexandria, 272n14
Pico della Mirandola, Giovanni, 233–34, 277n8, 277n9
picturesque, the, 55–57, 60, 63, 90, 116, 263n20
Plato, 73, 79–80, 95, 192, 234–35, 259n9, 264n4, 275n10, 277n10
Plato and Platonism (Pater), 234–35, 277n9
Plotinus, 192, 197
Plotz, Judith A., 268n8
poetry, idea of decline in, 9, 11, 14–15, 113–25, 129–35
Poetry of Architecture, The (Ruskin), 46, 60–62
Pope, Alexander, 40
positivism, 93–94, 98
Posner, Donald, 258n4
postmodernism, 3–4, 11, 21, 225–26
Poussin, Nicolas, 24
"Preface to *Poems*" (Arnold), 193–94, 206, 209
"Prevailing Epidemic, The" (Kingsley), 131–34, 160, 163, 194
Price, Uvedale, 56
Prickett, Stephen, 275n12
primitive hut, idea of the, 59–62

294

Princess, The (Tennyson), 14–15, 139–68, 201, 223, 268–69n1, 269n4, 269n5, 269n6, 269n7, 270n8
Proclus, 77, 95
Proust, Marcel, 265n10
provincialism, 217
Pugin, A. W. N., 44, 50–54, 59, 113, 196. See also *Contrasts*
Pusey, Edward, 271n8

Queen Victoria, 44
Quinet, Edgar, 208, 276n4

Racine et Shakespeare (Stendhal), 89–90, 265n14
Radcliffe, Ann, 48
Raphael, 22, 24, 33, 35, 125, 259n4
rationalism, 91–92
Ravaisson, Félix, 263n1
Reformation, 8, 50–51, 173, 229
Reid, Thomas, 94
Renaissance, 8, 15, 22–23, 27, 29, 35, 42, 51, 117, 166, 214–15, 221, 224–37, 241, 257n1, 259–60n10, 275n11
Renaissance, The (Pater), 225–33, 235–37, 243–44, 247, 276n5
Renan, Ernest, 192, 213–16, 219–20, 229–30, 274n5, 275–76n12
Reynolds, Sir Joshua, 12, 32–43, 59, 231–32, 244, 260n12, 261n14, 261n15
Ricks, Christopher, 269n2
Rintoul, Robert Stephen, 275n9
Robbins, Bruce, 249, 254
Rogers, Pat, 38
romance, 13, 15–16, 57–58, 225–26, 237–47, 276n2
romanticism, 3, 32, 79, 82–83, 230, 240, 260n11, 260n13, 265n13, 265n14, 272n17. See also Romantic Movement
Romantic Movement, 13, 43–44, 114, 117. See also romanticism
Rothschild, Lincoln, 20–21
Rousseau, Jean-Jacques, 85, 103
Royal Academy (London), 12, 27–28, 32–33, 39, 125, 144, 260n12, 261n15
Royal Institute of British Architects (London), 58

Royer-Collard, Pierre-Paul, 95, 264n4
Ruskin, John, 12–13, 32, 38, 40–41, 43–50, 52–55, 59–64, 113, 135, 155, 196, 246, 259n8, 261n15, 262n17. See also *Modern Painters; The Poetry of Architecture; The Stones of Venice;* "Traffic"
Ryan, Alan, 265n15, 266n17

Sainte-Beuve, Charles Augustin, 13, 67, 82–85, 88, 191–92, 208, 226, 229–30, 265n10, 274n5, 276n5, 276n6, 276n7
Saintsbury, George, 276n12
Sand, George, 90, 197, 265n13, 274n4
Sartor Resartus (Carlyle), 249–52, 275n11
Schelling, F. W. J., 91, 104–5
Schiller, Friedrich, 276n4
Schmidt-Biggemann, Wilhelm, 75, 264n8
Schneider, Ulrich, 263n1
"The Scholar-Gypsy" (Arnold), 209, 274n3
Scott, George Gilbert, 54
Scott, Sir Walter, 12–13, 43–50, 54, 57, 90, 116, 124–25, 261–62n16, 262n17, 262n18. See also Abbotsford; *Ivanhoe; The Lady of the Lake*
"Second Best, The" (Arnold), 191, 204–5
Sedding, J. D., 54
Seddon, J. P., 54
Sells, Iris, 273n1
Shakespeare, William, 47, 122–23, 125, 129, 196, 198–99, 262n18, 270n1
Shannon, Edgar Finley, 268–69n1
Shaw, Richard Norman, 63–64
Shelley, Percy, 162, 167
Shorey, Paul, 235
Sidgwick, Henry, 143, 157
"Signs of the Times" (Carlyle), 125–27, 194
Simo, Melanie Louise, 56
Simon, Jules, 66, 77, 192
Simon, W. M., 98, 267n19, 267n20
skepticism, 13, 73–74, 184, 254, 264n8, 275n10
Smith, Alexander, 195, 197, 242

Society for the Diffusion of Useful
    Knowledge, 268n5
Society for the Protection of Ancient
    Buildings (SPAB), 241
Socrates, 79, 264n4
Song, Misook, 259n9
Sophocles, 197
Southey, Robert, 14, 108–11, 116, 215
Spinoza, 197
spiritualism, 79, 81, 84, 132, 264n4,
    265n11, 267n1, 273n18
Staël, Mme Germaine de, 77, 79, 83, 85,
    90, 264n4, 265n12
"Stanzas from the Grande Chartreuse"
    (Arnold), 191, 206
Stendhal, 13, 79–82, 85, 89, 100, 102,
    192, 261n16, 265n14. See also *Racine et Shakespeare*
Stephens, James Fitzjames, 270n2
Sterling, John, 144
Stewart, Dugald, 94–95
Stoicism, 73, 204, 245, 274n4, 275n10
Stones of Venice, The (Ruskin), 13, 43,
    55, 259n8
Strachey, Lytton, 2–3, 6
Strawberry Hill, 44–45
Strayed Reveller, and Other Poems, The
    (Arnold), 197–201
Summerson, Sir John, 13, 42–43, 59, 64
Sutherland, John, 262n17
Swift, Jonathan, 242
syncretism, 68, 72, 180, 245, 267n2,
    272n12
Synesius, 182–83, 186

Tafuri, Manfredo, 262n19
Taine, Hippolyte, 13, 65, 85–89,
    100–101, 105, 163, 261n16, 265n12
Taylor, Jeremy, 117
Tennyson, Alfred, 14, 133–34, 139–68,
    183, 190–91, 196, 201–2, 223, 242,
    269n1, 269n2, 269n3, 269n4, 269n7,
    270n8. See also *In Memoriam;* "The
    Palace of Art"; *The Princess*
Tennyson, Hallam, 141
Thiers, Adolphe, 274n5
Tillotson, Geoffrey, 228

Tintoretto, 22
Titian, 22, 30
Toqueville, Alexis de, 103
Tractarians, the, 173–74, 176–77, 180
"Traffic" (Ruskin), 52–53
Transcendentalism, 174, 268n6, 271n6
translation/translatability, 6, 10, 249–54
Tucker, Herbert F., 146
Tucker, Irene, 4
Tulloch, John, 182–83
Turner, J. M. W., 12, 40–41, 49–50

Unitarianism, 174

Vathek (Beckford), 45
Vermeren, Patrice, 263n1
Vico, Giambattista, 76, 113, 192,
    213–14, 243, 264n9, 268n7, 275n11
Victorian Society, The, 64
Victorian Studies, 4, 273n1
Vigny, Alfred de, 265n13
Villemain, Abel-François, 265n10,
    274n5
Viollet-le-Duc, Eugène, 59–60
Voltaire, 75, 103, 150
Voysey, C. F. A., 63

Walpole, Horace, 44–45. See also *The
    Castle of Otranto;* Strawberry Hill
Waterhouse, John William, 261n15
Watts, G. F., 261n15
Wightwick, George, 57–58
Willey, Basil, 173, 180
Williams, Carolyn, 276n8
Winckelmann, Johann Joachim, 19–21,
    23–29, 35, 127, 194, 235–37, 241, 244
Wittkower, Rudolf, 23, 25
Wordsworth, William, 44, 114, 116,
    202, 243
"World and the Quietist, The" (Arnold), 192, 199, 274n8

Yeats, William Butler, 240
Young, Edward, 34–35, 232

Zeller, Eduard, 73–74, 172, 184, 264n6
Zeuxis, 37

www.ingramcontent.com/pod-product-compliance
Lightning Source LLC
Chambersburg PA
CBHW030107010526
44116CB00005B/142